Welcome to the East of England

Read on, for hundreds of ideas for great days out in Bedfordshire, Cambridgeshire, Essex, Hertfordshire, Norfolk and Suffolk! Whether you're a visitor to the East of England, or a local person who likes to get out and about, this guide is your expert companion, giving you the complete picture of places to visit in the region, as well as places to eat, drink and shop.

Co

Visit our website at www.visiteastofengland.com

east of england

How to use this Guide

Entries within this guide include contact details for each attraction, along with a short description, details of opening times, fees and facilities available.

Lower Stondon
Stondon Museum Map ref. F8 ———— ❶
Station Road
Tel: (01462) 850339 Web: www.transportmuseum.co.uk
The largest private transport museum in the country, with over 400 exhibits covering 100 years of motoring, mostly undercover. Full size replica of Captain Cook's ship 'The Endeavour'.
Times: Open all year, daily, 1000-1700. ———— ❷
Please contact for Christmas opening.
Fee: £6.00/£3.00/£5.00/£16.00. ———— ❸
Facilities: ⊛ ℙ T(1½ hrs) 🕺 ⑨ 🎋 🐕 ———— ❹
SAMPLE ENTRY

---

❶ **MAP REFERENCE**
Map references are given for each attraction. Please see the maps on pages 212-216.

❷ **OPENING TIMES**
Opening times are correct at the time of going to press, but we strongly recommend you contact the attraction prior to your visit.

❸ **FEE**
All prices for attractions appear in the order of Adult/Child/Concessions/Family. You may wish to check prices with the attractions before you visit, in case these have changed since our publication date.

❹ **FACILITIES**

⊛ Indicates that the attraction is in the Commercial Membership Scheme of the East of England Tourist Board.

Q These places to visit participate in the Visitor Attraction Quality Assurance Service. They have all been independently assessed and offer an assured level of quality for the visitor.

G Green Tourism Business Award Winner

ℙ Parking (on site)

🚌 Indicates a public bus service stops within ¼ mile of the attraction.

� Indicates a train station within 1 mile of the attraction.

T(1 hr) Indicates the time that should be allowed for a visit to this attraction.

🕺 Guided Tours (for individuals) available

⑨ Restaurant/Café

🎋 Picnic Site

🐕 Dogs Permitted

♿ Indicates that all/most of the attraction is accessible to the wheelchair visitor. But we strongly recommend you telephone in advance of your visit to check the exact details, particularly regarding access to toilets and refreshment facilities.

EH English Heritage

NT National Trust

All of the places to visit in this guide have signed the National Code of Practice for Visitor Attractions.

Compiled and published by:
East of England Tourist Board
Toppesfield Hall, Hadleigh, Suffolk IP7 5DN
Tel: 0870 225 4800 Fax: 0870 225 4890
Email: information@eetb.org.uk
Web: www.visiteastofengland.com

Editor and Production Manager: Elizabeth Woolnough
Production Assistant: Lyn Mowat
Graphic Design & Production: PRS Advertising Ltd, Ipswich, Suffolk
Maps: ©Maps in Minutes™2004. ©Crown Copyright, Ordnance Survey 2004
Printed: in the UK by Warners Midlands PLC
ISBN: 1 873246 722

PLEASE NOTE

All information contained in this guide is given in good faith, based on the information supplied by the individual establishments listed. Whilst every care has been taken to ensure the accuracy of the information published herein, the East of England Tourist Board cannot accept responsibility in respect of any error or omission which may have occurred.

Getting to know the East of England

There are hundreds of interesting places to discover in the East of England, as well as plenty of opportunity to get away from it all. Relax, breathe in the fresh air, and enjoy the lovely countryside.

Seaside towns and beaches stretch all the way from west-facing Hunstanton to the traditional fishing village of Leigh on Sea. It's a coastline renowned for tasty sea food such cockles, whelks, jellied eels and crabs – all for sale from seaside stalls. Meander along the outstandingly beautiful Norfolk coastline, habitat for birds, seals and wildlife. Enjoy the old-fashioned seaside charm of Aldeburgh and Southwold or join in the fun of the fair at Great Yarmouth or Southend.

Drift around the Norfolk Broads or the Fenland waterways by boat, or hop on a bike to explore the forests of Thetford and Rendlesham, or the country lanes of the Dedham Vale, inspiration for Constable's paintings. Follow walking trails on heaths or shady woodland, or climb the chalky hills of the Dunstable Downs for magnificent views. Take your binoculars to the Lee Valley Park, a unique mosaic of lakes, waterways and green open spaces, and a haven for birds.

Visit our historic towns & cities. Take a punt along "the Backs" to see the famous medieval university city of Cambridge from a different angle. Norwich, with its castle and cobbled streets of half-timbered houses, was also prosperous in medieval times thanks to the textile industry. Many other towns flourished with wealth from the wool trade, and you will see huge churches built by wealthy merchants in the attractive "wool" towns of Lavenham, Long Melford, Saffron Walden, Coggeshall, Thaxted and Braintree. Explore St Albans and its excellent museums to find out about the city in Roman times. Discover a wealth of antique and craft shops in the shadow of Ely's magnificent cathedral. Or visit historic Woburn, its houses and shop fronts beautifully preserved from Georgian times.

In the East of England you will find plenty of big attractions, as well as a host of less well-known places – quirky museums, grand houses, secret gardens and lovely countryside places. And lots of places for family fun – all yours to discover.

Southwold

SeaEast

With 250 miles of coastline, the East of England is full of fascinating maritime influences and connections to discover.

Follow in the footsteps of some of England's greatest seafarers, from Lord Nelson and Captain George Vancouver, to lifeboat man Henry Blogg and the Pilgrim Fathers. Enjoy a day's sailing or two aboard a traditional Thames Sailing Barge. Taste and try the fruits of the sea, from Cromer crabs and samphire, to oysters and Leigh-on-Sea cockles. Discover unspoilt saltmarshes, sand dunes, crumbling cliffs, river estuaries and shingle spits - a paradise for nature lovers and fossil hunters. Let the kids loose on our award-winning beaches. Explore picturesque fishing villages and historic maritime towns, such as King's Lynn, Great Yarmouth, Southwold and Maldon - where time has literally stood still. Stroll atop the timbers of our historic seaside piers, including the world's longest at Southend-on-Sea. Learn about tales of bravery and courage at the region's lifeboat stations.

Come and visit us in 2005, and be part of SeaBritain - a national maritime celebration. This includes the Trafalgar Festival, marking the 200th anniversary of Britain's greatest naval victory in 1805, under the command of the region's very own son - Admiral Lord Nelson.

He was born in September 1758 at Burnham Thorpe in Norfolk, where his father was rector at the 13th C. All Saints Church. Nelson was christened here, and inside are maritime artefacts, plus the lectern is made from the timbers of his flagship HMS "Victory".

In 1771, at the age of twelve, Nelson began his seafaring career joining the crew of the "Raisonnable", a vessel captained by his mother's brother. It was not until 1788, that he returned on leave to the Parsonage House in Burnham Thorpe, and over the next five years, he farmed in the area. Then in 1793, at the outbreak of war with revolutionary France, he was made Captain of the "Agamemnon". Then began his twelve years of fame when more than any other man, he halted the march of the great French dictator Napoleon Bonaparte with his command of the seas.

In the town of Great Yarmouth (also in Norfolk) you can visit the Norfolk Nelson Museum which tells his story. You can even sit onboard a re-creation of HMS "Victory" and hear cannon fire - but watch out for the rats! Don't miss the Nelson's Monument which was built in 1819 by the citizens of the town in honour of the great seafarer.

As part of SeaBritain, the East of England will be holding a host of special maritime events and activities. Full details and listings can be found at www.visiteastofengland.com where you can also download our free 44-page information sheet which includes a tour of the coastline, including places to visit, beaches, piers and famous people.

escape

to East Anglia with 'one'

'one' offers the convenient way to travel in comfort to and around the heart of this picturesque region and with our new 2005 timetable there's even more choice and flexibility for travelling by rail around the East of England.

We've added new services, provided more direct trains and introduced additional stops to help you to make more journeys without the need to change trains. And with our great value tickets and more air conditioned trains you can sit back, relax and really enjoy your trip with 'one'.

For more information visit
www.onerailway.com

Towns & Cities

MD: Market Day		**FM**:Farmers' Market	
EC: Early Closing			
i	Tourist Information Centre (see page 209)		
ↀ	Guided Tours (see page 21)		

BEDFORDSHIRE

Ampthill Map ref. D7
Ancient market town, beside the Greensand Ridge with picturesque narrow streets lined with fine Georgian buildings and quaint antique shops. **MD**: Thurs. **FM**: last Sat in month.

Bedford Map ref. D5/6
Ancient county town, dating back to before Saxon times. Fine buildings and mound of Norman castle. The Embankment is one of the country's finest river settings, with tree-lined walkways, gardens, bandstand and elegant suspension bridge. Connections to John Bunyan, preacher/author ('The Pilgrim's Progress'); Glenn Miller, the World War II bandleader; and the former Bedfordshire lace industry. **MD**: Wed and Sat. **FM**: 2nd Thurs in month. *i ↀ*

Biggleswade Map ref. F6
Set on the River Ivel, this busy town is in the heart of market gardening country. During the 18th C. it was an important coaching centre on the Great North Road, and many old inns remain today. **MD**: Sat.

Dunstable Map ref. C/D10
Set at the junction of the 4,000 year old Icknield Way and 'Roman' Watling Street, this ancient market town was started in the 12th C. by Henry I. The Augustinian priory, founded in 1131, was chosen by Henry VIII for the divorce proceedings of his first wife Katherine of Aragon. **MD**: Wed and Sat, plus small market on Fri. *i*

Leighton Buzzard Map ref. B10
On the Grand Union Canal, with fine Georgian buildings lining the wide High Street, alongside a medieval market cross,19th C. town hall and charming mews. **MD**: Tues and Sat. **FM**: 3rd Sat in month. **EC**: Thurs.

Luton Map ref. E10
On the edge of the Chiltern Hills, Luton is a thriving town with a long history. From the 17th C. it was noted for its straw plait and hat making industries. There is also a long association with the car industry. St. Mary's Church has one of the finest double arch stone screens in Europe. The famous Luton Shopping Centre, excellent entertainment/leisure facilities and several landscaped parks are other key attractions. **MD**: Mon to Sat. *i*

Sandy Map ref. F6
Against a backdrop of greensand hills, with parklands, woodlands and heath, Sandy is one of the earliest places in the county where market gardening was recorded. An Elizabethan-style mansion (The Lodge) is now the headquarters of the RSPB. **MD**: Fri. ▨

Woburn Map ref. B8
Surrounded by wooded countryside and parkland, this beautifully preserved Georgian town is acknowledged as one of the most historically important in Britain. 18/19th C. houses and period shop-fronts line the High Street. Today it has become an excellent centre for antiques and collectables. The old church is now a Heritage Centre.

CAMBRIDGESHIRE

Cambridge Map ref. G/H11/12
Famous university city, noted for its historic colleges (the first founded in 1284), complete with their courtyards and bridges across the River Cam. The crowning glory is King's College Chapel, noted for its fan-vaulted ceiling. Enjoy a walking tour of the city, or take a river trip through the watermeadows and gardens of 'The Backs', aboard the famous punts. Explore medieval churches, parks, bookshops and specialist museums.
MD: Mon to Sat. **FM**: Sun. ▨ 🛪

Leighton Buzzard, Bedfordshire

Ely Map ref. I8
One of England's most beautiful cities, dominated by its spectacular cathedral. Ely was once an island surrounded by marshes. Narrow streets and lanes are lined with historic buildings, such as the former home of Oliver Cromwell, now a museum. Attractive riverside area with marina and antique shops. **MD**: Thurs and Sat. **FM**: 2nd and 4th Sat in month. **EC**: Tues. ▨ 🛪

Godmanchester Map ref. D9/10
Delightful little town, separated from Huntingdon by water meadows and a 13th C. bridge. Elegant 17/18th C. town houses and timber-framed cottages. The charming Island Hall and Chinese Bridge were originally built in 1827 by the architect Gallier.

Huntingdon Map ref. D9
Historic market town, the birthplace (1599) of Oliver Cromwell. The town grew up around an important crossing of the River Great Ouse, then from the 16-18th C. prospered as a coaching stop on the Great North Road. The old stone river bridge is one of England's finest medieval bridges. Close by is the Hinchingbrooke Country Park and the National Hunt Racecourse. **MD**: Wed and Sat. **FM**: alternate Fri. ▨

March Map ref. G5/6
Busy market town with old cottages and attractive gardens. St. Wendreda's Church is noted for its outstanding timber roof, a double hammer-beam with 120 carved angels. **MD**: Wed and Sat.

Peterborough Map ref. C/D5/6
Peterborough was originally founded around a Saxon monastery. It has developed into a modern city, that tastefully combines the old with the new. The historic centre is dominated by the magnificent Norman cathedral, and the excellent undercover Queensgate Shopping Centre. To the west of the city centre is the Nene Park, with its landscaped parkland and lakes, nature reserves, sporting activities and steam train rides. **MD**: Tues to Sat.  𝓚

Ramsey Map ref. E7
This quiet market town grew up around its 10th C. abbey, founded on the edge of the Fens. In the 12/13th C. it became one of the most important in England. **MD**: Sat.

St. Ives Map ref. E/F9
Attractive, riverside market town. The Chapel of St. Leger is one of only four surviving bridge chapels in the country, set midstream on the 15th C. stone bridge spanning the river. On the Market Hill is the statue of Oliver Cromwell, who lived here from 1631-1636. **MD**: Mon (main) and Fri.

St. Neots Map ref. C/D11
Set beside the River Great Ouse, this is the largest town in the county. The large market square is overlooked by the 15th C. church - the 'Cathedral of Huntingdonshire'. **MD**: Thurs. **FM**: 2nd Sat in month.

Wisbech Map ref. H3/4
Prosperous market town, which grew up around its port. After the Fen drainage, it became a busy agricultural centre, evident today in some of the finest Georgian street architecture in Britain (such as North Brink, The Crescent and Museum Square). The town remains at the heart of a fruit and flower growing area. **MD**: Thurs and Sat. **FM**: alternate Fri, swaps with Whittlesey. **EC**: Wed.

Ely Cathedral, Cambridgeshire

ESSEX

Braintree Map ref. G4/5
Bustling market town standing on the old Roman road. The textile industry has brought prosperity here for more than 400 years, firstly with wool, then from the 19th C. silk-weaving. Close by is the Freeport Designer Outlet village. **MD**: Wed and Sat.

Brentwood Map ref. D/E9
The town grew up in the late 12th C. as a convenient stopping place for pilgrims travelling from East Anglia and the Midlands to Canterbury. Surrounding the town are rural areas of countryside and parkland.

Brightlingsea Map ref. L6
At the mouth of the River Colne, this maritime heritage town is a major yachting centre with one of the best stretches of sailing on the East Coast. It is also home to one of England's oldest timber-framed buildings, the 13th C. Jacobes Hall. Superb walks alongside the creek and river. **EC**: Thurs.

Burnham-on-Crouch Map ref. J9
Quiet, unspoilt riverside town, one of England's leading yachting centres. Known as the 'Cowes of the East Coast', the attractive quayside is lined with colour-washed houses, boat-building yards and sailing clubs. The famous clock tower dates from 1877. **EC**: Wed.

Castle Hedingham Map ref. H2/3
The winding lanes of this medieval village are lined with timber-framed buildings and elegant Georgian houses. Dominating the village is the magnificent 12th C. castle keep.

Chelmsford Map ref. F7
Founded in 1199, Chelmsford has been the county town of Essex for more than 700 years. Imposing 18th C. Shire Hall, and 15th C. parish church, designated a cathedral in 1914. Pedestrianised shopping areas and excellent entertainment/ leisure facilities. **MD**: Tues, Wed, Fri and Sat (second hand/collectable market on Thurs).

Clacton-on-Sea Map ref. N6
The capital of the 'Essex Sunshine Coast', Clacton is a popular seaside town with tree-lined streets, long sandy beaches and beautiful seafront gardens. The 19th C. pier offers a range of entertainment and attractions. Water sports, two theatres and good shopping area. Close by is the Clacton Factory Shopping Village. **MD**: Tues and Sat (covered market Mon to Sat).

●●●●● colchester
EXPLOR**E**XPERIENC**E**NJOY

If variety's the spice of life, Colchester's the place to savour it!

Into art? We're just buzzing! Choose firstsite @ the Minories art gallery, art cafés or other local exhibitions. Go shopping at temptingly distinctive specialist shops, big name stores or award-winning independent department store Williams & Griffin – you'll see that Colchester can really put the 'ping' in shopping!

Sample the cosmopolitan food scene with our café culture, à la carte restaurants, cosy English pubs or trendy wine bars. Then enjoy night-time vibes with 'Coolchester's' thriving club scene, cutting edge comedy or evening of exceptional theatre.

Add internationally important historical treasures and sweeping lush landscapes and you'll be full to bursting with everything that's just right for a day trip or short break.

MORE THAN
BRITAIN'S OLDEST
RECORDED TOWN

☎ **01206 282828**   vic@colchester.gov.uk

COLCHESTER

www.visitcolchester.com

Brightlingsea

Frinton-on-Sea Map ref. O5
With a reputation as an exclusive resort, Frinton retains an atmosphere of the 1920s and 30s. Tree-lined residential avenues sweep down to the elegant Esplanade and cliff-top greensward. The long stretch of sandy beach is quiet and secluded. The main shopping street (Connaught Avenue) has been dubbed the "Bond Street" of East Anglia. **EC**: Wed.

Halstead Map ref. H3
Lively and picturesque town with a 600 year old church and interesting country-style shops and a weather-boarded mill, which straddles the River Colne, now a large antiques centre. **MD**: Tues, Fri and Sat.

Harlow Map ref. B7
Designed to relieve the congestion of London in 1947, this New Town has the first tower block built in Britain in 1951, now listed for preservation. Wide range of sculpture. **MD**: Mon, Tues, and Thurs to Sat (bric-a-brac on Mon).

Harwich and Dovercourt Map ref. O3
Harwich is famous for its sea-faring history and heritage. It was once the headquarters of the King's Navy, and home of Christopher Jones 'Master of the Mayflower' Narrow streets, historic buildings and museums, including the Redoubt Fort. Adjacent is the Edwardian style resort of Dovercourt with its sandy beaches, boating lake and park. **MD**: Fri. **EC**: Wed.

Coggeshall Map ref. I5
Once an important place in the trade of wool and lace making, Coggeshall is now a major antiques centre. There are many fine timber-framed buildings, including 16th C. Paycockes, once home to a wealthy wool merchant. **MD**: Thurs. **FM**: at nearby Marks Hall Garden and Arboretum, last Sat in month. **EC**: Wed.

Colchester Map ref. K4
Britain's oldest recorded town, with over 2,000 years of history to explore. Discover the largest Norman castle keep in Europe (now an award-winning museum), and Britain's best preserved Roman gateway. Close by are the quaint narrow streets of the Dutch Quarter, where the cloth industry once flourished. Excellent shopping and leisure facilities. Lovely parkland and gardens. **MD**: Fri and Sat. **FM**: 1st Fri in month.

Dedham Map ref. L3
Set by the River Stour, Dedham is in the heart of Constable Country. It was here that the 18th C. landscape artist went to school. The attractive main street is lined with Georgian-fronted houses, old inns and a large arts/crafts centre. East of the village is the former home of the artist Sir Alfred Munnings. **EC**: Wed.

Epping Map ref. B8
The long, wide High Street is full of attractive buildings and old inns. To the north is the famous Epping Forest, covering some 6,000 acres. This former royal hunting ground was the haunt of legendary highwayman Dick Turpin. **MD**: Mon. **EC**: Wed.

Maldon Map ref. I7
Ancient hilltop town, port and sailing centre, at the head of the Blackwater estuary. Famed for its unique crystal salt and majestic Thames Sailing Barges. Attractive lanes and 'chases', with many historic buildings, including the 15th C. Moot Hall and 17th C. Dr Plume's Library. Edwardian Promenade Park. **MD**: Thurs and Sat. **FM**: 1st Tues in month. **EC**: Wed.

Manningtree and Mistley Map ref. M3
At the head of the Stour Estuary, these two small towns are joined by a waterfront area, noted for its swans. Both places are connected with Matthew Hopkins, the infamous 17th C. 'Witchfinder General'. **MD**: Wed and Sat. **EC**: Wed.

Saffron Walden Map ref. C/D2
This ancient town takes its name from the Saffron Crocus, which grew here in the 16th C. Once a centre for wool production, the wealth generated has left many lovely timber framed buildings, some decorated with pargetting. The parish church, with its elegant spire, is one of the largest in Essex. Also remains of Norman castle and rare turf maze. **MD**: Tues and Sat. **FM**: at nearby Great Chesterford, 2nd Sat in month.

there's more to Chelmsford...

...more parks
...more shops
...more history
...more entertainment
...more places to eat

Chelmsford has more to offer than you realise. It really is a great place for a day out or short break, with a fabulous choice of restaurants, superb shops, easy parking and loads of great places to explore and discover. We're not short of entertainment either, so you really should pay Chelmsford a visit!

Southend-on-Sea Map ref. I11
Traditional family seaside resort with seven miles of
seafront, award-winning beaches, and magnificent parks
and gardens. The famous 100 year old pier is the longest in
the world - take a ride to the end aboard the little trains.
Also excellent shopping centre, Kursaal entertainment
complex, Adventure Island theme park, bandstand
concerts, theatre and full calendar of special events.
MD: Thurs. **FM**: 3rd Wed in month. Also at nearby Leigh-
on-Sea, last Fri in month. **EC**: Thurs. 🔲

Thaxted Map ref. E3
Quaint streets are lined with fine medieval buildings,
including the 15th C. Guildhall and thatched almshouses.
Beautiful church with 181 foot high tower, and John
Webb's 19th C. windmill. Home of the highwayman Dick
Turpin. **MD**: Fri.

Waltham Abbey Map ref. A8
Well preserved town, home to one of the county's most
outstanding Norman buildings, 'Waltham Abbey'. It was
endowed by King Harold, who was reputedly buried here.
MD: Tues and Sat. **FM**: 3rd Thurs in month. **EC**: Thurs. 🔲

Walton-on-the-Naze Map ref. O5
Family seaside resort with clean sandy beaches, seafront
gardens and quaint narrow streets. The pier is the second
longest in Britain. The Naze is a headland jutting into the
sea, where the heathland nature reserve is a haven for
birdwatchers. **MD**: Mon (Jun-Sept) and Thurs.

Baldock, Hertfordshire

HERTFORDSHIRE

Baldock Map ref. G8
The town has retained much of its old-world charm, with
handsome 16-18th C. buildings. **MD**: Wed. **FM**: at nearby
Sandon, 3rd Sat in month. **EC**: Thurs.

Berkhamsted Map ref. C12/13
This thriving town is steeped in history, with a large section
of the elegant High Street designated a conservation centre.
Close by are the romantic ruins of the former 11th C.
castle. Just to the north is the 4,000 acres of The National
Trust's 'Ashridge Estate'. **MD**: Sat. **EC**: Wed.

Bishop's Stortford Map ref. K10/11
Set on the River Stort, this ancient market town has many
fine 16/17th C. buildings, and the remains of a Norman
castle. **MD**: Thurs and Sat. **FM**: at nearby Little Hadham,
last Sat in month. **EC**: Wed. 🔲

Harpenden Map ref. E/F11/12
Designated a conservation area, the tree-lined High Street
has many listed 17/18th C. buildings, interesting shops and
a variety of pubs and restaurants.

Hatfield Map ref. G12
The old town dates back to Saxon times, with Georgian
houses and former coaching inns. The 'new town' of
Hatfield was established in 1948. **MD**: Wed and Sat. **FM**:
1st Sat in month. **EC**: Thurs.

Hemel Hempstead Map ref. D12/13
Unlike most New Towns, Hemel Hempstead developed
around a charming old settlement, centred on St. Mary's
Church. The preserved High Street has 17/18th C. houses,
specialist shops and a lively arts centre. The New Town is a
vibrant centre with an undercover shopping mall, parkland
and water gardens. **MD**: Thurs to Sat (antiques market on
Wed). 🔲

Colchester Castle, Essex

Hertford Map ref. H/I12
Historic county town. The former castle with its Norman mound, massive walls and 15th C. gatehouse stand in attractive gardens. Impressive 18th C. Shire Hall, and the oldest 'Quaker' Friend's Meeting House (c.1670) in the world. The town has also become famed as an antiques centre, especially along St. Andrew Street.
MD: Sat. **EC**: Thurs. *ℹ*

Hitchin Map ref. F9
This ancient market town, dating back to Saxon times prospered from the wool trade, and retains its medieval plan with narrow streets and lanes. The large market square is surrounded by Tudor and Georgian buildings, and overlooked by the largest parish church in the county. **MD**: Tues, Fri and Sat. **FM**: Tues. **EC**: Wed.

Letchworth Garden City Map ref. G8
The world's first Garden City, founded in 1903 - its unique design based on the ideas of Ebenezer Howard. His dream was to combine "the health of the country with the comfort of the town", with carefully planned and well designed housing and industries. Wide tree-lined avenues, parks and gardens add to its unique appeal. Famous black squirrels. **MD**: (indoor market) Mon to Sat (except Wed). **EC**: Wed. *ℹ*

Royston Map ref. I7
Busy market town, which grew up around a cross erected around 1066, marking the intersection of the ancient Icknield Way and 'Roman' Ermine Street. Several historic buildings, award-winning gardens and an unusual man-made cave, with medieval carvings. **MD**: Wed and Sat. **EC**: Thurs.

St. Albans Map ref. F13
An historic city shaped by 2,000 years of history. Named after St. Alban, Britain's first Christian martyr, the city is built beside the site of Verulamium, the third largest Roman town in Britain. Today's settlement developed in Saxon times, around the precincts of the 10th C. monastery. Discover Roman remains, the magnificent 11th C. Cathedral/Abbey Church, historic buildings, parkland and bustling shopping areas. **MD**: Wed and Sat. **FM**: 2nd Sun in month. *ℹ 𝑌*

Sawbridgeworth Map ref. K11
Described as 'one of the best small towns in the county', Sawbridgeworth prospered from the malting industry. The riverside maltings have been converted into an antiques centre. The town centre is a conservation area with picturesque streets and Georgian/Victorian buildings. **EC**: Thurs.

Stevenage Map ref. G10
Stevenage was a small market town until 1946, when it was designated Britain's first New Town. It is noted for its parks, leisure facilities and Britain's first pedestrianised shopping centre. **MD**: Wed and Sat (outdoor); and Wed to Sat (indoor). **FM**: at nearby Dane End, 2nd Sat in month.

Tring Map ref. B12
Lying amidst the wooded Chiltern Hills, on the Grand Union Canal, this small attractive market town was the home of the wealthy Rothschild family, whose mansion (now a private school) is set in 300 acres of landscaped parkland. Famous zoological museum, beautiful memorial garden and brick maze. **MD**: Fri. **FM**: Sat bi-monthly. **EC**: Wed.

Ware Map ref. I11/12
Once a major centre for brewing, this delightful town is set on the navigable section of the River Lea. The town has many historic buildings, including old coaching inns, 18th C. riverside gazebos and the unique flint and shell decorated Scott's Grotto. **MD**: Tues. **EC**: Thurs.

Watford Map ref. E14/15
Hertfordshire's largest town is a busy and prosperous regional centre for shopping and entertainment. To the south is Cassiobury Park with open space, woodland and boat trips on the Grand Union Canal. **MD**: Tues, Fri and Sat.

Welwyn Garden City Map ref. G12
The town was developed from 1920, as England's second Garden City (after Letchworth). Based on the ideas of Ebenezer Howard, with residential and industrial areas laid out amongst landscaped parkland and tree-lined boulevards. The neo-Georgian town centre has shopping areas set around a fountain and lawns.

St. Albans, Hertfordshire

NORFOLK

Aylsham Map ref. K5
The open market place of this picturesque small town is surrounded by handsome 18th C. buildings. Humphry Repton, the famous 18th C. landscape gardener is buried in the churchyard. The town is noted for its regular antique auctions. **MD**: Mon and Fri. **FM**: 1st Sat in month. **EC**: Wed.

Cromer Map ref. K3
Dominated by the tower of its parish church (the tallest in the county), this sedate seaside town stands on a cliff top, with wide sandy beaches running down to the sea. Cromer is famous for its crabs, caught by its little fishing boats which still work from the beach. The fine pier is noted for its end-of-the-pier theatre and lifeboat station. **MD**: Fri. **EC**: Wed.

Cromer, Norfolk

Diss Map ref. J11
Set in the Waveney Valley, this thriving market town borders a six acre mere, home to a variety of wildfowl. A maze of streets clusters around St. Mary's Church, and 16th C. timber-framed houses, and later buildings of the 18/19th C. surround the market place. **MD**: Fri (also auction). **FM**: 2nd Sat in month. **EC**: Tues.

Downham Market Map ref. C8
Dating back to Saxon times, this small hillside settlement is one of Norfolk's oldest market towns. Lying on the edge of the Fens, Downham Market is noted for its 19th C. black and white clock tower and local carrstone buildings, some showing a Dutch influence. **MD**: Fri and Sat. **EC**: Wed.

Little Walsingham, Norfolk

Fakenham Map ref. G4
Thriving market town set on the River Wensum. The large market place is surrounded by handsome 18/19th C. buildings, interesting courtyards and tiny lanes. **MD**: Thurs. **FM**: 4th Sat in month. **EC**: Wed.

Great Yarmouth Map ref. P7
One of Britain's most popular seaside resorts with wide sandy beaches, colourful gardens and traditional seaside attractions and entertainment. Built on a spit of sand, between the sea and the River Yare, the town's wealth comes from its port, and the former herring industry. The historic quayside has old merchants' houses and 'rows' (narrow medieval alleys). Remains of the town wall and the largest parish church in England. **MD**: Wed, Fri (summer only) and Sat. **EC**: Thurs.

Holt Map ref. I3
One of the most attractive small towns in Norfolk, with a main street lined with elegant Georgian buildings. The town is best known for Greshams, a public school founded in 1555 by Sir John Gresham, a former Lord Mayor of London. Holt is a mecca for antique and bric-a-brac collectors. **EC**: Thurs.

Hunstanton Map ref. D3
This is England's only east coast resort which faces west. Hunstanton is a traditional seaside town with a range of attractions, large sandy beaches and gardens. Ornate Victorian and Edwardian houses overlook wide open greens. To the north is Old Hunstanton, a residential village with distinctive red and white striped cliffs. **MD**: Wed and Sun. **EC**: Thurs.

King's Lynn Map ref. C5/6
Historic port and market town, dating back to the 12th C. and steeped in maritime history. Two magnificent market places and two medieval guildhalls; one is the largest in Britain, the other houses the town's regalia. Former merchants' houses, and attractive waterfront area with 18th C. Custom House. **MD**: Tues, Fri and Sat.

Little Walsingham Map ref. G/H3
Picturesque village, and famous pilgrimage centre. Timber-framed buildings and Georgian facades line the High Street and Market Place, with its 16th C. pump-house. Also extensive ruins of Augustinian abbey set in attractive parkland. 🏛

Mundesley Map ref. M3
This is one of Norfolk's best kept secrets. The town prospered at the start of the 20th C. when the railway arrived, and for a time it was something of a health resort. Today Mundlesey is a quiet holiday town with a clean beach, and shallow pools left by the turning tide.
EC: Wed.

North Walsham Map ref. L4
This busy market town became a centre for the wool industry in the late medieval period. The 16th C. market cross is the focal point of the town. Lord Nelson spent his schooldays at 'The Paston School'. **MD**: Thurs. **EC**: Wed.

Norwich Map ref. K/L7
East Anglia's capital, and the most complete medieval city in Britain. Surrounded by its old walls are over 1,500 historic buildings, and an intricate network of winding streets and lanes, such as cobbled Elm Hill. Norwich is dominated by its magnificent cathedral, and impressive 12th C. castle keep. Lively cultural scene with museums, galleries, theatres, restaurants and pubs. Excellent shopping centre, including the Castle Mall, famous Mustard Shop and colourful open air market. **MD**: Mon to Sat. **FM**: 2nd Sat in month. 🛈 🏛

Sheringham Map ref. J/K2
This traditional seaside town grew up around its old fishing village, and a band of little boats still bring in the daily catch. A mixture of Edwardian and Victorian buildings, Sheringham is home of the North Norfolk Railway (The Poppy Line), which operates steam train rides to Holt. At low tide the large sandy beach reveals rock pools.
MD: Sat. **EC**: Wed. 🛈

Swaffham Map ref. F7
Charming old market town. The triangular-shaped market place has handsome Georgian buildings and a butter market. The 15th C. church is one of the finest in the region, with its double hammerbeam angel roof, and memorial to the famous Pedlar of Swaffham. **MD**: Sat. 🛈

Thetford Map ref. F/G11
Thriving market town, which a thousand years ago was the capital of East Anglia. Its importance continued during the early Middle Ages, and has left a legacy of historic sites, such as the Iron Age earthworks, a Norman castle mound and the remains of the 12th C. priory. The town centre is a conservation area with fine medieval and Georgian buildings. **MD**: Tues and Sat. **EC**: Wed.

Wells-next-the-Sea Map ref. G2
Picturesque small town, a busy port for coasters and the local whelk and shrimp boats. Wells has narrow streets lined with traditional flint buildings. A little railway takes visitors from the port to the nearby sandy beach.
EC: Thurs. 🛈

Wroxham and Hoveton Map ref. L/M6
The adjoining villages of Wroxham and Hoveton are known as the 'capital of the Broads'. Linked together by a hump-backed bridge over the River Bure, Hoveton is the main shopping and tourist centre with its boatyards, chandleries and 'Roys' (the largest village store in the world). Various boat excursions available. 🛈

Wymondham Map ref. J8
Wymondham (pronounced "Win-dum") retains all the character of a historic market town. The town has more listed buildings than any similar sized town in the county, including the 17th C. octagonal market cross. The twin towers of the beautiful abbey dominate the skyline. **MD**: Fri. **FM**: 3rd Sat in month. **EC**: Wed. 🛈

Norwich Castle, Norfolk

SUFFOLK

Aldeburgh Map ref. N8
Charming and sedate seaside town, whose wide High Street has attractive Georgian shop-fronts. Historic buildings include the Moot Hall (c.1520) and the 15th C. church. Fishermen still pull their boats onto the steep shingle beach, and sell their catch each morning. The famous music festival is held in June. **EC**: Wed. *☑*

Beccles Map ref. N2/3
Set on the River Waveney, this fine market town is now a major boating centre for the Broads. It has red-brick Georgian houses and unusual 18th C. octagonal town hall. The magnificent 14th C. church has a detached bell tower. Nearby Roos Hall is one of England's most haunted houses. **MD**: Fri. **FM**: at nearby Barsham, last Sat in month. Also Beccles Heliport, 1st and 3rd Sat in month. **EC**: Wed. *☑*

Brandon Map ref. C3
Small town, beside the Little Ouse River, surrounded by forest and heathland. Brandon stands on flint, is largely built from flint, and was for long the home of England's oldest industry, flint knapping. Heritage Centre and country park. **MD**: Thurs and Sat. **FM**: at nearby Elveden, last Sat in month. **EC**: Wed.

Bungay Map ref. L3
Unspoilt market town, beside a loop of the River Waveney. After a great fire in 1688, Bungay rebuilt itself as a Georgian town with red-brick facades and Dutch gables. **MD**: Thurs. **EC**: Wed.

Aldeburgh, Suffolk

Bury St. Edmunds Map ref. D/E6/7
Named after St. Edmund (the Saxon King of East Anglia), this ancient market town has played an important part in English history. For it was here in 1214, that the barons of England vowed to extract from King John the concessions set out in the 'Magna Carta'. The ruins of the 12th C. abbey are overlooked by the cathedral's new gothic tower. Bury is also noted for its award-winning gardens, Georgian theatre, and the smallest pub in Britain 'The Nutshell'. **MD**: Wed and Sat. *☑ ⚐*

Clare Map ref. C10
Delightful small town, with colour-washed and timber-framed buildings, many decorated with pargetting. The country park is dominated by the 100ft high motte of the former Norman castle. Close by is the 13th C. priory, the first Augustinian house in England. **MD**: Mon and Sat. **EC**: Wed.

Felixstowe Map ref. L11/12
Edwardian resort, retaining much of its original charm, with beautiful south-facing gardens, paved promenade, leisure centre, pier and theatre. Its popularity began with the arrival of the railway in 1887, and a visit in 1891 by the Empress of Germany. **MD**: Thurs and Sun. **FM**: 1st Sat in month. **EC**: Wed. *☑*

Framlingham Map ref. K/L7
Ancient market town, noted for its well-preserved 12th C. castle, built by the Bigod Family (Earls of Norfolk), and the church with its magnificent tombs and effigies. **MD**: Sat. **EC**: Wed.

Halesworth Map ref. M4
Nestled in a curve of the River Blyth, Halesworth has many fine buildings, including the carved Gothic House, a Tudor Rectory and Elizabethan almshouses. **MD**: Wed. **EC**: Thurs.

Ipswich Map ref. I/J10
Dating back to Saxon times, Ipswich is one of England's oldest towns, with historic buildings, such as the Ancient House, renowned for its plasterwork. Twelve medieval churches stand testimony to the importance of the town as it developed in the Middle Ages. Close by is 16th C. Christchurch Mansion, which stands in a beautiful landscaped park. Ipswich has a rich maritime heritage, its port founded in the 6/7th C. The redeveloped waterfront has a marina, restaurants and bars. **MD**: Tues, Fri and Sat. **FM**: at nearby Harkstead, 3rd Sat in month. 🚻 𝕏

Lavenham Map ref. E/F9
England's best-preserved medieval town. From the 14-16th C. it was a major wool and cloth-making centre. The wealth generated has left a beautiful legacy of timber-framed houses set along narrow streets and lanes, such as the Guildhall and Swan Hotel. The 13th C. church is noted for its magnificent 141 feet high tower. Numerous gift, craft and tea shops. **EC**: Wed. 🚻 𝕏

Long Melford Map ref. E10
This former wool town is now the 'Antiques Capital of Suffolk'. Its wide, tree-lined High Street is full of antique shops and centres. At one end of the village is the large green, dominated by Melford Hall (c.1550s), and the magnificent 15th C. church, built of carved stone and flint. Moated Kentwell Hall and Gardens is renowned for its annual recreations of Tudor life. **FM**: 3rd Sat in month. **EC**: Wed.

Lowestoft Map ref. P2
Attractive seaside resort at Britain's most easterly point (Lowestoft Ness). It has one of Britain's best sandy beaches, backed by a long promenade. Once a flourishing fishing port, visitors can see the yacht harbour and neighbouring docks. Impressive, glass Edwardian-style pavilion. **MD**: Tues, Fri and Sat. **EC**: Thurs. 🚻 𝕏

Newmarket Map ref. A7
Associated with horses and royalty since Queen Boadicea's day. Over 35 race days a year, two racecourses, The National Horseracing Museum, the heathland "gallops", training yards, studs, a horse hospital and Tattersall's sales rooms. **MD**: Tues and Sat. **EC**: Wed. 🚻 𝕏

Orford Map ref. N9
This attractive small town is overlooked by its 12th C. castle keep built by Henry VII for coastal defence. From the top, there are panoramic views over the town and marshes. Brick and timber buildings line the streets to the little quayside, where there are boat trips to the mysterious Orfordness (a shingle spit).

Oulton Broad Map ref. O2
Forming the southern gateway to The Broads, this is one of the finest stretches of inland water in England. A haven for lovers of watersports, Oulton Broad is perfect for sailing, rowing or cruising. Regular sailing regattas and motorboat racing events. **EC**: Wed.

Southwold Map ref. O5
The land mark of this charming town is the white lighthouse built in 1890. Nine open greens are surrounded by period houses and fisherman's cottages. Picturesque harbour, colourful beach huts, specialist shops and real ale from the town's own brewery. **MD**: Mon and Thurs. **EC**: Wed. 🚻

Stowmarket Map ref. H7/8
This bustling market town in the Gipping Valley is a popular shopping centre and home of the Museum of East Anglian Life. **MD**: Thurs and Sat. **EC**: Tues. 🚻

Sudbury Map ref. E10
Set on the River Stour, this ancient market town is surrounded by water meadows. Sudbury has thrived on the textile industry, firstly with wool, then silk. The famous artist Thomas Gainsborough was born here in 1727, and his statue stands on the Market Place. **MD**: Thurs and Sat. **EC**: Wed. 🚻

Woodbridge Map ref. K9
Set on the River Deben, this attractive market town was once a port, noted for its shipbuilding and sail-making industries. Narrow streets hide many historic buildings, including fine examples of Georgian architecture. On the quayside is the famous Tide Mill, and on the opposite bank of the river, Sutton Hoo, the burial site of Anglo-Saxon kings. **MD**: Thurs. **FM**: 2nd Sat in month. **EC**: Wed. 🚻

Lavenham, Suffolk

Guided Tours

EETB
Registered
GUIDE

Explore the region's towns and cities with the experts. Our guides know all the best places to show you, as well as the stories and history behind them.

Most of the tours are conducted by qualified Blue Badge Guides who have attended a training course sponsored by the East of England Tourist Board.

* indicates tours are conducted by Blue Badge Guides.

BEDFORDSHIRE

Bedford

● **Regular town tours:** summer programme of Sun morning guided walks which take place at 1100, departing from the Tourist Information Centre. Walks last approximately 90 mins and pre-booking is essential.
● **Group tours:** available throughout the year by prior arrangement. A choice of six titles on offer, plus ghost walks which are available throughout the winter months.
● For further information contact the Tourist Information Centre on (01234) 215226.

CAMBBRIDGESHIRE

Cambridge Tour

Cambridge *

● **Daily walking tours:** of the city and colleges depart from the Tourist Information Centre up to four times a day in summer. Ticket price includes entrance to either King's or St. John's College, other colleges included as available. For further information contact the Tourist Information Centre on (01223) 457574.
● **Group tours:** tours for groups can be arranged in ten different languages, and can include city and colleges, walking/punting, science tours, Royal Cambridge, ghost tours and other themed tours. Coach tours of Cambridge and East Anglia can also be arranged. For bookings and

enquiries, Tel: (01223) 457574. Fax: (01223) 457588. Email: tours@cambridge.gov.uk
Web: www.visitcambridge.org
● **Important information:** all parties of ten or more who intend to tour the colleges should be accompanied by a Cambridge Registered Blue Badge Guide. Colleges which charge for admission are only included on request (cost added to tour price). Most colleges are closed to the public during University examination time, mid Apr-end Jun.

Ely *

● **Cathedral and city tours, and city only tours:** guides available for pre-booked groups by appointment. Tours can include the cathedral and city, or Oliver Cromwell's House. For cathedral tours, please contact The Chapter Office on (01353) 667735.
● **Oliver Cromwell's House, tours and visits:** available for pre-booked groups. Evening tours can be arranged. Special rate for school parties and costumed guides are popular.
● **Ghost tours and alternative Ely tours:** with costumed guides, can be arranged direct with the guides.
● For further information contact the Tourist Information Centre on (01353) 662062.

Peterborough *

● **Group tours:** guides are available for city and cathedral tours at any time for private groups, each tour lasts approximately 1½ hours. For further information contact the Tourist Information Centre on (01733) 452336.

Wisbech

● **Regular town tours:** themed guided walks on Wed evenings from May-Jul, lasting 1½ hours.
● **Group tours:** town tour and themed walks can be arranged for groups.
● For further information contact the Tourist Information Centre on (01945) 583263.

ESSEX

Colchester *

● **Regular town tours:** depart from the Visitor Information Centre. Duration of 1¾ hours. For further information (including times and costs) contact the Visitor Information Centre on (01206) 282920, or visit www.visitcolchester.com
● **Group tours:** may be booked at any time of year.

Harwich

● **Regular town tours:** meet at the Ha'penny Pier Visitor Centre on Wed and Sat at 1400, between the 1 May-mid Sept. Free guided walks in Harwich.
● **Group tours:** for pre-booked groups. Guided tour of

Harwich, visit to museums, including Harwich Redoubt Fort. Charges include museum entrance and small charge for guide.
● For further information contact Weston Gray on (01255) 880568 or email : weston.lesley@virgin.net

Saffron Walden and surrounding areas *
● **Group tours:** guides available at any time to conduct tours for private groups. Variety of walking tours in Saffron Walden, Great and Little Dunmow, Thaxted and Newport - some tours themed (eg Saffron Walden Quakers). Can design tours to meet specific needs of groups. Tours last for about 2 hours - but can be scaled down to fit into existing itinerary. Prices on application.

● **Day or half day coach tours:** Uttlesford and Essex guides available to guide tours in a large area of North West Essex, and well into Hertfordshire and Suffolk. Wide range of standard tours (visits to churches a speciality). Can also assist with the design of special and themed tours for particular interests and occasions.
● For further information contact the Tours Organiser on (01799) 526109.

Colchester Tour

HERTFORDSHIRE

St. Albans *
● **Regular city walks:** depart from the Tourist Information Centre. Easter-end Oct, Sun and Bank Hols at 1100 and 1500.
● **Ghost walk:** departs from the Tourist Information Centre. 8pm on Weds (once monthly in summer; twice monthly in winter).
● **Verulamium walk:** departs from the Verulamium Museum. Easter-end Oct, Sun at 1500. Guides also on duty at Roman Theatre from Easter-end Oct, on Sat and Sun at various times.

● **Themed coach tours:** in Bedfordshire and Hertfordshire in your own coach.
● For further information contact the Tourist Information Centre on (01727) 864511.

St. Albans, Hertfordshire (courtesy of St. Albans Museum)

NORFOLK

Great Yarmouth
● **Regular town tours:** a choice of four heritage walks running on certain dates between May-Oct. Medieval Town Walls; Maritime Connections; Historic Town Centre and Old Yarmouth. All accompanied by an official town guide.
● Private tours may be booked throughout the year.
● For further information contact the Tourist Information Centre on (01493) 842195.

King's Lynn *
● **Regular town tours:** individuals may join the tours which depart from The Tales of the Old Gaolhouse, from May-Oct. For further information of days and times contact the Tourist Information Centre on (01553) 763044.
● **Group tours:** guided tours can be arranged throughout the year for groups by contacting King's Lynn Town Guides on (01553) 765714.

Little Walsingham
Walking guided tours around the historic village of Walsingham. Easter-30 Sept, Wed and Thurs at 1100. Also Sat from Jun-Sept at 1400. Group tours throughout the year by arrangement. For further information contact the Tours Organiser on (01328) 820250.

Norwich *
● **Regular city tours:** 'Norwich - City of Century' walking tours lasting 1¹/2 hours, depart from the Tourist

Information Centre in the Forum. Up to three times daily from Apr-Oct, plus Suns from Jun-Sept.

● **Evening tours:** themed tours including 'Tales of the Riverside' and 'When George was King', twice weekly at 1830 from Jun-Sept.

● **Group tours:** a variety of themed walking tours are available for pre-booked groups. A 'Panoramic Norwich' coach tour can be arranged. Itineraries can also be arranged for longer half or full day tours, including the Norfolk Broads or North Norfolk Coast.

● For further information contact the Tourist Information Centre on (01603) 727927. Fax: (01603) 765389. Email: tourism@norwich.gov.uk

Visitors to King's Lynn

SUFFOLK

Bury St. Edmunds *

● **Regular town tours:** lasting 1¹/2 hours, depart from the Tourist Information Centre. Tickets can be purchased in advance, or on the day. Tours run daily in the summer, including Sat at 1430. Also available are themed walks on summer evenings.

● **Group tours:** guides can be arranged for groups at any time if enough notice is given. Special themes also available.

● For further information (including comprehensive leaflet) contact the Tourist Information Centre on (01284) 764667.

Ipswich *

● **Regular town tours:** individuals may join the tours (lasting approximately 1¹/2 hours) departing from the

Tourist Information Centre - May-Sept on Tues and Thurs at 1415.

● **Group tours:** can be arranged for groups anytime all year around.

● For further information contact the Tourist Information Centre on (01473) 258070.

Lavenham *

● **Regular town tours:** weekend walks (with Blue Badge Guides) running from end Mar-end Oct, Sat at 1430 and Sun at 1100 and 1430. Tickets can be purchased in advance or on the day. Tours last approximately 1¹/4 hours, departing from the Tourist Information Centre.

● **Group tours:** can be arranged for groups - contact for details.

● For further information contact the Tourist Information Centre on (01787) 248207.

Lowestoft

● **Regular town tours:** lasting 2 hours, depart from the Town Hall. Tours feature historic tales and ghost stories, and run every Tues and Thurs from Apr-Oct at 1930.

● **Group tours:** can be arranged for groups - contact for details.

● For further information contact the Tourist Information Centre on (01502) 533600.

Expert help from staff at Bury St. Edmunds Tourist Information Centre

Events 2005

The East of England offers a range of exciting and varied events to suit all tastes, from air shows to arts festivals, from historical re-enactments and cheese rolling contests to craft fairs and agricultural shows. Or for the more unusual, try the World Snail Racing and Pea Shooting Championships, all held in the region throughout the year. On the following pages we have brought together a selection of events taking place during the year. For more information on the events listed or other events taking place during 2005, please contact the East of England Tourist Board on 0870 225 4800 or visit us at www.visiteastofengland.com.

* - Provisional

January

2 Jan	Maldon Mud Race, Promenade Park, Town Centre, Maldon
2 Jan-27 Feb	Floodlit Swan Evenings, Wildfowl and Wetlands Trust, Welney, Cambs
8-9 Jan	Whittlesey Straw Bear Festival, Whittlesey, Cambs
21-23 Jan	Chilford Hall's Home Design and Interiors Exhibition, Balsham Road, nr. Linton, Cambs
28-30 Jan	Woburn Abbey Home Design and Interiors Exhibition, Woburn, Beds

February

1-28 Feb	Walsingham Abbey Snowdrop Walks, Little Walsingham, Norfolk

8 Feb	Pancake Races, Town Centre, Hitchin, Herts
8 Feb	Pancake Races, Town Centre, Huntingdon, Cambs
8 Feb	Lowestoft Pancake Races, High Street, Lowestoft, Suffolk
12-22 Feb	King's Lynn Mart, Tuesday Market Place, King's Lynn, Norfolk
13 Feb-13 Mar	Lambing Sundays and Spring Bulb Days, Kentwell Hall, Long Melford, Suffolk
19/20 Feb	Lee Valley Birdwatching Fair, Lee Valley Park Farms, Stubbins Hall Lane, Crooked Mile, nr. Waltham Abbey, Essex
22 Feb	Primrose/Spring Plant Festival, By-pass Nurseries, Capel St. Mary, Suffolk
26 Feb-5 Mar	Bedfordshire Festival of Music, Speech and Drama, Corn Exchange, Bedford, Beds

March

Mar-Oct	Grand National Exhibition, National Horseracing Museum, High Street, Newmarket, Suffolk
Mar-Oct	Racing Post Exhibition, National Horseracing Museum, High Street, Newmarket, Suffolk
2 Mar-17 Apr	Lambing Weekends, Wimpole Hall and Home Farm, Arrington, nr. Royston, Cambs
5/6 Mar	Bedfordshire Spring Craft Show at Woburn Safari Park, Woburn, Beds
7-12 Mar	Celebration of Schools Music, Snape Maltings, Snape, Suffolk
11-13 Mar	Fiction Festival, Town Hall, Saturday Market Place, King's Lynn, Norfolk
11-19 Mar	St. Patrick's Day Festival, various venues, Luton, Beds
12-31 Mar	Early Spring Flowers, Fairhaven Woodland and Water Garden, School Road, South Walsham, Norfolk
19/20 Mar	The Shire Horse Society Spring Show, East of England Showground, Peterborough, Cambs
19/20 Mar	Thriplow Daffodil Weekend, Thriplow, Cambs
25-27 Mar	Aldeburgh Easter Music Festival, various venues, Aldeburgh, Suffolk
25-28 Mar	Blickling Easter Craft Show, Blickling Hall, Blickling, nr. Aylsham, Norfolk
25-28 Mar	Tudor Easter, Kentwell Hall, Long Melford, Suffolk
26-28 Mar	2005 Twinwood Classic Motor Transport, Steam and Country Fair, Twinwood Airfield, Clapham, Beds
26-28 Mar	Easter Thunderball (National Drag Racing Championships), Santa Pod Raceway, Podington, Beds
27/28 Mar	Easter Fun Days, Barleylands Farm Centre, Barleylands Road, Billericay, Essex
27/28 Mar *	Medieval Jousting, Knebworth House, nr. Stevenage, Herts
28 Mar	Easter Family Fun Day, Roots of Norfolk, Gressenhall, nr. Dereham, Norfolk

April

1 Apr-31 Oct	Nelson Portraits, Norfolk Nelson Museum, Great Yarmouth, Norfolk
3 Apr	Haverhill Country Music Festival, Leisure Centre, Ehringshausen Way, Haverhill, Suffolk
9-end Apr	Wild Primrose Week, Fairhaven Woodland and Water Garden, School Road, South Walsham, Norfolk
15-17 Apr	Suffolk Spring Garden Show, Suffolk Showground, Ipswich, Suffolk
18-23 Apr	Hertford Theatre Week, Castle Hall, Hertford, Herts
27-30 Apr	The East Anglian Beer Festival, The Corn Exchange, Cornhill, Bury St. Edmunds, Suffolk
22-24 Apr	The National Motorhome Show, East of England Showground, Peterborough, Cambs
23/24 Apr	Minsmere Bird Fair, RSPB Minsmere Nature Reserve, Westleton, nr. Saxmundham, Suffolk

30 Apr- 2 May	Tudor May Day Celebrations, Kentwell Hall, Long Melford, Suffolk
30 Apr- 2 May	Southend Spring Garden Show, Garons Park, Southend-on-Sea, Essex

May

May-Oct	The Shuttleworth Collection Flying Displays, Old Warden, nr. Biggleswade, Beds
1-31 May	Candelabra Primula Weeks, Fairhaven Woodland and Water Garden, School Road, South Walsham, Norfolk
1 May	Heritage Coast Run or Walk, Thorpeness Sports Ground, nr. Aldeburgh, Suffolk
1-31 May	Hertford Music Festival, various venues, Hertford, Herts
1 May	34th Ipswich to Felixstowe Historic Vehicle Run, Ipswich/Felixstowe, Suffolk
1 May	King's Lynn May Garland Procession, Town Centre, King's Lynn, Norfolk
1/2 May	Suffolk Game and Country Fair, Glemham Hall, Little Glemham, Suffolk
1/2 May	Mendlesham Street Fayre and Art Exhibition, Mendlesham, Suffolk
1/2 May	Truckfest 2005, East of England Showground, Peterborough, Cambs

1/2 May *	Knebworth Country Show, Knebworth House, nr. Stevenage, Herts
1/3 May	Sagitta Guineas Festival, Rowley Mile Racecourse, Newmarket, Suffolk
2 May	Ickwell May Festival, Ickwell Green, nr. Biggleswade, Beds
2 May	Dunstable Carnival, Bennett Memorial Recreation Ground, Dunstable, Beds
2 May	Woodbridge Horse Show, Suffolk Showground, Ipswich, Suffolk
2 May	Stilton Cheese Rolling, Stilton, nr. Peterborough, Cambs
2 May	Breckland Family Show, Watton Airfield, Watton, Norfolk
4-14 May	Norfolk and Norwich Festival, various venues, Norwich, Norfolk
5-8 May	Living Crafts Exhibition, Hatfield House, Hatfield, Herts
6-8 May	St. Neots Folk Festival, The Priory Centre, St. Neots, Cambs
6-15 May	The Harleston and Waveney Festival 2005, various venues, Harleston, Norfolk
7-14 May	Chelmsford Cathedral Festival, Chelmsford, Essex
7/8 May	VE Day Anniversary Air Show, Imperial War Museum, Duxford

3 May	South Suffolk Show, Ampton Racecourse, Ampton, nr. Bury St. Edmunds, Suffolk
3 May	Peterborough Dragon Boat Festival, The Embankment (opposite Key Theatre), Peterborough, Cambs
3 May	Reach Fair, Village Green, Reach, Cambs
13-15 May	Norfolk Garden Show, Norfolk Showground, Norwich, Norfolk
13-29 May	Bury St. Edmunds Festival, various venues, Bury St. Edmunds, Suffolk
14/15 May *	8th Suffolk International Kite Festival, Rougham Airfield, nr. Bury St. Edmunds, Suffolk
14-30 May	Norfolk Open Studios, various venues, Norfolk
20-22 May	Essex Garden Show, Brentwood Centre, Doddinghurst Road, Brentwood, Essex
21 May	Hadleigh Farmer's Agricultural Association May Show, Holbecks Park, Hadleigh, Suffolk
21/22 May	BMF Bike Show, East of England Showground, Peterborough, Cambs
21/22 May	Rickmansworth Canal Festival, Grand Union Canal, Rickmansworth, Herts
21/22 May	Hertfordshire Garden Show, Knebworth House, nr. Stevenage, Herts
26 May *	Tour de Tendring (Cycle Race), various venues, Tendring district, Essex
27-30 May	The Main Event (FIA European Drag Racing Championships), Santa Pod Raceway, Podington, Beds
28/29 May	Hertfordshire County Show, Hertfordshire County Showground, Redbourn, Herts
28-30 May	Aldenham Country Park Craft Fair, Elstree, Herts
28-30 May	Felbrigg Coast and Country Show, Felbrigg Hall, Felbrigg, Norfolk
28-30 May	WWII Re-Creation and 1940's Charity Fete, Kentwell Hall, Long Melford, Suffolk
28 May- 1 Jun	Walpole St Peter Annual Flower Festival, Walpole St Peter Church, Walpole St Peter, Wisbech, Cambs
28 May- 6 Jul	East Coast Regatta, various venues, Lowestoft, Suffolk
29/30 May	Bury St Edmund Flower and Continental Market, The Buttermarket, Bury St. Edmunds, Suffolk
29/30 May	Southend Air Show, Seafront, Southend-on-Sea, Essex
29/30 May	Tring Canal Festival, Grand Union Canal, Tring, Herts

29 May- 5 Jun	Downham Market Festival, various venues, Downham Market, Norfolk
30 May	Framlingham Gala, Town Centre, Framlingham, Suffolk
30 May	Luton International Carnival, Town Centre and Wardown Park, Luton, Beds
30 May	Harwich Redoubt Fort Fete, off Main Road, Harwich, Essex
30 May	Norfolk History Fair, Roots of Norfolk, Gressenhall, nr. Dereham, Norfolk

June

Jun/Aug*	Theatre in the Parks, various venues, Norwich, Norfolk
1-2 Jun	Suffolk Show, Suffolk Showground, Ipswich, Suffolk
3/4 Jun	Thaxted Morris Ring Meeting, various venues in Thaxted and surrounding villages, Essex
3-5 June	East of England Garden Show, Wood Green Animal Shelter, Godmanchester, Cambs
4 Jun	Newmarket Carnival, Town Centre, Newmarket, Suffolk
4/5 Jun	Woolpit Steam Rally, Warren Farm, Wetherden, nr. Stowmarket, Suffolk
5 Jun	Cambridgeshire County Show, Wimpole Hall and Home Farm, Arrington, nr. Royston, Cambs
6 Jun- 3 Sept	Stamford Shakespeare Festival, Rutland Open Air Theatre, Lincolnshire.
9-19 Jun	Woolpit Festival, various venues, Woolpit, Suffolk
10-12 Jun	Flower Festival, Hatfield House, Hatfield, Herts
10-26 Jun	58th Aldeburgh Festival of Music and the Arts, Snape Maltings, Snape, Suffolk

11 Jun	Strawberry Fair, Shenfield Common, Ingrave Road, Brentwood, Essex
11 Jun	Braintree and Bocking Carnival, various venues, Braintree, Essex
11/12 Jun	Deepdale Jazz Festival, Marsh Barn, Burnham Deepdale, Norfolk
11/12 Jun	Campaign 2005 WWII Living History Show, Twinwood Airfield, Clapham, Beds
11/12 Jun	Cressing Temple Craft Festival, Cressing Temple Barns, Cressing, nr. Braintree, Essex
11/12 Jun	Eye Open Gardens, Eye, Suffolk
11/12 Jun	Whitwell Steam and Country Fair, St. Pauls Walden, nr. Whitwell, Herts
11/12 Jun	Woburn Garden Show, Woburn Abbey, Woburn, Beds
12 Jun	Aldham Gardens Open Day, Aldham, nr. Colchester, Essex
12 Jun	15th Euston Park Rural Pastimes Show, Euston Hall, Euston, nr. Thetford, Suffolk
12 Jun*	Peterborough Kite Festival, Ferry Meadows Country Park, Peterborough, Cambs
17-19 Jun	South East Essex Garden Show, Barleylands Farm Centre, Billericay, Essex
17-19 Jun	The East of England Country Show, East of England Showground, Peterborough, Cambs
17-19 Jun	A1 Festival of Music and Dance, Sacrewell Farm and Country Centre, Thornhaugh, nr. Peterborough, Cambs
18 Jun	Brightlingsea Carnival, various venues, Brightlingsea, Essex

8 Jun	Lowestoft Fish Fayre, The Docks, Lowestoft, Suffolk
8 Jun	Woburn Village Open Gardens Day, Woburn, Bedfordshire
8 Jun-Jul	Haverhill Festival, Arts Centre, Haverhill, Suffolk
9 Jun	The Hidden Gardens of Bury St. Edmunds, Bury St. Edmunds, Suffolk
9 Jun	Nowton Park Country Fair, Nowton Road, Bury St. Edmunds, Suffolk
9 Jun	Lavenham's Hidden Gardens, Lavenham, Suffolk
9 Jun	Grease/Mania, Royal Green, Lowestoft
9 Jun-0 Jul	Great Annual Re-creation of Tudor Life, Kentwell Hall, Long Melford, Suffolk
4-27 Jun	Leigh Folk Festival, various venues, Leigh-on-Sea, Essex
4 Jun-7 Jul	Thaxted Festival, Parish Church and various venues, Thaxted, Essex
5/26 Jun	Bedford International Kite Festival, Russell Park, Bedford, Beds
5/26 Jun	Wings and Wheels Model Spectacular, North Weald Airfield, Epping, Essex
5/26 Jun	Summer Nationals (National Drag Racing Championships), Santa Pod Raceway, Podington, Beds
25/26 Jun	Wings, Wheels and Steam, Rougham Airfield, nr. Bury St. Edmunds, Suffolk
25/26 Jun	Sandringham Country Show and Horse Driving Trials, Sandringham Estate, Norfolk
25 Jun-10 Jul	Peterborough Festival, various venues, Peterborough, Cambs
25 Jun-10 Jul	IP-Art, various venues, Ipswich, Suffolk
26 Jun	Ampthill Festival, Gala Day, Ampthill Park, Ampthill, Beds
26 Jun	Castle Point Borough Show, Waterside Farm Showground, Canvey Island, Essex
26 Jun	Chelsworth Open Gardens Day, Chelsworth, nr. Hadleigh, Suffolk
26 Jun	Vintage Vehicle Rally, Leighton Buzzard Railway, Page's Park Station, Leighton Buzzard, Beds
29-30 Jun	Royal Norfolk Show, Norfolk Showground, Norwich, Norfolk
29 Jun-3 Jul	Wisbech Rose Fair, St. Peter's Parish Church, Wisbech, Cambs

July

1-10 Jul	Harwich Festival of the Arts, various venues, Harwich, Essex

1-17 Jul	Hitchin Festival, various venues, Hitchin, Herts
1-10 Jul	Wymondham Music, various venues, Wymondham, Norfolk
2 Jul	Families Day in Meadow Park, Borehamwood, Herts
2 Jul	Pin Mill Barge Match, River Orwell, Pin Mill, Suffolk
2 Jul	Ware Carnival Day, various venues, Ware, Herts
2 Jul	North Watford Show, Billeverett Community Centre, Watford, Herts
2 Jul	Zum, Wymondham Abbey
2-3 Jul	Bungay Hog Fair and Carnival
2-17 Jul	Bungay Festival, various venues, Bungay, Suffolk
3 Jul	Aquafest, Riverside (Willow Walk/Maltings area), Ely, Cambs
3 Jul*	Hunstanton Rotary Carnival, The Green, Hunstanton, Norfolk
3 Jul	Ipswich Music Day, Christchurch Park, Ipswich, Suffolk
3 Jul	Model Railway Mania, Leighton Buzzard Railway, Page's Park Station, Leighton Buzzard, Beds
7-10 Jul	Lord Mayor's Celebrations, City Centre, Norwich, Norfolk

7-17 Jul	Cambridge Film Festival, Arts Picture House, Cambridge, Cambs
8-10 Jul	20th Ely Folk Weekend, beside A10, Ely, Cambs
9 Jul	Hoddesdon Vintage and Classic Car Display, Town Centre, Hoddesdon, Herts
9 Jul	Ipswich Community Carnival, Town Centre, Ipswich, Suffolk
9 Jul	Tendring Hundred Show, Lawford House Park, Lawford, nr. Manningtree, Essex
9 Jul	World Pea Shooting Championships, Village Green, Witcham, Cambs
9/10 Jul	Bedfordshire Country Show, Old Warden Park, nr. Biggleswade, Beds
9/10 Jul	Flying Legends Air Show, Imperial War Museum, Duxford, Cambs
9-31 Jul	27th East Anglian International Summer Music Festival, The Old School, Bridge Street, Hadleigh, Suffolk
10-17 Jul	Swaffham Carnival Week, various venues, Swaffham, Norfolk
14-17 Jul	Bures Music Festival, various venues, Bures, Suffolk
14-17 Jul	Southwold Festival of the Sea, Blackshore, The Harbour, Southwold, Suffolk
15-17 Jul	Hacheston Rose Festival, various venues, Hacheston, Suffolk

5-17 Jul	Weeting Steam Engine Rally, Fengate Farm, Weeting, nr. Brandon, Suffolk	27 Jul	Sandringham Flower Show, Sandringham Park, Sandringham, Norfolk
5 Jul-3 Aug	26th Cambridge Summer Music Festival, various venues, Cambridge, Cambs	28/29 Jul	Lowestoft Seafront Air Festival 2005, Seafront, Lowestoft, Suffolk
6 Jul	World Snail Racing Championships, The Cricket Field, Grimston, nr. King's Lynn, Norfolk	28 Jul-2 Aug	Southend's International Jazz Festival, various venues, Southend-on-Sea, Essex
6-17 Jul	Holkham Country Fair, Holkham Hall, Holkham, Norfolk	29 Jul-2 Aug	Cambridge Folk Festival, Cherry Hinton Hall Grounds, Cherry Hinton, nr. Cambridge, Cambs
6-17 Jul	38th Snape Antiques and Fine Art Fair, Snape Maltings, nr. Aldeburgh, Suffolk	30/31 Jul	West Bergholt Historic Vehicle Rally, Nayland Road, West Bergholt, Essex
7 Jul	Swaffham Carnival	31 Jul-6Aug	Wells Carnival, various venues, Wells-next-the-Sea, Norfolk
8-31 Jul	Festival of Music and the Arts, various venues, King's Lynn, Norfolk		
8-31 Jul	King's Lynn Festival, various venues, King's Lynn, Norfolk	**August**	
9-21 Jul	East of England July Show, East of England Showground, Peterborough, Cambs	3 Aug	Sheringham Carnival, various venues, Sheringham, Norfolk
2-24 Jul	Bug Jam VW Beetle Festival, Santa Pod Raceway, Podington, Beds	4/5 Aug	Minsmere Family Event, RSPB Minsmere Nature Reserve, Westleton, nr. Saxmundham, Suffolk
3 Jul*	Clare World Music Festival, Clare Castle Country Park, Clare, Suffolk	4/6 Aug	12th Annual Rhythm and Booze Festival, The Angel Inn, Larling, Norfolk
3 Jul	Duxford Flying Proms, Imperial War Museum, Duxford, Cambs	5-7 Aug	Felixstowe Carnival, various venues, Felixstowe, Suffolk
4 Jul	London to Southend Classic Car Run, Western Esplanade, Southend-on-Sea, Essex	5-7 Aug	Art in Clay - National Pottery and Ceramics Festival, Hatfield House, Hatfield, Herts

6 Aug	Maldon Carnival, various venues, Maldon, Essex
6/7 Aug	Thurlow and Haverhill Steam and Country Show, Horseheath Racecourse, Haverhill, Suffolk
6/7 Aug	WWII: Re-Creation, Kentwell Hall, Long Melford, Suffolk
6-13 Aug	The Mundlesey Festival, Coronation Hall, Mundlesey, Norfolk
7 Aug	Duxford Military Vehicle Show, Imperial War Museum, Duxford, Cambs
7 Aug	Frettenham Festival, various venues, Frettenham, Norfolk
7 Aug	Helmingham Festival of Classics, Helmingham Hall, Helmingham, Suffolk
7 Aug	Royston Kite Festival, Therfield Heath, nr. Royston, Herts
7 Aug	Green Environmental Festival, Fairhaven Woodland and Water Garden, School Road, South Walsham, Norfolk
7 Aug	National Amber Hunt, Southwold Beach, Suffolk
7 Aug	Wayland Show, The Meadows, Brandon Road, Watton, Norfolk
7-14 Aug	Sunrise Carnival Procession, various venues, Lowestoft, Suffolk
8 Aug	Lifeboat Day, The Promenade, Cromer, Norfolk
13 Aug	Clacton Carnival, Town Centre, Clacton-on-Sea, Essex
13 Aug	Blackwater Barge Race, River Blackwater, Maldon, Essex

14 Aug	Hemsby Lifeboat Day, Hemsby Beach, Norfolk
14 Aug	25th Crabbing Championship, Ferry Car Park, Walberswick, Suffolk
14 Aug	Woburn Commercial Rally and Road Run, Woburn Abbey, Woburn, Beds
15 Aug	Aldeburgh Olde Marine Regatta and Carnival, High Street and Seafront, Aldeburgh, Suffolk
16-20 Aug	Summer Championship Show, East of England Showground, Peterborough, Cambs
17 Aug	Cromer Carnival, various venues, Cromer, Norfolk
18/19 Aug	Thorpeness Regatta and Fireworks, Thorpeness, nr. Aldeburgh, Suffolk
20 Aug *	Illuminated Carnival Procession and Firework Spectacular, Seafront, Southend-on-Sea, Essex
20 Aug	Walton Carnival, various venues, Walton-on-the-Naze, Essex
20/21 Aug	V Festival, Hylands Park, Chelmsford, Essex
20/21 Aug	Rougham Air Display 2005, Rougham Airfield, nr. Bury St. Edmunds, Suffolk
21 Aug	Great Yarmouth Carnival, various venues, Great Yarmouth, Norfolk
21 Aug*	Hunstanton Rotary Kite Festival, Smithdon School Playing Field, Hunstanton, Norfolk
23/24 Aug	Basildon Festival, Wat Tyler Country Park, Pitsea, nr. Basildon, Essex
25/26 Aug	Clacton Air Show, Marine Parade, Clacton-on-Sea, Essex
25-29 Aug	Clacton Jazz Festival, various venues, Clacton-on-Sea, Essex

6-29 Aug   Suffolk Villages Festival, Boxford/Hadleigh/Stoke-by-Nayland Churches, Suffolk

6-29 Aug   High Summer Re-Creation of Tudor Life, Kentwell Hall, Long Melford, Suffolk

7 Aug   RNLI Street Fayre, Aldeburgh, Suffolk

7/28 Aug   Ely Horticultural Society Show, Paradise Sports Centre, Ely, Cambs

7-29 Aug   The Annual Glenn Miller Festival, Twinwood Airfield, nr. Bedford, Beds

7-29 Aug   Southend Summer Garden Show, Garon Park, Southend-on-sea

7 Aug-Sept   Burnham Week, various venues, Burnham-on-Crouch, Essex

8 Aug   Mini Adventure, St Felix School, Southwold

8/29 Aug   Eye Show, Eye Showground, Dragon Hill, Eye, Suffolk

8/29 Aug   Village at War, Roots of Norfolk, Gressenhall, nr. Dereham, Norfolk

8/29 Aug *   Classic Motor Show, Knebworth House, nr. Stevenage, Herts

8/29 Aug   Fenland Country Fair, Quy Park, Stow Cum Quy, Cambs

8 Aug-6 Sept   Festival of Bowls, Seafront, Great Yarmouth, Norfolk

29 Aug   Aylsham Agricultural Show, Blickling Park, Blickling, nr. Aylsham, Norfolk

29 Aug   Lavenham Carnival, various venues, Lavenham, Suffolk

29 Aug   Lowestoft Lions Charity Gala Day, Nicholas Everitt Park, Oulton Broad, Suffolk

September

2-4 Sept   Suffolk Autumn Garden Show, Suffolk Showground, Ipswich, Suffolk

2-4 Sept   Walton Folk Festival, various venues, Walton-on-the-Naze, Essex

2-4 Sept*   Woburn Oyster Festival, Market Place, Woburn, Beds

3/4 Sept   English Wine Festival and Country Craft Fair, New Hall Vineyards, Purleigh, Essex

4 Sept   Burston Strike School Annual Rally, Burston, nr. Diss, Norfolk

4 Sept   Herring Day, Hemsby Beach, nr. Great Yarmouth, Norfolk

6-10 Sept   19th Chappel Beer Festival, East Anglian Railway Museum, Wakes Colne, nr. Colchester, Essex

8-11 Sept   The European Finals (FIA European Drag Racing Championships), Santa Pod Raceway, Podington, Beds

9-11 Sept	Reedham Ferry Folk Festival, Reedham Ferry Inn, Reedham, Norfolk	24 Sept	Burnham Carnival, various venues, Burnham on-Crouch, Essex
10 Sept	Norfolk Churches Trust - Sponsored Cycle Ride, various locations, Norfolk	24 Sept	Maldon Regatta, various venues, Maldon, Essex
10/11 Sept	Essex Country Show, Barleylands Farm Centre, Billericay, Essex	24 Sept	Soham Pumpkin Fayre, Recreation Ground, Soham, Cambs
10/11 Sept	Duxford 2005 Air Show, Imperial War Museum, Duxford, Cambs	24/25 Sept	Cressing Temple Craft Festival, Cressing Temple Barns, Cressing, nr. Braintree, Essex
10/11 Sept	Great Yarmouth Maritime Festival, South Quay, Great Yarmouth, Norfolk	24/27 Sept	Re-Creation of Tudor Life at Michaelmas, Kentwell Hall, Long Melford, Suffolk
10/11 Sept	Haddenham Steam Rally, Haddenham, nr. Ely, Cambs	25 Sept	The Mascot Grand National 2005, Huntingdon Racecourse, Brampton, nr. Huntingdon, Cambs
10/11 Sept	Steam-Up Weekend, Leighton Buzzard Railway, Page's Park Station, Leighton Buzzard, Beds		

October

11 Sept	Medieval Jousting, Knebworth House, nr. Stevenage, Herts	1 Oct	Enthusiasts Day, Leighton Buzzard Railway, Page's Park Station, Leighton Buzzard, Beds
17/18 Sept	Bedfordshire Steam and Country Fayre, Shuttleworth Park, Old Warden, nr. Biggleswade, Bedfordshire	1/2 Oct	National Finals (National Drag Racing Championships), Santa Pod Raceway, Podington, Beds
17/18 Sept*	Old Leigh Regatta, Old Leigh Town, nr. Southend-on-Sea, Essex	1/2 Oct	Ploughs to Propellers, Rougham Airfield, nr. Bury St. Edmunds, Suffolk
17/18 Sept	Grand Henham Steam Rally, Benacre Hall, Wrentham, Suffolk	1-31 Oct	Bedford Film and Book Festival
21-24 Sept*	Ipswich Beer Festival, Corn Exchange, Ipswich, Suffolk	5-8 Oct *	Bedford Beer Festival, Corn Exchange, Bedford, Beds
23-25 Sept	King's Lynn Poetry Festival, Thoresby College, College Lane, King's Lynn, Norfolk	9 Oct	World Conker Championships 2005, The Village Green, Ashton, Cambs

9 Oct	East of England Autumn Show, East of England Showground, Peterborough, Cambs
14-16 Oct	Crafts for Christmas at Chilford Hall Vineyard, Balsham Road, nr. Linton, Cambs
16 Oct	Autumn Air Show, Imperial War Museum, Duxford, Cambs
21-23 Oct	Trafalgar Weekend, nation-wide
24-27 Oct	Norwich Beer Festival, St. Andrews and Blackfriars Hall, Norwich, Norfolk
29/30 Oct	WWII: The House Requisitioned, Kentwell Hall, Long Melford, Suffolk
29/30 Oct	Cambridge Gift Show, Wood Green Animal Shelters, London Road, Godmanchester, Cambs

November

4 Nov	37th Big Night Out, Melford Hall Park, Long Melford, Sudbury, Suffolk
4-6 Nov*	Aldeburgh Poetry Festival, Jubilee Hall, Aldeburgh, Suffolk
5 Nov	Harwich Guy Carnival, Main Road, Harwich, Essex
5 Nov	Annual Firework Display, Christchurch Park, Ipswich, Suffolk
5 Nov *	Guy Fawkes Night Bonfire and Fireworks, Promenade Park, Maldon, Essex
5 Nov	Luton Fireworks Spectacular, Popes Meadow, Old Bedford Road, Luton, Beds
5 Nov	Gala Fireworks Celebration at St. Albans, Verulamium Park, St. Albans, Herts
5 Nov	Sparks in the Park, Earlham Park, Norwich, Norfolk
5-6 Nov	Christmas Craft Show, Woburn Safari Park, Woburn, Beds

10-14 Nov	Southwold Literary Festival, St. Edmunds Hall, Southwold, Suffolk
12 Nov	Southend Christmas Spectacular and Lights, High Street, Southend
12/13 Nov	Colchester Gift Show, Leisure World, Cowdray Road, Colchester, Essex
12/13 Nov	East of England Christmas Festival, East of England Showground, Peterborough
16 Nov-* 23 Dec	The Thursford Christmas Spectacular Thursford, nr. Fakenham, Norfolk
19 Nov	Dunstable Tudor Festival, Town Centre, Dunstable, Beds
19/20 Nov	Festival of Swans, Wildfowl and Wetlands Trust, Welney, Cambs
25/27 Nov	Norfolk Christmas Gift Show, Norfolk Showground, Norwich, Norfolk

December

1 and 8 Dec	Maldon Victorian Evenings, High Street, Maldon, Essex
3/4 Dec	Christmas Craft Fair, Knebworth House, nr. Stevenage, Herts
4 Dec	Brentwood Christmas Craft and Gift Show, Brentwood Centre, Doddinghurst Road, Brentwood, Essex
9-11 Dec	Magic of Christmas, Blickling Hall, Blickling, nr. Aylsham, Norfolk
9-11 Dec	Victorian Christmas Fair, Town Centre, Bedford, Beds
11 Dec	The Celebration of the Life and Music of Glenn Miller, Twinwood Airfield, nr. Bedford, Beds
11 Dec	Hitchin Winter Gala Day, Town Centre, Hitchin, Herts

Horseracing (contact relevant racecourse for fixture list)

Fakenham, Norfolk - (01328) 862388
www.fakenhamracecourse.co.uk

Great Yarmouth, Norfolk - (01493) 842527
www.greatyarmouth-racecourse.co.uk

Huntingdon, Cambridgeshire - (01480) 453373
www.huntingdon-racecourse.co.uk

Newmarket, Suffolk - (01638) 675500
www.newmarketracecourses.co.uk

Motor Sports (contact relevant venue for fixture list)

Oulton Broad Powerboat Racing, nr. Lowestoft, Suffolk
(regular race meetings) - www.lobmbc.co.uk

Santa Pod Raceway, Podington, Bedfordshire
(drag-racing and other events) - (01234) 782828
www.santapod.com

Snetterton Circuit, nr. Attleborough, Norfolk
(various car and bike events) - (01953) 887303
www.snetterton.co.uk

Stock car/banger racing:
Arena Essex, Purfleet, Essex - (01708) 867728
www.arenaessex.co.uk

Also stadiums at Bovingdon, Hertfordshire; Great Yarmouth,
Norfolk; Swaffham, Norfolk; and Ipswich, Suffolk. More
information on these on (01420) 588020
www.spedeworth.co.uk

Open Gardens

British Red Cross (on-line listing of gardens open) -
(0207) 235 5454 www.redcross.org.uk

County offices (for programmes):
Bedfordshire (01234) 349166
Cambridgeshire (01223) 868686
Essex (01245) 291014
Hertfordshire (01992) 586609
Norfolk (01603) 426361
Suffolk (01284) 767215

The National Gardens Scheme - (01483) 211535
www.ngs.org.uk

St. John's Ambulance - Essex (01245) 265678,
Norfolk (01603) 621649

Miscellaneous
The following organisations have a wide and varied range of
events at their properties in the East of England.

English Heritage - (01223) 582700
www.english-heritage.org.uk

Forestry Commission (Enterprise) - (01842) 810271
www.forestry.gov.uk

The National Trust - 0870 609 5388
www.nationaltrust.org.uk

RSPB (Royal Society for the Protection of Birds) -
(01603) 661662 www.rspb.org.uk

The Wildlife Trusts - www.wildlifetrusts.org
County offices:
Bedfordshire and Cambridgeshire (01223) 712400
Essex (01621) 862960
Hertfordshire (01727) 858901
Norfolk (01603) 625540
Suffolk (01473) 890089

Historic Houses

BEDFORDSHIRE

Elstow (nr. Bedford)
Elstow Moot Hall Map ref. D6
Elstow Green, Church End
Tel: (01234) 266889 Web: www.bedfordshire.gov.uk
A medieval market hall containing exhibits of 17th C. life, including beautiful period furniture. Publications and antique maps for sale.
Times: Open 25 Mar and 27 Mar-30 Sept, Tues-Thurs, Sun and Bank Holidays 1300-1600.
Fee: £1.00/50p/50p.
Facilities: ⊛ 🅿 🚌 T(40 mins)

Moggerhanger (nr. Bedford)
Moggerhanger Park Map ref. E6
Park Road
Tel: (01767) 641007
Web: www.moggerhangerpark.com
Recently restored Georgian Grade I listed building designed by Sir John Soane, with grounds landscaped by Humphry Repton. Guided tours, tea rooms, exhibition and visitor centre.
Times: Park, visitor centre and tea rooms open all year daily 1100-1600. Historic house and guided tours June-Sept daily 1100-1600. Please contact for further details.
Fee: Guided Tours/£5.00/free.
Facilities: ⊛ 🅿 T(1 hr) 🏌 🐕 (park only) 🔲

Shefford
Chicksands Priory Map ref. E7
Tel: (01525) 860497
12th C. priory of the Gilbertine Order - only one cloister remains. After the dissolution, it became the ancestral seat of the Osborn Family until 1936. Medieval roof timbers and 13th C. vaulting.
Times: By appointment only - 1st and 3rd Sun of each month from Apr-Oct at 1400.
Fee: Donations welcome (suggested £5, includes refreshments).
Facilities: 🅿 T(1 hr) 🏌

Woburn
Woburn Abbey Map ref. C8
Tel: (01525) 290666 Web: www.woburnabbey.co.uk
An 18th C. Palladian mansion, altered by Henry Holland, the Prince Regent's architect, containing a collection of English silver, French and English furniture and art.
Times: Open 24 Mar-2 Oct, Mon-Sat, Sun and Bank Hols, 1100-1600*(* last entry); Deer Park open daily 1000-1700. Nov and Dec opening to be advised, please telephone for details.
Fee: £9.50/£5.00/£8.50.
Facilities: ⊛ 🅿 T(2 hrs) 🏌 🍴 🐕 (park only)

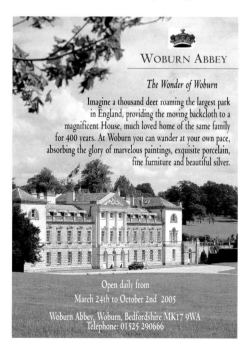

CAMBRIDGESHIRE

Arrington (nr. Royston)
Wimpole Hall and Home Farm Map ref. F12
Tel: (01223) 206000 Web: www.wimpole.org
An 18th C. house in a landscaped park with a folly and
Chinese bridge. Plunge bath and yellow drawing room in
the house, the work of John Soane. Home Farm with rare
breeds centre.
Times: Hall, Farm and garden open 19 Mar-30 Oct, Sat-
Wed, 1300-1700, (farm and garden 1030-1700); farm and
garden only also open 1 Jan-18 Mar Sat and Sun, 1100-
1600; 1 Nov-31 Dec, Sat and Sun, 1100-1600. Open Bank
Holiday Mondays and 25 Mar. Park - open all year, dawn
to dusk.
Fee: Estate Ticket £10.20/5.50/26.00 (family)Hall and
garden only £6.90/£3.40. Farm and garden £5.40/£3.40.
Garden £2.70/free
Facilities: ⊛ ▣ T(3½ hrs) ⊕ ⋒ ✝ (park only on
leads) **NT**

Elton (nr. Peterborough)
Elton Hall Map ref. B6
Tel: (01832) 280468
An historic house and gardens open to the public with a
fine collection of paintings, furniture, books and Henry
VIII's prayer book. There is also a restored rose garden.
Times: Open 29 and 30 May; Jun, Wed; Jul-Aug, Wed
Thurs and Sun; 29 Aug, 1400-1700.
Fee: £6.00. School parties £3.00.
Facilities: ⊛ ▣ T(50 mins) ⋔ ⊕

Wimpole Hall and Home Farm, Arrington

Ely
Oliver Cromwell's House Map ref. I8
29 St. Mary's Street
Tel: (01353) 662062 Web: www.eastcambs.gov.uk
The family home of Oliver Cromwell with a 17th C. kitchen,
parlour, a haunted bedroom, a Tourist Information Centre,
souvenirs and a craft shop.
Times: Open 1 Apr-31 Oct, daily, 1000-1730. 1 Nov-31
Mar, Sun-Fri, 1100-1600; Sat, 1000-1700.Closed 25 and
26 Dec.
Fee: £3.75/£2.50/£3.25/£10.00 (family).
Facilities: ⊛ Q ⊨ T(45 mins) ⋔

Godmanchester
Island Hall Map ref. D9/10
Tel: (01480) 459676
A mid-18th C. mansion of architectural importance on the
Great Ouse river. A family home with interesting ancestral
possessions.
Times: Open by appointment for groups only, May-Sept.
Closed Aug.
Fee: £4.00/£2.00.
Facilities: ⊛ ▣ T(2½hrs) ⊕

Hemingford Grey (nr. St. Ives)
The Manor Map ref. E9
Tel: (01480) 463134 Web: www.greenknowe.co.uk
The 'Green Knowe' children's books were based on this
ancient house. Also see the Lucy Boston patchworks.
Garden is 4½ acres with topiary.
Times: Garden open all year, daily, 1100-1700 (dusk in
winter). House tours during May 1100 and 1400 or by
appointment.
Fee: House £5.00/£1.50/£4.00. Garden £2.00.
Facilities: ⊨ T(1½ hrs) ⋔ ✝

Kimbolton
Kimbolton Castle Map ref. B10
Tel: (01480) 860505 Web: www.kimbolton.cambs.sch.uk
A Tudor house, remodelled by Vanbrugh with Pellegrini
mural paintings, an Adam gatehouse and fine parklands.
The castle is now occupied by an independent school.
Times: Open 6 Mar and 6 Nov, Sun, 1300-1600.
Fee: Please contact for details of admission prices.
Facilities: ▣ T(1½ hrs) ⊕ ⋒

Lode (nr. Cambridge)
Anglesey Abbey, Gardens and Lode Mill Map ref. I11
Quy Road
Tel: (01223) 810080
Web: www.nationaltrust.org.uk/angleseyabbey
A 13th C. abbey with a later Jacobean house and the
famous Fairhaven collection of paintings and furniture.
There is also an outstanding 100-acre garden and
arboretum. Watermill.
Times: Garden, house and mill open 23 Mar-6 Nov, Wed-
Sun 1030-1730 (house and Mill 1300-1700). Garden only
also open 1 Jan-23 Mar, Wed-Sun 1030-1630, 4 July-28
Aug, Mon-Sun 1030-1730, 9 Nov-18 Dec and 28-31 Dec,
Wed-Sun, 1030-1630. Closed 25 Mar.
Fee: Abbey, gardens and mill summer £7.00/£3.50.
Gardens and mill only £4.30/£2.20. Winter season
£3.60/£1.80.
Facilities: ⊛ Q 🅿 ⬛ T(4 hrs) ⚙ 🍴 NT

Nassington (nr. Peterborough)
The Prebendal Manor Medieval Centre Map ref. B6
Church Street
Tel: (01780) 782575 Web: www.prebendal-manor.co.uk
Discover life during the Middle Ages at this 13th C. Grade I
listed building, once King Cnut's Royal Manor. Europe's
largest recreated medieval garden, rare breed animals and
tithe barn exhibition.
Times: Open 28 Mar-end Sept, Wed, Sun and Bank Hol
Mon 1300-1730.
Fee: £5.50/£2.50/£5.00. Gardens only £5.00/£2.00/£5.00
Facilities: 🅿 T(2-3 hrs) 🏹 (audio tours) ⚙ 🍴 🗃

Stamford
Burghley House Map ref. A4
Tel: (01780) 752451 Web: www.burghley.co.uk
Immense Elizabethan stately home. Built by William Cecil
in 1587, and occupied by his descendants ever since. 18
state rooms including art collections, woodcarvings and
magnificent ceilings.
Times: Open 25 Mar-30 Oct, daily, 1100-1700 (last
admission 1630). Mon-Sat - guided tours only; Sun - free
flow in house. Closed 3 Sept.
Fee: £8.20/£3.70/£7.20/family £21.00.
Facilities: 🅿 ⬛ ⇌ T(3-4 hrs) 🏹⚙ 🍴 🗃

Wisbech
Peckover House and Gardens Map ref. H4
North Brink
Tel: (01945) 583463 Web: www.nationaltrust.org.uk
A merchant's house on the North Brink of the River Nene,
built in 1722, with a plaster and wood rococo interior and
a notable 2 acre Victorian garden with unusual trees.
Times: Open 19 Mar-6 Nov, Sat, Sun, Tues, Wed,1200-
1700.
Fee: House and gardens £4.50/£2.25/family £14.00
Facilities: ⊛ T(3 hrs) ⚙ NT

ESSEX

Chingford
Queen Elizabeth's Hunting Lodge Map ref. A9
Rangers Road
Tel: (0208) 529 7090
Web: www.cityoflondon.gov.uk/openspaces
Timber-framed hunting lodge built for King Henry VIII in
1543. Surrounded by the ancient forest of Epping.
Times: Open all year, Wed-Sun and Bank Hols, 1300-1600,
closed 24 Dec-1 Jan.
Fee: Free.
Facilities: 🅿 ⬛ ⇌ T(45 mins) 🍴

Coggeshall
Paycockes Map ref. I5
West Street
Tel: (01376) 561305 Web: www.nationaltrust.org.uk
A half-timbered merchant's house, built in the 16th C. with
a richly-carved interior and a small display of Coggeshall
lace. Very attractive garden.
Times: Open 27 Mar-9 Oct, Tues, Thurs, Sun 1400-1730.
Fee: £2.40/£1.20. Joint ticket with Grange Barn
£3.50/£1.80.
Facilities: ⊛ T(45 mins) NT

Hartford End (nr. Braintree)
Leez Priory Map ref. F5
Tel: (01245) 362555 Web: www.brideshead.co.uk
13th C. priory ruins and 16th C. redbrick Tudor mansion
and tower. 40 acres of parkland, lakes, walled gardens,
Tudor tunnels and oak-panelled Great Hall.
Times: Open all year, by appointment only.
Fee: Free.
Facilities: 🅿 T(3 hrs)

Ingatestone
Ingatestone Hall Map ref. E9
Hall Lane
Tel: (01277) 353010
Tudor house and gardens, the home of the Petre family
since 1540. Family portrait collection, furniture and other
heirlooms on display.
Times: Open 26 Mar-25 Sept, Sat, Sun and Bank Hol
Mons, 1300-1800. 20 Jul-2 Sept, Wed-Fri, 1300-1800.
Fee: House and Garden £4.00/£2.00/£3.50.
Facilities: ⊛ 🅿 ⇌ T(1½ hrs) ⚙ 🍴

For even more
information visit
our website at
www.visiteastofengland.com

Layer Marney (nr. Colchester)
Layer Marney Tower Map ref. J5
Tel: (01206) 330784 Web: www.layermarneytower.co.uk
A 1520 Tudor-brick gatehouse, 8 storeys high with
Italianate terracotta cresting and windows. Gardens, park,
rare breed farm animals and also the nearby church.
Times: Open 20 Mar-2 Oct, Sun-Thurs, 1200-1700.
Fee: £3.50/£2.00/£10.00 (family).
Facilities: ⊛ Q 🄿 T(2 hrs) 🕐 🎪 🏇

Rayleigh
Dutch Cottage Map ref. H10
Crown Hill
Tel: (01702) 318150 Web: www.rochford.gov.uk
This tiny octagonal cottage, based on the design of the
17th C. Dutch settlers, must be one of the smallest, and
certainly most unusual 'council houses' in Britain.
Times: Open all year (by appointment), Wed, 1330-1630.
Fee: Free.
Facilities: 🚌 ⇌ T(40 mins) 🏇

Rochford
The Old House Map ref. I10
South Street
Tel: (01702) 318144 Web: www.rochford.gov.uk
History is revealed in the rooms of this elegant house,
originally built in 1270, lovingly restored and now housing
the District Council offices.
Times: Open all year (by appointment), Wed, 1400-1630.
Fee: Free.
Facilities: 🚌 ⇌ T(40 mins) 🏇

Ingatestone Hall

Saffron Walden
Audley End House and Park Map ref. C2
Audley End
Tel: (01799) 522399 Web: www.english-heritage.org.uk
Visit a former wonder of the nation and experience the
sumptuous splendour enjoyed by royalty in one of
England's grandest stately homes. Wonder at the lavish
interiors and relax in the lovingly restored 19th century
parterre garden and beautiful Elysian garden cascade.
Times: House open 3-21 Mar, Thurs-Mon, 1000-1600; 23
Mar-3 Oct, Wed-Mon, 1200-1700; 6-31 Oct, Thurs-Mon,
1000-1600. Gardens 3-21 Mar, Thurs-Mon, 1000-1700; 23
Mar-3 Oct, Wed- Mon, 1000-1800; 6-31 Oct, Thurs- Mon,
1000-1700. Closed 24, 25, Dec, 1 Jan.
Fee: House and Gardens £8.95/£4.50/£6.70. Gardens only
£4.60/£2.30/£3.50.
Facilities: ⊛ Q 🄿 ⇌ T(3 hrs) 🕐 🎪 🏇 (on leads) EH

Widford (nr. Chelmsford)
Hylands House Map ref. F8
Hylands Park, London Road
Tel: (01245) 496800 Web: www.chelmsfordbc.gov
Originally built in 1730. Currently nine restored rooms are
available to view. Exhibitions on the history of the house, as
well as monthly art exhibitions are on display.
Times: All year, Mon 1100-1600, Sun 1100-1800 (1 Apr-30
Sept closes 1800 on Mon). Closed 25 Dec
Fee: £3.20/free/£2.20.
Facilities: ⊛ 🄿 🚌 T(1½ hrs) 🕐 🎪 ♿

See also:
Southchurch Hall Museum page 78

**For even more
information visit
our website at
www.visiteastofengland.com**

HERTFORDSHIRE

Ayot St. Lawrence (nr. Welwyn Garden City)
Shaw's Corner Map ref. F11
Tel: (01438) 820307
Web: www.nationaltrust.org.uk/shawscorner
The home of George Bernard Shaw from 1906 until his death in 1950, with literary and personal effects on display. 3¹/2 acre garden.
Times: Open 19 Mar-30 Oct, Wed-Sun and Bank Hol Mon, Garden 1200-1730, House 1300-1700.
Last admission 1630.
Fee: £3.80/£1.90/£9.50 (family).
Facilities: ☺ �ＰＴ(1¹/2 hrs) ⧘ NT

Gorhambury (nr. St. Albans)
Gorhambury Map ref. E13
Tel: (01727) 855000
A classical-style mansion, built from 1777-1784 by Sir Robert Taylor. 16th C. enamelled glass, 17th C. carpet and historic portraits of the Bacon and Grimston families.
Times: Open 5 May-29 Sept, Thurs, 1400-1700.
Fee: £6.00/£3.00/£4.00.
Facilities: Ｐ Ｔ(1¹/2 hrs) ⧘

Hatfield

Hatfield House Map ref. G12/13
Tel: (01707) 287010 Web: www.hatfield-house.co.uk
Magnificent Jacobean house, home of the Marquess of Salisbury. Exquisite gardens, model soldiers and park trails. Childhood home of Queen Elizabeth I.
Times: Open 26 Mar-28 Sept, Sat-Wed, house, 1200-1600. Gardens, park, gift shop and restaurant, 1100-1730. Guided tours on Mon, except Bank Hols.
Fee: House, park and gardens
£8.00/£4.00/£22.00(family). Park and gardens
£4.50/£3.50. Park £2.00/£1.00. Park and gardens (Mon)
£6.50/£6.50. House tour extra (Mon) £5.00/£5.00.
Facilities: ☺ Ｑ Ｐ ⬛ ⮐ Ｔ(2¹/2 hrs) ⧘ ⬙ ⧘
⧘ (park only) ▦

'U-think-he-saw-us' on the Dino Trail...

Knebworth
HOUSE, GARDENS, PARK, ADVENTURE PLAYGROUND & DINOSAUR TRAIL

Home of the Lytton family for over 500 years, where Elizabeth I visited, Dickens acted and Churchill painted. With its ever-changing architecture and colourful family history, peppered throughout with famous names, a visit to Knebworth House, Gardens and Park is full of surprising discoveries. The extensive Gardens, Maze, Indian Raj Display, Dino Trail, Adventure Playground, Miniature Railway, Gift Shop and Garden Terrace Tea Room, all set in 250 acres of deer park.

FOR A LIST OF EVENTS IN THE PARK, FROM EASTER THROUGH TO SEPTEMBER - PLEASE VISIT OUR WEBSITE OR PHONE FOR MORE INFORMATION AND ENTRANCE PRICES.

www.knebworthhouse.com

The Estate Office, Knebworth Park, Nr Stevenage, Herts SG3 6PY
Tel: 01438 812661   Fax: 01438 811908
email: info@knebworthhouse.com   website: www.knebworthhouse.com
Immediate access off the A1(M), via our own slip road at Junction 7, 15 miles from M25 (J23).

Hoddesdon
Rye House Gatehouse Map ref. J12
Rye House Quay, Rye Road
Tel: (01992) 702200 Web: www.leevalleypark.com
A 15th C. moated building, the scene of the 'Rye House Plot' to assassinate King Charles II in 1683. Features include an exhibition and a shop.
Times: Open 25 Mar-25 Sept, Sat, Sun and Bank Hol Mon, 1100-1700.
Fee: £1.45/90p/90p
Facilities: ⊛ 🄿 ⇌ T(30 mins) 🛱

Knebworth (nr. Stevenage)
Knebworth House, Gardens and Park Map ref. G10/11
Tel: (01438) 812661 Web: www.knebworthhouse.com
Tudor manor house, re-fashioned in the 19th C., housing a collection of manuscripts, portraits and Jacobean banquet hall. Formal gardens and adventure playground.
Times: Open 19-20 Mar, Sat and Sun; 25 Mar-10 Apr, daily; 16 Apr-22 May Sat, Sun and Bank Hols; 28 May-5 Jun, daily; 11-26 Jun, Sat and Sun; 2 Jul-4 Sept daily; 11-25 Sept, Sat and Sun. House open 1200-1700 (last admission at 1615). Park open 1100-1730.
Fee: House, park, gardens and playground £8.50/£8.00/£8.00/£29.00(family).
Park, gardens and playground £6.50/£6.50/£6.50/£25.00.
Facilities: ⊛ 🄿 T(2½ hrs) 🎟 🛱 🛉 (park only on leads)

Ware
Ware Priory Map ref. I11/12
High Street
Tel: (01920) 460316 Web: www.warepriory.co.uk
Grade I Listed, the Priory stands in 7 acres of picturesque riverside grounds. Founded as a Franciscan Friary in 1338.
Times: Open 10 and 11 Sept.
Fee: Free.
Facilities: ⊛ 🄿 ⇌ T(1-2 hrs) 🛱 🄿

NORFOLK

Blakeney
Blakeney Guildhall Map ref. H/12
Tel: (01223) 582700 Web: www.english-heritage.org.uk
The remains of the 14th C. basement to a merchant's house which was most likely used for storage.
Times: Open at any reasonable time.
Fee: Free.
Facilities: ⊛ T(30 mins) EH

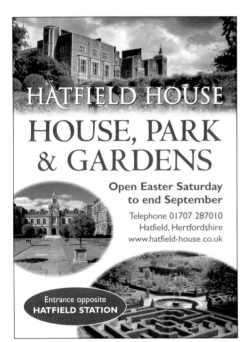

HATFIELD HOUSE
HOUSE, PARK & GARDENS

Open Easter Saturday to end September

Telephone 01707 287010
Hatfield, Hertfordshire
www.hatfield-house.co.uk

Entrance opposite
HATFIELD STATION

HOLKHAM
Much more than a stately home

OPEN from 2 June to 30 September
Discounts for Group Visits
Private Guided Tours also
available, please contact
Tel: (01328) 710227 for details

Holkham Beach — Palladian Hall
Cafés — Bygones Museum
The Victoria Hotel — Pottery Shop
Art, Crafts and Fine Food Centre
Deer Park — Holkham Ice Cream

www.holkham.co.uk

Blickling (nr. Aylsham)

Blickling Hall, Garden and Park Map ref. K4

Tel: (01263) 738030 Web: www.nationaltrust.org.uk

A Jacobean redbrick mansion with garden, orangery, parkland and lake. Spectacular long gallery, superb plasterwork ceilings and fine collections of furniture, pictures, books and tapestries. Walks. Cycle hire available.

Times: House open - 19 Mar-2 Oct, Wed-Sun, 1300-1700. 5-30 Oct, Wed-Sun, 1300-1600. Garden open 5 Jan-18 Mar Thurs-Sun, 1100-1600; 19 Mar-31 July, Wed-Sun, 1015-1715; 2-31 Aug, Tues-Sun,1015-1715; 1 Sep-30 Oct, Wed-Sun 1015-1715; 3 Nov-23 Dec, Thurs-Sun, 1100-1600. Park open all year, daily, dawn-dusk.

Fee: House and garden £7.30/£3.65. Garden only £4.20/£2.10.

Facilities: T(2 hrs) NT

Erpingham (nr. Aylsham)

Wolterton Park Map ref. K4

Tel: (01263) 584175 Web: www.manningtongardens.co.uk

A beautiful Georgian house with lake and extensive parkland. Park has a playground, walks and orienteering. House with fascinating history.

Times: Park open all year, daily, 0900-dusk. Hall open 1 Apr-28 Oct, 1400-1700. Last admission 1600.

Fee: Hall £5.00/£2.50. Park free, but car park charge of £2.00.

Facilities: T(2 hrs) (park only on leads)

Felbrigg (nr. Cromer)

Felbrigg Hall Map ref. K3

Tel: (01263) 837444 Web: www.nationaltrust.org.uk

A 17th C. country house with original 18th C. furniture and pictures. There is also a walled garden, orangery, park and woodland with way-marked walks, shops and catering.

Times: Open 19 Mar-30 Oct, Hall Sat-Wed, 1300-1700; Gardens Sat-Wed 1100-1700, 21 Jul-9 Sept, daily, 1100-1700. Closed 25 Mar.

Fee: Hall and gardens £6.30/£3.10/£16.20 (family). Gardens only £2.70.

Facilities: T(2 hrs) (Not Hall, garden or catering)**NT**

Houghton

Houghton Hall Map ref. E4

Tel: (01485) 528569 Web: www.houghtonhall.com

Splendid Palladian house built by Sir Robert Walpole. Magnificently furnished State Rooms. 5-acre walled garden - full of colour all summer. 20,000 Model Soldier Museum. Restaurant and Shop.

Times: Open Easter-29 Sept, Wed, Thurs, Sun and Bank Hol Mon. Gates, Garden, Solider Museum, Restaurant and Shop 1100-1700. House 1330-1730 (last admission 1630)

Fee: £7.00/£3.00, £16.00(family).

Excluding house £4.50/£2.00.

Facilities: T(2 hrs)

Norwich

Dragon Hall Map ref. K/L7

115-123 King Street

Tel: (01603) 663922

Web: www.dragonhall.org

Medieval merchant's hall with outstanding timber-framed structure. The 15th C. Great Hall has a crown-post roof with an intricately carved and painted dragon.

Times: Closed for extensive renovation until Aug 2005. Exact re-opening to be confirmed, please contact for details.

Fee: £4.50/£2.95/£3.45.

Facilities: T(1 hr)

Oxborough (nr. Swaffham)

Oxburgh Hall Map ref. E8

Tel: (01366) 328258 Web: www.nationaltrust.org.uk

A 15th C. moated redbrick fortified manor-house with an 80ft gatehouse, Mary Queen of Scot's needlework, a Catholic priest's hole, garden, woodland walks and a Catholic chapel.

Times: House open 19 Mar-30 Oct, Sat-Wed, 1300-1700. Garden open 8 Jan-13 Mar, Sat and Sun, 1100-1600. 19 Mar-31 Jul, Sat-Wed, 1100-1730. 1-31 Aug, daily, 1100-1730. 3 Sept-30 Oct, Sat-Wed, 1100-1730. 5 Nov-18Dec, Sat and Sun, 1100-1600. Closed 25 Mar, 19 Dec-7 Jan .

Fee: House and garden £6.00/£3.00/£15.50 (family). Garden and estate £3.00/£1.50.

Facilities: T(3 hrs) NT

Sandringham (nr. King's Lynn)
Sandringham Map ref. D4/5
Tel: (01553) 612908 Web: www.sandringhamestate.co.uk
The country retreat of HM The Queen. A delightful house set in 60 acres of gardens and lakes. Museum of royal vehicles and memorabilia. 600 acre country park, with visitor centre.
Times: Open daily, 26 Mar-late July and early Aug-30 Oct, 1100-1645.
Fee: House and gardens £7.00/£4.50/£5.50. Gardens only £5.00/£3.00/£4.00/£13.00.
Facilities: ⊛ ☐ 🚾 T(3½ hrs) ⊕ ☵ 🔲

Thetford
Thetford Warren Lodge Map ref. F11
Tel: (01223) 582700 Web: www.english-heritage.org.uk
The ruins of a small two storey medieval gamekeeper's lodge which can only be viewed from the outside.
Times: Open at any reasonable time.
Fee: Free.
Facilities: ⊛ T(20 mins) 🐕 (on leads) **EH**

Wells-next-the-Sea
Holkham Hall Map ref. G2
Tel: (01328) 710227 Web: www.holkham.co.uk
A classic 18th C. Palladian-style mansion. Part of a great agricultural estate, and a living treasure house of artistic and architectural history. Bygones Museum with over 4,000 items from cars and crafts to kitchens and steam.
Times: Hall open 5-27 May, Thurs-Mon, 1500 for audio tour; 2 Jun-30 Sept, Thurs-Mon 1300-1700. Bygones open 2 Jun-30 Sept, Thurs-Mon 1200-1700. Hall and Bygones open Bank Hol weekends 1200-1700. Last admissions 1630. Closed 25 Mar.
Fee: Hall £6.50/£3.25. Bygones Museum £5.00/£2.50. Hall and Bygones Museum £10.00/£5.00/£25.00 (family).
Facilities: ⊛ Q ☐ T(2 hrs) ⊕ ☵ 🐕(on leads).

See Also:
Elizabethan House Museum page 87
Guildhall of St George page 88
Strangers' Hall Museum page92

SUFFOLK

Flatford (nr. East Bergholt)
Bridge Cottage Map ref. H12
Tel: (01206) 298260 Web: www.nationaltrust.org.uk
A 16th C. thatched cottage, just upstream from Flatford Mill, and housing an exhibition on landscape painter John Constable. Tearoom, shop, information centre and guided walks.
Times: Open 8 Jan -27 Feb, Sat and Sun, 1100-1530. 2 Mar -30 Apr, Wed-Sun, 1100-1700. 1 May-30 Sept, daily, 1000-1730.1-30 Oct, daily, 1100-1600. 2 Nov-18 Dec, Wed-Sun, 1100-1530.
Fee: Free.
Facilities: ⊛ ☐ T(1½ hrs) 🖌⊕ 🐕 (not in restaurant).**NT**

Hadleigh
Guildhall Map ref. G10
Market Place
Tel: (01473) 823884
Large medieval timber-framed complex, Grade I Listed (with a Victorian addition) dating from the 15th C.
Times: Open 12 Jun-25 Sept, daily, except Sat. 1430-1700. Cream teas in the garden, Sun-Fri, 1430-1700. Please contact for details on tours.
Fee: Free. Donations appreciated.
Facilities: 🚾 T(45 mins) 🖌 ⊕ 🐕

Haughley (nr. Stowmarket)
Haughley Park Map ref. G7
Tel: (01359) 240701 Web: www.haughleyparkbarn.co.uk
Imposing redbrick Jacobean manor house (1620), set in gardens, park and woodland. Walled kitchen garden, three woodland walks and 17th C. barn.
Times: Open 24 Apr and 1 May. Bluebell Suns, 1400-1730. 3 May-30 Sept, Tues, 1400-1730.
Fee: Gardens, wood and barn £3.00. House £2.00.
Facilities: ☐ T(1½ hrs) 🐕 (on leads)🔲

For even more
information visit
our website at
www.visiteastofengland.com

Hengrave (nr. Bury St. Edmunds)
Hengrave Hall Map ref. D6
Tel: (01284) 701561 Web: www.hengravehallcentre.org.uk
Hengrave Hall stands in 44 acres, with a lake, varied
gardens and parkland. This unique Tudor house is
renowned for its Oriel above the gatehouse and stained
glass window.
Times: Open by appointment only, please contact for
details.
Fee: Tour: £4.00, Tours with refreshments £6.00
Facilities: ▣ ▦ T(2hrs) 𝄁 🛈 🛉(on leads).

Horringer (nr. Bury St. Edmunds)
Ickworth House, Park and Gardens Map ref. D7
Tel: (01284) 735270 Web: www.nationaltrust.org.uk
An extraordinary oval house with flanking wings, begun in
1795. Fine paintings, a beautiful collection of Georgian
silver, an Italian garden and stunning parkland. Waymarked
woodland walks and vineyard.
Times: Park open all year, daily, 0700-1900. Gardens open
1 Jan-24 Mar, daily, 1000-1600; 25 Mar-30 Oct, daily,
1000-1700; 31 Oct-23 Dec, Mon-Fri, 1000-1600. House
open 25 Mar-30 Sept, Mon, Tues, Fri-Sun 1300-1700; 1-30
Oct, Mon, Tues, Fri-Sun 1300-1630. Garden and park
closed 25 Dec.
Fee: House, park and gardens £6.70/£3.00. Park and
gardens £3.10/90p.
Facilities: ◈ ▣ T(3 hrs) 🛈 ⴷ 🛉 (on leads) NT

Ipswich
The Ipswich Unitarian Meeting House Map ref. I/J10
Friars Street
Tel: (01473) 218217 Web: www.unitarianipswich.org.uk
A Grade I Listed building, built 1699 (opened in 1700).
One of the finest surviving meeting houses, and one of the
most important historic structures in Ipswich.
Times: Open 1 May-30 Sept, Tues and Thurs, 1200-1600;
Sat, 1000-1600. Closed Easter and Christmas except
services.
Fee: Free.
Facilities: ▦ ⴷ T(30 mins)

Ipswich
Pykenham Gatehouse Map ref. I/J10
Northgate Street
Tel: (01473) 255591
15th C. Grade II* timber framed gatehouse to the former
residence of Archdeacon Pykenham. Major restoration in
1982/3. Displays on the work of the Ipswich Building
Preservation Trust.
Times: Open 7 May, 4 Jun, 2 Jul, 6 Aug, 3 Sept, 1 Oct, Sat,
1030-1230.
Fee: Free.
Facilities: ▦ ⴷ T(30 mins) 𝄁

Lavenham
Lavenham Guildhall of Corpus Christi Map ref. E/F9
Market Place
Tel: (01787) 247646 Web: www.nationaltrust.org.uk
Impressive timber-framed building dating from 1530.
Originally the hall of the Guild of Corpus Christi, now a
local museum with information on the medieval cloth
trade. Walled garden.
Times: Open 5-27 Mar, Sat and Sun, 1100-1600. 2-30 Apr,
Wed-Sun, 1100-1700. 1 May-31 Oct, daily, 1100-1700.
5-27 Nov, Sat and Sun, 1100-1600.
Fee: £3.25.
Facilities: ⊛ 🛏 T(1 hr) 🕈 NT

Lavenham
Little Hall Map ref. E/F9
Market Place
Tel: (01787) 247019 Web: www.suffolksociety.com
A 14th C. hall house with a crown-post roof. Contains the
Gayer-Anderson collection of furniture, pictures, sculpture
and ceramics. There is also a small walled garden.
Times: Open 23 Mar-30 Oct, Wed, Thurs, Sat and Sun,
1400-1730. Bank Hols, 1000-1730.
Fee: £2.00.
Facilities: ⊛ 🛏 T(40 mins) 🕈

*Boy carving at the Tudor Re-Creation
at Kentwell Hall and Gardens*

Long Melford
Kentwell Hall and Gardens Map ref. E9
Tel: (01787) 310207 Web: www.kentwell.co.uk
A beautiful mellow redbrick Tudor Mansion, with intact
medieval service building, surrounded by a broad moat.
Extensive gardens with massed spring bulbs, herb garden,
potager and woodland walks. Rare Breeds Farm, icehouse,
camera obscura, 60ft sculpted tree and more. Best known
for award-winning large-scale Re-creations of Tudor Life,
and WWWII daily life, on selected weekends, in which
visitors are transported back in time.
Times: Gardens & Farms: 13-18, 20-25, 27 Feb; 6, 13, 20-
24 Mar, 1100-1600. House, Gardens & Farm: 29-31 Mar;
1, 3-6, 10-13, 17-20, 24-27 Apr; 3-4, 8-11, 15-18, 22-25,
31 May; 1-3, 5-8, 12-15 Jun; 13-15, 17-22, 24-31 Jul; 1-5,
8-12, 14-19, 21-25, 30-31 Aug; 1-2, 4-7, 11-14, 18-21, 28
Sept; 2, 9, 16, 23-28 Oct, 1200-1700. The Great Annual
Tudor Re-Creation: 19, 25-26 Jun, 2-3, 6, 9-10 Jul, 1200-
1700. Other Tudor Re-Creations: 25-28 Mar; 30 Apr-2
May; 26-29 Aug; 24-27 Sept, 1100-1800. WWII Re-
Creations: 28-30 May; 6-7 Aug, 1100-1800; 29-30 Oct,
1100-1700.
Fee: House, garden and Farm: £7.15/£4.60/£6.15 Gardens
and farm only £5.00/£3.30/£4.30 Special prices apply for
Bank Holiday weekends, Re-Creations and events. Please
telephone for details.
Facilities: ⊛ 🅿 T(5 hrs) ⑴ ⚲ 🅱

Long Melford
Melford Hall Map ref. E9/10
Tel: (01787) 379228 Web: www.nationaltrust.org.uk
Turreted brick Tudor mansion with 18th C. and Regency
interiors. Collection of Chinese porcelain, gardens and a
walk in the grounds. Memorabilia of Beatrix Potter.
Times: Open 26 Mar-1 Apr, daily, 1400-1730. 2-30 Apr,
Sat, Sun 1400-1730. 1 May-30 Sept, Wed-Sun and Bank
Hols, 1400-1730. 1-30 Oct, Sat and Sun, 1400-1730. Last
admission at 1700. Closed 25, 29 Mar. Contact for
Christmas openings.
Fee: £4.50/£2.25/£11.25 (family).
Facilities: ⊛ 🅿 ⎓ T(1½hr) ⚲ ⚲ 🐾 (park and car park
only on lead) **NT**

Newbourne (nr. Woodbridge)
Newbourne Hall Map ref. K10
Tel: (01473) 736277
Hall house with timber framing of c.1480, Tudor brick
work, pargetting and plaster work of around 1600.
Times: Open all year, by written application only
Fee: £6.00/£10.00.
Facilities: 🅿 T(1 hr) ⚲ ⚲

Somerleyton (nr. Lowestoft)
Somerleyton Hall and Gardens Map ref. O1
Tel: (0871) 2224244 Web: www.somerleyton.co.uk
Early Victorian stately mansion in Anglo-Italian style, with
lavish features and fine state rooms. Beautiful 12 acre
gardens, with historic Yew hedge maze. Gift shop.
Times: Open 19 Mar-30 Oct, Sun, Thurs and Bank Hol
Mon, plus Tues and Wed in Jul and Aug, 1100-1730 (hall
1300-1700).
Fee: £6.50/£4.50/£5.50. Garden only; £4.50/£2.50/£3.50
Facilities: ⊛ Q 🅿 ⇌ T(3 hrs) ⑴ ⚲ 🅱

South Elmham (nr. Harleston)
South Elmham Hall Map ref. L3/4
St. Cross
Tel: (01986) 782526 Web: www.southelmham.co.uk
Grade I Listed medieval bishops palace. Also South
Elmham Minster, a ruined Norman chapel in fortified
enclosure. Wildlife walks around farm.
Times: Walk and Minster, open at any reasonable time.
Tearoom open 25 Mar-30 Sept, Sun, Thurs and Fri, 1 Oct-
24 Mar, Sun only, 1000-1700. Hall open 1 May-30 Sept,
Thurs and Bank Hol Mon, guided tour at 1400, Sun 1100
and 1500.
Fee: Walks free. Hall £6.00/£3.00.
Facilities: 🅿 T(1 hr) ⚲ ⑴ 🐾 (grounds only)

Thetford
Euston Hall Map ref. E4
Tel: (01842) 766366 Web: www.eustonhall.co.uk
18th C. hall housing paintings by Van Dyck, Lely and
Stubbs, with pleasure grounds designed by John Evelyn and
'Capability Brown'. 17th C. church of St. Genevieve.
Times: Open 16 Jun-15 Sept, Thurs, 1430-1700. Also
26 Jun, 17 Jul and 4 Sept, Sun, 1430-1700.
Fee: House and gardens £5.00/£2.00/£4.00. Gardens only
£3.00/£2.00/£3.00.
Facilities: ⊛ 🅿 T(2 hrs) ⑴ ⚲

See Also:
Christchurch Mansion page 96
Gainsborough's House page 100

Melford Hall, Long Melford

Looking for even more Great Days Out in the East of England?

Then why not visit our web site at **www.visiteastofengland.com**

You can search for the latest information on places to visit and events, plus discover great deals on short breaks and holidays in the region. Alternatively explore our special sections on aviation heritage, cathedrals, cycling, food and drink, gardens, golf and shopping.

EAST OF ENGLAND
TOURIST BOARD

www.visiteastofengland.com

Ancient Monuments

BEDFORDSHIRE

Ampthill
Houghton House Map ref. D7
Tel: (01234) 228337 Web: www.english-heritage.org.uk
The ruins of a 17th C. country house, built in the heights
near Ampthill, and believed to be the House Beautiful in
Bunyan's The Pilgrim's Progress.
Times: Open at any reasonable time.
Fee: Free.
Facilities: ⌖ 🅿 **T(45 mins)** 🐾 EH

Colmworth (nr. Bedford)
Bushmead Priory Map ref. E4
Tel: (01525) 860152 Web: www.english-heritage.org.uk
A small Augustinian priory founded in about 1195, with a
magnificent 13th C. timber roof of crown-post
construction. Medieval wall paintings and stained glass.
Times: 1 Jul-31 Aug, Sat and Sun for groups by
appointment only.
Fee: £2.00/£1.00/£1.50
Facilities: ⌖ 🅿 **T(45 mins)** 🔥 EH

Dunstable
Priory Church of St. Peter Map ref. C/D10
Church Street
Tel: (01582) 477422
Web: www.dunstableparish.freeserve.co.uk
A Grade I Listed building which is an active parish church.
It is the surviving part of an Augustinian priory founded in
1131. Scene of the annulment of Henry VIII's marriage to
Katherine of Aragon.
Times: Open daily, 0900-1600.
Fee: Free.
Facilities: 🚌 **T(45 mins)** 𝄜 🔥 🖼

Flitton
De Grey Mausoleum Map ref. D8
Tel: (01525) 860094 Web: www.english-heritage.org.uk
A large mortuary chapel of the de Greys of Wrest Park,
containing fine sculptured tombs of monuments from
16th-19th C. and some brass and alabaster.
Times: Open all year, Sat and Sun. Please contact Mrs
Stimson (key keeper) on (01525) 860094 in advance.
Fee: Free.
Facilities: ⌖ **T(1 hr)** EH

Willington (nr. Bedford)
Willington Dovecote and Stables Map ref. E6
Church End
Tel: (01480) 301494 Web: www.nationaltrust.org.uk
A distinctive 16th C. stable and stone dovecote, lined
internally with nesting boxes for 1,500 pigeons. They are
the remains of an historical manorial complex.
Times: Open Bank Hol Mons, 1300-1700. At other times
by appointment.
Fee: £1.00/£1.00/£1.00.
Facilities: ⌖ 🅿 **T(1 hr)** 🔥 (on leads) NT

CAMBRIDGESHIRE

Cambridge
King's College Chapel Map ref. H11
Tel: (01223) 331212 Web: www.kings.cam.ac.uk
The chapel, founded by Henry VI, includes the breathtaking
fan-vault ceiling, stained glass windows, a carved oak screen
and Ruben's masterpiece 'The Adoration of the Magi'.
Times: Open all year, during term - Mon-Fri, 0930-1530; Sat,
0930-1515; Sun, 1315-1430. Out of term - Mon-Sat, 0930-
1630; Sun 1000-1700.
Fee: £4.50/£3.00/£3.00. Audio Guides £2.00
Facilities: Q **T(1 hr)** 𝄜 🖼

Coton (nr. Cambridge)
Cambridge American Cemetery Map ref. G11
Tel: (01954) 210350
A cemetery with a visitor reception for information, the graves
area and a memorial chapel. Operated and maintained by the
American Battle Monuments Commission.
Times: Open all year, daily, 0900-1700. Closed 25 Dec-1 Jan.
Fee: Free.
Facilities: 🅿 **T(40 mins)** 🖼

Ely
Ely Cathedral Map ref. I8
Tel: (01353) 667735 Web: www.cathedral.ely.anglican.org
One of England's finest cathedrals with guided tours and
tours of the Octagon and West Tower. Monastic precincts,
brass rubbing centre and Stained Glass Museum.
Times: Open 1 Jan-27 Mar, Mon-Sat, 0730-1800; Sun,
0730-1700. 28 Mar-30 Oct, daily, 0700-1900. 31 Oct-31
Dec, Mon-Sat, 0730-1800; Sun, 0730-1700.
Fee: £4.80/free/£4.20.
Facilities: ⛁ ≈ T(1½ hrs) ⚐ ⊕ ⤢ ▣

Isleham
Isleham Priory Church Map ref. J9
Tel: (01223) 582700 Web: www.english-heritage.org.uk
Rare example of early Norman church with herringbone
masonry. Little altered despite later conversion to a barn.
Times: Open at any reasonable time.
Fee: Free.
Facilities: ⊕ T(30 mins) EH

Longthorpe (nr. Peterborough)
Longthorpe Tower Map ref. C5
Thorpe Road
Tel: (01733) 268482 Web: www.english-heritage.org.uk
The 14th C. tower of a fortified manor house, with wall
paintings which form the most complete set of domestic
paintings of the period in northern Europe.
Times: Jul-Aug, Sat, 1200-1700.
Fee: £2.30/£1.20/£1.70.
Facilities: ⊕ T(1 hr) ⚐ EH

March
Saint Wendreda's Church Map ref. G6
Church Street
Tel: (01354) 654783
This church is noted for its exceptional double hammerbeam
timber roof which contains 120 carved angels. Probably the
finest of all such East Anglian timber roofs.
Times: Open all year, Mon-Fri, 1100-1600, Sun, outside
service times. Church key obtainable from 'Stars' public
house which is 50yds away.
Fee: Free.
Facilities: ▣ ⛁ T(30 mins) ⚐ ⤢ ▣

For even more information visit our website at www.visiteastofengland.com

Peterborough
Flag Fen Bronze Age Centre Map ref. D5
The Droveway, Northey Road
Tel: (01733) 313414 Web: www.flagfen.com
Visitor Centre with landscaped park, summer
archaeological excavation, rare breed animals, roundhouses
and museum of the Bronze Age.
Times: Open all year, daily, 1000-1700. Closed 24 Dec-2 Jan.
Fee: £4.00/£3.00/£3.50/£11.00(family).
Facilities: ❀ Q 🅿 T(2 hrs) ◑ ⊼

Peterborough
Peterborough Cathedral Map ref. D5
Tel: (01733) 343342
Web: www.peterborough-cathedral.org.uk
Norman cathedral with an Early English west front, a 13th C.
painted nave ceiling and the tomb of Katherine of Aragon. It
was also the former burial place of Mary Queen of Scots.
Times: Open all year, Mon-Sat, 0900-1700; Sun, 1200-1700.
Closed 25 and 26 Dec.
Fee: Donations requested.
Facilities: ❀ ▭ ⇌ T(1½ hr) ⚲ ◑ ⊼ ▨

Peterborough Cathedral

Ramsey
Ramsey Abbey Gatehouse Map ref. E7
Tel: 0870 609 5388 Web: www.nationaltrust.org.uk
The ruins of a 15th C. gatehouse.
Times: Open 1 Apr-31 Oct, daily, 1000-1230, 1330-1700.
Fee: Free.
Facilities: ❀ 🅿 T(30 mins) NT

St. Ives
Saint Ives Bridge Chapel Map ref. E/F9
Bridge Street
Tel: (01480) 497314
A 15th C. chapel built onto the bridge in midstream. One
of only four in England, with a balcony over the river.
Times: Open 1 Jan-30 Apr, Mon-Sat, 1000-1700. 1 May-30
Sept, Mon-Sat, 1000-1700; Sun, 1400-1700. 1 Oct-31
Dec, Mon-Sat, 1000-1700.
Fee: Free.
Facilities: ▭ T(20 mins) ⇞

Round houses at Flag Fen

Thorney
Thorney Abbey Church Map ref. E4
Tel: (01733) 270388
Abbey church with a Norman nave (c.1100), a fine church
organ originally built in 1787-1790 and a stained glass east
window depicting the miracles of St. Thomas Becket.
Times: Open all year, daily, 1000-dusk.
Fee: Free.
Facilities: 🅿 T(1 hr) ⚲ ⊼ ▨

Whittlesford
Duxford Chapel Map ref. H13
Tel: (01223) 713180 Web: www.english-heritage.org.uk
A 14th C. chapel which was once part of the Hospital of
St. John.
Times: Open at any reasonable time.
Fee: Free.
Facilities: ❀ ⇌ T(1 hr) ⇞ EH

See Also:
Farmland Museum and Denny Abbey, Waterbeach, page 69

St. Peter's-on-the-Wall, Bradwell on Sea

ESSEX

Billericay
St. Mary Magdalene Church Map ref. F10
Church Street, Great Burstead
Tel: (01277) 652701
Web: www.greatburstead.freewire.co.uk
Saxon church with 14th C. medieval wall paintings.
Christopher Martin, the church warden, led the Pilgrim
Fathers' journey to Billericay (nr. Boston) in the USA.
Times: Open all year, daily, dawn to dusk.
Fee: Free.
Facilities: 🅿 🚻 T(30 mins) 🎋 🐕 🖼

Bradwell-on-Sea
Saint Peters-on-the-Wall Map ref. L7
East End Road
Tel: (01621) 776203
Built by St. Cedd of Lindisfarne in AD654, this is England's
oldest Saxon church. Small exhibition about its history.
Bookstall. Evening services every Sun at 1800 during Jul
and Aug.
Times: Open at any reasonable time.
Fee: Free.
Facilities: 🅿 T(30 mins) 🐕

Brentwood
Cathedral Church of St. Mary and St. Helen
Map ref. D/E9
Ingrave Road
Tel: (01277) 265235
Web: www.brentwood-cathedral.co.uk
Roman Catholic cathedral designed by Mr Quinlan Terry in
the Classical style. Dedicated in May 1991.
Times: Open all year, Mon-Sat, 1000-1800; Sun, 1400-
1700. Please contact for Christmas and Easter openings.
Fee: Free.
Facilities: 🅿 🚻 ♿ T(1 hr) 🖼

Castle Hedingham
Hedingham Castle Map ref. H2
Tel: (01787) 460261 Web: www.hedinghamcastle.co.uk
The finest Norman keep in England, built in 1140 by the de
Veres, Earls of Oxford. Visited by Kings Henry VII and VIII
and Queen Elizabeth I, and besieged by King John. Lake
walks and woodland.
Times: Open Apr-end Sept, Sun 1000-1700. Also during
Essex school hols, Sun-Thurs, 1000-1700.
Fee: £4.50/£3.50/£4.00.
Facilities: ⊛ 🅿 T(3 hrs) ⊕ 🎋 🐕

Chelmsford
Chelmsford Cathedral Map ref. F7
Tel: (01245) 294480
Web: www.cathedral.chelmsford.anglican.org
A late-medieval church, reordered in 1983 and blending old
with new. Became a cathedral in 1914, when the Diocese
of Chelmsford was created. Modern sculpture and tapestry.
Times: Open all year, Mon-Sat 0800-1800, Sun 0745-
1230, 1400-1900.
Fee: Free.
Facilities: ⊛ 🚻 ♿ T(1 hr) 🍴(by arrangement) 🎋 🖼

Coggeshall
Grange Barn Map ref. I5
Grange Hill
Tel: (01376) 562226 Web: www.nationaltrust.org.uk
One of the oldest surviving timber framed barns in Europe,
dating from around 1240, and originally part of a
Cistercian Abbey. Restored in the 1980s.
Times: Open 27 Mar-9 Oct, Tues, Thurs, Sun and Bank
Hol Mon, 1400-1700.
Fee: £1.80/90p. Joint ticket with Paycockes £3.50.
Facilities: ⊛ 🅿 T(30 mins) 🎋 NT

Saint Botolphs Priory, Colchester

Colchester
Saint Botolphs Priory Map ref. K4
Tel: (01206) 282931 Web: www.english-heritage.org.uk
The remains of a 12th C. priory near the town centre, with
a nave which has an impressive arcaded west end. One of
the first Augustinian priories in England.
Times: Open at any reasonable time.
Fee: Free.
Facilities: ⊛ Q ⇌ T(45 mins) EH

Colchester
Saint Michael and All Angels Church Map ref. J5
Church Road, Copford Green
Tel: (01621) 815434
A 12th C. church in Romanesque style, with an apse that is
decorated with medieval wall paintings.
Times: Open all year, daily, 0915-1730 (or dusk). Sun
service, 1100-1200.
Fee: Free.
Facilities: ⊒ T(30 mins)

Cressing (nr. Braintree)
Cressing Temple Barns Map ref. H5
Witham Road
Tel: (01376) 584903 Web: www.essexcc.gov.uk
The site of a Knights Templar settlement dating from 1137.
Two magnificent 13th C. timber-framed barns and Tudor
walled garden.
Times: Open 6 Mar-30 Oct, Sun, 1030-1700; also 4 May-
30 Sept, Wed-Fri, 1030-1630. Open 28 Mar 1030-1700.
Fee: £3.50/£2.50/£2.50.
Facilities: ⊛ ⊒ T(2½ hrs) ⓘ ⊓

East Tilbury
Coalhouse Fort Map ref. F12
Princess Margaret Road
Tel: (01375) 844203
Web: www.coalhousefort.freeserve.co.uk
Best example of a Victorian armoured casemate fortress in
the south east. Built as a frontline defence for the Thames.
Guided tours and displays, including Thameside Aviation
Museum.
Times: Open Apr-Sep, last Sun of each month and Bank
Hols, 1100-1600.
Fee: £2.50/free/£2.00.
Facilities: ⊒ T(2 hrs) ⓘ ⓘ ⊓ ⊓(kept on leads at all times)

Great Dunmow
Great Dunmow Maltings Map ref. E5
Mill Lane
Tel: (01371) 878979
Dating from 1560, the Maltings retain much of the original
malting infrastructure used to produce malt by hand. They
are superb examples of 16th C. and 18th C.
architecture. Houses town museum.
Times: Open 8 Jan-18 Dec, Sat, Sun, 1100-1600; 29 Mar-
25 Oct, Tues, 1100-1600. Last admission is 30 mins before
closing.
Fee: £1.00/50p/50p.
Facilities: ⊟ T(1½ hrs) ⓘ

Greensted (nr. Chipping Ongar)
St. Andrews Church Map ref. C8
Church Lane, Greensted Road
Tel: (01992) 524005
The oldest wooden church in the world, and the oldest
wooden (stave built) building in Europe.
Times: Open all year, daily, 0900-sunset.
Fee: Free.
Facilities: ⊒ ⊟ T(1 hr) ⓘ

St. Andrew's (Minster) Church, Ashingdon, Southend-on-Sea

Hadleigh
Hadleigh Castle Map ref. H11
Tel: (01760) 755161 Web: www.english-heritage.org.uk
Familiar from Constable's painting, the castle stands on a
bluff overlooking the Leigh Marshes with a single, large
50ft tower and 13th C. and 14th C. remains.
Times: Open at any reasonable time.
Fee: Free.
Facilities: ❀ **T(45 mins)** EH

Harwich
Harwich Redoubt Fort Map ref. O3
Behind 29 Main Road
Tel: (01255) 503429 Web: www.harwich-society.com
An anti-Napoleonic circular fort commanding the harbour.
Eleven guns on battlements.
Times: Open 4 Jan-25 Apr, Sun and Bank Hols 1000-1600.
1 May-31 Aug, daily, from 1000 (last admission 1600).
5 Sept-Dec, Sun, 1000-1600. Closed Christmas.
Fee: £1.00/free/50p.
Facilities: **T(1½ hrs)** ⫰

Little Tey (nr. Coggeshall)
St. James the Less Church Map ref. I4
Church Lane
Tel: (01206) 211481
A 12th C. church with 13/14th C. wall paintings, which
have been uncovered and conserved without any
restoration. They are virtually untouched since their original
painting.
Times: Open all year. Key available on request.
Fee: Free. Donations appreciated.
Facilities: ◻ 🍴 ⇌ **T(30 mins)** ⼌

Mistley
Mistley Towers Map ref. M3
Tel: (01206) 393884 Web: www.english-heritage.org.uk
Two towers designed by Robert Adam in 1776, as part of
the parish church. A rare example of Robert Adam's
ecclesiastical work. Key from Mistley Quay Workshops.
Times: Open at any reasonable time.
Fee: Free.
Facilities: ❀ ⇌ **T(45 mins)** EH

Rayleigh
Rayleigh Mount Map ref. H10
Tel: 0870 609 5388 Web: www.nationaltrust.org.uk
Former site of the Domesday castle built by Sweyn of Essex.
Times: Open summer, daily, 0700-1800; winter, daily,
0700-1700.
Fee: Free.
Facilities: ❀ ⇌ **T(1 hr)** ⫰ NT

Rivenhall (nr. Witham)
Saint Mary and All Saints Church Map ref. H5
Church Road
Tel: (01376) 511161 Web: www.rivenhall.org.uk
A Saxon church on the earthworks of a Roman villa,
restored by early Victorians with 12th C. glass and
interesting monuments.
Times: Open 1 May-2 Oct, Sun, 1430-1630; Wed,
0900-1130. At other times key available to casual callers.
Fee: Free. Donations appreciated.
Facilities: ◻ 🍴 **T(30 mins)** ⼌ 🛈

Southend-on-Sea
St. Andrew's (Minster) Church Map ref. I9
Church Road, Ashingdon
Tel: (01702) 203358
Built by Canute in 1020, this small hilltop church offers
panoramic views. Very peaceful, and with many features of
great historic interest.
Times: Open 28 Mar-30 Sept, daily (except Sun),
1400-1600. Contact for Christmas opening.
Fee: Free.
Facilities: ◻ **T(45 mins)** ⼌ 🛈 🛈

Mistley Towers

Mountfitchet Castle, Stansted Mountfitchet

Southminster
Rural Discovery Church Map ref. J8
Saint Lawrence
Tel: (01621) 779319
An active church, sited on a hill overlooking the River
Blackwater. Exhibitions of local interest.
Times: Open 28 May-25 Sept, Sat, Sun and Bank Hols,
1430-1630.
Fee: Free.
Facilities: ⊡ T(1 hr) ⚊ ⋔ (on lead)

Stansted Mountfitchet
Mountfitchet Castle Map ref. C4
Tel: (01279) 813237 Web: www.mountfitchetcastle.com
A re-constructed Norman motte-and-bailey castle, and
village of the Domesday period. Grand Hall, church, prison
and siege tower. Domestic animals roam the site.
Times: Open Mid Mar-Mid Nov, daily, 1000-1700.
Fee: £6.00/£5.00/£5.50. 10% discount on admission to
castle and toy museum next door, if visiting both places on
the same day.
Facilities: ⊛ ⊡ ⋞ T(2 hrs) ⚊ ⋒

Tilbury
Tilbury Fort Map ref. F12
Tel: (01375) 858489 Web: www.english-heritage.org.uk
One of Henry VIII's coastal forts, re-modelled and extended
in the 17th C. in continental style. The best and largest
example of 17th C. military engineering in England.
Times: 2 Jan-23 Mar, Thurs-Mon,1000-1600; 24 Mar-30
Sept, daily, 1000-1800; 1-31 Oct, daily, 1000-1700;
1 Nov-31 Dec, Thurs-Mon, 1000-1600. Closed 24-26 Dec
and 1 Jan.
Fee: £3.30/£1.70/£2.50.
Facilities: ⊛ ⊡ T(2 hrs) ⋔ (audio tours) ⋔ (on leads) EH

Waltham Abbey
Waltham Abbey Church Map ref. A8
Highbridge Street
Tel: (01992) 767897
Web: www.walthamabbeychurch.co.uk
A Norman church, the reputed site of King Harold's tomb.
The Lady Chapel and crypt (now a visitors' centre and
shop) date from the 14th C.
Times: Open 1 Jan-26 Mar, Mon-Sat, 1000-1600; (Wed
opens 1100), Sun, 1200-1600. 27 Mar-29 Oct, Mon-Sat,
1000-1800, (Wed opens 1100), Sun, 1200-1800; 30 Oct-
31 Dec, Mon-Sat, 1000-1600 (Wed opens 1100), Sun
1200-1600. Closed 25 Mar and 25 Dec.
Fee: Donations welcome.
Facilities: ⊡ ⚊ ⋞ T(1 hr) ⋒

Widdington
Priors Hall Barn Map ref. D3
Tel: (01223) 582700 Web: www.english-heritage.org.uk
One of the finest surviving medieval barns in south east
England, representative of the type of aisled barn in North
West Essex, 124 x 30 x 33 ft high.
Times: 24 Mar-30 Sept, Sat and Sun, 1000-1800.
Fee: Free
Facilities: ⊛ T(30 mins) EH

Willingale (nr. Chipping Ongar)
Willingale Churches Map ref. D7
Tel: (01277) 896353
Two ancient churches in one churchyard, side by side. On
this site since Norman times. A village setting on The Essex
Way.
Times: Open all year, daily, dawn-dusk.
Fee: Free.
Facilities: ⊡ T(1½ hrs) ⋒

See Also:
Colchester Castle Museum, page 70, 73
Thaxted Guildhall, page 79

Waltham Abbey Church

HERTFORDSHIRE

Berkhamsted
Berkhamsted Castle Map ref. C12
Tel: (01536) 402840 Web: www.english-heritage.org.uk
The extensive remains of an 11th C. motte-and-bailey castle
which was the work of Robert of Mortain, half brother of
William of Normandy, who learnt he was king here.
Times: All year, daily, 1000-1800 in summer, 1000-1600 in
winter. Closed 25 Dec and 1 Jan.
Fee: Free.
Facilities: ⊛ ⇌ T(30 mins) EH

Bishop's Stortford
Castle Mound Map ref. K10/11
The Castle Gardens
Tel: (01279) 655831 Web: www.bishopsstortford.org
Remaining mound of a castle built by William I, set in the
gardens just minutes from the town. Key to gate available
from Bishop's Stortford Tourist Information Centre.
Times: Open all year, Mon-Sat, by appointment only.
Closed Bank Hols. Key needs to be collected from Bishop's
Stortford Tourist Information Centre.
Fee: Free.
Facilities: ⊛ 🅿 🚌 ⇌ T(30 mins) 🐕

Gorhambury (nr. St. Albans)
Roman Theatre of Verulamium Map ref. E13
Tel: (01727) 835035
The only completely exposed Roman theatre in Britain, with
the remains of a townhouse and underground shrine.
Times: Open 1 Jan-28 Feb, daily, 1000-1600. 1 Mar-31
Oct, daily, 1000-1700. 1 Nov-31 Dec, daily, 1000-1600.
Closed 25 and 26 Dec.
Fee: £2.00/£1.00/£1.50.
Facilities: 🅿 T(20 mins) 🐕 (on leads)

Roman Theatre of Verulamium

Hertford
Hertford Castle Map ref. H/I12
The Castle
Tel: (01992) 552885
A 15th C. Edward IV gatehouse, Mayor's parlour and
robing room with 15th C. stone, brick and timber screens.
The town's insignia is also on display on special open days.
Times: Castle grounds open all year, close at dusk. Only by
arrangement within the castle gatehouse.
Fee: Free.
Facilities: ⊛ 🅿 T(1½ hrs) 🏃 🎋 🐕 (on leads)

Royston
Royston Cave Map ref. I7
Melbourn Street
Tel: (01763) 245484 Web: www.roystoncave.com
A man-made cave with medieval carvings made by the
Knights Templar dated from around the beginning of the
14th C. Possibly a secret meeting place for initiations.
Times: Open 26 Mar-25 Sept, Sat, Sun and Bank Hol Mon,
1430-1730, also throughout Aug, Wed 1430-1730.
Fee: £2.00/free/£1.00.
Facilities: ⇌ T(45 mins) 🏃

St. Albans
Cathedral and Abbey Church of St. Alban Map ref. F13
Tel: (01727) 860780 Web: www.stalbanscathedral.org.uk
A Norman abbey church on the site of the martyrdom of
St. Alban, Britain's first Christian martyr. The 13th C.
shrine has been restored and is a centre of ecumenical
worship.
Times: Open all year, daily, 0900-1745.
Fee: Free. Donations requested
Facilities: ⊛ Q 🚌 ⇌ T(1½ hrs) 🏃🄯 🎋

St. Albans
Clock Tower Map ref. F13
Market Street
Tel: (01727) 866380
A curfew tower, built in approximately 1405, with small
exhibitions on aspects of local history. The belfry and 1866
clock mechanism can be viewed. Fine views from the roof.
Times: Open 25 Mar-18 Sept, Sat, Sun and Bank Hols,
1030-1700.
Fee: 40p/20p.
Facilities: 🚌 ⇌ T(30 mins)

Waltham Cross
Eleanor Cross Map ref. I14
High Street
Tel: (01992) 785537 Web: www.broxbourne.gov.uk
One of 12 crosses erected between 1291 and 1294 to mark
the overnight stops of Eleanor of Castile's funeral cortege
(wife of King Edward I), on its way to Westminster Abbey.
Times: Open all year, daily - can be viewed at anytime.
Fee: Free.
Facilities: ⊛ ⇔ ⇌ T(15 mins) ⋔ ▣

Ware
Scott's Grotto Map ref. I11/12
Scotts Road
Tel: (01920) 464131 Web: www.scotts-grotto.org
Grotto extending 67ft into the hillside, including passages
and six chambers decorated with fossils, shells, pebbles and
flints. Unlit so torches are necessary.
Times: Open 2 Apr-24 Sept, Sat and Bank Hol Mons,
1400-1630.
Fee: Free.
Facilities: ⇔ ⇌ T(30 mins)

Welwyn
Welwyn Roman Baths Map ref. G11
Welwyn Bypass
Tel: (01707) 271362 Web: www.welhat.gov.uk
The baths are a small part of a villa which was built at the
beginning of the 3rd C. and occupied for over 150 years.
The villa had at least four buildings.
Times: Open 1 Jan-27 Nov, Sat, Sun and Bank Hols,
1400-1700 (or dusk if earlier). Also Hertfordshire school
holidays.
Fee: £1.00/free.
Facilities: ▣ ⇔ T(1½ hrs) ⋏ ⊓ ⋔ ▣

Scott's Grotto

NORFOLK

Baconsthorpe (nr. Holt)
Baconsthorpe Castle Map ref. J3
Tel: (01223) 582700 Web: www.english-heritage.org.uk
A 15th C. part-moated, semi-fortified house. The remains
include the inner and outer gatehouse and the curtain wall.
Baconsthorpe Post Office sells guide books and postcards.
Times: Open at any reasonable time.
Fee: Free.
Facilities: ⊛ ▣ T(45 mins) ⋔ (on leads) EH

Binham
Binham Priory Map ref. H3
Tel: (01604) 230320 Web: www.english-heritage.org.uk
Extensive remains of an early 12th C. Benedictine priory.
The original nave of the church is still used as the parish
church.
Times: Open at any reasonable time.
Fee: Free.
Facilities: ⊛ T(45 mins) EH

Burnham Market
Creake Abbey Map ref. F3
Tel: (01223) 582700 Web: www.english-heritage.org.uk
Remains of an abbey church dating from the 13th C.,
including presbytery and north transept with chapels.
Times: Open at any reasonable time.
Fee: Free.
Facilities: ⊛ ▣ T(45 mins) ⋔ (on leads) EH

Caistor St. Edmund (nr. Norwich)
Caistor Roman Town Map ref. L8
Web: www.norfarchtrust.org.uk
The site of Venta Icenorum, the Roman capital of Norfolk.
The Roman fortifications can be seen in several places.
Series of interpretation boards on signposted walks.
Times: Open at any reasonable time.
Fee: Free.
Facilities: ▣ T(1½ hrs) ⊓ ⋔(on leads)

Castle Acre (nr. Swaffham)
Castle Acre Castle Map ref. F6
Tel: (01760) 755394 Web: www.english-heritage.org.uk
The remains of a Norman manor-house which became a
castle with earthworks, set by the side of a village.
Times: Open at any reasonable time.
Fee: Free.
Facilities: ⊛ Q ▣ T(½ hrs) ⊓ ⋔ (on leads) EH

**For even more
information visit
our website at
www.visiteastofengland.com**

Castle Rising (nr. King's Lynn)
Castle Rising Castle Map ref. D5
Tel: (01553) 631330 Web: www.castlerising.co.uk
Castle Rising Castle is a fine example of a Norman castle.
The rectangular keep, one of the largest, was built around
1140 by William D'Albini.
Times: 1 Jan-18 Mar, Wed-Sun, 1000-1600; 19 Mar-1 Nov,
daily, 1000-1800 or dusk if earlier in October; 2 Nov-31
Dec, Wed-Sun, 1000-1600. Closed 24-27 Dec.
Fee: £3.85/£2.20/£3.10.
Facilities: ◉ 🅿 T(1½ hrs) 🎋 🐾 EH

Castle Acre (nr. Swaffham)
Castle Acre Priory Map ref. F6
Stocks Green
Tel: (01760) 755394 Web: www.english-heritage.org.uk
Castle Acre is the site of one of the greatest Norman
settlements in England. First visit Britain's best Cluniac
priory. Take time to explore this romantic and atmospheric
priory and learn all about the daily life of the Monks.
Castle Acre castle nearby, is also well worth a visit.
Times: 2 Jan-23 Mar, Wed-Sun, 1000-1600; 24 Mar-30
Sept, daily, 1000-1800; 1 Oct-31 Dec, Wed-Sun, 1000-
1600. Closed 24-26 Dec, 1 Jan.
Fee: £4.30/£2.20/£3.20.
Facilities: ◉ Q 🅿 T(1 hr) 🎋(audio tours) ⑨ 🎋
🐾 (on leads) EH

Great Yarmouth
Burgh Castle Map ref. O8
Church Farm, Burgh Castle
Tel: (01223) 582700 Web: www.english-heritage.org.uk
The remains of a 3rd C. Roman fort overlooking the River
Waveney. The monument is only approached on foot.
There is information and a tearoom available from Easter-
Oct.
Times: Open at any reasonable time.
Fee: Free.
Facilities: ◉ T(45 mins) 🐾 (on leads) EH

Castle Rising Castle

Great Yarmouth
Caister Roman Site Map ref. P7
Caister-on-Sea
Tel: (01223) 582700 Web: www.english-heritage.org.uk
The remains of a Roman commercial port which was
possibly a fort. The footings of walls and buildings are seen
all along the main street.
Times: Open at any reasonable time.
Fee: Free.
Facilities: ☉ T(45 mins) ⋔ (on leads) EH

Little Walsingham
Shrine of our Lady of Walsingham Map ref. G/H3
Holt Road
Tel: (01328) 820239 Web: www.walsingham.org.uk
A pilgrimage church containing the Holy House, standing
in extensive grounds.
Times: Open all year, daily, 0700-1800.
Fee: Free.
Facilities: ▣ ᕦ T(1 hr) ⊕ ⼐ ▣

Little Walsingham
Slipper Chapel: Roman Catholic National Shrine
Map ref. G3/4
Houghton St Giles
Tel: (01328) 820217 Web: www.walsingham.org.uk
The Roman Catholic National Shrine of Our Lady. A small
14th C. chapel, plus the new Chapel of Reconciliation.
Bookshop and tearoom.
Times: Open all year, please contact for details.
Fee: Free.
Facilities: ▣ T(20 mins) ⊕ ⼐ ▣

Loddon
Hales Hall Barn and Gardens Map ref. M9
Tel: (01508) 548507 Web: www.haleshall.com
Fortified manor with fabulous 15th C. brick barn, built by
Henry VII's attorney general, Sir James Hobart. Gardens
with topiary, fruit, pottager, greenhouses and exotic plants.
Times: Open 9 Jan-18 Dec, Mon-Sat, 1030-1600. 27 Mar-
31 Oct, Sun, 1100-1600. Closed 25 Mar. Some Sats are
closed for private functions, please contact for details.
Fee: £2.00/free/£2.00.
Facilities: ▣ T(1 hr) ⼐ ▣

Ludham
Saint Benets Abbey Map ref. N6
Web: www.norfarchtrust.org.uk
The ruins of a monastery founded in AD1020 by King
Canute. A gatehouse with interesting carvings, 18th C.
windmill tower, perimeter wall and fishponds.
Times: Open at any reasonable time.
Fee: Free
Facilities: ▣ T(1 hr) ⋔(on leads)

Lynford (nr. Thetford)
Grimes Graves Map ref. F10
Tel: (01842) 810656 Web: www.english-heritage.org.uk
Neolithic flint mines. Five thousand years old and first
excavated in the 1870s, with over 300 pits and shafts. One
open to the public, 30ft deep with radiating gallery.
Times: 24-31 Mar, Thurs-Mon, 1000-1700; 1 Apr-30 Sept,
daily, 1000-1800; 1-31 Oct, Thurs-Mon, 1000-1700.
Fee: £2.60/£1.30/£2.00
Facilities: ☉ Q ▣ T(1½ hrs) ⋔ (on leads) EH

New Buckenham (nr. Attleborough)
New Buckenham Castle Map ref. J10
Tel: (01953) 860251
A Norman castle and keep, said to be the largest in
diameter in England. Remains of later additions.
Times: Open at any reasonable time.
Fee: £1.00.
Facilities: T(30 mins) ⼐ ⋔(strickly on leads)

North Elmham (nr. Dereham)
North Elmham Chapel Map ref. H5/6
High Street
Tel: (01223) 582700 Web: www.english-heritage.org.uk
The remains of a Norman chapel, later converted into a
house and enclosed by earthworks.
Times: Open at any reasonable time.
Fee: Free.
Facilities: ☉ T(45 mins) ⋔ (on leads) EH

Exploring Grimes Graves

Norwich
Norwich Cathedral Map ref. K/L7
Tel: (01603) 218321 Web: www.cathedral.org.uk
A Norman cathedral from 1096, with 14th C. roof bosses
depicting bible scenes from Adam and Eve to the Day of
Judgement. Cloisters, Cathedral Close, shop and
restaurant.
Times: Open daily, 0730-1800 (closes 1900 mid May-Mid
Sept).
Fee: Free. Donations requested.
Facilities: ⊛ 🅿 🛏 ⇌ T(1½ hrs) 🏃 ⊛ 🎋 🖼

Norwich
Roman Catholic Cathedral of St. John The Baptist
Map ref. K/L7
Unthank Road
Tel: (01603) 624615 Web: www.stjohncathedral.co.uk
A particularly fine example of 19th C. gothic revival by
George Gilbert Scott Junior, with fine stained glass,
exquisite stonewalk and Frosterley marble.
Times: Open all year, daily, Mon-Fri, 0730-1930;
Sat, 0900-1900; Sun, 0800-1930.
Fee: Free.
Facilities: 🅿 🛏 ⇌ T(1 hr) 🏃 🖼

Norwich
Saint Peter Mancroft Church Map ref. K/L7
Haymarket
Tel: (01603) 610443
A church with a Norman foundation (1075). The present
church was consecrated in 1455, with a 1463 font, a 1573
Flemish tapestry, an east window with medieval glass and
the Thomas Browne memorial.
Times: Open all year, Mon-Fri, 1000-1600, Sat 1000-1230.
Fee: Free.
Facilities: T(30 mins) 🏃 ⊛

Tasburgh (nr. Norwich)
Tasburgh Hillfort Map ref. K9
Web: www.norfarchtrust.org.uk
Remains of an earthworks fort, probably Iron Age, with the
parish church standing within it. The earthwork and
northern bank of the fort can be clearly seen. Interpretative
panels.
Times: Open at any reasonable time.
Fee: Free.
Facilities: 🅿 T(1 hr) 🎋 🐾(on leads)

Thetford
Thetford Priory Map ref. F/G11
Tel: (01223) 582700 Web: www.english-heritage.co.uk
The 14th C. gatehouse is the best preserved part of this
Cluniac priory, built in 1103. The extensive remains include
a plan of the cloisters.
Times: Open at any reasonable time.
Fee: Free.
Facilities: ⊛ ⇌ T(30 mins) 🐾 (on leads) EH

Walpole St. Peter (nr. Wisbech)
Walpole St. Peter's Church Map ref. B6
Church Road
Tel: (01945) 780206
A masterpiece of 14th C. architecture. Famous annual
flower festival.
Times: Open all year, daily, 0930-1700.
Fee: Free.
Facilities: 🅿 T(1 hr) 🏃

Weeting
Weeting Castle Map ref. E10
Tel: (01223) 582700 Web: www.english-heritage.org.uk
The ruins of an early medieval manor-house within a
shallow rectangular moat.
Times: Open at any reasonable time.
Fee: Free.
Facilities: ⊛ T(45 mins) 🐾 (on leads) EH

Wymondham
Wymondham Abbey Map ref. J8
Vicar Street
Tel: (01953) 602269
Web: www.wymondham-norfolk.co.uk
Magnificent Norman church built in 1107, with ruins of
former Benedictine abbey. Splendid interior with 15th C.
Lady Chapel, richly carved angel roofs, two 18th C.
organs and gold-faced reredos.
Times: Open 1 Jan-31 Mar, Mon-Sat, 1000-1500. 1 Apr-31
Oct, Mon-Sat, 1000-1600. 1 Nov-31 Dec Mon-Sat, 1000-
1500.
Fee: Free.
Facilities: 🅿 🛏 T(45 mins) 🎋 🖼

See Also:
Norwich Castle Museum and Art Gallery, page 91
Shirehall Museum and Abbey Gardens, Little Walsingham,
page 89

For even more information visit our website at www.visiteastofengland.com

SUFFOLK

Bungay

Bungay Castle Map ref. L3
Tel: (01986) 896156
The remains of an original Norman castle with Saxon mounds. Built by the Bigods in 1165. Massive gatehouse towers and curtain walls. Visitor centre with cafe.
Times: Open all year, daily, 1000-1600. Closed Sun in winter (please telephone to confirm).
Fee: £1.00/50p/50p.
Facilities: T(30 mins) 𝑋 ☺ 𝍖 𝔥

Bury St. Edmunds

Bury St. Edmunds Abbey Map ref. D/E6/7
Tel: (01223) 582700 Web: www.english-heritage.org.uk
The remains of a Benedictine abbey in beautifully kept gardens. The two great gateways (one being 14th C.) are the best preserved buildings.
Times: Open any reasonable time.
Fee: Free.
Facilities: ☺ 🚌 ≽ T(1 hr) 𝔥 (on leads) EH

Bury St. Edmunds

Saint Edmundsbury Cathedral Map ref. D/E6/7
Tel: (01284) 754933 Web: www.stedscathedral.co.uk
Come and see the magnificent Millennium Tower which now completes the last unfinished Anglican cathedral in England. Rising 150ft above the Central Crossing, the Lantern Tower is built of English limestone, brick and lime mortar to late Gothic design, using medieval craft skills.
Times: Open all year, daily, 0730-1800 (1900, 14 May-29 Aug).
Fee: Free.
Facilities: 🚌 ≽ T(1 hr) 𝑋 (summer only) 𝔥 (not in restaurant)

Leiston Abbey

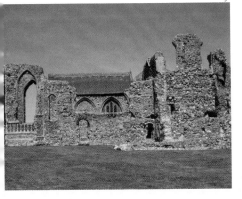

Eye

Eye Castle Map ref. I5
Castle Street
Tel: (01449) 676800 Web: www.midsuffolkleisure.co.uk
A Norman motte-and-bailey, with medieval walls and a Victorian folly. The castle has always had close associations with royalty since the Norman conquest.
Times: Open 25 Mar-Oct, daily, 0900-1900 (or dusk if earlier).
Fee: Free.
Facilities: ☺ 🚌 T(30 mins) 𝍖

Felixstowe

Landguard Fort Map ref. K/L12
Tel: (07749) 695523 Web: www.landguard.com
An ancient monument, a 1744 fort with 1875 modifications, and additions in 1890, 1901 and 1914.
Times: Open 27 Mar-31 May, daily, 1000-1700; 1 Jun-31 Aug, daily, 1000-1800; 1 Sep-30 Oct, daily, 1000-1700. Last admission 1hr before closing time.
Fee: £3.00/£1.00/£2.50.
Facilities: ☺ 🅿 T(1½ hrs) 𝍖 𝔥 (on leads) EH

Framlingham

Framlingham Castle Map ref. K/L7
Tel: (01728) 724189 Web: www.english-heritage.org.uk
Framlingham is a splendid example of a 12th Century castle. Walk around the impressive wall-walk, explore the magnificent Mere, outer courts and moats and admire the fine castle gatehouse.
Times: Open 2 Jan-23 Mar, daily, 1000-1600; 24 Mar-30 Sept, daily, 1000-1800; 1-31 Oct, daily, 1000-1700; 1 Nov-31 Dec, daily, 1000-1600. Closed 24-26 Dec and 1 Jan.
Fee: £4.30/£2.20/£3.20.
Facilities: ☺ Q 🅿 T(1½ hrs) 𝑋 (audio tours) 𝔥 (on leads) EH

Herringfleet (nr. Lowestoft)
Saint Olave's Priory Map ref. N1
Tel: (01223) 582700 Web: www.english-heritage.org.uk
Remains of an Augustinian priory, with an early 14th C.
undercroft and a brick vaulted ceiling.
Times: Open at any reasonable time.
Fee: Free.
Facilities: ☺ **T(45 mins)** ✝ (on leads) **EH**

Leiston
Leiston Abbey Map ref. N7
Tel: (01223) 582700 Web: www.english-heritage.org.uk
The remains of a 14th C. abbey for premonstratensian
canons, including the transepts of the church, a range of
cloisters and a restored chapel.
Times: Open at any reasonable time.
Fee: Free.
Facilities: ☺ 🅿 **T(45 mins)** 🛏 ✝ (on leads) **EH**

Lindsey (nr. Hadleigh)
Saint James's Chapel Map ref. G10
Tel: (01223) 582700 Web: www.english-heritage.org.uk
A small 13th C. medieval chapel, once attached to the
nearby castle. Thatched roof and lancet windows.
Times: Open all year, daily, 1000-1600.
Fee: Free.
Facilities: ☺ **T(30 mins) EH**

Orford
Orford Castle Map ref. N9
Tel: (01394) 450472 Web: www.english-heritage.org.uk
Visit the great keep of Henry II built between 1165 and
1173. Enjoy the spectacular panoramic views over Orford
Ness from the top of the keep. Climb the spiral staircase
leading to a maze of rooms and passageways. Explore the
charming village Orford, with its church, shops and
smokery.
Times: 2 Jan-23 Mar, Thurs-Mon, 1000-1600; 24 Mar-30
Sept, daily, 1000-1800; 1 Oct-31 Dec, Thurs-Mon, 1000-
1600. Closed 24-26 Dec and 1 Jan.
Fee: £4.30/£2.20/£3.20
Facilities: ☺ 🇶 🅿 **T(1 hr)** 𝒦(audio tours) **EH**

Walpole (nr. Halesworth)
Walpole Old Chapel Map ref. M5
Halesworth Road
Tel: (01986) 798308
17th C. conversion of a hall house into an independent
chapel. Many original fittings of late 17th C. - pulpit,
chandelier and galleries. Later box pews. Graveyard
managed for wildlife.
Times: Open 28 May-10 Sept, Sat, 1400-1630.
Fee: Free. Donations appreciated.
Facilities: 🅿 **T(30 mins)** 𝒦

West Stow (nr. Bury St. Edmunds)
West Stow Anglo-Saxon Village Map ref. D5
Icklingham Road
Tel: (01284) 728718
Web: www.stedmundsbury.gov.uk/weststow.htm
Unique reconstructed Anglo-Saxon village built on the site
of an original settlement. Archaeological finds are displayed
in a specially built centre.
Times: Open all year, daily, 1000-1700. Last admission
1600 (1530 in winter). Closed 25-26 Dec.
Fee: £5.00/£4.00/£4.00/£15.00(family).
Facilities: ☺ 🅿 **T(2 hrs)** 🕮 🛏

Woodbridge
Sutton Hoo Burial Site Map ref. K/L9
Tel: (01394) 389700 Web: www.nationaltrust.org.uk
An Anglo-Saxon royal burial site, where the priceless Sutton
Hoo treasure was discovered in a huge ship grave.
Exhibition tells story including original objects/replicas of
treasure. Estate with walks
Times: Open 2 Jan-13 Mar, Sat and Sun, 1000-
1600.(Open 12-20 Feb, daily 1000-1600), 19 Mar-2 Oct,
daily, 1100-1700. 3-31 Oct, Wed-Sun, 1100-1700. 1 Nov-
31 Dec, Fri-Sun, 1100-1600. Closed 23, 24, 25 Dec.
Fee: £5.00/£2.50/£12.50(family).
Facilities: ☺ 🅿 **T(2½ hrs)** 𝒦🕮 🛏 (on leads) 🌳 **NT**

See Also:
Clare Castle Country Park, page 194
South Elham Hall Minster, nr Harleston, page 47

West Stow Anglo-Saxon Village

Museums & Galleries

EDFORDSHIRE

edford
CA Gallery Map ref. D5/6
3 Castle Lane
el: (01234) 273580 Web: www.bedfordcreativearts.org
ontemporary art gallery offering a changing programme
f lens based work by local, national and international
ving artists. Shows include photography, film and
ew media work.
imes: Open all year, Tues-Sat, 1100-1700. Please contact
or Christmas openings.
ee: Free.
acilities: ▱ ▭ ≈ T(15 mins)

edford
edford Museum Map ref. D5/6
astle Lane
el: (01234) 353323 Web: www.bedfordmuseum.org
oused in the former Higgins and Sons Brewery, Bedford
Museum is situated within the gardens of bygone Bedford
astle. Changing programme of temporary exhibitions.
imes: Open all year, Tues-Sat, 1100-1700; Sun and Bank
ol Mon, 1400-1700. Closed Mon. Closed 25 Mar, 25, 26
ec, 1 Jan.
ee: Free.
acilities: ⊛ Q ▱ ▭ ≈ T(1½ hr) ㅋ ▨

Bedford Museum

Bedford
Cecil Higgins Art Gallery Map ref. D5/6
Castle Lane
Tel: (01234) 211222
Web: www.cecilhigginsartgallery.org
A Victorian mansion, furnished in late 19th C. style. A large
collection of watercolours, prints, drawings, glass,
ceramics, porcelain and lace.
Times: Open all year, Tues-Sat, 1100-1700; Sun and Bank
Hol Mon, 1400-1700. Closed 9 Apr, 23-28 Dec and 1 Jan.
Fee: Free entry
Facilities: ⊛ ▭ ≈ T(1½ hrs) ① ㅋ

Bedford
John Bunyan Museum and Bunyan Meeting Free Church
Map ref. D5/6
Mill Street
Tel: (01234) 213722
Museum housing the personal effects of John Bunyan
(1628-1688) and copies of The Pilgrim's Progress in over
170 languages, together with other works by Bunyan.
Times: Open 1 Mar-29 Oct, Tues-Sat, 1100-1600. Last
admission 1545. Closed 25 Mar.
Fee: Free. Donations appreciated.
Facilities: ▭ ≈ T(1 hr) ㅋ ① ▨

**For even more
information visit
our website at
www.visiteastofengland.com**

Clapham (nr. Bedford)

Twinwood Arena and The Glenn Miller Museum
Map ref. D5
Twinwood Road
Tel: (01234) 350413 Web: www.twinwoodevents.com
Restored airfield control tower housing an audio and visual
exhibition dedicated to the famous band leader Glenn
Miller. RAF room, aviation art gallery and collection of
military vehicles. Landscaped showground arena.
Times: Open Mar-Dec, Sat, Sun and Bank Hols, 1030-
1600. Closed 24-26 Dec and 1 Jan.
Fee: £3.00/free/£3.00.
Facilities: P T(2½ hrs) 🕎⑪ 🎋

Luton

Stockwood Park Museum Map ref. E10
Farley Hill
Tel: (01582) 738714
Web: www.luton.gov.uk/enjoying/museums
The craft museum illustrates the crafts and trades of pre-
industrial Bedfordshire; period gardens; the Mossman
Collection of carriages, sculpture gardens and tea room.
Times: Open 2 Jan-21 Mar, Sat and Sun, 1000-1600. 22 Mar-
30 Oct, Tues-Sun, 1000-1700. 31 Oct-19 Dec, Sat and Sun,
1000-1600.
Fee: Free.
Facilities: ⊛ P T(3 hrs) ⑪ 🎋 🖳

Luton

Wardown Park Museum Map ref. E10
Wardown Park
Tel: (01582) 546722
Web: www.luton.gov.uk/enjoying/museums
Housed in a Victorian mansion, displays present the
development of Luton from prehistory to the present day.
Free parking and admission. Gift shop.
Times: Open all year, Tues-Sat, 1000-1700; Sun, 1300-
1700. Closed Mon (except Bank Hol Mon), 25, 26 Dec and
1 Jan.
Fee: Free.
Facilities: ⊛ P ⇌ T(1½ hrs) ⑪ 🎋 🖳

Sandy

Roman Sandy Story Map ref. F6
Council Offices, 10 Cambridge Road
Tel: (01767) 681491 Web: www.roman-sandy.com
Permanent exhibition (mini museum) telling the story of
Roman Sandy, using many of the artefacts of a five year
programme of archaeology. Artists impressions and finds.
Times: Open all year, Mon-Fri, 0900-1600. Closed 25-28
Mar, 25, 26 Dec, 1, Jan.
Fee: Free.
Facilities: P 🚌 ⇌ T(1 hr) 🕎 🎋 🖳

Thurleigh (nr. Bedford)

306th Bombardment Group Museum Map ref. D4
Bedford Autodrome, Thurleigh Airfield Business Park
Tel: (01234) 708715
Museum commemorating the 306th Bombardment Group,
and the social impact of the 'Friendly Invasion' on the
surrounding area during the war years. Large collection of
artefacts, uniforms and photographs.
Times: Open 5 Mar-30 Oct, Sat, Sun and Bank Hols, 1030-
1600. At other times by arrangement.
Fee: £3.00/free.
Facilities: P T(1½ hrs) 🕎 🎋 🖳

Woburn

Woburn Heritage Centre Map ref. B8
Old St. Mary's Church, Bedford Street
Tel: (01525) 290631
Small registered museum covering the local history of
Woburn. Housed in the redundant Old St. Mary's Church.
Tourist Information Point.
Times: Open 25 Mar-30 Sept, Mon-Fri, 1400-1630; Sat,
Sun and Bank Hols, 1000-1700. 1-31 Oct, Sat and Sun,
1000-1700.
Fee: Free.
Facilities: 🚌 T(45 mins) 🖳

See Also:
Elstow Moot Hall page 37

BEDFORD MUSEUM

* FUN FOR ALL THE FAMILY *
* MONTHLY ACTIVITIES *
* QUIZZES * EVENTS *
* CHANGING EXHIBITIONS *
www.bedfordmuseum.org
See our entry on page 63 for opening times
Admission Free
Facilities for people with disabilities

AMBRIDGESHIRE

assingbourn (nr. Royston)
assingbourn Tower Museum Map ref. F14
assingbourn Barracks
el: (01763) 243500
useum housed in original airfield control tower. Exhibits,
notographs and documents covering the history of this
nportant military establishment, including the RAF,
SAAF 91st BG (H) and British Army.
imes: Open by appointment only - 1Apr-31 Oct, Wed and
un, 1000-1300.
ee: £3.00/Free/£3.00
acilities: P ⊞ T(3 hrs) ⫟

ourn (nr. Cambridge)
vysing Arts Map ref. F12
ox Road
el: (01954) 718881 Web: www.wysingarts.org
rt centre and gallery exhibiting contemporary art.
ontinuous programme of courses for adults and children.
leven acre site open all year round.
imes: Open all year, Mon-Fri, 1000-1700, Sat 1130-1700.
losed 24 Dec-3 Jan.
ee: Free.
acilities: P T(1½ hrs) ⫟ ⫯ ⊓

Burwell Museum of Fen Edge Village Life

Burwell
Burwell Museum of Fen Edge Village Life Map ref. J10
Mill Close
Tel: (01638) 605544
Web: www.burwellmuseum.org.uk
A rural village museum housed in a re-erected 18th C.
timber-framed barn. Also war memorabilia, forge, wagons
and carts. Displays of village shop and old school room.
Roman potter's display.
Times: Open 27 Mar-30 Oct, Thurs, Sun and Bank Hol
Mon, 1400-1700.
Fee: £2.00/50p.
Facilities: ⊞ T(2 hrs) ⊡

Cambridge
Cambridge and County Folk Museum Map ref. G11
2-3 Castle Street
Tel: (01223) 355159 Web: www.folkmuseum.org.uk
A part timber-framed 17th C. inn, retaining many original
fittings. Established as a museum of Cambridgeshire life in
1936. Strong collections. Extra display room from Jun
2004.
Times: May-end Sept, Mon-Sat, 1030-1700, Sun 1400-
1700; Oct-Mar, Tues-Sat 1030-1700, Sun 1400-1700.
Please telephone to confirm opening times and prices.
Fee: £2.50/75p/£1.50.
Facilities: ⊞ T(1 hr) ⊡

Cambridge
Cambridge Contemporary Art Map ref. H11
6 Trinity Street
Tel: (01223) 324222 Web: www.cambridgegallery.co.uk
Changing exhibitions highlight paintings, sculpture, hand-
made prints and crafts. With work by acknowledged
masters and established artists.
Times: Open all year, Mon-Sat, 0900-1730. Closed Bank
Hols.
Fee: Free.
Facilities: ⊞ T(1 hr) ⊡ ⫯

Cambridge
Fitzwilliam Museum Map ref. H11
Trumpington Street
Tel: (01223) 332900 Web: www.fitzmuseum.cam.ac.uk
A large, internationally-renowned collection of antiquities,
applied and fine arts. The original buildings are mid-
19th C. with later additions.
Times: Open all year, Tues-Sat and Bank Hol Mon, 1000-
1700; Sun, 1200-1700. Closed 24-26, 31 Dec
and 1 Jan.
Fee: Free.
Facilities: ⊛ ⊞ ⫞ T(2 hrs) ⫟

Cambridge
Kettle's Yard Map ref. G11
Castle Street
Tel: (01223) 352124 Web: www.kettlesyard.co.uk
A major collection of 20th C. paintings and sculpture,
exhibited in a house of unique character. Also changing
contemporary art exhibitions in the gallery.
Times: House, 1 Apr-31 Aug, Tues-Sun, 1330-1630;
1 Sept-31 Mar, Tues-Sun, 1400-1600; Gallery, open all
year, Tues-Sun, 1130-1700. Please phone for Christmas-
New Year opening times.
Fee: Free.
Facilities: ▦ T(1½ hrs)

Cambridge
Rupert Brooke Museum Map ref. G12
The Orchard, 45-47 Mill Way, Grantchester
Tel: (01223) 551118 Web: www.rupertbrooke.com
Small, privately owned museum depicting the life in words
and photographs of the poet Rupert Brooke (1887-1915),
who lived at Orchard House whilst at University.
Times: Open all year, daily, 1100-1730. Closed 25, 26 Dec.
Fee: Free.
Facilities: ▣ ▦ T(15 mins) ◔ ✝(Orchard and footpath
only)

Cambridge
Sedgwick Museum Map ref. H11
Department of Earth Sciences, Downing Street
Tel: (01223) 333456 Web: www.sedgwickmuseum.org
A large collection of fossils from all over the world, both
invertebrate and vertebrate with some mounted skeletons
of dinosaurs, reptiles and mammals. Mineral gallery.
Times: Open all year, Mon-Fri, 0900-1300 and 1400-1700;
Sat, 1000-1300. Closed 25-28 Mar and 24 Dec-3 Jan.
Fee: Free.
Facilities: T(1 hr)

Cambridge
University Museum of Archaeology and Anthropology
Map ref. H11
Downing Street
Tel: (01223) 333516
Web: http://museum.archanth.cam.ac.uk
Displays relating to world prehistory and local archaeology
with anthropology displays, opened in July 1990.
Times: Open all year, Tues-Sat, 1400-1630. Extended
opening hours from Jun-Sept.
Fee: Free.
Facilities: T(2 hrs) ⏜ ▩

Cambridge
University Museum of Zoology Map ref. H11
Downing Street
Tel: (01223) 336650 Web: www.zoo.cam.ac.uk/museum
Spectacular displays of internationally important
specimens, including fossils, mammal skeletons, birds,
dinosaurs, beautiful shells and a huge whale. Temporary
exhibitions throughout the year.
Times: Open all year, Mon-Fri, 1000-1300, 1400-1645.
Closed 25-28 Mar and 24 Dec-1 Jan.
Fee: Free.
Facilities: ▦ ⇌ T(45 mins) ⏜ ▩

Cambridge
Whipple Museum of the History of Science
Map ref. H11
Free School Lane
Tel: (01223) 330906 Web: www.hps.cam.ac.uk/whipple
The Whipple Museum houses a designated collection of
scientific instruments and models, dating from the Middle
Ages to the present.
Times: Open all year, Mon-Fri, 1330-1630. Closed Bank
Hols.
Fee: Free.
Facilities: T(1 hr) ▩

Fitzwilliam Museum, Cambridge

Chatteris
Chatteris Museum Map ref. G7
14 Church Lane
Tel: (01354) 696319
A small museum with artefacts, ephemera and
photographs relating to the history of the town of
Chatteris, its people and its environs.
Times: Open 6 Jan-31 Mar, Thurs, 1400-1600; Sat, 1000-
1200. 1 Apr-31 Oct, Thurs, 1400-1630; Sat, 1000-1300.
1 Nov-15 Dec, Thurs, 1400-1600; Sat, 1000-1200.
Fee: Free.
Facilities: ▣ ▭ T(1 hr) 🖼

Ely
Babylon Gallery Map ref. I8
Waterside
Tel: (01353) 669022 Web: www.babylongallery.co.uk
The Babylon Gallery offers a mixture of national touring
exhibitions, and high quality curated exhibitions of work by
local and regional artists.
Times: Open all year, Tues-Sat, 1000-1600; Bank Hol Sun
and Mon, 1100-1700. Please contact for Christmas
opening.
Fee: Free.
Facilities: ▭ ⇝ T(1 hr) 🖼

Ely
Ely Museum Map ref. I8
The Old Gaol, Market Street
Tel: (01353) 666655 Web: www.ely.org.uk
Tells the story of Ely from prehistory to the present day.
Collections include archaeology and social history, as well
as displays of the condemned gaol cells. Events throughout
the year.
Times: Open 2 Jan-27 Mar, Mon, Wed-Sat, 1030-1600;
Sun, 1300-1600. 28 Mar-30 Oct, Mon-Sat, 1030-1700;
Sun, 1300-1700. 31 Oct-18 Dec, Mon, Wed-Sat, 1030-
1600; Sun, 1300-1600.
Fee: £3.00/free /£2.00.
Facilities: ▭ T(1 hr) 🖼

Ely
Stained Glass Museum Map ref. I8
Ely Cathedral
Tel: (01353) 660347 Web: www.sgm.abelgratis.com
A museum housing examples of stained glass from the
13th C. to the present day in specially lighted display
boxes, with models of a modern workshop.
Times: Open 1 Jan-31 Mar, Mon-Fri, 1030-1700; Sat,
1030-1700; Sun, 1200-1630. 1 Apr-31 Oct, Mon-Fri, 1030-
1700; Sat, 1030-1730; Sun, 1200-1800. 1 Nov-31 Dec,
Mon-Fri, 1030-1700; Sat, 1030-1700; Sun, 1200-1630.
Closed 25 Mar and 25, 26 Dec.
Fee: £3.50/£2.50/£2.50/£7.00.
Facilities: ▭ ⇝ T(40 mins) 🖋 ⊕ ⛩

Eynesbury (nr. St. Neots)
St. Neots Picture Gallery Map ref. D11
23 St. Mary's Street
Tel: (01480) 215291
Watercolours, pastels and photographs of St. Neots and
surrounding area. Comprehensive range of artists materials.
Times: Open all year, Tues-Fri, 0900-1730; Sat, 0900-1630.
Closed 25 and 28 Mar and 25 Dec-1 Jan.
Fee: Free.
Facilities: ⊛ ▣ ▭ ⇝ T(30 mins) 🐾

Great Staughton (nr. St. Neots)
Taggart Tile Museum Map ref. C10
Robin Hood Cottage
Tel: (01480) 860314 Web: www.taggartgallery.co.uk
15th C. cottage (next to the church), housing a permanent
and extensive exhibition of tiles covering the period of
1650-2000.
Times: Open all year, Wed-Sat, 1000-1700; Sun (Oct-
May), 1100-1500. Closed 28 Mar, 25 Dec-4 Jan.
Fee: Free.
Facilities: ▣ T(30 mins)

Huntingdon
Blacked-Out Britain War Museum Map ref. D9
1 St. Marys Street
Tel: (01480) 450998
Everyday items of life from 1939-45. From evacuation to
rationing, bus tickets to bombs.
Times: Open all year, Mon-Sat, 0900-1700; Sun, 1000-1400.
Closed 27 Mar and 25, 26 Dec.
Fee: Free.
Facilities: ▣ T(30 mins) ⊕ 🐾

Thorney Heritage Museum
(© Fens Tourism)

Huntingdon
Cromwell Museum Map ref. D9
Grammar School Walk
Tel: (01480) 375830 Web: www.cromwell.argonet.co.uk
A museum with portraits, signed documents and other
articles belonging to Cromwell and his family.
Times: 2 Jan-31 Mar, Tues- Fri 1300-1600, Sat 1100-1300,
1400-1600, Sun 1400-1600; 1 Apr-31 Oct, Tues-Fri 1100-
1300, 1400-1700, Sat and Sun 1100-1300, 1400-1600; 1
Nov-31 Dec, Tues-Fri 1300-1600, Sat 1100-1300, 1400-
1600, Sun 1400-1600.
Fee: Free.
Facilities: ⊕ ▭ ⇌ T(1 hr) ▨

March
March and District Museum Map ref. G5/6
High Street
Tel: (01354) 655300
A general collection of artefacts relating to social history,
agricultural tools, many local photographs and 19th C
record material. A restored blacksmith's forge and
Victorian cottage parlour.
Times: Open all year, Wed and Sat, 1030-1530. Suns -1
May, 5 Jun; 3 Jul; 7 Aug, 1400-1700. Closed 18 Dec-5 Jan.
Fee: Free.
Facilities: ▣ ▭ ⇌ T(1 hr) ♥ ▨

Parson Drove (nr. Wisbech)
The Cage Map ref. F4
The Village Green, Station Road
Tel: (01945) 700501
Built in 1829 by John Peck as a lock-up. The clock tower
was added in 1897. Houses displays covering the history of
the building and local land drainage.
Times: Open 10 Apr-11 Sept, Wed and Sun, Bank Hol
1400-1700.
Fee: Free.
Facilities: ▣ ▭ T(45 mins) ⊓

Peterborough
Peterborough Museum and Art Gallery Map ref. D5
Priestgate
Tel: (01733) 343329
Web: www.peterboroughheritage.org.uk
Museum of local history, geology, archaeology, natural and
social history. World-famous collection of Napoleonic
POW work. A period shop and many cultural exhibitions.
Times: Open all year, school term time, Tues-Fri, 1200-
1700, Sat 1000-1700. School hols, Tues-Sat, 1000-1700;
Sun and Bank Hol Mon, 1200-1600. Closed 1 Jan, 25-27
Mar and 25-26 Dec.
Fee: Free.
Facilities: ⊕ ▭ ⇌ T(2½ hrs) ⅄

Ramsey
Ramsey Rural Museum Map ref. E7
Wood Lane
Tel: (01487) 814304 Web: www.ramseytown.com
17th C. farm buildings with collection covering the history
of Fenland life. Well restored agricultural machinery,
Victorian chemists, cobblers, blacksmiths and schoolroom.
Local and family history archive.
Times: Open 3 Apr-29 Sept, Thurs, 1000-1700; Sun and
Bank Hols, 1400-1700.
Fee: £3.00/£2.00/£2.00.
Facilities: ▣ T(1-3 hrs) ⅄ ⊛ ⊓ ▨

St. Ives
Norris Museum Map ref. E/F9
The Broadway
Tel: (01480) 497314
Museum displaying the history of Huntingdon from earliest
times to the present day with fossils, archaeology, history,
an art gallery and library.
Times: Open 4 Jan-30 Apr, Mon-Fri, 1000-1300, 1400-
1600, Sat 1000-1200; 1 May-30 Sept, Mon-Fri, 1000-
1300, 1400-1700; Sat, 1000-1200, 1400-1700; Sun, 1400-
1700. 1 Oct-31 Dec, Mon-Fri, 1000-1300, 1400-1600; Sat,
1000-1200. Closed 25-27 Mar, 25-27 Dec.
Fee: Free.
Facilities: ▭ T(1 hr) ⊓ ♥ ▨

St. Neots
Saint Neots Museum Map ref. C/D11
The Old Court, 8 New Street
Tel: (01480) 214163
A former police station and Magistrates' Court, now
housing the local history museum.
Times: Open 2 Feb-25 Mar, Wed-Sat, 1030-1630; 26 Mar-
17 Dec, Tues-Sat 1030-1630.
Fee: £2.00/£1.00/£1.00.
Facilities: ▭ ⇌ T(45 mins) ▨

Cromwell Museum, Huntingdon

Thorney
Thorney Heritage Museum Map ref. E4
Station Road
Tel: (01733) 270780
Showing the development from monastic days, Walloon and Flemish influence after Vermuydens drainage; also 19th C. model housing by the Duke of Bedford.
Times: Open 26 Mar-25 Sept, Sat and Sun, 1200-1500. Please contact to confirm.
Fee: Free.
Facilities: 🅿 ⬛ T(1½ hrs) 🕏 🚹 ♿

Thornhaugh (nr. Peterborough)
Sacrewell Farm and Country Centre Map ref. B5
Sacrewell
Tel: (01780) 782254 Web: www.sacrewell.org.uk
Farm animals, pets, tractor rides and children's play areas. Range of listed buildings including working watermill, gardens, farm bygones, farm trails, restaurant and shop.
Times: Open all year, daily, 1 Mar-30 Sept, 0930-1700; 1Oct-29 Feb, 1000-1600. Closed 24 Dec-2 Jan.
Fee: £4.25/£2.75/£3.25/£12.00(family).
Facilities: ⊕ Q 🅿 ⬛ T(3 hrs) ⓘ 🚹 ♣(on leads)

Waterbeach (nr. Cambridge)
The Farmland Museum and Denny Abbey Map ref. H10
Ely Road
Tel: (01223) 860988/860489
Web: www.dennyfarmlandmuseum.org.uk
An agricultural estate since medieval times, with an abbey and an interactive museum. Remains of 12th C. Benedictine abbey, and a 14th C. hall of a religious house.
Times: Open 27 Mar-31 Oct daily, 1200-1700
Fee: £3.80/£1.60/£2.90/£9.60(family)
Facilities: ⊛ 🅿 ⬛ T(1½ hrs) ⓘ 🚹 ♣(on leads and outside areas) **EH**

Wendy (nr. Royston)
British Museum of Miniatures Map ref. F13
Maple Street
Tel: (01223) 207025 Web: www.maplestreet.co.uk
Dolls house and miniatures museum, including the largest dolls house in the world. Dolls house and miniatures shop. New crafts and toy department.
Times: Open all year, Mon-Sat, 1000-1700; Sun, 1200-1600. Closed 25, 26 Dec.
Fee: £2.50/£1.50.
Facilities: 🅿 T(2 hrs) ⓘ

Whittlesey
Whittlesey Museum Map ref. E5/6
Town Hall, Market Street
Tel: (01733) 840986
Museum of archaeology, agriculture, hand tools, brickmaking, local photographs, a Sir Harry Smith exhibition, costume display and temporary exhibitions.
Times: Open all year, Fri and Sun, 1430-1630; Sat, 1000-1200.
Fee: 50p/20p.
Facilities: T(1 hr) 🕏

Wisbech
Octavia Hill Birthplace House Map ref. H4
1 South Brink Place
Tel: (01945) 476358 Web: www.octaviahillmuseum.org
Grade II* Georgian house in which Octavia Hill, social reformer and co-founder of the National Trust was born. Museum commemorates her life, work and legacy.
Times: Open 16 Mar-30 Oct, Wed, Sat, Sun and Bank Hol Mon, 1300-1630 (last admission 1600). Open all year by appointment.
Fee: £2.00/accompanied child free/£1.50.
Facilities: T(1 hr)

Wisbech and Fenland Museum (© Fens Tourism)

A 2000 Year Adventure

See history
Some of the most important historical finds in Britain can be seen here

Hear history
Audio visual dramas explain Colchester's involvement in some of the most important events in British history

Touch history
Try on a toga, catch up with medieval fashions and touch real Roman pottery

Discover history
A variety of events take place during the school holidays

A visit to **Colchester Castle Museum** takes you through 2000 years of some of the most important events in British history. Once capital of Roman Britain, Colchester has experienced devastation by Boudica *(Boadicea)*, invasion by the Normans and siege during the English Civil War.

Since the 16th century, the Castle has been a ruin, a library and a gaol for witches. Today it is an award-winning museum featuring many hands-on displays to help explain the townspeople's experience of Colchester's varying fortunes.

The Castle itself is the largest keep ever built by the Normans. It was constructed on the foundations of the Roman Temple of Claudius, which can still be seen today.

ColchesterCastleMuseu

Enquiries telephone: **01206 282939**
www.colchestermuseums.org.uk

Peckover House, Wisbech, see page 36

Wisbech
Skylark Studios Map ref. G2/3
Hannath Road, Tydd Gote
Tel: (01945) 420403 Web: www.skylarkstudios.co.uk
An art gallery showing monthly exhibitions by local and national artists, along with a permanent display of art and crafts.
Times: Open all year, Tues-Sat, 1000-1700. Closed 27 Mar and 25 Dec-4 Jan.
Fee: Free.
Facilities: 🅿 T(45 mins) 🐾 ♿

Wisbech
Wisbech and Fenland Museum Map ref. H4
Museum Square
Tel: (01945) 583817
One of the oldest purpose-built museums in the country, situated next to Wisbech's fine Georgian crescent. Displays on Fen landscape, local history, geology and archaeology.
Times: Open Jan-Mar, Tues-Sat, 1000-1600. Apr-Sept, Tues-Sat, 1000-1700. Oct-Dec, Tues-Sat, 1000-1600.
Fee: Free.
Facilities: 🅿 🚌 T(45 mins) 🚶 ♿

See Also:
Flag Fen Bronze Age Centre, Peterborough page 50, 51
Oliver Cromwell's House, Ely page 10, 38

ESSEX

Billericay
Cater Museum Map ref. F9
74 High Street
Tel: (01277) 622023
A folk museum of bygones with a Victorian sitting room, bedroom and kitchen, as well as a World War II exhibition.
Times: Open all year, Mon-Sat, 1400-1700. Closed all Bank Hols, 24 Dec-3 Jan.
Fee: Free.
Facilities: ⇌ T(1 hr) 🚶

Braintree
Braintree District Museum Map ref. G4/5
Manor Street
Tel: (01376) 325266 Threads of Time is a permanent exhibition housed in a converted Victorian school, telling the story of Braintree district and its important place in our history.
Times: Open all year, Mon-Sat, 1000-1700. Sun afternoons in Nov and Dec.
Fee: £2.00/£1.00
Facilities: 🅝 🅿 🚌 ⇌ T(1 hrs) 🚶 🚻 ♿

Braintree
The Town Hall Centre Map ref. G4/5
Market Square
Tel: (01376) 557776 Web: www.braintree.gov.uk
Art gallery in Grade II* listed building with Tourist Information Centre on site. Situated in historic market square dating back to 1199.
Times: Open all year, Mon-Sat, 1000-1700. Please contact for details of Christmas and Easter opening times.
Fee: Free.
Facilities: 🅿 🚌 ⇌ T(1 hr) 🚶 ♿

Brentwood
Brentwood Museum Map ref. D/E9
Cemetery Lodge, Lorne Road
Tel: (01277) 223326
A small cottage museum covering social and domestic history with special reference to Brentwood. It includes a 1930s kitchen, toys and exhibits from two World Wars.
Times: Open 3 Apr, 1 May, 5 Jun, 3 Jul, 7 Aug, 4 Sept, 2 Oct, Sun, 1430-1630.
Fee: Free.
Facilities: 🅝 🅿 🚌 ⇌ T(40 mins) ♿

Brentwood
Kelvedon Hatch Nuclear Bunker Map ref. D8
Kelvedon Hall Lane, Kelvedon Hatch
Tel: (01277) 364883 Web: www.secretnuclearbunker.co.uk
A large, 3-storey, ex-government regional headquarters buried some 100ft below ground, complete with canteen, BBC studio, dormitories, plant room and plotting floor.
Times: Open 1 Jan-28 Feb, Thurs-Sun, 1000-1600. 1 Mar-31 Oct, Mon-Fri, 1000-1600, Sat, Sun and Bank Hol, 1000-1700; 1 Nov-31 Dec, Thurs-Sun, 1000-1600. Closed 25 Dec.
Fee: £5.00/£3.00/£12.00 (family).
Facilities: 🅝 Q 🅿 T(2 hrs) 🚻 ♿

Brightlingsea
Brightlingsea Museum Map ref. L6
1 Duke Street
Tel: (01206) 303286
The maritime and social history museum of Brightlingsea (a limb of the Cinque Port of Sandwich) showing collections relating to the town's Cinque Port connections.
Times: Open 26 Mar -26 Sept, Sun and Mon, 1400-1700; Sat, 1000-1600.
Fee: Free.
Facilities: 🚌 T(1 hr) 𝄢

Burnham-on-Crouch
Burnham Museum Map ref. J9
Tucker Brown Boathouse, Coronation Road
Tel: (01621) 782184
A small museum devoted to local history with maritime and agricultural features of the Dengie Hundred.
Times: Open 26 Mar-30 Nov, Wed, Sat, Sun and Bank Hols and daily in school hols, 1400-1700.
Fee: £1.00/20p.
Facilities: T(30 mins) 🔲

Canvey Island
Dutch Cottage Museum Map ref. H11
Canvey Road
Tel: (01268) 794005
An early 17th C. cottage of one of Vermuyden's Dutch workmen who was responsible for drainage schemes in East Anglia.
Times: Open 30 May; 5-26 Jun, Sun, 1430-1700; 3 Jul-31 Aug, Wed, Sun, 1430-1700; 29 Aug, 1430-1700; 4 Sep, Sun, 1430-1700.
Fee: Free.
Facilities: 🅿 🚌 T(45 mins)

Canvey Island
Heritage Centre Map ref. H11
Canvey Village, Canvey Road
Tel: (01268) 512220
The Heritage Centre is housed in the now redundant parish church of St. Katherine, built in 1876. It contains an art and craft centre and a folk museum.
Times: Please telephone for opening times.
Fee: Free.
Facilities: 🅿 🚌 ⇌ T(30 mins) ⑨

Chelmsford
Chelmsford Museum Map ref. F7
Oaklands Park, Moulsham Street
Tel: (01245) 615100
Web: www.chelmsfordbc.gov.uk/museums
Local and social history, from prehistory to present day.
Essex Regiment history, fine and decorative arts (ceramics,
costume, glass), coins, natural history, events and talks.
Times: Open all year, Mon-Sat, 1000-1700; Sun, 1300-
1600 (or 1400-1700 in summer). Closed 25 Mar, 25, 26
Dec.
Fee: Free.
Facilities: ⊛ 🅿 T(2 hrs) 🛏

Chelmsford
Essex Police Museum Map ref. F7
Essex Police Headquarters, Springfield
Tel: (01245) 457150 Web: www.essex.police.uk/museum
Covers the history of policing in Essex, from its Victorian
origins to the present day, including Moat Farm murder
and the death of PC Gutteridge. Hands-on police
equipment.
Times: Open by appointment only. All year, please contact
for details.
Fee: Free.
Facilities: 🚗 ⇌ T(1½ hrs)🛏 🖼

Coggeshall
Coggeshall Heritage Centre Map ref. I5
St. Peter's Hall, Stoneham Street
Tel: (01376) 563003
Web: www.btinternet.com/~coggeshall
Ever-changing historical depiction of this medieval wool
and market town. Large exhibition of Coggeshall lace,
working wool loom and old photographs.
Times: Open 27 Mar-30 Oct, Sun, Bank Hol Sat and Mon,
1415-1645.
Fee: Free.
Facilities: T(45 mins) 🛏 🖼

Colchester
Colchester Castle Museum Map ref. K4
Tel: (01206) 282939
Web: www.colchestermuseums.org.uk
A Norman keep on the foundations of a Roman temple.
The archaeological material includes much on Roman
Colchester (Camulodunum). Exciting hands-on displays.
Times: Open all year, Mon-Sat, 1000-1700; Sun, 1100-
1700. Closed 25, 26 and 27 Dec and 1 Jan.
Fee: £4.50/£2.90/£2.90.
Facilities: ⊛ Q 🚗 ⇌ T(2½ hrs) 🛏 🛏 🖼

Colchester
firstsite @ The Minories Art Gallery Map ref. K4
74 High Street
Tel: (01206) 577067 Web: www.firstsite.uk.net
firstsite presents a diverse programme of innovative
contemporary art exhibitions and events at the Minories
Art Gallery - an inpressive Georgian townhouse with a
shop, cafe and beautiful walled garden.
Times: Open 2 Jan-22 Dec, Mon-Sat, 1000-1700.
Fee: Free.
Facilities: ⊛ Q 🚗 ⇌ T(2 hrs) ⓘ 🛏 🐕(garden only)

Colchester
Gallery Schomberg Map ref. K4
12 St. Johns Street
Tel: (01206) 769458
Gallery situated in centre of town with changing exhibition
programme. Featuring a wide range of ceramics, glass,
jewellery, wood textiles, prints and paintings.
Times: Open all year, Fri, Sat, 1030-1730; 1-31 Dec, Mon-
Sat, 1030-1700, Sun 1100-1700. Please telephone for
exhibition opening times. Closed 25 Dec.
Fee: Free.
Facilities: 🚗 ⇌ T(1 hr)

The Sir Alfred Munnings Art Museum, Dedham

Colchester
Hollytrees Museum Map ref. K4
High Street
Tel: (01206) 282940
Web: www.colchestermuseums.org.uk
A collection of toys, costumes and decorative arts from the 18th-20th C., displayed in an elegant Georgian town house, built in 1718.
Times: Open all year, Mon-Sat, 1000-1700; Sun, 1100-1700. Closed 25, 26 and 27 Dec and 1 Jan.
Fee: Free.
Facilities: ◎ Q 🚾 ⇌ T(1 hr) 🎋 🄫

Colchester
Natural History Museum Map ref. K4
All Saints Church, High Street
Tel: (01206) 282932
Web: www.colchestermuseums.org.uk
Hands-on displays and events giving the whole family an interesting perspective on the local natural history of Essex.
Times: Open all year, Mon-Sat, 1000-1700; Sun, 1100-1700. Closed 25, 26 and 27 Dec and 1 Jan.
Fee: Free.
Facilities: ◎ Q 🚾 ⇌ T(40 mins) 🄫

Colchester
Tymperleys Clock Museum Map ref. K4
Trinity Street
Tel: (01206) 282931
Web: www.colchestermuseums.org.uk
A fine collection of Colchester-made clocks from the Mason collection, displayed in a 15th C. timber-framed house which Bernard Mason restored and presented to the town.
Times: Open 1 Apr-31 Oct, Tues-Sat, 1000-1300 and 1400-1700.
Fee: Free.
Facilities: ◎ Q T(45 mins) 🄫

Dedham
The Sir Alfred Munnings Art Museum Map ref. L3
Castle House, Castle Hill
Tel: (01206) 322127
The home, studios and grounds where Sir Alfred Munnings, KCVO, lived and painted for 40 years. A large collection, also includes pictures on loan from private collections.
Times: Open 27 Mar-2 Oct, Sun, Wed and Bank Hol Mon, 1400-1700. Also Thurs and Sat in Aug, 1400-1700
Fee: £4.00/£1.00/£3.00.
Facilities: ◎ Q 🄿 T(1½ hrs) 🎋 🐎(on leads)

Finchingfield
Finchingfield Guildhall and Heritage Centre Map ref. F3
Church Hill
Tel: (01371) 810525
The Guildhall is open for exhibitions, lectures and meetings. Heritage Centre is open for details of the Guildhall, church and other ancient properties in the village.
Times: Open 1 May-25 Sept, Sun, 1400-1700.
Fee: Free.
Facilities: T(1½ hrs)

Goldhanger (nr. Maldon)
Maldon and District Agricultural and Domestic Museum Map ref. J7
47 Church Street
Tel: (01621) 788647
An extensive collection of farm machinery, domestic items of every kind, products of Maldon Ironworks, printing machines from 1910, photographs and stuffed birds.
Times: 27 Mar-end Nov, Sun, 1000-1800.
Fee: £3.00/£1.50/£1.50.
Facilities: 🄿 T(1 hr)

Tymperleys Clock Museum, Colchester

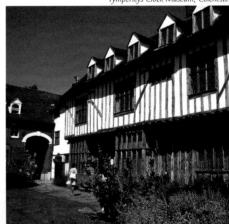

Grays
Thurrock Museum Map ref. E12
Thameside Complex, Orsett Road
Tel: (01375) 382555
Over 1,500 artefacts interpreting 250,000 years of Thurrock's Heritage. From prehistory through to our recent industrial developments.
Times: Open all year, Mon-Sat, 0900-1700. Closed Bank Hols.
Fee: Free.
Facilities: P T(1 hr)

Great Bardfield
Bardfield Cage Map ref. F3
Bridge Street
Tel: (01371) 810516
Great Bardfield Cage is a 19th C. village lock-up. There is a figure of a man in the cage and an audio tape player.
Times: Open 25 Mar-26 Sept, Sat, Sun and Bank Hol Mon, 1400-1700.
Fee: Free. Donations appreciated.
Facilities: P T(20 mins)

Great Bardfield
Cottage Museum Map ref. F3
Dunmow Road
Tel: (01371) 810516
A 16th C. charity cottage with a collection of 19th C. and 20th C. domestic and agricultural artefacts and some rural crafts. Mainly straw plaiting and corn dollies.
Times: Open 26 Mar-25 Sept, Sat, Sun and Bank Hol Mon, 1400-1700.
Fee: Free. Donations appreciated.
Facilities: P T(1 hr)

Great Warley (nr. Brentwood)
Hazle Ceramics Workshop Map ref. D10
Stallion's Yard, Codham Hall
Tel: (01277) 220892 Web: www.hazle.com
Discover the background to our award-winning designs, especially 'A Nation of Shopkeepers'. Learn how to cast clay into moulds, and watch demonstrations of the whole ceramic process. Hobby painting.
Times: Open 7 Jan-24 Dec Tues-Sat and Bank Hols, 1100-1700. Closed 23-31 Dec.
Fee: Free.
Facilities: P T(1½ hr)

Harlow
The Museum of Harlow Map ref. B7
Muskham Road, Off First Avenue
Tel: (01279) 454959 Web: www.tmoh.com
Museum showing the history of Harlow from earliest times to the present day. Also includes a bicycle collection, local history library and three walled gardens.
Times: Open all year, Tues-Fri, 1000-1700; Sat, 1000-1230 and 1330-1700. Closed 25, 26, and 28 Mar; 25 Dec-1 Jan.
Fee: Free.
Facilities: P T(1½ hrs)

Harwich
Ha'penny Pier Visitor Centre Map ref. O3
The Quay
Tel: (01255) 503429 Web: www.theharwich-society.com
Visitor information centre for everything in Harwich. Includes a small Harwich and the New World exhibition.
Times: Open 1 May-31 Aug, daily, from 1000-1700.
Fee: Free.
Facilities: P T(20 mins)

Harwich
Harwich Lifeboat Museum Map ref. O3
Timberfields, off Wellington Road
Tel: (01255) 503429 Web: www.harwich-society.com
The Harwich Lifeboat Museum contains the last Clacton off-shore 37ft lifeboat, the Oakley class, and a fully-illustrated history of the lifeboat service in Harwich.
Times: Open 1 May-31 Aug, Tues-Sun from 1100. Last admission 1430.
Fee: 50p/25p.
Facilities: P T(30 mins)

Harwich
Harwich Maritime Museum Map ref. O3
Low Lighthouse, Harbour Crescent
Tel: (01255) 503429 Web: www.harwich-society.com
A museum with special displays related to the Royal Navy and commercial shipping, with fine views over the unending shipping movements in the harbour.
Times: Open 1 May-31 Aug, daily, 1000-1630.
Fee: 50p.
Facilities: T(30 mins)

Harwich
Radar Tower (Beacon Hill Fort) Map ref. O3
Barrack Lane
Tel: (01255) 503429 Web: www.harwich-society.com
One of the earliest radar installations in World War II
(1941). Now fully restored by The Harwich Society.
Times: Open 1 May, 5 Jun, 3 Jul, 7 Aug, Sun, 1400-1600.
Fee: £1.00/free/£1.00
Facilities: ▣ T(30 mins)

Kelvedon (nr. Coggeshall)
Feering and Kelvedon Local History Museum Map ref. I5
Aylett's School, Maldon Road
Tel: (01376) 571206
Artefacts from the Roman settlement of Canonium,
manorial history, agricultural tools and bygones.
Times: Open 8 Jan-26 Feb, Sat,1030-1230. 5 Mar-31 Oct,
Mon, 1400-1700; Sat, 0930-1230. 5 Nov-17 Dec, Sat,
1030-1230.
Fee: Free.
Facilities: ▣ ⇄ T(1 hr) ✝ 🕭

Lindsell (nr. Great Dunmow)
Lindsell Art Gallery Map ref. E4
Tel: (01371) 870777
Art gallery specialising in paintings, prints, sculptures and
greeting cards by local artists. Pictures of local interest.
Times: Open all year, Mon, Tues, Thur-Sat, 0930-1730.
Closed 25-31 Dec.
Fee: Free.
Facilities: ▣ T(30 mins) 🕭

Linford (nr. Tilbury)
Walton Hall Museum Map ref. F12
Walton Hall Road
Tel: (01375) 671874 Web: www.waltonhallmuseum.com
The main collection is housed in a 17th C. English barn and
other farm buildings. Bygones, tools, wagons, militaria,
domestic and motoring displays. Old-time dairy, blacksmith
and printshop displays.
Times: Open 19 Mar-30 Oct, Thurs-Sun , Bank Hol Mon and
school hols, 1000-1700. Please contact for school holiday
openings.
Fee: £3.00/£1.50/£1.50.
Facilities: ▣ T(3 hrs) ⑪ ⼕ ✝

Maldon
Combined Military Services Museum Map ref. I7
Station Road
Tel: (01621) 841826 Web www.cmsm.co.uk
The museum has collections of British military artefacts and a
number of items on display are of national importance for
example: the only surviving MK2 'Cockle' canoe.
Times: Open 2 Jan-24 Dec, Wed-Sun, 1030-1700.
Fee: £3.50/£2.00/£2.00/£10.00(family).
Facilities: ▣ T(2 hrs) 🖅 🕭

Maldon
Maeldune Heritage Centre Map ref. I7
Plume Building
Tel: (01621) 851628
The Maeldune Centre houses the celebrated Maldon
embroidery and exhibitions of paintings and local history.
Large archive of old Maldon photographs.
Times: Open 3 Feb-31 Mar, Thurs-Sat, 1300-1600; 1 Apr-
31 Oct, Mon-Sat, 1300-1600; 3 Nov-23 Dec, Thurs-Sat,
1300-1600. May open Sat mornings, please telephone to
check. Closed 25, 26 Dec and 1 Jan.
Fee: Free.
Facilities: T(1 hr) ⼕ 🕭

Maldon
Maldon District Museum Map ref. I7
47 Mill Road
Tel: (01621) 842688
Web: www.maldonmuseum.fsnet.co.uk
A small museum devoted to Maldon town with many
articles of a general and domestic nature.
Times: Open 26 Mar-31 Oct, Wed, Fri, Sat, Sun and Bank
Hol Mon, 1400-1700.
Fee: £1.00/25p.
Facilities: ▣ 🖾 T(1 hr) 🖅 ⼕ 🕭

Maldon
Thames Barge Heritage Centre Map ref. I7
SB Glenway
Cooks Barge Yard, The Hythe
Tel: (01621) 857567 Web: www.cooksbargeyard.co.uk
Cooks Barge Yard Heritage Centre tells the story from
evolution in the early 1800's to their heyday at the turn of
the century.
Times: Open 25 Mar-25 Sept, Sat, Sun, 1200-1700; 2 Oct-
18 Dec, Sun 1200-1600(weather permitting).
Fee: Free.
Facilities: T(1½ hrs) ⼕

Ha'penny Pier Visitor Centre, Harwich

Manningtree
Dragonflies Craft Gallery Map ref. L/M3
8 Station Road
Tel: (01206) 399099 Web: www.dragonfliesgallery.com
Dragonflies philosophy is to bring togather a collection of
good quality local arts and crafts, which can inspire,
enhance, decorate or be of practical use. We have a range
of unique jewellery but specialise in amber. Watercolour
painting and Tiffany glass.
Times: Open all year, Tues-Sat, 1000-1600. Closed 25-28
Mar, 24 Dec-3 Jan.
Fee: Free.
Facilities: ⇌ T(1 hr) ⊕ 🔲

Manningtree
Manningtree and District Local History Museum
Map ref. M3
Manningtree Library, High Street
Tel: (01206) 392747
Displays of old photographs, artefacts, books and local
maps. Some permanent displays, with two exhibitions
yearly.
Times: Open 3 Jan-24 Dec, Wed, 1000-1200; Fri, 1400-
1600; Sat, 1000-1200. Closed 25, 26 Mar and 25-31 Dec.
Fee: Free. Donations welcome.
Facilities: 🚻 ⇌ T(1 hr) 🗛

Purfleet
Purfleet Heritage and Military Centre Map ref. D12
Royal Gunpowder Magazine, Centurion Way
Tel: (01708) 866764/523409
The Royal Gunpowder Magazine dates from 1760. The
heritage centre displays local history, photographs,
artefacts and memorabilia.
Times: Open Nov-Mar, Thurs and Sun, 1000-1500. Apr-
Oct, Thurs, Sun and Bank Hols, 1000-1630.
Fee: £2.00/75p (2004 prices).
Facilities: 🅿 T(4 hrs) 🏃⊕ 🗛

Ridgewell
Ridgewell Airfield Commemorative Museum Map ref. G2
Tel: (01787) 277310 Web: www.381st.com
Small private collection of military/civilian memorabilia,
dedicated to the USAAF 381st Bomb Group and 90
Squadron, RAF who flew from Ridgewell. Housed in US
base hospital building.
Times: Open 10 Apr, 8 May, 12 Jun, 10 Jul, 14 Aug, 11
Sept 1100-1700.
Fee: Free.
Facilities: 🅿 T(1hrs) 🗛 🏃 🔲

Edward Bawden

Saffron Walden
Fry Public Art Gallery Map ref. C/D2
Bridge End Gardens, Castle Street
Tel: (01799) 513779 Web: www.fryartgallery.org
Permanent exhibition of 20th C. British artists who have
lived and worked in North West Essex: including Edward
Bawden, Eric Ravilious, Michael Rothenstein, Bernard
Cheese, John Aldridge. Additionally two or three changing
exhibitions are on show in parallel.
Times: Open 26 Mar-30 Oct, Tues, Sat, Sun and Bank
Hols, 1400-1700.
Fee: Free.
Facilities: 🚻 T(45 mins) 🏃 🔲

Saffron Walden
Saffron Walden Museum Map ref. C/D2
Museum Street
Tel: (01799) 510333
A friendly, family-sized museum of local history, decorative
arts, ethnography, archaeology and natural history.
Museum of the Year Award: Best Museum of Social
History.
Times: Open 1 Jan-29 Feb, Mon-Sat, 1000-1630; Sun and
Bank Hols, 1400-1630. 1 Mar-31 Oct, Mon-Sat, 1000-
1700; Sun and Bank Hols, 1400-1700. 1 Nov-31 Dec,
Mon-Sat, 1000-1630; Sun and Bank Hols, 1400-1630.
Closed 24 and 25 Dec.
Fee: £1.00/free/50p.
Facilities: ⊛ 🅿 T(1 hr) 🗛 🔲

Southend-on-Sea
Central Museum and Planetarium Map ref. I11
Victoria Avenue
Tel: (01702) 434449 Web: www.southendmuseums.co.uk
An Edwardian building housing displays of archaeology,
natural history, social and local history. Hands-on
Discovery Centre. Planetarium.
Times: Open 5 Jan-31 Dec, 1000-1700. Closed 25-29 Mar,
24-28 Dec and 1 Jan.
Fee: Museum free. Charge for Planetarium, please contact
for details
Facilities: ⊛ 🅿 🚻 ⇌ T(1 hr) 🗛

Southend-on-Sea
Focal Point Gallery Map ref. I11
Southend Central Library, Victoria Avenue
Tel: (01702) 612621 Web: www.focalpoint.org.uk
A regularly changing exhibition programme of the best of
contemporary photography, digital and video art. Artists'
talks and workshops accompany most shows.
Times: Open all year, Mon-Fri, 0900-1900; Sat, 0900-
1700. Closed Bank Hols, 25, 28 Mar, 26-27 Dec and 2
Jan. Closed between exhibitions, please contact for details.
Fee: Free.
Facilities: 🅿 🛏 ⇌ T(1 hr) 🛈 ♿

Southend-on-Sea
Prittlewell Priory Map ref. I11
Priory Park, Victoria Avenue
Tel: (01702) 342878 Web: www.southendmuseums.co.uk
The remains of a 12th C. priory with later additions
housing displays of medieval religious life, radios,
gramophones and televisions.
Times: Open all year, Tues-Sat, 1000-1300 and 1400-1700
(or dusk). Closed 25 Mar, 25, 26 Dec and 1 Jan.
Fee: Free.
Facilities: ⊛ 🅿 🛏 ⇌ T(30 mins) 🚻

Southend-on-Sea
Southchurch Hall Museum Map ref. I11
Southchurch Hall Gardens, Southchurch Hall Close
Tel: (01702) 467671 Web: www.southendmuseums.co.uk
A moated, timber-framed 14th C. manor-house with Tudor
extensions set in attractive gardens. Rooms in period
settings.
Times: Open all year, daily, 1000-1300 and 1400-1700.
Mornings reserved for schools during term time.
Closed 25-29 Mar, 24-29 Dec.
Fee: Free.
Facilities: ⊛ 🛏 ⇌ T(1 hr) 🍴 🚻

Southchurch Hall Museum, Southend-on-Sea

Southend-on-Sea Pier

Southend-on-Sea
Southend Pier Museum Map ref. I11
Southend Pier, Marine Parade
Tel: (01702) 611214/614553
Situated in redundant pier workshops underneath the pier
station (Shore End). Depicts the history of the longest pier
in the world from 1830. Pictures and antique slot
machines.
Times: Open early May-31 Oct, Tues, Wed, Sat, Sun and
Bank Hols, 1100-1700 (1730 on school hols).
Fee: £1.00.
Facilities: 🛏 ⇌ T(1 hr) 🍴 ♿ (by arrangement)

Southend-on-Sea
Southend Planetarium Map ref. I11
Central Museum, Victoria Avenue
Tel: (01702) 434449 Web: www.southendmuseums.co.uk
Projector provides a clear illusion of the night sky with stars
and the Milky Way which lasts 40 minutes. No children
under 5 admitted.
Times: Open all year, Wed-Sat, shows at 1100, 1400 and
1600. Closed 25-28 Mar, 24-31 Dec.
Fee: £2.40/£1.70.
Facilities: ⊛ T(45 mins) 🍴 🚻

Stansted Mountfitchet
House on the Hill Toy Museums Adventure Map ref. C4
Tel: (01279) 813237 Web: www.mountfitchetcastle.com
An exciting, animated toy museum covering 7,000 sq ft and
featuring a huge collection of toys from Victorian times to
the 1970s. Offers a nostalgic trip back to childhood.
Times: Open all year, daily, 1000-1700. Closed 24, 25, 26
Dec.
Fee: £4.00/£3.20/£3.50. 10% discount on admission to toy
museum and castle next door, if visiting both places on the
same day.
Facilities: ⊛ 🅿 T(2 hrs)

Thaxted

Thaxted Guildhall Map ref. E3
Town Street
Tel: (01371) 830226 Web: www.thaxted.co.uk
A 15th C. building housing a permanent display of old photographs and relics, mainly relating to the history of Thaxted. Exhibitions on some weekends and small museum.
Times: Open 25 Mar-25 Sept, Sun and Bank Hol weekends, 1400-1730.
Fee: 50p/25p.
Facilities: 🅿 🚌 T(30 mins) 🕈

Tiptree

Tiptree Tearoom, Museum and Shop Map ref. I6
Wilkin and Sons Ltd
Tel: (01621) 814524 Web: www.tiptree.com
Tearoom and shop with a museum displaying how life was and how the art of jam-making has advanced over the years at Tiptree.
Times: Open 3 Jan-30 Apr, Mon-Sat, 1000-1700. 1 May-31 Aug, Mon-Sat, 1000-1700; Sun, 1200-1700. 1 Sept-24 Dec, Mon-Sat, 1000-1700.
Fee: Free.
Facilities: Q 🅿 T(1½ hrs) 🚼 📷

Waltham Abbey

Epping Forest District Museum Map ref. A8
39-41 Sun Street
Tel: (01992) 716882
Web: www.eppingforestdistrictmuseum.org.uk
Tudor and Georgian timber-framed buildings with a herb garden, a Tudor-panelled room, temporary exhibitions, the social history of Epping Forest and many special events.
Times: Open 1 Jan-30 Apr, Mon, 1400-1700; Tues, 1200-1700; Fri, 1400-1700; Sat, 1000-1700. 1 May-30 Sept, Mon, 1400-1700; Tues, 1200-1700; Fri, 1400-1700; Sat, 1000-1700; Sun, 1400-1700. 1 Oct-31 Dec, Mon, 1400-1700; Tues, 1200-1700; Fri, 1400-1700; Sat, 1000-1700. Contact for Christmas opening.
Fee: Free.
Facilities: 🚌 ⚲ T(1 hr) 🎍

Waltham Abbey

Royal Gunpowder Mills Map ref. A8
Beaulieu Drive
Tel: (01992) 707370 Web: www.royalgunpowdermills.com
Combining fascinating history, exciting science and 175 acres of natural parkland, the Royal Gunpowder Mills offers a truly unique day out for the family. Exhibitions and displays.
Times: Open 30 Apr-25 Sept, Sat, Sun and Bank Hols, 1100-1700 (last entry at 1530).
Fee: £5.50/£3.00/£4.70/£17.00(family).
Facilities: ⊕ Q 🅿 🚌 ⚲ T(3 hrs) 🕈 🚼 🎍

Colchester Castle Museum

Walton-on-the-Naze
Walton Maritime Museum Map ref. O5
East Terrace
Tel: (01255) 678259
A 120-year-old former lifeboat house, carefully restored with exhibitions of local interest, particularly maritime, urban, geological seaside and development.
Times: Open 25-28 Mar, Fri-Mon,1400-1600; 30 Apr-2 May, 28 May-30 May, 2 Jul-25 Sept, Sat, Sun, 1400-1600.
Fee: £1.00/free.
Facilities: 🅿 🚻 ≈ T(30 mins) 🚼 🖼

Westcliff-on-Sea
Beecroft Art Gallery Map ref. I11
Station Road
Tel: (01702) 347418 Web: www.beecroft-art-gallery.co.uk
An Edwardian building housing a permanent collection of works of art. Varied programme of temporary exhibitions. Panoramic estuary views.
Times: Open 4 Jan-31 Dec, Tues-Sat, 1000-1300 and 1400-1700. Closed 25 Mar, 25, 26 Dec and 1 Jan.
Fee: Free.
Facilities: ⊛ 🚻 ≈ T(1½ hrs)

West Mersea
Mersea Island Museum Map ref. K6
High Street
Tel: (01206) 385191
Museum of local, social and natural history with displays of methods and equipment used in fishing and wildfowling. Fossils and a mineral display. Also special exhibitions.
Times: Open 1 May-25 Sept, Wed-Sun and Bank Hol Mon, 1400-1700.
Fee: 50p/25p/25p.
Facilities: 🅿 🚻 T(1 hr) 🖼

On the Quayside at Maldon

Witham
Dorothy L. Sayers Centre Map ref. H6
Witham Library, 18 Newland Street
Tel: (01376) 519625
A reference collection of books by/about Dorothy L. Sayers. The centre is only 100m from the house where Sayers lived, and a statue of her stands just across the road.
Times: Open by appointment only.
Fee: Free.
Facilities: T(30 mins) 𝆏

See also:
Barleylands Farm Centre, Billericay, page 131
Blake Hall Gardens and Museum, Ongar, page 116
Great Dunmow Maltings, page 53
Great Notley Country Park and Discovery Centre, Braintree, page 184
Langdon Visitor Centre and Nature Reserve, Basildon, page 184
Norpar Flowers, Navestock, nr Romford, page 116
Rayleigh Windmill and Museum, page 198.

HERTFORDSHIRE

Ashwell (nr. Baldock)
Ashwell Village Museum Map ref. G7
Swan Street
Tel: (01462) 742956
A collection of village bygones and agricultural implements set in a small but interesting timber building.
Times: Open all year, Sun and Bank Hol Mon, 1430-1700. Please phone for Christmas openings.
Fee: £1.00/25p.
Facilities: T(40 mins)

Baldock
Baldock Museum Map ref. G8
Town Hall, Hitchin Street
Tel: (01462) 892640
Permanent display on the history of Baldock. Plus series of changing displays focusing on particular aspects of the town's history.
Times: Open 2 Jan-18 Dec, Wed, 1000-1500 and Sun, 1400-1600.
Fee: 25p/free/25p.
Facilities: 🚻 ≈ T(1 hr)

For even more
information visit
our website at
www.visiteastofengland.com

Bushey
Bushey Museum and Art Gallery Map ref. E/F15
Rudolph Road
Tel: (0208) 950 3233 Web: www.busheymuseum.org
Community museum telling the story of Bushey.
Archaeology, social history, local trades and industries. Art
galleries show changing exhibitions.
Times: Open all year, Thurs-Sun, 1100-1600. Closed 20
Aug, 24, 25 Dec, 1 Jan.
Fee: Free.
Facilities: ⊛ Q ₽ T(1½ hrs) ⌧

Hertford
Hertford Museum Map ref. H/I12
18 Bull Plain
Tel: (01992) 582686 Web: www.hertfordmuseum.org
e.mail: info@hertfordmuseum.org
A 17th C. building with main exhibits on the archaeology,
natural and local history of Hertfordshire, with a collection
of Hertfordshire Regiment regalia and changing exhibitions.
Times: Open all year, Tues-Sat, 1000-1700.
Closed 24-28 Dec.
Fee: Free.
Facilities: ⊛ ⇌ T(1 hr)

Hatfield
Mill Green Museum and Mill Map ref. G12
Mill Green
Tel: (01707) 271362 Web: www.welhat.gov.uk
An 18th C. watermill, restored to working order, with a
museum in the adjoining miller's house displaying local and
social history and archaeology. Riverside gardens
Times: Open all year, Tues-Fri, 1000-1700; Sat, Sun and
Bank Hols, 1400-1700. Closed 25-26 Dec.
Fee: Free.
Facilities: ₽ ⇌ ⇌ T(1½ hr) ⫯ ⊓ ⫯(garden only)

Hertford
Courtyard Arts Centre Map ref. H/I12
Port Vale
Tel: (01992) 509596 Web: www.courtyardarts.org.uk
Courtyard contemporary art gallery is housed in an
attractive listed building. The gallery has 1000sq ft of wall
space and the exhibition programme changes fortnightly,
shows include exhibits from well established and emerging
artists.
Times: Open all year, 6 Jan-20 Dec, Wed-Sun, 1000-1600.
Closed 21 Dec-5 Jan.
Fee: Free.
Facilities: ⊛ ₽ T(1 hr) ⫯⊛ ⊓ ⫯ ⌧

Hitchin
The British Schools Museum, Hitchin Map ref. F9
41/42 Queen Street
Tel: (01462) 420144
Web: www.hitchinbritishschools.org.uk
Historic elementary school buildings including unique
1837 monitorial school room for 330 boys and rare 1853
galleried classroom. Displays of the history of elementary
education. Family trail activities.
Times: Open 1 Feb-29 Nov, Tues, 1000-1600. Mar - Oct,
Sat 1000-1300 and Sun 1430-1700.
Fee: £3.00/£1.00.
Facilities: ⇌ ⇌ T(2 hrs) ⫯⊛

Mill Green Museum and Mill

Hitchin
Hitchin Museum and Art Gallery Map ref. F9
Paynes Park
Tel: (01462) 434476 Web: www.north-herts.gov.uk
A converted 19th C. house on two floors with displays of
costume, local history, a Victorian chemist's shop and a
physic garden. Changing temporary exhibitions and active
events programme.
Times: Open all year, Mon-Sat, except Wed, 1000-1700.
Closed on Bank Hols.
Fee: Free.
Facilities: ⊛ 🅿 T(40mins)

Hoddesdon
Lowewood Museum Map ref. I12
High Street
Tel: (01992) 445596 Web: www.lowewood.com
A listed Georgian building housing a museum of artefacts
and photographs concerning the Borough of Broxbourne,
along with temporary exhibitions.
Times: Open 1 Jan-31 Dec, Wed-Sat, 1000-1600. Closed
25 Mar.
Fee: Free.
Facilities: 🅿 ⊟ ⇌ T(1 hr) ⊓

Ivinghoe (nr. Tring)
Pitstone Green Museum Map ref. B11
Vicarage Road (off B489)
Tel: (01582) 605464
Web: http://website.lineone.net/~pitstonemus
Rural life museum, with displays and exhibits relating to
farming, country life, trades and professions. Also model
railway, stationary engines and WWII military aviation
room.
Times: 28 Mar, 2 and 30 May, 12 June, 10 Jul, 14 and 29
Aug, 11 Sept, 1100-1700.
Fee: £3.00/£1.50/£3.00.
Facilities: 🅿 T(3-4 hrs) ⊼ 🔲

Letchworth Garden City
First Garden City Heritage Museum Map ref. G8
296 Norton Way South
Tel: (01462) 482710 Web: www.letchworth.com
A museum housing displays relating to the Garden City
movement and the social history of Letchworth including a
collection of Parker and Unwin architectural drawings.
Times: Open all year, Mon-Sat, 1000-1700. Closed 25, 26
Dec and 1 Jan.
Fee: Non-residents £1.00/free. Residents 50p/free.
Facilities: ⊛ ⊟ ⇌ T(1 hr) ⊓

Letchworth Garden City
Letchworth Museum Map ref. G8
Broadway
Tel: (01462) 685647 Web: www.north-herts.gov.uk
A museum which features local wildlife, archaeological
displays and a programme of temporary exhibitions.
Times: Open all year, Mon, Tues and Thurs-Sat,
1000-1700. Closed Bank Hols.
Fee: Free.
Facilities: ⊛ ⊟ ⇌ T(45 mins)

Much Hadham
The Forge Museum and Victorian Cottage Garden
Map ref. J11
High Street
Tel: (01279) 843301 Web: www.hertsmuseums.org.uk
Grade II Listed building. Houses displays on blacksmithing,
beekeeping, the parish of Much Hadham and the Page
family who were blacksmiths for over 150 years.
Times: Open 1 Apr-17 Dec, Fri-Sun and Bank Hol Mon,
1100-1700.
Fee: £1.00/50p/50p/£2.00.
Facilities: ⊟ T(1 hr) 🧑 ⊼ 🐕

Batchworth Lock Canal Centre, Rickmansworth, Hertfordshire

Much Hadham
The Henry Moore Foundation Map ref. J11
Dane Tree House, Perry Green
Tel: (01279) 843333 Web: www.henry-moore-fdn.co.uk
A sculpture garden and studios with a permanent
exhibition of monumental sculptures by Henry Moore.
Times: Open Apr-Oct, by appointment only. Closed all
Bank Hols.
Fee: £7.00/free/£3.00.
Facilities: ▣ T(2½ hrs) 𝖋 🗚 🖾

Potters Bar
Potters Bar Museum Map ref. G14
Wyllyotts Centre, Darkes Lane
Tel: (01707) 645005
Local history museum tracing the development of Potters
Bar from pre-history, through Roman, medieval and recent
history, up to the present day. Also temporary exhibitions
throughout year.
Times: Open all year, Tues and Wed, 1230-1630; Sat,
1100-1300.
Fee: Free.
Facilities: ▣ 🛏 ⇌ T(1 hr) ⑪ 🐕 🖾

Redbourn
Redbourn Village Museum Map ref. E12
Silk Mill House, The Common
Tel: (01582) 793397 Web: www.redbourn.org.uk
History of Redbourn and surrounding area from Iron Age
to present day. Housed in a Grade II listed building
standing in its own grounds.
Times: Open all year, Sat, 1400-1700; Sun, 1200-1700.
Please contact for Bank Hol Mon opening times.
Fee: £1.00/50p.
Facilities: ▣ 🛏 T(1 hr) 🗚

*St. Albans
Organ Museum*

Rickmansworth
Batchworth Lock Canal Centre Map ref. D15
99 Church Street
Tel: (01923) 778382
Batchworth Lock provides information to boaters and
walkers using the Rickmansworth area. Canal history,
narrowboat 'Roger' and shop. Model canal landscape with
remote contrl boats. Boat trips in summer.
Times: Open 25 Mar-end Sept, Mon, 0900-1700; Tues, 0900-
1300; Sat, 1200-1700; Sun, 0900-1700.
Fee: Free.
Facilities: 🛏 ⇌ T(30 mins) ⑪ 🗚 🐕

St. Albans
Museum of St. Albans Map ref. F13
Hatfield Road
Tel: (01727) 819340 Web: www.stalbansmuseums.org.uk
Displays include craft tools and local/natural history,
telling the St. Albans story from Roman times to the
present day. Wildlife garden.
Times: Open all year, Mon-Sat, 1000-1700; Sun, 1400-
1700. Closed 24 Dec to 4 Jan.
Fee: Free.
Facilities: ◉ Q ▣ T(1½ hrs) 🗚

St. Albans
Saint Albans Organ Museum Map ref. F13
320 Camp Road
Tel: (01727) 873896
Web: www.saintalbansorganmuseum.org.uk
A collection of mechanical organs by Mortier, DeCap,
Bursens; Weber and Steinway duo-art reproducing pianos;
Mills violano-virtuoso; music boxes and Wurlitzer and Rutt
theatre pipe organs.
Times: Open all year, Sun, 1400-1630. Closed 25 Dec.
Fee: £4.00/£1.50.
Facilities: ◉ ▣ T(2 hrs) 𝖋 🖾

St. Albans

Verulamium Museum Map ref. F13

St. Michaels

Tel: (01727) 751810 Web: www.stalbansmuseums.org.uk

The museum of everyday life in Roman Britain. Award-winning displays of re-created Roman rooms, 'hands-on' areas and videos of Roman Verulamium.

Times: Open all year, Mon-Sat, 1000-1730; Sun, 1400-1730. Closed 24 Dec to 4 Jan.

Fee: £3.30/£2.00/£2.00/£8.00.

Facilities: ◉ Q 🄿 🛏 T(2 hrs) 🙽 🛗

Stevenage

The Boxfield Gallery Map ref. G10

Stevenage Arts and Leisure Centre, Lytton Way

Tel: (01438) 242642 Web: www.stevenage-leisure.co.uk

Contemporary art gallery exhibiting a variety of work by both local and national artists. Approximately twelve exhibitions a year, ranging from paintings and textiles to sculptures and installations.

Times: Open all year, daily, 0800-2200. Closed 27 Mar, 25 Dec and 1 Jan.

Fee: Free.

Facilities: 🄿 ⇌ T(1 hr) 🙽 🛗

Stevenage

Stevenage Museum Map ref. G10

St. George's Way

Tel: (01438) 218881 Web: www.stevenage.gov.uk/museum

Award-winning museum which tells the story of Stevenage from the Stone Age to the present. Displays include a 1950s living room and a programme of exhibitions.

Times: Open all year, Mon-Sat, 1000-1700; Sun, 1400-1700.

Fee: Free.

Facilities: ◉ ⇌ T(1½ hrs) 🛏 🛗

Tring

The Walter Rothschild Zoological Museum Map ref. B12

Akeman Street

Tel: (0207) 942 6171 Web: www.nhm.ac.uk/museum/tring

The former private zoological collection of Lionel Walter, 2nd Baron Rothschild. More than 4,000 mounted animal and bird specimens on display in a unique Victorian setting.

Times: Open all year, Mon-Sat, 1000-1700; Sun, 1400-1700. Closed 24-26 Dec.

Fee: Free.

Facilities: 🄿 🛏 T(2 hrs) 🙽 🛏

Ware

Ware Museum Map ref. I11/12

The Priory Lodge, High Street

Tel: (01920) 487848 Web: www.waremuseum.org.uk

An independent museum featuring the story of Ware from the Roman town through to the malting industry. Also a World War II command bunker and changing exhibitions.

Times: Open summer - Tues, Thurs and Sat, 1100-1700; Sun, 1400-1700. Winter - Tues, Thurs and Sat, 1100-1600; Sun, 1400-1600. Please phone for Easter and Christmas openings.

Fee: Free. Donations welcome.

Facilities: 🛏 ⇌ T(30 mins) 🛗

Watford

Watford Museum Map ref. E14/15

194 High Street

Tel: (01923) 232297 Web: www.hertsmuseums.org.uk

A museum building, built in 1775, with displays of local history, brewing, printing and archaeology.

Times: Open all year, Thurs-Sat, 1000-1700.

Fee: Free.

Facilities: 🄿 🛏 ⇌ T(1½ hrs)

See also:

Standalone Farm, Letchworth Garden City, page 133

College Lake Wildlife Centre, Tring, page 189

Walter Rothschild Zoological Museum

NORFOLK

Burston (nr. Diss)
Burston Strike School Map ref. J11
Tel: (01379) 741565 Web: www.burstonstrikeschool.org
Scene of the longest strike in British history which lasted 25 years. The building was erected to house a school for scholars of the strike. Artefacts, documents and photographs.
Times: Open all year, daily, during daylight hours key available. Closed for local and national polling days.
Fee: Free.
Facilities: P ⛵ T(1 hr) ⊼ ✝ ▣

Cockley Cley (nr. Swafham)
Iceni Village and Museums Map ref. E8
Tel: (01760) 724588
Iceni tribal village reconstruction, believed to be on the original site. Medieval cottage and forge with museum, Saxon church 630 AD, carriage/vintage engine and farm museum.
Times: Open 24 Mar-30 Oct, daily, 1100-1730. Jul and Aug, 1000-1730.
Fee: £5.00/£2.00/£3.00.
Facilities: P T(2 hrs) ⊼ ✝ (on leads)

Cromer
Cromer Museum Map ref. K3
East Cottages, Tucker Street
Tel: (01263) 513543
Web: www.museums.norfolk.gov.uk
A late-Victorian fisherman's cottage with displays of local history (fishing, bathing resort), geology, natural history and archaeology.
Times: Closed for refurbishment, hope to re-open Summer 2005, please telephone for details and prices.
Facilities: ✿ T(2 hr) ✝

Burston Strike School

Cromer
Henry Blogg Museum Map ref. K3
The Old Boathouse, The Promenade
Tel: (01263) 511294/513018
World War II Watson Class lifeboat 'H.F Bailey' - Bloggs boat which saved 500 lives between 1935-1945. History of nearly 200 years of Cromer lifeboats.
Times: Open 25 Mar-24 Dec, daily, 1000-1600 but closing for two months during the summer for move, please telephone to check dates.
Fee: Free. Donations appreciated.
Facilities: T(1 hr) ⅄⊕ ✝ ▣

Cromer
Little Gems Map ref. K3
2a Mount Street
Tel: (01263) 519519 Web: www.littlegems.info
An Aladdin's cave - fossils, crystals and minerals from around the globe - most for sale, but also many museum pieces, including a 'baby dinosaur' skeleton and 0.25 ton amethyst cave.
Times: Open all year, Mon-Sat, 1000-1700; Sun, 1200-1600. Limited opening hours over Christmas and New Year - please contact for details.
Fee: Free.
Facilities: ⇌ T(30 mins) ▣

Dereham
Bishop Bonners Cottage Museum Map ref. H6/7
St. Withburga Lane
Tel: (01362) 850293
A timber-framed building, built in 1502 with walls of brick, flint, wattle and daub. It has a thatched roof, coloured pargetting, local artefacts and bygones from local trades.
Times: Open 3 May-30 Sept, Tues and Thurs-Sat, 1400-1630.
Fee: 50p/25p
Facilities: ⛵ T(1 hr) ⅄

Dereham
Hobbies Museum of Fretwork and Craft Centre
Map ref. H6/7
34-36 Swaffham Road
Tel: (01362) 692985 Web: www.hobbies-dereham.co.uk
A museum of fretwork machines dating back to 1880, with magazines and hobbies weeklies from 1895, and samples of old fretwork designs.
Times: Open 4 Apr-26 Aug, Mon-Fri, 1000-1200 and 1400-1600.
Fee: Free.
Facilities: 🅿 T(1 hr) 🐾

Dickleburgh (nr. Diss)
100th Bomb Group Memorial Museum Map ref. K11
Common Road
Tel: (01379) 740708
A museum housed in an original World War II control tower and other buildings, showing the history of the 100th Bomb Group, plus 8th Air Force exhibits. Visitor Centre.
Times: Open 5 Feb-30 Oct, Sat, Sun and Bank Hol Mon, 1000-1700. 1 May-28 Sept, Wed, Sat, Sun and Bank Hol Mon, 1000-1700.
Fee: Free.
Facilities: 🅿 T(1³/4 hrs) 🍴 🛏 🐾

Diss
Diss Museum Map ref. J11
Market Place
Tel: (01379) 650618
Housed in the historic Shambles building, award-winning Diss Museum provides visitors with a variety of changing displays on local history and prehistory.
Times: Open 16 Mar-30 Nov, Wed and Thurs, 1400-1600; Fri and Sat, 1030-1630; also 1 May-28 Aug, Sun, 1400-1600.
Fee: Free.
Facilities: 🚻 ♿ T(45 mins)

Downham Market
The Collectors World of Eric St. John-Foti Map ref. C8
Hermitage Hall, Bridge Farm
Tel: (01366) 383185 Web: www.collectors-world.org
The Collectors World contains unique collections amassed by Eric St. John-Foti - cars, carriages, dolls, farming and household items. Whilst the Magical Dickens Experience takes you back in time.
Times: Open all year, daily, 1100-1700.
Fee: £4.50/£3.50/£4.00/£14.00(family).
Facilities: ⊛ 🅿 T(2¹/2 hrs) 🍴 ⊛ 🛏 🐾

Fakenham
Fakenham Museum of Gas and Local History
Map ref. G4
Hempton Road
Tel: (01328) 863150
A complete small-town gasworks with a local history section and displays of working gas meters and working exhausters.
Times: Open all year, Thurs 1030-1300; Jun-Aug, Thurs and Bank Hol Mon 1030-1530. Other days by appointment.
Fee: Free. Donations appreciated.
Facilities: T(2 hrs)

Cromer Museum

Glandford (nr. Holt)
Glandford Shell Museum Map ref. I3
Tel: (01263) 740081
Sir Alfred Jodrell's unique collection of shells. Various other exhibits including evocative John Craske tapestry showing panorama of the Norfolk coast.
Times: Open 26 Mar-30 Oct, Tues-Sat and Bank Hol Mon, 1000-1230 and 1400-1630.
Fee: £1.75/75p/£1.25.(2004 prices)
Facilities: 🅿 🚻 T(30 mins)

Great Yarmouth
Elizabethan House Museum Map ref. P7
4 South Quay
Tel: (01493) 855746
Web: www.museums.norfolk.gov.uk
A 16th C. merchant's house displaying rooms as though
still lived in by families in the past. Includes Victorian
kitchen/scullery, Tudor bedroom and conspiracy room.
Times: Open 21 Mar-30 Oct, Mon-Fri, 1000-1700; Sat and
Sun, 1315-1700.
Fee: £2.90 (£2.30 in a family group)/£1.50 /£2.40.
Facilities: ⊛ ⌷ ⇌ T(1 hr) NT

Great Yarmouth
Great Yarmouth Potteries Map ref. P7
18/19 Trinity Place
Tel: (01493) 850585
Web: www.greatyarmouthpotteries.co.uk
Full working pottery - from liquid clay to finished ware.
Herring smoking museum. Video showing fishing era and
town wall, 700 years ago. Nautical oil paintings, carvings
and sculptures.
Times: Open all year, Mon-Fri 1000-1600, also some Sats.
Closed 20 Jan-6 Feb, 25-28 Mar, 24, 25, 31 Dec and 1 Jan.
Fee: £3.50/£2.00/£3.00.
Facilities: ⌷ ⇌ T(1 hr) ⑪ ⊁ ⛭

Great Yarmouth

Great Yarmouth
Great Yarmouth Row Houses Map ref. P7
South Quay
Tel: (01493) 857900 Web: www.english-heritage.org.uk
Typical 17th C. town houses, one with splendid plaster
ceilings containing local original architectural and domestic
fittings salvaged from other 'Row' houses. Also remains of
Franciscan friary.
Times: 24 Mar-31 Oct, Thurs-Sun, 1200-1700.
Fee: £3.30/£1.70/£2.50.
Facilities: ⊛ Q ⇌ T(1 hr) ✗ EH

Great Yarmouth
Norfolk Nelson Museum Map ref. P7
26 South Quay
Tel: (01493) 850698 Web: www.nelson-museum.co.uk
Find out about Nelson's amazing career, famous battles
and heroic death. Learn about his scandalous personal life
and about the times in which he lived. An interactive
maritime courtyard.
Times: Open 1 Apr-31 Oct, Mon-Fri, 1000-1700; Sat and
Sun, 1400-1700.
Fee: £2.50/£1.30/£2.00/£6.00(family).
Facilities: P ⌷ ⇌ T(1½ hrs) ⼊ ⛭

Great Yarmouth
Time and Tide Map ref. P7
Blackfriars Road
Tel: (01493) 745526 Web: www.museums.norfolk.gov.uk
Museum in Great Yarmouth's Tower Curing Works, telling
the story of Great Yarmouth over time, and celebrating the
town's maritime and fishing heritage.
Times: 1 Jan-24 Mar, Mon-Fri 1000-1600, Sat and
Sun 1200-1600; 25 Mar-31 Oct, daily, 1000-1700, 1 Nov-
31 Dec, Mon-Fri 1000-1600, Sat and Sun 1200-1600.
Closed 24, 25, 26 Dec.
Fee: £5.45(£4.80 in family group)/£3.50/£4.90.
Facilities: ⊛ T(3 hrs) ⑪ ⼊ ⛭

Great Yarmouth
Tolhouse Museum Map ref. P7
Tolhouse Street
Tel: (01493) 858900
Web: www.museums.norfolk.gov.uk
One of the oldest municipal buildings in England, once the
town's courthouse and gaol. Prison cells can still be seen
with displays illustrating the long history of the town.
Times: Open 21 Mar-30 Oct, Mon-Fri, 1000-1700; Sat and
Sun, 1315-1700.
Fee: £2.90 (£2.30 in a family group)/£1.50/£2.40.
Facilities: ⊛ ⌷ ⇌ T(1 hr)

Gressenhall (nr. Dereham)
Roots of Norfolk Map ref. H6
Norfolk Rural Life Museum
Tel: (01362) 860563
Web: www.museums.norfolk.gov.uk
Georgian workhouse in extensive grounds. Stunning
displays on rural life. Rare breed animals on working 1920s
farm. Trails, re-enactments, events and activities. Gardens
and adventure playground.
Times: Open 13-20 Feb, daily, 1100-1600. 27 Feb-13 Mar,
Sun, 1100-1600. 20 Mar-30 Oct, daily, 1000-1700. 6-27
Nov, Sun, 1100-1600.
Fee: £5.70/£4.40/£5.00.(2004 prices).
Facilities: ◎ Q P ⛟ T(6 hrs) ⑨ ⛱ 🅿

Hanworth (nr. Cromer)
The Straw Museum Map ref. K3
Conifer Cottage, Buck Bridge, Colby
Tel: (01263) 761615
Beautiful and fascinating straw items from around the
world. Corn dollies, plain and dyed marquetry, Swiss straw
lace, plaits, embroidery, jewellery and quilling. Courses are
available.
Times: Open 26 Mar-31 Oct, Wed and Sat, 1100-1600.
Fee: Free.
Facilities: P T(2 hrs) ⫟ ⛱ 🐾 🅿

Harleston
Harleston Museum Map ref. L11
King Georges Hall, Broad Street
Tel: (01379) 852844
A museum housing an exhibition of items of historical
interest relating to Harleston and the district.
Times: Open 7 May-1 Oct, Wed, 1000-1200 and 1400-
1600; Sat, 1000-1200.
Fee: Free. Donations appreciated.
Facilities: T(30 mins)

Holt
Bircham Contemporary Arts Map ref. I3
14 Market Place
Tel: (01263) 713312 Web: www.birchamgallery.co.uk
Exhibitions of contemporary paintings, prints, ceramics,
sculpture and jewellery by the finest artists and
craftspeople.
Times: Open all year, Mon-Sat, 0900-1700. Please phone
for Bank Hol opening times. Closed 25, 26 Dec and 1 Jan.
Fee: Free.
Facilities: ◎ ⛟ T(20 mins) 🅿

**For even more
information visit
our website at
www.visiteastofengland.com**

Holt
Picturecraft of Holt Map ref. I3
North Norfolk's Art Centre, 23 Lees Courtyard,
Off Bull Street
Tel: (01263) 711040
Web: www.picturecraftgallery.com
The newly refurbished gallery is now divided into 32
individual exhibition spaces, and the displays are changed
every three weeks. Picture framing specialists and a premier
artists' material centre.
Times: Open all year, Mon-Wed, 0900-1700; Thurs, 0900-
1300; Fri and Sat, 0900-1700. Closed 24 Dec-6 Jan.
Fee: Free.
Facilities: ◎ P ⛟ T(1 hr) 🅿

King's Lynn
Caithness Crystal Visitor Centre Map ref. C6
Paxman Road, Hardwick Industrial Estate
Tel: (01553) 765111 Web: www.caithnessglass.co.uk
See glass making at close quarters, watching the skill of our
glass makers as they shape and blow the glass in the
manner used for centuries. Factory shop.
Times: Open all year, Mon-Sat, 0900-1700; Sun, 1015-
1615. Please contact for glassmaking times. Closed 25, 26
Dec, 1, 2 Jan.
Fee: Free.
Facilities: ◎ P ⛟ T(1½ hrs) ⫟ ⑨ 🅿

King's Lynn
Custom House - Maritime Exhibition Map ref. C5/6
Tourist Information Centre, Purfleet Quay
Tel: (01553) 763044
The town's most famous landmark. Displays on the
merchants, customs men, smugglers and famous mariners
(Vancouver and Nelson) of the past. Superb views over the
River Great Ouse.
Times: Open 2 Jan-20 Mar, Mon-Sat 1030-1600, Sun
1200-1600; 21 Mar-30 Sept, Mon-Sat 1000-1700; 1
Oct-31 Dec, Mon-Sat 1030-1600, Sun 1200-
1600. (Closed Wed, Jan-Mar and Oct-Dec). Closed 25, 26
Dec and 1 Jan.
Fee: Free.
Facilities: ◎ T(1 hr)

King's Lynn
Guildhall of St. George Map ref. C5/6
27-29 King Street
Tel: (01553) 765565 Web: www.kingslynnarts.co.uk
A regional arts centre, the medieval Guildhall now houses a
theatre with a regular programme of daytime and evening
events: film, concerts and galleries.
Times: Open all year, Mon-Fri, 1000-1400. Access to view
building is dependent on performance schedule.
Fee: Free.
Facilities: ◎ ⛟ ⇌ T(20 mins) ⫟ ⑨ NT

King's Lynn
Tales of the Old Gaol House Map ref. C5/6
The Old Gaol House, Saturday Market Place
Tel: (01553) 774297 Web: www.west-norfolk.gov.uk
A personal stereo tour through Lynn's 1930s police station
and into the old cells beyond. True stories of infamous
smugglers, murderers, highwaymen and even witches. Also
Lynn treasury.
Times: Open Jan-30 Mar, Mon, Tues, Fri and Sat, 1000-
1600; Sun, 1200-1600. 1 Apr-31 Oct, Mon-Wed, Fri and
Sat, 1000-1700; Sun, 1200-1700. 1 Nov-end Dec, Mon.
Tues, Fri and Sat, 1000-1600; Sun, 1200-1600. Closed 22
Dec-4 Jan
Fee: Tour: £2.50/£1.80/£2.20/£7.00(family).
Facilities: ◉ Q ⇌ T(1 hr) 🖳

King's Lynn
Town House Museum of Lynn Life Map ref. C5/6
46 Queen Street
Tel: (01553) 773450
Web: www.museums.norfolk.gov.uk
The past comes to life in this friendly museum with historic
room displays including costumes, toys, a working
Victorian kitchen and a 1950s living room.
Times: Open Jan-Apr, Mon-Sat, 1000-1600. May-Sept,
Mon-Sat, 1000-1700; Sun 1400-1700. Oct-Dec, Mon-Sat,
1000-1600. Closed Bank Hols.
Fee: £1.80/90p/£1.40 (2004 prices).
Facilities: ◉ 🛏 ⇌ T(40 mins)

King's Lynn

King's Lynn
True's Yard Museum Map ref. C5/6
3-5 North Street
Tel: (01553) 770479 Web: www.welcome.to/truesyard
Two fully-restored fisherman's cottages with research
facilities for tracing ancestry in King's Lynn. There is a
museum, gift shop and tearoom.
Times: Open 1 Jan-31 Mar, Tues-Sat, 1000-1600; 1 Apr-30
Sept, daily, 1000-1600; 1 Oct-31 Dec, Tues-Sat, 1000-
1600.
Fee: £2.25/£1.00/£1.75/£6.00(family).
Facilities: ◉ 🛏 ⇌ T(1 hr) 🐾 ◉ 🖳

Langham (nr. Holt)
Langham Glass Map ref. H3
The Long Barn, North Street
Tel: (01328) 830511 Web: www.langhamglass.co.uk
Glassmakers can be seen working with molten glass from
the furnace using blowing irons. Also enclosed children's
playground, museum/video, walled garden and 7 acre
maize maze in 2005.
Times: Open all year. Glass making , 1 Apr-31 Mar, daily,
1000-1700; 1 Nov-31 Mar, Mon-Fri, 1000-1430. Maize
maze open mid Jul-mid Sept. Closed 25, 26 Dec and 1 Jan.
Fee: Langham Glass £3.75/£2.75/£2.75. Maize Maze
£3.75/£2.75/£2.75.
Facilities: ◉ Q 🄿 T(2½ hrs) 🐾 ◉ 🎋 🖳

Litcham (nr. Dereham)
Litcham Village Museum Map ref. G6
'Fourways'
Tel: (01328) 701383
A local village museum and underground lime kiln. The
museum houses local artifacts from Roman times to date,
and a local photograph collection of over 1,000 items.
Times: Open 2 Apr-2 Oct, Sat and Sun, 1400-1700.
Fee: Free.
Facilities: 🄿 🛏 T(2 hrs) 🐾 🎋

Little Walsingham
Shirehall Museum and Abbey Gardens Map ref. G/H3
Common Place
Tel: (01328) 820510 Web: www.walsingham.uk.com
A Georgian country courthouse, local museum and Tourist
Information Point. Ruins of the Augustinian abbey,
peaceful gardens and woodland walks set in approximately
20 acres.
Times: Open 29 Jan-27 Feb, daily, 1000-1600. 19 Mar-30
Oct, daily, 1000-1630. 5 Nov-18 Dec, Sat and Sun, 1000-
1600.
Fee: Combined ticket (grounds and museum)
£3.00/£1.50/£1.50/£7.50 (2004 prices).
Facilities: ◉ 🛏 T(1 hr) 🐾 🎋 🐕

Ludham
Toad Hole Cottage Museum Map ref. N6
How Hill
Tel: (01692) 678763 Web: www.broads-authority.gov.uk
A small 18th C. cottage with a Broads information area.
Museum giving the impression of the home and working
life of a family on the marshes.
Times: Open Easter-31 May, Mon-Fri, 1100-1300 and
1330-1700, Sat and Sun 1100-1700. 1 Jun-30 Sept, daily,
1000-1800. 1-31 Oct, Mon-Fri, 1100-1300 and 1330-
1700, Sat and Sun 1100-1700.
Fee: Free.
Facilities: ⊛ 🅿 T(30 mins) ⊼

Mundesley
Mundesley Maritime Museum Map ref. M3
Beach Road
Tel: (01263) 720879
Museum housed in former coastguard lookout.
Photographs, prints and artefacts illustrating Mundesley's
maritime and village history. First floor reinstated as a
lookout of the 1930/40 era.
Times: Open Easter Week-end and 1 May-30 Sept, daily,
1100-1300 and 1400-1600.
Fee: 50p/free.
Facilities: 🚌 T(30 mins) ⊼

Trace the history of Norfolk at Origins, Norwich

Norwich
The Amber Room Map ref. K/L7
2 Fishers Lane
Tel: (01603) 627347
Displays of amber, from around the world with examples of
amulets and beads from pre-historic to modern. Exhibition
of inclusions in amber. Modern amber goods from the
Baltic region.
Times: Open Tues, Wed, Fri 0930-1630. Closed Good Fri,
24 Dec-3 Jan.
Fee: Free
Facilities: 🅿 T(30 mins) ⑴ ⊼

Norwich
Bridewell Museum Map ref. K/L7
Bridewell Alley
Tel: (01603) 629127
Web: www.museums.norfolk.gov.uk
A museum with displays illustrating local industry during
the past 200 years, with a re-created 1920s pharmacy and
a 1930s pawnbroker's shop. Also temporary exhibits.
Times: 3 May-29 Oct, school terms, Tues-Fri, 1000-1630,
Sat 1000-1700; half term, Easter and summer holiday,
Mon-Sat 1000-1700.
Fee: £2.20/£1.30/£1.80/£5.00(family) (2004 prices).
Facilities: ⊛ 🚌 ⇌ T(1 hr)

Norwich
Inspire Discovery Centre Map ref. K/L7
St. Michael's Church, Coslany Street
Tel: (01603) 612612
Web: www.science-project.org/inspire
Inspire is a hands-on science centre housed in a medieval
church. Suitable for all ages, it allows everyone to explore
and discover the wonders of science for themselves.
Times: Open all year, daily, 1030-1730. Closed 24 Dec-
1 Jan.
Fee: £4.70/£3.60/£3.60/£12.00(family).
Facilities: ⊛ 🚌 ⇌ T(2 hrs) ⑴ ⊼ 🅑

Norwich
John Jarrold Printing Museum Map ref. K/L7
Whitefriars
Tel: (01603) 660211
John Jarrold was a pioneering figure in British printing, and
this museum charts the history of the printing industry over
the last 160 years. Impressive collection of printing
machines.
Times: Open all year, Wed, 0900-1200.
Fee: Free.
Facilities: 🅿 🚌 ⇌ T(2 hrs) 𝑘 🅑

Norwich
The Mustard Shop Map ref. K/L7
15 The Royal Arcade
Tel: (01603) 627889 Web: www.mustardshop.com
A decorated 19th C. style shop which houses a museum, with a series of displays illustrating the history of Colman's Mustard.
Times: Open all year, Mon-Sat, 0930-1700. Bank Hols, 1100-1600. Closed 25, 26 Dec and 1 Jan.
Fee: Free.
Facilities: ▦ ⚹ T(15 mins) ⚹ ⚹ ▦

Norwich
Norwich Castle Museum and Art Gallery Map ref. K/L7
Shine Hall, Market Avenue
Tel: (01603) 493625
Web: www.museums.norfolk.gov.uk
Ancient Norman keep, one of the most important buildings of its kind in Europe. Houses fine regional collections of archaeology, art and natural history.
Times: Core times - Mon-Fri, 1000-1630; Sat, 1000-1700; Sun, 1300-1700. School half-term, Easter and summer holidays, Mon-Sat, 1000-1800; Sun 1300-1700. Closed 24-27 Dec and 1 Jan.
Fee: £5.25/£3.70/£4.50.
Facilities: ▦ ▦ ⚹ T(2 hrs) ⚹ ⚹ ▦

Norwich
Norwich Gallery Map ref. K/L7
Norwich School of Art and Design, St. George Street
Tel: (01603) 610561 Web: www.norwichgallery.co.uk
Gallery showing temporary exhibitions of contemporary art, design and crafts.
Times: Open all year, Mon-Sat, 1000-1700. Closed all Bank Hols.
Fee: Free.
Facilities: ⚹ T(1 hr) ▦

Norwich
Norwich Puppet Theatre Map ref. K/L7
St. James, Whitefriars
Tel: (01603) 629921
Web: www.puppettheatre.co.uk
Medieval church converted to a puppet theatre in 1980. Theatre open for viewing, except on performance days. Foyer houses a display of puppets from the last 20 years.
Times: Open all year, Mon-Fri, 0930-1700. Closed Bank Hols. Contact for Christmas openings.
Fee: Free. There are charges for performances days.
Facilities: ▦ ▦ ▦ ⚹ T(30 mins) ▦ ▦

Norwich
Origins Map ref. K/L7
The Forum, Millennium Plain
Tel: (01603) 727922 Web: www.originsnorwich.com
Origins is Norfolk's most original and interactive experience, tracing 2,000 years of Norfolk and Norwich through exhibits and multimedia presentations. Includes England's only 180 degree projected panorama.
Times: Open 1 Jan-31 Mar, Mon-Sat, 1000-1715; Sun, 1100-1645. 1 Apr-31 Oct, Mon-Sat, 1000-1745; Sun, 1100-1645. 1 Nov-31 Dec, Mon-Sat, 1000-1715; Sun, 1100-1645. Closed 25 and 26 Dec.
Fee: £5.95/£3.95/£3.95/£16.80(family).
Facilities: ▦ ▦ ▦ ▦ ⚹ T(1½ hrs) ▦

Norwich
The Royal Air Force Air Defence Radar Museum
Map ref. M6
RAF Neatishead
Tel: (01692) 633309 Web: www.radarmuseum.co.uk
History of the development and use of radar, in the UK and overseas, from 1935 to date. Housed in an original 1942 building.
Times: Open 8 Jan, 12 Feb, 12 Mar, 28 Mar, 1000-1700. 5 Apr-27 Oct, Tues, Thurs, Bank Hol Mon and 2nd Sat of month, 1000-1700. 12 Nov, 10 Dec, 1000-1700.
Fee: £4.00/free/£3.50.
Facilities: ▦ ▦ T(3 hrs) ▦ ▦ ▦

Norwich
Royal Norfolk Regimental Museum Map ref. K/L7
Market Avenue
Tel: (01603) 493649
Web: www.museums.norfolk.gov.uk
A modern museum with displays about the county
regiment from 1685. Includes a reconstructed World War I
communication trench.
Times: Open all year, school terms and Christmas holidays,
Tues-Sat, 1000-1630. School half terms, Easter and
Summer holidays, Mon-Sat, 1000-1630. Closed 24-27 Dec
and 1 Jan.
Fee: £2.20/£1.30/£1.80/£5.00(family).
Facilities: ⊛ ⇔ ⇌ T(1¹/₂ hrs) ⼝

Norwich
Sainsbury Centre for Visual Arts Map ref. K7
University of East Anglia
Tel: (01603) 593199 Web: www.uea.ac.uk/scva
Housing the Sainsbury collection of works by artists such
as Picasso, Bacon and Henry Moore, alongside many
objects of pottery and art from across cultures and time.
Times: Closed until late 2005, please phone for details.
Fee: Please contact for details.
Facilities: ⊛ 🅿 ⇔ T(2hr) ⼁⑪ ⼝ ⼵

Norwich
Second Air Division Memorial Library Map ref. K/L7
The Forum, Millennium Plain
Tel: (01603) 774747 Web: www.2ndair.org.uk
An American library, and a war memorial to those who
served in the Second Air Division of the 8th Air Force in
World War II.
Times: Open all year, Mon, 0900-1700, Tues, 1000-1700,
Wed-Sat, 0900-1700. Closed 25, 26, 28 Mar, 24-27 Dec.
Fee: Free.
Facilities: ⊛ 🅿 ⇔ ⇌ T(1 hr) ⼁ ⼵

Norwich
Strangers' Hall Museum Map ref. K/L7
Charing Cross
Tel: (01603) 667229
Web: www.museums.norfolk.gov.uk
Medieval town house with period rooms. Displays from
Tudor to Victorian times. Toy collection on display.
Times: Open all year, Wed, Sat 1030-1630.
Fee: £2.50/£1.50/£2.00.
Facilities: ⊛ ⇔ ⇌ T(1¹/₂ hr) ⼁

Sea Palling
Waxham Barn Map ref. OO
Tel: (01692) 598824
Waxham Barn is a fully restored, magnificent Elizabethan
barn set in North Norfolk's area of outstanding beauty.
The thatched barn is the longest in the country. It houses a
lively exhibition featuring Elizabethan agriculture, the
Woodhouses who built the barn, smuggling and shipwrecks
along the coast and the resident owls and bats.
Times: Open 26 Mar-31 Oct, Thur-Tues, 1030-1630.
Fee: £2.50/free.
Facilities: 🅿 T(30 mins) ⑪ ⼝

Seething (nr. Loddon)
Seething Airfield Control Tower Map ref. M9
Station 146, Seething Airfield
Tel: (01508) 550787
A renovated original wartime control tower holding the
448th Bomb Group honour roll and World War II exhibits.
Also pictures/stories from 448th veterans from 1943-1945.
Times: Open 1 May, 5 Jun, 3 Jul, 7 Aug, 4 Sept, 2 Oct,
Sun, 1000-1700.
Fee: Free.
Facilities: 🅿 T(1¹/₂ hrs) ⼁⑪ ⼍

Norwich Castle Museum and Art Gallery

Sheringham
The Henry Ramey Upcher Lifeboat Museum
Map ref. J/K2
West Cliff
Tel: (01263) 824343
The 'Henry Ramey Upcher' (private) lifeboat is a sailing and pulling boat in service from 1894-1935. Now on display in her original boatshed with original photographs.
Times: Open 24 Mar-30 Sept, daily, 1200-1630.
Fee: Free.
Facilities: ⇌ T(30 mins) 🖍

Sheringham
Sheringham Museum Map ref. J/K2
Station Road
Tel: (01263) 821871
Local social history museum. Displays on lifeboats and fishing heritage, boat-building, the 1¹/₂ million year old 'Weybourne Elephant', flint picking, fossils, Roman kiln and art gallery.
Times: Open 25 Mar-30 Oct, Tues-Sat 1000-1600; Sun 1400-1600. Also 1-29 Aug, Mon 1400-1600.
Fee: £1.50/75p/£1.00
Facilities: 🚌 ⇌ T(1 hr) 🖍

Stalham
The Museum of the Broads Map ref. N5
Stalham Staithe
Tel: (01692) 581681
Web: www.norfolkbroads.com/broadsmuseum
Displays of tools from the traditional Broads industries. Many Broads boats, including gunpunts and steam launch.
Times: Open 25 Mar-31 Oct, Mon-Fri, 1100-1700. Daily during school hols.
Fee: £3.00/£2.00/£2.00/£6.50(family).
Facilities: T(1¹/₂ hrs) 🎋 🖳

Stalham
Stalham Old Firehouse Museum Map ref. N5
High Street (corner of St. Mary's Church ground)
Tel: (01692) 580553
Tiny Grade II building (c.1833) showing 173 years of fire fighting history in the town. Photographs, a 1902 fire engine, brigade log books, uniforms and other artefacts.
Times: Open Apr-end Oct, Mon, Tues, Thurs, Fri, 1000-1600, also by appointment at other times.
Fee: Free.
Facilities: 🚎 T(25 mins) 🖳

Swaffham
Ecotech Map ref. F7
Turbine Way
Tel: (01760) 726100 Web: www.ecotech.org.uk
Climb the UK's largest windturbine. Take a guided tour (pre-bookings is advisable). Free admission to organic/heritage garden, shop and café.
Times: Open Jan-24 Mar, Mon-Fri 1100-1400; 25 Mar-30 Sept, Mon-Fri 1000-1600; 1 Oct-Dec, Mon-Fri 1100-1400.
Fee: £5.00/£3.00/£4.00.
Facilities: ⊛ 🅿 T(1 hr) 🖍⟨⟩ 🖳

Swaffham
Swaffham Museum Map ref. F7
Town Hall, London Street
Tel: (01760) 721230 Web: www.aboutswaffham.co.uk
An 18th C. building, formerly a brewer's home. Small social history museum for Swaffham and the surrounding villages. Annual exhibitions, plus displays from Stone Age to 20th C.
Times: Closed for refurbishment until after July, please telephone for details.
Fee: Please telephone for details.
Facilities: Q 🚎 T(1 hr) 🖍 🖳

The Forum at Norwich

Thetford
Charles Burrell Museum Map ref. F/G11
Minstergate
Tel: (01842) 765840
The Charles Burrell Steam Museum draws together an
impressive collection of exhibits to tell the story of Charles
Burrell and Son (1770-1932).
Times: Please contact for details of opening times.
Fee: Please contact for details of admission prices.
Facilities: ⊕ Q ▣ T(1 hr)

Wymondham
Wymondham Heritage Museum Map ref. J8
10 Bridewell, Norwich Road
Tel: (01953) 600205
Web: www.wymondham-norfolk.co.uk
Museum housed in a prison built in 1785, and telling the
story of the Bridewell as a prison, police station and
courthouse. Many local history displays. Cell, dungeon and
shop.
Times: Open 1 Mar-30 Nov, Mon-Sat, 1000-1600; Sun,
1400-1600.
Fee: £2.00/50p/£1.50.
Facilities: ▥ ⇌ T(1 hr) ⑪ ▣

See also:
Green Quay Environmental Discovery Centre, King Lynn,
page 191
Holkham Hall Bygones Museum, page 42, 44
Houghton Hall, Model Soldier Museum, page 43
Mid-Norfolk Railway, County School Station, North
Elmham, nr Dereham, page 107
Sandringham, nr Kings Lynn, page 44.

SUFFOLK

Aldeburgh
The Aldeburgh Museum Map ref. N8
The Moot Hall
Tel: (01728) 454666
A 16th C. Listed ancient building with a museum displaying
items of local interest, such as photographs and artefacts
depicting life in Aldeburgh (fishing, lifeboat and Anglo-
Saxon finds).
Times: Please telephone to check opening times.
Fee: £1.00/free (2004 prices).
Facilities: ▥ T(45 mins) ⫝

Beccles
Beccles and District Museum Map ref. N2/3
Leman House, Ballygate
Tel: (01502) 715722 Web: www.becclesmuseum.org.uk
A Grade I Listed building concerning printing, Waveney,
agricultural costumes, cultural and domestic items. Also a
model of the town in 1841, and a natural history diorama.
Times: Open 1 Apr-31 Oct, Tues-Sun and Bank Hol Mon,
1430-1630.
Fee: Free.**Facilities:** ▥ ⇌ T(1½ hrs) ⫝ ▣

Brandon
Brandon Heritage Centre Map ref. C3
George Street
Tel: (01842) 814955
The centre gives details of the flint, fur and forestry
industries in the Brandon area, together with a local
interest section housed in the former fire station premises.
Times: Open 25 Mar-30 Oct, Sat and Bank Hol Mon,
1030-1700; Sun, 1400-1700.
Fee: 50p/40p/40p.
Facilities: ⊕ ▣ ▥ ⇌ T(1 hr) ⫝ ⨅ ▣

Bungay
Bungay Museum Map ref. L3
Waveney District Council Office, Broad Street
Tel: (01986) 894463
The museum consists of two small upstairs rooms which
are inter-connecting. These contain showcases of general
items from Norman to Victorian periods.
Times: Open 2 Jan-24 Dec, Mon-Fri, 0900-1630. Closed
Bank Hols.
Fee: 50p/30p/30p.
Facilities: ⊕ ▥ T(30 mins) ⫞

Bury St. Edmunds
Bury St. Edmunds Art Gallery Map ref. D/E6/7
The Market Cross, Cornhill
Tel: (01284) 762081
Web: www.burystedmundsartgallery.org
A programme of changing exhibitions of fine and applied
arts, educational activities and craft shop in a magnificent
Robert Adam building, the Market Cross.
Times: Open all year, Tues-Sat, 1030-1700.
Closed 24-28 Dec.
Fee: £1.00/free/50p.
Facilities: ▥ ⇌ T(30 mins)

For even more information visit our website at www.visiteastofengland.com

Bury St. Edmunds
Manor House Map ref. D/E6/7
5 Honey Hill
Tel: (01284) 757076 Web: www.stedmundsbury.gov.uk
A collection of clocks, watches, costumes and textiles, with fine and decorative arts of national importance in a magnificent 18th C. building.
Times: Open all year, Wed-Sun, 1100-1600. Closed 25, 28 Mar, 25, 26 Dec and 1 Jan.
Fee: £2.50/£2.00/£2.00/£8.00(family).
Facilities: ⊛ 🄿 🚻 ♨ T(2 hrs) 🏃 ⑨ 🗚 🗒

Bury St. Edmunds
Moyse's Hall Museum Map ref. D/E6/7
Cornhill
Tel: (01284) 706183 Web: www.stedmundsbury.gov.uk
Dating back over 800 years, Moyse's Hall contains local history and archaeology collections, Murder in the Red Barn artifacts and highlights from the Suffolk Regiment.
Times: Open all year, Mon-Fri, 1030-1630; Sat and Sun, 1100-1600. Closed 25 Mar, 25, 26 Dec and 1 Jan.
Fee: £2.50/£2.00/£2.00/£8.00(family).
Facilities: ⊛ 🚻 ♨ T(4 hrs) 🏃 🗒

Bury St. Edmunds
Theatre Royal Map ref. D/E6/7
Westgate Street
Tel: (01284) 769505 Web: www.theatreroyal.org
Built in 1819 by William Wilkins, this is a rare example of a late Georgian playhouse. Presents a full programme of drama to comedy and dance. Theatre tours.
Times: Closing for major restoration work from June 2005. Until end May, Mon-Sat, 1100-1600, subject to theatrical activity. Guided tours for groups, pre-booking essential.
Fee: Free. Group Tours £2.00.
Facilities: ⊛ T(40 mins) 🏃 NT

Cavendish (nr. Sudbury)
Sue Ryder Museum Map ref. D9
High Street
Tel: (01787) 282591
Museum depicting the life and work of Sue Ryder - past present and future.
Times: Open all year, daily, 1000-1700. Closed 24-27 Dec.
Fee: £1.00/50p/50p.
Facilities: 🄿 T(1 hr) ⑨ 🗒

Clare
Ancient House Museum Map ref. C10
26 High Street
Tel: (01787) 277662
Web: www.clare-ancient-house-museum.co.uk
Set in a 14th C. building, renowned for its pargeting, the museum tells the story of Clare, with graphic displays, computerised records and census returns.
Times: Open 24-28 Mar and 28 Apr-30 Sept, Thurs, Fri and Sun, 1400-1700; Sat and Bank Hols, 1130-1700.
Fee: £1.00/free/£1.00.
Facilities: 🚌 T(45 mins)

Dunwich
Dunwich Museum Map ref. O6
St James's Street
Tel: (01728) 648796
A museum showing the history of Dunwich from Roman times, chronicling its disappearance into the sea and local wildlife.
Times: Open 1-31 Mar, Sat and Sun, 1400-1630. 1 Apr-30 Sept, daily, 1130-1630. 1-31 Oct, daily 1200-1600.
Fee: Free.
Facilities: ⊛ 🅿 T(40 mins) 🎏 🔳

Felixstowe
Felixstowe Museum Map ref. K/L12
Landguard Point, Viewpoint Road
Tel: (01394) 674355 Web: www.fhms.org.uk
The museum is housed in the Ravelin block adjacent to Landguard Fort. There are exhibits covering local, social and military history of the Felixstowe area.
Times: Open Easter to 31 Oct, Wed, Sun and Bank Hol Mon, 1300-1730.
Fee: £1.00/50p.
Facilities: T(1 hr) 🕙 🐕 (on leads) 🔳

Framlingham
Lanman Museum Map ref. K/L7
Framlingham Castle
Tel: (01728) 724189
A museum with rural exhibits relating to everyday life in Framlingham and the surrounding area, including paintings and photographs.
Times: Open 1 Jan-30 Apr, daily,1000-1600; 1 May-30 Sept, daily, 1000-1800; 1-31 Oct, daily, 1000-1700; 1 Nov-31 Dec, daily, 1000-1600. Closed 25, 26 Dec.
Fee: Free.
Facilities: 🅿 T(1 hr) 🏃

Halesworth
Halesworth and District Museum Map ref. M4
The Railway Station, Station Road
Tel: (01986) 875351
Museum housed in the 19th C. railway station building, alongside unique movable platforms. Changing local history displays, railway information and important residents. Also displays of local geology and archaeology.
Times: Open 11 Jan-30 Apr, Tues, Thurs, 1030-1230; 2 May-29 Oct, Tues-Fri, 1000-1230, also Tues, Wed and Bank Hol 1400-1600; 1 Nov-15 Dec, Tues, Thurs, 1030-1230.
Fee: Free.
Facilities: 🅿 🚌 ⇌ T(1½ hr)

Haverhill
Haverhill and District Local History Centre
Map ref. B9/10
Town Hall Arts Centre, High Street
Tel: (01440) 714962
A collection of over 6,000 items relating to Haverhill and district. There is also a vast collection of photographs.
Times: Open all year, Tues, 1900-2100; Thurs and Fri, 1400-1600; Sat, 1030-1530. Closed 25,28 Mar and 23-28 Dec, 1-2 Jan.
Fee: Free.
Facilities: 🅿 🚌 T(1 hr) 🕙 🔳

Ipswich
Christchurch Mansion Map ref. I/J10
Christchurch Park
Tel: (01473) 433554 Web: www.ipswich.gov.uk
Fine Tudor mansion built between 1548-50. Collection of furniture, panelling, ceramics, clocks and paintings from the 16-19th C. Art exhibitions in Wolsey Art Gallery.
Times: Open 1 Jan-31 Mar, Tues-Sat, 1000-1600; Sun, 1430-1600. 1 Apr-31 Oct, Tues-Sat, 1000-1700; Sun, 1430-1630. 1 Nov-31 Dec, Tues-Sat, 1000-1600; Sun, 1430-1600.
Fee: Free.
Facilities: ⊛ 🚌 T(2 hrs) 🕙 🎏

Ipswich
Ipswich Museum Map ref. I/J10
High Street
Tel: (01473) 433550 Web: www.ipswich.gov.uk
Displays of Roman Suffolk, Suffolk wildlife, Suffolk and world geology, the Ogilvie Bird Gallery, 'People of the World' and 'Anglo-Saxons come to Ipswich' displays.
Times: Open all year, Tues-Sat, 1000-1700. Closed 25, 28 Mar, 24, 25 Dec and 1 Jan.
Fee: Free.
Facilities: ⊛ 🚌 T(2 hrs)

Ipswich

The John Russell Gallery Map ref. I/J10
4-6 Wherry Lane
Tel: (01473) 212051 Web: www.artone.co.uk
Contemporary art galleries, representing over 160 of the
region's painters and sculptors. Demonstrations.
Times: Open 5 Jan-13 Aug, Mon-Sat, 0930-1700; 30 Aug-
24 Dec, Mon-Sat, 0930-1700. Closed 25, 27, 28 Mar.
Fee: Free.
Facilities: ▣ 🛏 ⇌ T(30 mins) ⬛

Ipswich

Wattisham Airfield Museum Map ref. H9
Wattisham Airfield
Tel: (01449) 678189
Web: www.wattishamairfieldmuseum.fsnet.co.uk
Museum houses an extensive photographic record, models,
artefacts and memorabilia depicting the history and
squadrons based at the station.
Times: Open 28 Mar-30 Oct, Sun, 1400-1630 also all year
by appointment
Fee: Free.
Facilities: ▣ T(2 hrs) ⬛

Kentford (nr. Newmarket)

Animal Health Trust Visitor Centre Map ref. B6
Lanwades Park
Tel: 08700 502424 Web: www.aht.org.uk
The John MacDougall Visitor Centre gives an insight into
the veterinary work of the Animal Health Trust charity.
Exhibitions and touch screen information. Coffee shop
serves light refreshments.
Times: Open all year, Mon-Fri, 0900-1700. Closed 25-28
Mar, 25, 26 Dec and 1 Jan.
Fee: Free.
Facilities: ▣ ⇌ T(1 hr) ⑬ 🐾 ⬛

Lowestoft and East Suffolk Maritime Museum

Laxfield (nr. Framlingham)

Laxfield and District Museum Map ref. L5
The Guildhall, High Street
Tel: (01986) 798026
Museum housed in the early 16th C. Guildhall opposite the
church. Displays relate to the domestic and working life of
the village in the 19/20th C.
Times: Open 30 Apr-25 Sept, Sat, Sun and Bank Hol Mon,
1400-1700.
Fee: Free.
Facilities: 🛏 T(1 hr)

Lowestoft

Heritage Workshop Centre Map ref. P2
Old School House, 80a High Street, Wilde Score
Tel: (01502) 587500
Old school built in 1788, the first to offer free education to
sons of fisherfolk. Interactive model beach village.
Changing exhibitions and workshops. Archives of local
newspapers available to browse.
Times: Open all year, Mon-Fri, 1000-1600.
Fee: Free. Beach Village and exhibitions
£4.00/£1.50/£3.50/£9.00(family).
Facilities: ▣ 🛏 ⇌ T(1 hr) ⏃ ⬛

Lowestoft

Lowestoft and East Suffolk Maritime Museum
Map ref. P2
Sparrow's Nest Park, Whapload Road
Tel: (01502) 561963
The museum houses models of fishing and commercial
ships, shipwrights' tools, fishing gear, a lifeboat display, an
art gallery and a drifter's cabin with models of fishermen.
Times: Open 25 Mar-2 Apr, then 30 Apr-9 Oct, daily,
1000-1700.
Fee: 75p/25p/50p.
Facilities: ▣ 🛏 ⇌ T(1½ hrs) ⏃ 🗏 ⬛

Lowestoft

Lowestoft Museum Map ref. O2
Broad House, Nicholas Everitt Park
Tel: (01502) 511457
A museum housing displays on local history, Lowestoft
porcelain, fossils, flint implements, medieval artefacts from
local sites and domestic history.
Times: Open 31 Mar-2 Nov, Mon-Fri, 1030-1630; Sat and
Sun, 1300-1630.
Fee: Free.
Facilities: 🛏 ⇌ T(1 hr) 🗏

**For even more
information visit
our website at
www.visiteastofengland.com**

Lowestoft
Lowestoft Porcelain Map ref. P2
Redgrave House, 10 Battery Green Road
Tel: (01502) 572940 Web: www.lowestoftporcelain.com
A little piece of history - the rebirth of an 18th C. English
porcelain factory. An opportunity to see fine heritage
porcelain and new studio ranges being painted by our
artists.
Times: Open 4 Jan-24 Dec, Tues-Sat, 1000-1600. Closed
1,2 Jan.
Fee: Free.
Facilities: ⊛ 🅿 🚌 ≋ T(1 hr) ⑪ 🎋 🔳

Lowestoft
Lowestoft War Memorial Museum Map ref. P2
Sparrow's Nest Gardens, Whapload Road
Tel: (01502) 587500
Museum and chapel dedicated to all who served in World
War II, both service and civillian.
Times: Open 30 May-1 Oct, Sun-Fri, 1300-1600.
Fee: Donations appreciated.
Facilities: 🚌 ≋ T(45 mins) ⑪ 🎋

Lowestoft
Royal Naval Patrol Service Association Museum
Map ref. P2
Sparrow's Nest Gardens, Whapload Road
Tel: (01502) 586250
A museum with photographs and models of World War II
officers and crews, minesweepers and anti-submarine
vessels.
Times: Open 5 May-mid Oct, Mon, Wed and Fri, 0900-
1200. Other times by appointment.
Fee: Free.
Facilities: 🅿 🚌 ≋ T(2 hrs) 𝘐 ⑪ 🎋

Moot Hall, Aldeburgh

Martlesham Heath
Martlesham Heath Control Tower Museum Map ref. K10
Off Parkers Place
Tel: (01473) 435104 Web: www.mhas.org.uk
Original World War II control tower built in 1942. Museum
depicts history of this famous airfield 1917-1979. Once
important Battle of Britain base and former home to
USAAF 356FG.
Times: Open 3 Apr-30 Oct, Sun, 1400-1630.
Fee: Free.
Facilities: 🅿 🚌 T(1 hr) 𝘐

Mildenhall
Mildenhall and District Museum Map ref. B5
6 King Street
Tel: (01638) 716970 Web: www.mildenhallmuseum.co.uk
A local voluntary museum housed in 19th C. cottages, with
modern extensions. Displays include RAF Mildenhall,
Fenland and Breckland local archaeology and local history.
Complete replica of Mildenhall Treasure.
Times: Open 2 Mar-22 Dec, Wed, Thurs, 1430-1630; Fri,
1100-1630. Sat 1430-1630. Closed 25 Mar.
Fee: Free.
Facilities: 🚌 T(1 hr)

Newmarket
The National Horseracing Museum and Tours
Map ref. A7
99 High Street
Tel: (01638) 667333 Web: www.nhrm.co.uk
Award-winning display of the people and horses involved in
racing's amazing history. Minibus tours to gallops, stables
and equine pool. Hands-on gallery with horse simulator.
Times: Open Easter-31 Oct, Tues-Sun, 1100-1630. Last
admission 1600.
Fee: Museum £4.50/£2.50/£3.50/£10.00. Minibus tours
£20.00/£18.50/£18.50.
Facilities: ⊛ 🅿 🚌 ≋ T(2 hrs) 𝘐 ⑪ 🎋 🔳

Orford
Dunwich Underwater Exploration Exhibition Map ref. N9
The Orford Craft Shop
Tel: (01394) 450678
Exhibits show progress in the underwater exploration of the
former city of Dunwich, and underwater studies off the
Suffolk coast. Attraction is not suitable for small children.
Times: Open all year, daily, 1030-1700. Closed 25 and 26
Dec.
Fee: 50p/50p.
Facilities: 🅿 T(1 hr)

Parham (nr. Framlingham)
Parham Airfield Museum Map ref. L7
Tel: (01728) 621373 (open hours), or (01376) 320848
Museum housed in the original control tower, with aircraft engines, uniforms, photographs and memorabilia. UK Museum of the British Resistance Organisation (Churchill's Secret Army), with many artefacts.
Times: Open 6 Mar-30 Oct, Sun, 1100-1700. Also Wed from 1 Jun-28 Sept, 1100-1600.
Fee: Free.
Facilities: 🅿 T(2 hrs) 🚶 ⛱ 🐕

Shotley Gate (nr. Ipswich)
HMS Ganges Association Museum Map ref. K11
Old Sail Loft, Shotley Marina
Tel: (01473) 684749 Web: www.hmsgangesassoc.org
The history of HMS Ganges, a training establishment for boys aged 15-16 years (closed in 1976). Photographs, artifacts and documentation.
Times: Open 25 Mar-30 Oct, Sat, Sun and Bank Hol Mons, 1100-1700.
Fee: Free.
Facilities: 🅿 🚻 T(1 hr) 🚶 ⓘ

Southwold
Alfred Corry Museum Map ref. O5
Ferry Road
Tel: (01502) 722103
The old Cromer lifeboat station transported by sea to Southwold. Restored, and now housing the old Southwold lifeboat. One hundred and ten years old.
Times: Open 31 Mar-2 Nov, daily, 1030-1230.
Fee: Free.
Facilities: 🅿 T(40 mins) 🚶 ⓘ ⛱ 🐕 ⓘ

Christchurch Mansion, Ipswich

Southwold
The Amber Museum Map ref. O5
15 Market Place
Tel: (01502) 723394 Web: www.ambershop.co.uk
A purpose-built museum telling the story of amber, the precious gem found on the Suffolk shores. Discover how it is formed through historical uses to spectacular modern pieces.
Times: Open all year, Mon-Sat, 0900-1700; Sun, Bank Hol, 1100-1600. Closed 25 and 26 Dec.
Fee: Free.
Facilities: 🚻 T(30 mins) 🐕 ⓘ

Southwold
Southwold Museum Map ref. O5
9-11 Victoria Street
Tel: (01502) 723374 Web: www.southwoldmuseum.org
Museum housing local history, archaeology, natural history and domestic bygones. Exhibits relating to the Southwold railway and The Battle of Sole Bay.
Times: Open 25 Mar-31Oct, daily, 1400-1600; 1-31 Aug, daily, 1030-1200, 1400-1600.
Fee: Free.
Facilities: T(1 hr) ⓘ

Southwold
Southwold Sailors' Reading Room Map ref. O5
East Cliff
A building of character where retired seamen have a social club and reading room. There are maritime exhibits and local history. No unaccompanied children.
Times: Open 1 Jan-25 Mar, daily, 0900-1530. 26 Mar-30 Oct, daily, 0900-1700. 31 Oct-31 Dec, daily, 0900-1530. Closed 25 Dec.
Fee: Free.
Facilities: 🚻 T(15 mins) ⓘ

Steeple Bumpstead (nr. Haverhill)
Steeple Bumpstead Pottery and Gallery Map ref. B10
Church Street
Tel: (01440) 730260
Traditional working pottery set in a Victorian village school.
Gallery displaying the pots made here.
Times: Open all year, days and times vary - please contact
for details.
Fee: Free.
Facilities: ▣ ⏴ T(30 mins) ⧉

Stowmarket
Museum of East Anglian Life Map ref. H7/8
Tel: (01449) 612229
Web: www.eastanglianlife.org.uk
East Anglia's open-air museum, set in 70 acres of Suffolk
countryside. Displays and special events to interest visitors
of all ages. Historic buildings. Suffolk breeds of animals.
Times: Open 25 Mar-31 Oct, Mon-Sat, 1000-1700; Sun,
1100-1700.
Fee: £6.50/£3.50/£5.50/£17.50.
Facilities: ⊛ ⏴ ⇌ T(3 hrs) ⧉ ⊓ ⋔

Sudbury
Gainsborough's House Map ref. E10
46 Gainsborough Street
Tel: (01787) 372958 Web: www.gainsborough.org
Birthplace of Thomas Gainsborough (1727-88). An elegant
Georgian townhouse, which displays more of the artist's
work than any other gallery. Walled garden, print workshop
and programme of temporary exhibitions.
Times: Open all year, Mon-Sat, 1000-1700; Bank Hol Sun
and Mon, 1400-1700. Closed 25 Mar and 24 Dec-1 Jan.
Fee: £3.50/£1.50/£2.80/£8.00 (family).
Facilities: ⊛ Q ⏴ ⇌ T(1 hr) ⧉

Walberswick
Walberswick Visitor Centre Map ref. O5
Village Green
Tel: (01394) 384948
Web: www.suffolkcoastandheaths.org.uk
Visitor centre with photographic coverage of the village's
history. Fascinating film 'Wild Coasts and Ancient Heaths',
containing archive and present day footage on this Area of
Outstanding Natural Beauty.
Times: Open 25-28 Mar; May, Sat and Sun and Bank Hol
Mon; June, Sat and Sun; July, Wed, Fri, Sat and Sun; Aug,
daily; 3, 4, 10 and 11 Sept, 1400-1700.
Fee: Free.
Facilities: T(30 mins) ⋔

Wingfield (nr. Diss)
Wingfield Arts Map ref. J/K4/5
College Yard, Church Road
Tel: (01379) 384505 Web: www.wingfield-arts.co.uk
Award-winning arts centre with art galleries, sculpture
garden, shop and tea room. Quality programme of
exhibitions, concerts and arts activities for people of all
ages in rural settings.
Times: Open 26 Mar-18 Dec, Wed-Fri, 1200-1700; Sat,
Sun and Bank Hol Mon, 1400-1700.
Fee: £1.50/£1.00/£1.00.
Facilities: ⊛ ▣ T(2 hrs) ⫶ ⧉ ⧉

Woodbridge
Suffolk Horse Museum Map ref. K9
The Market Hill
Tel: (01394) 380643 Web: www.suffolkhorsesociety.org.uk
An indoor exhibition about the Suffolk Punch breed of
heavy horse. Paintings, photographs and exhibits.
Times: Open 28 Mar-30 Sept, Tues-Sun and Bank Hol
Mon, 1400-1700.
Fee: £2.00/£1.50/£1.50.
Facilities: ⏴ ⇌ T(1 hr)

Woodbridge
Woodbridge Museum Map ref. K9
5a Market Hill
Tel: (01394) 380502
The museum tells the story of Woodbridge and its people,
from pre-history to the present.
Times: Open Easter-Oct half term, Thurs-Sun, 1000-1600.
Daily in school holidays.
Fee: £1.00/30p.
Facilities: ⏴ ⇌ T(1 hr) ⫶ ⧉

Woolpit (nr. Bury St. Edmunds)
Woolpit and District Museum Map ref. F7
The Institute
Tel: (01359) 240822
A 17th C. timber-framed building with one permanent
display of brickmaking and other displays (changing
yearly), depicting the life of a Suffolk village.
Times: Open 26 Mar-25 Sept, Sat, Sun and Bank Hol Mon,
1430-1700.
Fee: Free.
Facilities: ▣ ⏴ ⇌ T(1 hr) ⫶⊓

See also:
Bridge Cottage, Flatford, page 44
Greene King Brewery Visitor Centre, Bury St Edmunds,
page 162
Lavenham Guildhall of Corpus Christi, page 46.

Machinery & Transport

BEDFORDSHIRE

Biggleswade
Shuttleworth Collection Map ref. F6
Old Warden Aerodrome
Tel: (01767) 627288 Web: www.shuttleworth.org
A unique historical collection of aircraft from a 1909
Bleriot to a 1942 Spitfire in flying condition, and cars
dating from an 1898 Panhard in running order.
Times: Open 1 Apr-31 Oct, 1000-1700 . 1 Nov-31 Mar,
1000-1600.
Fee: Non-event days - £7.50/free (up to 16yrs and
accompanied by an adult)/£6.00. Separate fees for air
displays/events.
Facilities: ⊛ 🅿 T(2½ hrs) 🕪 🎋 🐈 🔣

Leighton Buzzard
Leighton Buzzard Railway Map ref. B10
Page's Park Station, Billington Road
Tel: (01525) 373888 Web: www.buzzrail.co.uk
An authentic narrow-gauge light railway, built in 1919,
offering a 70-minute return journey into the Bedfordshire
countryside. Most trains hauled by historic steam locos.
Times: Open 13, 20, 25-28, 30 Mar; 3 Apr-30 May, Sun
and Bank Hol Mon, also 30 Apr and 28 May; 1, 2, 4 Jun; 5
Jun-31 Jul, Wed and Sun; 2-31 Aug, Tues, Wed, Thurs, Sat,
Sun and Bank Hol Mon; 4, 10, 11, 18, 25 Sept; 2-30 Oct,
Sun, also 1 and 26 Oct; 3-21 Dec, Wed, Sat and Sun; 26,
27, 28 Dec, 1040-1540.
Fee: £6.00/£3.00/£5.00/£14.00(family).
Facilities: ⊛ 🅿 T(2 hrs) 🕪 🎋 🐈 🔣

Lower Stondon
Stondon Museum Map ref. F8
Station Road
Tel: (01462) 850339 Web: www.transportmuseum.co.uk
The largest private transport museum in the country, with
over 400 exhibits covering 100 years of motoring, mostly
undercover. Full size replica of Captain Cook's ship 'The
Endeavour'.
Times: Open all year, daily, 1000-1700. Please contact for
Christmas opening
Fee: £6.00/£3.00/£5.00/£16.00.
Facilities: ⊛ 🅿 T(1½ hrs) 🎋 🕪 🎋 🐈

Luton
Mossman Collection Map ref. E10
Stockwood Craft Museum and Gardens, Farley Hill
Tel: (01582) 738714
Web: www.luton.gov.uk/enjoying/museums
The Mossman Collection is Britain's largest collection of
horse-drawn carriages, illustrating the history of road
transport from Roman times to the 1930s.
Times: Open 3 Jan-21 Mar, Sat and Sun, 1000-1600.
22 Mar-30 Oct, Tues-Sun, 1000-1700. 31 Oct-19 Dec, Sat
and Sun, 1000-1600.
Fee: Free.
Facilities: ⊛ 🅿 T(3 hrs) 🕪 🎋 🔣

See Also:
Pitstone Green Museum, Ivinghoe, nr Tring, page 82
Pitstone Green Museum, Ivinghoe, nr Tring, page 82
Twinwood Arena and The Glen Miller Museum, Clapham,
nr Bedford, page 64.

Stondon Museum, Lower Stondon, Bedfordshire

**For even more
information visit
our website at
www.visiteastofengland.com**

CAMBRIDGESHIRE

Cambridge

Museum of Technology Map ref. H11
The Old Pumping Station, Cheddars Lane
Tel: (01223) 368650
Web: www.museumoftechnology.com
A Victorian pumping station housing unique Hathorn
Davey steam pumping engines, electrical equipment and a
working letterpress print shop. Hands-on pumps.
Times: Steam days - 27, 28 Mar; 29, 30 May; 28, 29 Aug;
29, 30 Oct, 31 Dec, 1100-1700. Non-steam days - 2 Jan, 6
Feb, 6 Mar and 3 Apr-6 Nov, Sun, 1400-1700.
Fee: Steam days - £5.00 Non-steam days - £3.00.
Concessions available.
Facilities: P 🚂 T(1 hr) 🚻 🍴 🎏 🐕

Duxford (nr. Cambridge)

Imperial War Museum Map ref. H13
Tel: (01223) 835000 Web: www.iwm.org.uk
One of the world's most spectacular aviation heritage
complexes, with almost 200 aircraft on display. Collection
of military vehicles, tanks and guns. Special exhibitions and
air shows throughout the year.
Times: Open 1 Jan-18 Mar, daily, 1000-1600. 19 Mar-29
Oct, daily, 1000-1800. 31 Oct-31 Dec, daily, 1000-1600.
Please contact for Christmas and New Year openings.
Fee: Please contact for details of admission prices.
Facilities: 🅥 Q P 🚂 T(4 hrs) 🚻 🍴 🎏 🖼

Peterborough

Railworld Map ref. C5
Oundle Road
Tel: (01733) 344240 Web: www.railworld.net
Railworld highlights modern trains and the environment.
Superb model railway, films and hands-on displays for
children. 'Steam age' displays, large locomotives and
hovertrains. Visitors have all day free parking
Times: Open 1 Jan-28 Feb, Mon-Fri, 1100-1600. 1 Mar-31
Oct, daily, 1100-1600. 1 Nov-31 Dec, Mon-Fri, 1100-1600.
Closed 25 Mar. Open by arrangement at Christmas, please
contact for details.
Fee: £4.00/£2.00/£3.00/£10.00.
Facilities: 🅥 P 🚂 ⇌ T(1½ hr) 🚻 🍴 🎏 🐕 🖼

Prickwillow

Prickwillow Drainage Engine Museum Map ref. J8
Main Street
Tel: (01353) 688360
Web: prickwillow-engine-museum.co.uk
A museum housing a Mirrlees Bickerton and Day diesel
engine, a 5-cylinder, blast injection, 250 bhp working unit
and a Vicker-Petter, 2-cylinder, 2-stroke diesel and others.
Times: Open Mar-Apr, Sat, Sun and Bank Hols, 1100-
1630. 30 Apr-30 Sept, Mon, Tues, Fri-Sun, 1100-1630. 1-
30 Oct, Sat and Sun, 1100-1630.
Fee: £2.00/£1.00/£1.50/£5.00. Run days
£3.00/£1.50/£2.00/£7.00.
Facilities: P T(1 hr) 🚻 🍴 🎏 🐕

Visit Britain's International Steam Railway

All the sights and sounds of the golden age of steam come
alive at the Nene Valley Railway, travelling between Wansford
and Peterborough the 7½ miles of track passes through the
heart of the 500 acre Ferry Meadows Country Park. The ideal
outing for lovers of steam both young and old. NVR is also the
home of "Thomas" the children's favourite engine. Shop, Café
and Museum open on service days. Loco Yard and Station
open all year. **Services** operate Saturdays from January;
weekends from Easter to October; Wednesdays from May, plus
other mid-week services in summer. Santa Specials end
November and throughout December. Disabled visitors very
welcome. Free parking and picnic areas. Play Area.
Special Events held throughout the year.

Full Steam Ahead for a Great Day Out!

Enquiries: 01780 784444, Timetable: 01780 784404 or
visit www.nvr.org.uk

Wansford Station (next to A1), Stibbington,
PETERBOROUGH, PE8 6LR Registered Charity No. 263617

DUXFORD **2005**

Open daily from
10am all year round.*
Half an hour from the M25.
Junction 10 on the M11.
20 mins south of Cambridge. FREE parking.

CHILDREN GO FREE
www.iwm.org.uk
Tel: 01223 835000
*Except 24-26 December

DUXFORD
Imperial War Museum

Stibbington (nr. Peterborough)
Nene Valley Railway Map ref. B5
Wansford Station
Tel: (01780) 784444 Web: www.nvr.org.uk
A 7¹/₂ mile track between Wansford and Peterborough via
Yarwell Jct and Nene Park, with over 28 steam and diesel
locomotives. Regular steam trains operate over the line.
Times: Locomotive yard open all year, daily, 0930-1630.
Closed 25 Dec. Steam days 25 Mar-1 Apr, daily; 2 Apr-mid
May, Sat and Sun; mid May-end Aug, Wed, Sat and Sun,
also daily during summer school hols; Sept-end Oct, Sat
and Sun and daily during half term week.
Fee: Rover Ticket £10.00/£5.00/£7.50/£25.00.
Facilities: ⊛ 🅿 🚃 ≈ T(1-2 hrs) 🍴 ⊞ 🝙 🐕

See Also:
Burwell Museum, Burwell, page 65

ESSEX

Audley End (nr. Saffron Walden)
Audley End Miniature Railway Map ref. C2
Tel: (01799) 541354 Web: www.audley-end-railway.co.uk
Steam and diesel locomotives in 10.25 gauge, running through
attractive woodland for 1¹/₂ miles. The railway crosses the
River Cam twice.
Times: Open 19 Mar-30 Oct, Sat and Sun, 1400-1700.
Daily in school hols, 1400-1700. Bank Hols, 1100-1700.
Fee: Railway £2.50/£1.50.
Facilities: 🅿 ≈ T(1 hr) ⊞ 🝙 🐕

East Anglian Railway Museum, Colchester

Burnham-on-Crouch
Mangapps Railway Museum Map ref. J9
Tel: (01621) 784898 Web: www.mangapps.co.uk
A large collection of railway relics, two restored stations,
locomotives, coaches and wagons with a working railway line
of 1 mile.
Times: Open 1, 2, and 3 Jan; 12 Feb-20 Mar, Sat and Sun;
21 Mar-1 Apr daily; 2 Apr-31 Jul, Sat, Sun and Bank Hol;
1-31 Aug, daily, 3 Sept-18 Dec, Sat and Sun, 1130-1700.
Closed 25-31 Dec.
Fee: £5.00/£2.50.
Facilities: 🅿 T(2 hrs) ⊞ 🝙 🐕

Canvey Island
Canvey Railway and Model Engineering Club Map ref. H11
Waterside Farm Leisure Centre
Tel: (01268) 413235 Web: www.cramec.org
Two miniature railways, both live steam and/or diesel. Approx.
1 mile of track.
Times: Open 3 Apr-2 Oct, Sun, 1000-1600.
Fee: Free entry. Train rides 80p. 12 rides for £8.00.
Facilities: 🚃 ≈ T(1 hr) ⊞ 🝙 🐕 🖼

Canvey Island
Castle Point Transport Museum Map ref. H11
105 Point Road
Tel: (01268) 684272
A 1935 museum housing a collection of buses, coaches and
commercial vehicles in restored and unrestored condition.
Some examples of these vehicles are unique.
Times: Open Apr-Oct, first and third Sun of each month,
1000-1700.
Fee: Free.
Facilities: 🅿 🚃 T(1¹/₂ hr) 🍴 🐕(on leads)

Castle Hedingham
Colne Valley Railway Map ref. G2/3
Yeldham Road
Tel: (01787) 461174 Web: www.colnevalleyrailway.co.uk
An award-winning station. Ride in the most pleasant part of
the Colne Valley. A large, interesting collection of operational
heritage railway rolling stock.
Times: Open 25 Mar-31 Oct, Sun, 1100-1700. Also Wed and
Thurs in school hols, and daily in Aug.
Fee: Operational steam days (includes rides)
£6.00/£3.00/£5.00/£18.00.
Facilities: ⊛ 🅿 🚃 T(3 hrs) ⊞ 🝙

Colchester
East Anglian Railway Museum Map ref. I4
Chappel Station, Wakes Colne
Tel: (01206) 242524 Web: www.earm.co.uk
A large and varied collection of working and static railway
exhibits from the age of steam, set in original surroundings
of a once important Victorian country junction station.
Times: Open all year, daily, 1000-1630. Closed 25, 26 Dec.
Fee: £6.00/£3.00/£4.50/£15.00 (event days).
£3.00/£2.00/£2.50/£8.00 (non-event days).
Facilities: Q P ⛟ ≋ T(3 hrs) 𝄆 ⦿ ⴲ ⸙

Burwell Museum, Burwell, see page 65

Langford (nr. Maldon)
Museum of Power Map ref. H7
Steam Pumping Station, Hatfield Road
Tel: (01621) 843183 Web: www.museumofpower.org.uk
Housed in an impressive 1920s building. A large triple-
expansion steam engine is the main exhibit with many other
sources of power on show.
Times: Open 4 Mar-24 Mar, Fri, Sat and Sun 1000-1600;
25 Mar-end Oct, Wed-Sun and Bank Hols 1000-1700; 1
Nov-24 Dec, Fri, Sat and Sun 1000-1600.
Fee: Admission charges. Please telephone to check prices.
Facilities: P T(1½ hrs) 𝄆 ⦿ ⴲ

North Weald
North Weald Airfield Museum Map ref. C8
Astra House, Hurricane Way
Tel: (01992) 523010 Web: www.fly.to/northweald
A fine old house at the former main gate of North Weald
Airfield, standing adjacent to an impressive memorial.
Artifacts, photographs and models telling story of airfield.
Times: Open Easter-30 Oct, Sat and Sun 1200-1700.
Fee: £1.50/£1.00/£1.00.
Facilities: P ⛟ T(2½ hrs) ⴲ

Museum of Power, Langford

Pitsea (nr. Basildon)
The Motorboat Museum Map ref. G11
Wat Tyler Country Park
Tel: (01268) 550077 Web: www.motorboatmuseum.org.uk
A museum devoted to the history and evolution of the
motorboat in the sports and leisure field.
Times: Open all year, Mon and Thurs-Sun, 1000-1630.
Closed 24 Dec-6 Jan.
Fee: Free.
Facilities: P T(2½ hrs) ⦿ ⴲ ▣

St. Osyth (nr. Clacton-on-Sea)
East Essex Aviation Society and Museum Map ref. M6
Martello Tower, Point Clear
Tel: (01255) 428028
An exhibition of aircraft parts from local recoveries. There
are also displays from World War I up to the late 1940s.
Housed in a 19th C. Martello tower.
Times: Open all year, Mon, 1900-2130; 5 Feb-30 Oct, Sun,
1000-1400. 1 Jun-28 Sept, Wed, 1000-1400. Open 28
Mar, 1000-1400.
Fee: Free.
Facilities: P ⛟ T(1 hr) 𝄆 ⴲ ⸙

Thaxted
Glendale Forge Map ref. E3
Monk Street
Tel: (01371) 830466
Forge with a comprehensive range of wrought ironwork,
gates, lanterns, fireguards, blacksmith work and a small
collection of unusual half-size vehicles.
Times: Open all year, Mon-Sat, 0900-1700; Sun, 1000-
1200. Train shed open, Wed, 1400-1700; Sun, 1000-1200.
Please phone for Christmas openings.
Fee: Free. Donations appreciated.
Facilities: P ⛟ T(1½ hrs) ⴲ ▣

See Also:
Coalhouse Fort (Thameside Aviation Museum), East
Tilbury, page 53
Maldon and District Agricultural and Domestic Museum,
Goldhanger, nr Maldon page 76
Walton Hall Museum, Linford, nr Tilbury, page 76.

Bressingham Steam Experience and Gardens

HERTFORDSHIRE

London Colney
de Havilland Aircraft Heritage Centre Map ref. G14
Salisbury Hall
Tel: (01727) 822051 Web: www.dehavillandmuseum.co.uk
Museum showing the restoration and preservation of a
range of de Havilland aircraft, including the prototype
Mosquito. Also engines, propellers, missiles, memorabilia
and a de Havilland story board.
Times: Open 6 Mar-30 Oct, Tues, Thurs and Sat,
1400-1730; Sun and Bank Hols, 1030-1730.
Fee: £5.00/£3.00/£3.00/£13.00.
Facilities: 🅿 T(2½ hrs) 🏃 ⚡ ⚓ 🛈

NORFOLK

Aylsham
Bure Valley Railway Map ref. K5
Aylsham Station, Norwich Road
Tel: (01263) 733858 Web: www.bvrw.co.uk
A 15-inch narrow-gauge steam railway covering 9 miles of
track from Wroxham in the heart of the Norfolk Broads to
Aylsham which is a bustling market town.
Times: Open 13-20 Feb; 20 Mar-25 Sept; 22-30 Oct, daily,
0930-1730. Gala weekend 8-9 Oct.
Fee: Rover ticket: £9.00/£5.00/£8.50. Boat/train fare:
£14.00/£10.00/£13.50.
Facilities: 🅿 🚽 ⚡ T(2 hrs) 🛈 ⚓ ⚡ 🛈

Bressingham (nr. Diss)
Bressingham Steam Experience and Gardens Map ref. J11
Tel: (01379) 686900 Web: www.bressingham.co.uk
Steam train rides through four miles of woodland. Six acres of
island garden beds. Plant centre. Mainline locomotives, the
Victorian Gallopers and over 50 steam engines. Dad's Army
Collection.
Times: Open 28 Mar-30 Oct, daily, 1030-1730. (Apr and
Oct closes 1630). May close Mon and Tues, please
telephone to check.
Fee: £7.00/£5.00/£6.00 (2004 prices).
Extra charges for rides.
Facilities: 🅿 T(4 hrs) 🏃 ⚡ ⚓ 🛈

Dereham
Mid-Norfolk Railway (Dereham to Wymondham Line)
Map ref. H6/7
The Railway Station, Station Road
Tel: (01362) 690633 Web: www.mnr.org.uk
Victorian railway station at Dereham undergoing
restoration. Selection of diesel locomotives and heritage
railcars. Other vehicles undergoing restoration. Passenger
services to Wymondham
Times: Open 27 Feb-25 Mar, Sun and Bank Hol; 26 Mar-
10 May, Sat, Sun and Bank Hol; 11 May-27 Jul, Wed, Sat,
Sun and Bank Hol; 28 Jul-8 Sept, Wed, Thurs, Sat, Sun and
Bank Hol Mon; 9-28 Sept, Wed, Sat and Sun; 29 Sept-29
Oct, Sat and Sun; 30 Oct-18 Dec, Sun, 1000-1630 (Sun
opens 1030)
Fee: £5.50/£2.75/£5.00. Special prices apply for steam
days in May.
Facilities: ⊛ Q 🅿 T(2 hrs) 🐕 ⊞

Forncett St. Mary (nr. Long Stratton)
Forncett Industrial Steam Museum Map ref. K9
Low Road
Tel: (01508) 488277
Web: www.phoenixbooks.org
A unique collection of large industrial steam engines including
one that used to open Tower Bridge in London. Seven engines
can be seen working on steam days.
Times: Open 1 May, 5 Jun, 3 Jul, 7 Aug, 4 Sept, 2 Oct, 6 Nov,
steamdays.
Fee: £4.50/free/£4.00.
Facilities: 🅿 T(2 hrs) 🐾 ⊞

Horsham St. Faith (nr. Norwich)
City of Norwich Aviation Museum Map ref. K6
Old Norwich Road
Tel: (01603) 893080 Web: www.cnam.co.uk
A collection of aircraft and memorabilia showing the aviation
history of Norfolk. The collection features many aircraft which
have flown from Norfolk.
Times: Open 4 Jan-31 Mar, Wed and Sat, 1000-1600; Sun,
1200-1600; 1 Apr-31 Oct, Tues-Sat, 1000-1700, Sun 1200-
1700. Also Bank Hol Mons 1200-1700, and mid Jul-Aug
Mons, 1000-1700.
Fee: £2.60/£1.50/£2.30 (prov).
Facilities: 🅿 T(2½ hrs) ⊞ ⊞

Shuttleworth Collection see page 101

North Elmham (nr. Dereham)
Mid Norfolk Railway (County School Station)
Map ref. H5
Holt Road
Tel: (01362) 668181 Web: www.mnr.org.uk
Built in 1884, County School Station is the northern
outpost of the Mid Norfolk Railway. Situated in the heart
of the unspoilt Wensum Valley. Small exhibition and walks.
Times: Open May-end Sept, Sun and Bank Hol Mon 1030-
1630, also Sats in Aug.
Fee: Free.
Facilities: ⊛ Q ⊡ T(30 mins) ⑴ 굣 ⋔

North Walsham
Norfolk Motor Cycle Museum Map ref. L4
Railway Yard
Tel: (01692) 406266
A museum displaying a wide collection of motor cycles dating
from 1920-1960. Also old bicycles and die cast toys.
Times: Open all year, daily, 1000-1630. Closed Sun from
31 Oct-1 Apr. Closed 25, 26 Dec.
Fee: £3.00/£1.50/£2.50.
Facilities: ⊡ 🚐 ⇌ T(1 hr) 𝑘 굣 ⋔ ▣

Sheringham
The Poppy Line (North Norfolk Railway) Map ref. J/K2
Sheringham Station, Station Approach
Tel: (01263) 820800 Email : enquiries@nnrailway.com
Web: www.nnr.co.uk
Full-size heritage railway with steam trains from
Sheringham to Holt via Weybourne. Scenic views of coast
and heathland. Gift shop and buffet at Sheringham
Station.
Times: Trains on most days mid Mar-end Oct, plus Santa
Specials. Sheringham Station open daily (exc. Christmas
Day).
Fee: All day hop-on hop-off Rover tickets
£8.50/£5.00/£24.50 (2+2 or 3+1)
Facilities: ⊛ ⊡ 🚐 ⇌ T(1³/₄ hrs) ⑴ 굣 ⋔

North Norfolk Railway, Sheringham

Strumpshaw (nr. Norwich)
**Strumpshaw Old Hall Steam Museum
and Farm Machinery Collection** Map ref. M7/8
Strumpshaw Old Hall, Low Road
Tel: (01603) 714535
Many steam engines, beam engines, mechanical organs,
narrow gauge railway and a working toy train for children.
There is also a cafe, gift shop, picnic area and free parking.
Times: Open 25 Mar-1 Apr, daily; 3 Apr-25 May, Wed,
Sun and Bank Hol Mon; 28-30 May open for steam rally;
31 May-2 Oct, Mon-Fri and Sun, 1100-1600.
Fee: £5.00/£2.00/£4.00.
Facilities: ⊛ ⊡ ⇌ T(1 hr) 𝑘 ⑴ 굣 ⋔

Thursford (nr. Fakenham)
Thursford Collection Map ref. H4
Thursford Green
Tel: (01328) 878477
Our 'Treasures in Store' museum houses majestic old road
engines, mechanical organs and old-fashioned fairground
rides. Live Wurlizter shows, and music from mechanical pipe
organs. Old farm buildings, transformed into a small village
with a touch of Charles Dickens' England, house the gift
shops, famous Christmas shop and restaurants .
Times: 25 Mar-25 Sept, Sun-Fri, 1200-1700.
Fee: £5.50/£3.00/£5.20.
Facilities: ⊛ Q P T(2½ hrs) ⊕ ⩕ 🖼

Wells-next-the-Sea
Wells Harbour Railway Map ref. G2
Beach Road
Tel: (01328) 738835
This 10¼ inch narrow gauge railway, of approximately
1 mile, runs adjacent to Beach Road, carrying passengers
to the beach or harbour. Late trains available.
Times: Seasonal Easter-end Oct. Times vary according to
time of year.
Fee: Single fare £1.00/70p
Facilities: T(20 mins) ⩕

Wells-next-the-Sea
Wells Walsingham Railway Map ref. G2/3
Stiffkey Road
Tel: (01328) 711630
Four miles of railway. The longest 10¼ inch railway in the
world, with a new steam locomotive 'Norfolk Hero' now in
service (the largest of its kind ever built).
Times: Open 25 Mar-31 Oct, daily, 1000-1800.
Fee: £6.50/£4.50 (return ticket).
Facilities: P 🚻 T(1¼ hrs) ⊕ ⩕

West Walton (nr. Wisbech)
Fenland and West Norfolk Aviation Museum Map ref. A7
Bambers Garden Centre, Old Lynn Road
Tel: (01945) 463996 Web: www.fawnaps.co.uk
Vampire T11 and Lightning aircraft. Uniforms, aero engines,
aircraft components, artefacts, memorabilia, radio equipment,
souvenirs, models and a Jumbo Jet cockpit.
Times: Open 6 Mar-31 Oct, Sat, Sun and Bank Hol Mon,
0930-1700.
Fee: £1.50/75p.
Facilities: P 🚻 T(1½ hrs) 𝒳 ⩕ 🖼

Weybourne (nr. Holt)
Muckleburgh Collection Map ref. J2
Weybourne Old Military Camp
Tel: (01263) 588210 Web: www.muckleburgh.co.uk
Collection of over 136 military vehicles and heavy equipment
used by the allied armies during and since World War II,
including fighting tanks, armoured cars and artillery.
Times: Open 13-20 Feb, daily, 1000-1700. Then Suns until
20 Mar, 1000-1700. 21 Mar-6 Nov daily, 1000-1700.
Fee: £5.50/£3.00/£4.50/£13.50.
Facilities: ⊛ Q P 🚻 T(2½ hrs) ⊕ ⩕ ⩕ 🖼

Wells Walsingham Railway, Wells-next-the-Sea

Ipswich Transport Museum

Wroxham
Barton House Railway Map ref. M6
Hartwell Road, The Avenue
Tel: (01603) 782470
A 3¹/₂ gauge miniature steam passenger railway, and a 7¹/₄ gauge steam and battery-electric railway. Full-size M and GN accessories including signals and signal boxes.
Times: Open 28 Mar, 17 Apr, 15 May, 19 Jun, 17 Jul, 21 Aug, 18 Sept, 16 Oct, 1430-1730.
Fee: £1.50/75p.
Facilities: 🅿 🚾 ⇌ T(2 hrs) ⑪ ⊁

See Also:
Charles Burrell Museum, Thetford, page 94
Collectors World of Eric St John-Foti, Downham Market, page 86
Iceni Village and Museums, Cockley Cley, nr Swaffham, page 85
Museum of the Broads, Stalham, page 93
Norfolk Shire Horse Centre, West Runton, nr Sheringham, page 136

SUFFOLK

Barnham (nr. Thetford)
East England Tank Museum Map ref. E4
Tel: (01842) 890010 Web: www.tankmuseum.com
Exhibits of over 70 military vehicles, weapons, uniforms and associated equipment over the last 100 years. Outside and inside exhibits. Military vehicle displays and rides.
Times: Open 2 Apr-mid Oct, Fri, Sat and Bank Hols, 1100-1700; Sun 1100-1600. Mon-Thurs, by appointment only.
Fee: £3.50/£2.50/£2.50/£10.00.
Facilities: 🅿 T(1¹/₂ hrs) ⑪ ⊓

Carlton Colville (nr. Lowestoft)
East Anglia Transport Museum Map ref. O2
Chapel Road
Tel: (01502) 518459 Web: www.eatm.org.uk
A working museum with one of the widest ranges of street transport vehicles on display and in action. Developing street scene, vehicle rides and a 2ft gauge railway.
Times: Open 25 and 26 Mar; 27 Mar-3 Jun, Wed, Sun and Bank Hols; 4 Jun-18 Jul, Wed, Sat and Sun; 19 Jul-2 Sept, Tues-Sun and Bank Hols; 3 Sept-2 Oct, Wed, Sat and Sun, 1400-1700 (Sun and Bank Hols open at 1100).
Fee: £5.00/£3.50/£3.50 (includes rides).
Facilities: ⊛ 🅿 T(2 hrs) ⑪ ⊓ ⊁

Cotton (nr. Stowmarket)
Mechanical Music Museum and Bygones Trust
Map ref. H6
Blacksmith Road
Tel: (01449) 613876 Web: www.davidivory.co.uk
The Mechanical Music Museum and Bygones at Blacksmith Road, Cotton, nr. Stowmarket, houses a unique collection of music boxes, polyphons, street pianos, barrel organs, fair organs, Wurlitzer Theatre Organ and many unusual items all played.
Times: Open Jun-Sept, Sun, 1430-1730. Fair Organ Enthusiasts Day 2 Oct, 1000-1700. Weekday group tours by arrangement.
Fee: £4.00/£1.00.
Facilities: 🅿 T(1¹/₂ hrs) ⊁ ⊓ ▨

Flixton (nr. Bungay)
Norfolk and Suffolk Aviation Museum Map ref. L3
East Anglia's Aviation Heritage Centre, The Street
Tel: (01986) 896644 Web: www.aviationmuseum.net
A museum with forty aircraft on display, together with a
large indoor display of smaller items connected with the
history of aviation.
Times: Open 15 Jan-30 Mar, Tues, Wed and Sun, 1000-
1600. 1 Apr-30 Oct, Sun-Thurs, 1000-1700. 2 Nov-15 Dec,
Tues, Wed and Sun, 1000-1600.
Fee: Free. Donations appreciated.
Facilities: Q P T(2½ hrs) ⚲ ⵏ (on leads) 🗟

Ipswich
Ipswich Transport Museum Map ref. J10
Old Trolleybus Depot, Cobham Road
Tel: (01473) 715666
Web: www.ipswichtransportmuseum.co.uk
Over 100 historic vehicles, housed in a former trolleybus
depot. All have been built or used in the area. Also history
and products of local engineering companies.
Times: Open 20 Mar-27 Nov, Sun and Bank Hol Mon,
1100-1600. School hols, Mon-Fri, 1300-1600.
Fee: £3.00/£2.00/£2.50/£8.50.
Facilities: P 🚽 T(1 hr) ⵏ🐾 🗟

Leiston
Long Shop Museum Map ref. N7
Main Street
Tel: (01728) 832189
Award-winning museum, including Grade II* Listed Long
Shop, the first production line for portable steam engines.
Discover Leiston's unique history, and the home of the
Garrett collection.
Times: Open 1 Apr-31 Oct, Mon-Sat, 1000-1700; Sun,
1100-1700. Open other times by appointment.
Fee: £3.50/£1.00/£3.00.
Facilities: P T(1½ hrs) ⵏ 🗟

Lowestoft
Mincarlo Trawler Map ref. P2
Yacht Basin, Lowestoft Harbour
Tel: (01502) 565234
The Mincarlo is a mid-water side-fishing trawler launched
in 1962. Contains museum with photographs and displays
on the local fishing industries.
Times: Open 25 Mar-end Aug, daily 1030-1530. Moves to
Great Yarmouth 1-30 Sept, please telephone TIC to check
days open.
Fee: Free.
Facilities: 🚽 ⵏ T(45 mins)

Wetheringsett (nr. Stowmarket)
Mid-Suffolk Light Railway Museum Map ref. I6
Brockford Station
Tel: (01449) 766899 Web: www.mslr.org.uk
A re-created Mid-Suffolk light railway station. Exhibits
relating to the Mid-Suffolk Light Railway, and the
restoration of the station and trackwork on part of the
original route.
Times: Open Easter to end Sept, Sun and Bank Hols, 1100-
1700. 1-31 Aug, Wed, 1400-1700.
Fee: £2.50/£1.00/£2.50/£6.00. Special events
£5.00/£2.50/£4.50/£12.50.
Facilities: P T(2 hrs) 🗟 ⵏ🐾 🗟

East Anglia Transport Museum, Carlton Colville

Gardens

BEDFORDSHIRE

Old Warden (nr. Biggleswade)
The Swiss Garden Map ref. F6
Old Warden Park
Tel: (01767) 627666 Web: www.bedfordshire.gov.uk
19th C. landscape garden created in the picturesque/Swiss manner. A garden of continued vistas leading the eye to several significant architectural features. Tiny folly buildings and ornamental ponds and bridges.
Times: Open 4 Jan-31 Mar, daily, 1000-1600; 1 Apr-31 Oct, daily, 1000-1700; 1 Nov-24 Dec, daily, 1000-1600.
Fee: £3.00/£2.00/£2.00/£8.00(2004 prices).
Facilities: ☜ 🅿 T(1½ hrs) ⚔ ⑪ 🎏 ▣

Shefford
Hoo Hill Maze Map ref. E7
Hitchin Road
Tel: (01462) 813475
Hedge maze, 2m high and approx 30m by 30m square. Set in a small apple, pear and plum orchard of about 3 acres. Picnic areas and marquee/summer house for shelter.
Times: Open all year, Sat and Sun, 1000-1800. Also daily in school hols and by appointment.
Fee: £3.00/£3.00 (under 5's £2.00).
Facilities: 🅿 T(1-2 hrs) 🎏

Silsoe
Wrest Park Gardens Map ref. E8
Tel: (01525) 860152 Web: www.english-heritage.org.uk
One hundred and fifty years of English gardens laid out in the early 18th C. including painted pavilion, Chinese bridge, lakes, classical temple and orangery and bath house.
Times: Open 24 Mar-30 Sept, Sat and Sun, 1000-1800; Bank Hol 1000-1700; 1-31 Oct, Sat and Sun 1000-1700. Closed 24-26 Dec, 1 Jan.
Fee: £4.30/£3.20/£2.20
Facilities: ☜ Q 🅿 T(1 hr) ⚔ (audio tours) ⑪ 🎏 🐕 (on leads) EH

See Also:
RSPB Lodge Nature Reserve, Sandy, page 181
Stockwood Craft Museum and Gardens, Luton, page 64
Woburn Abbey, page 37.

CAMBRIDGESHIRE

Cambridge
Cambridge University Botanic Garden Map ref. H12
Bateman Street
Tel: (01223) 336265 Web: www.botanic.cam.ac.uk
Forty-acre oasis of beautiful gardens and glasshouses, with some 80,000 plant species. Rock, winter and dry gardens, tropical glasshouse and lake. Unique systematic beds.
Times: Open all year. Feb, Mar, and Oct, daily 1000-1700. Apr-Sept, daily, 1000-1800. Jan, Nov and Dec, daily 1000-1600. Glasshouses close ½ hour before Garden closing. Closed 25 Dec-1 Jan.
Fee: £3.00/£2.40 children 0-16 free (must be accompanied by an adult).
Facilities: 🚻 ⇌ T(3½ hrs) ⑪ (daily in summer, weekends only in winter) 🎏

Castle Park

an oasis in the
heart of colchester

A visit to Colchester is not complete without seeing this award-winning classic Victorian park! Once the site of major historical events which took place in and around the Castle 2000 years ago, Castle Park is now a delight for the senses all year round.

- 23 gently sloping acres
- Venue for fairs, open-air concerts & displays
- Formal flower beds and gardens
- Sensory Garden
- Children's playground
- Hollytrees Museum
- Pitch & Putt in the summertime
- Boating lake
- River walks
- Café
- Victorian bandstand
- Oldest Roman wall in Britain
- And of course, the award winning Castle Museum

COLCHESTER

colchester
EXPLOREXPERIENCENJOY

For further information about Colchester
and events in Castle Park call the
Colchester Visitor Information Centre on 01206 282920,
or drop in at 1 Queen Street, Colchester, Essex, CO1 2PG,
or click onto www.colchesterwhatson.co.uk

VISITOR
ATTRACTION

GREEN
FLAG
PARK

Shepreth
Crossing House Map ref. G13
78 Meldreth Road
Tel: (01763) 261071
The crossing keeper's cottage and a small plantsman's garden with a very wide variety of plants.
Times: Open all year, daily, dawn-dusk.
Fee: Free.
Facilities: T(1 hr)

Shepreth
Docwra's Manor Garden Map ref. G13
2 Meldreth Road
Tel: (01763) 261473
Walled gardens around an 18th C. red-brick house, approached by 18th C. wrought iron gates. There are barns, a 20th C. folly and unusual plants.
Times: Open all year, Wed and Fri, 1000-1600. 6 Mar; 3 Apr; 1 May; 5 Jun; 3 Jul; 7 Aug; 4 Sept; 2 Oct, Sun 1400-1600.
Fee: £3.00/free/£3.00.
Facilities: T(1½ hrs)

Walpole St. Peter (nr. Wisbech)
Walpole Water Gardens Map ref. H3
Chalk Road
Tel: 07718 745935
Dominated by water and rocks, with a sub-tropical atmosphere, 3/4 acres. Eucalyptus, rockeries and palms. Koi carp, black swans, ducks and peacocks.
Times: Open all year, daily, 1000-1900, May-Aug closes 2100.
Fee: Free.
Facilities: T(30 mins)

Elton Hall

The Orangery at Peckover House

Wilburton (nr. Ely)
Herb Garden Map ref. H9
Nigel House, 67 High Street
Tel: (01353) 740824
A herb garden laid out in collections: culinary, aromatic, medical, biblical, Shakespearean, dye bed and astrological.
Times: Open 1 May-30 Jun, daily, by apponitment only.
Fee: Free.
Facilities: T(1 hr)

See Also:
Anglesey Abbey, Gardens and Lode Mill, Lode, nr Cambridge, page 39
Elgood's Brewery and Garden, Wisbech, page 160
Elton Hall, nr Peterborough, page 38
The Manor, Hemingford Grey, nr St Ives, page 38
Peckover House and Gardens, Wisbech, page 39
The Prebendal Manor Medieval Centre, Nassington, nr Peterborough, page 39
Wimpole Hall and Home Farm, Arrington nr Royston, page 38.

ESSEX

Abridge (nr. Romford)
BBC Essex Garden Map ref. B/C9
Ongar Road
Tel: (01708) 688581 Web: www.gardeningwithken.com
Garden with lawn, borders and small vegetable area. Linked to Ken's programme 'Down to Earth' on Sats. Also farmyard pets, teashop, superb plants and clematis on sale.
Times: Open all year, daily, 0900-1730. Closed 24 Dec-2 Jan
Fee: Free.
Facilities: T(1 hr)

Ardleigh (nr. Colchester)

Green Island Garden Map ref. L4
Green Island, Park Road
Tel: (01206) 230455 Web: www.greenislandsgardens.co.uk
Beautiful gardens in 19 acres of woodland, with a huge
variety of unusual plants. Lots of interest all year. New
sculpture trail.
Times: Open 1Mar-31 Oct, Wed, Thurs also 27 Mar; 3,
10, 17 Apr; 1, 8, 15, and 22 May; 5, 12, 19 Jun; 3, 10, 17,
24 Jul; 7, 14, 21 Aug, 4, 11, 18 Sept; 2 Oct, 1300-1700.
Fee: £2.50/50p.
Facilities: 🅿 �" T(1½ hrs) ⑪ 🏕 🖫

Bocking

Roundwood Garden Centre Map ref. G4
Bocking Church Street
Tel: (01376) 551728
Drought and Millennium gardens, nature trail with ponds
and wildflower meadow. Aviary.
Times: Open all year, Mon-Fri, 0915-1700. Closed 25-28
Mar and 23 Dec-3 Jan.
Fee: Free.
Facilities: 🅿 T(1 hr) 🏃⑪ 🏕 🐕 🖫

Coggeshall

Marks Hall Garden and Arboretum Map ref. H/I4
Tel: (01376) 563796 Web: www.markshall.org.uk
Newly re-opened walled garden, designed for summer.
Winter walks and snowdrops. Wildlife walks through
woodland. Visitor centre with teashop and gift shop.
Times: Open 1 Jan-27 Mar, Fri-Sun, 1030-dusk. 1 Apr-30
Oct, Tues-Sun and Bank Hol Mon, 1030-1700. 5 Nov-31
Dec, Sat and Sun, 1030-dusk. Closed 25, 26 Dec.
Fee: £4.00 per car.
Facilities: ❀ 🅿 T(2½ hrs) 🏃⑪ 🏕 🐕 🖫

Dedham

Gnome Magic Map ref. L3
New Dawn, Old Ipswich Road (off A12)
Tel: (01206) 231390 Web: www.gnomemagic.co.uk
An unusual treat, with a delightful garden and an amazing
wood (5 acres) where gnomes and their friends live. Come
and meet them.
Times: Open 1 Apr-30 Sept, daily, 1000-1730 (last entry at
1630).
Fee: £3.50/£2.00/£3.00.
Facilities: ❀ 🅿 T(2 hrs) ⑪ 🏕

Elmstead Market
The Beth Chatto Gardens Map ref. L4
Tel: (01206) 822007 Web:
www.bethchatto.co.uk
Drought tolerant plants furnish the gravel
garden throughout the year, the dappled wood
garden is filled with shade lovers, while the
water garden fills the spring fed hollow.
Times: Open 4 Jan-28 Feb, Mon-Fri, 0900-1600.
1 Mar-31 Oct, Mon-Sat, 0900-1700. 1 Nov-22
Dec, Mon-Fri, 0900-1600. Closed 27 Mar and
23 Dec-3 Jan.
Fee: £4.00/free.
Facilities: Q P ⛽ T(3 hrs) ⅂ 🖫

Cressing Temple Barns, Cressing

Feering (nr. Coggeshall)
Feeringbury Manor Map ref. I5
Tel: (01376) 561946
A well designed 10 acre garden, intensively planted
with many rare and interesting plants for both dry and
damp areas.
Times: Open 31 Mar-29 Jul and 1-30 Sept, Thurs and Fri,
0800-1600.
Fee: £2.50/free.
Facilities: P T(1 hr) ⅂ 🐴

Harlow
The Gibberd Garden Map ref. B7
Marsh Lane, Gilden Way
Tel: (01279) 442112 Web: www.thegibberdgarden.co.uk
Important 20th C. garden designed by Sir Frederick
Gibberd, master planner for Harlow New Town, with some
fifty sculptures.
Times: Open 25 Mar-25 Sept, Wed, Sat, Sun and Bank Hol
Mon, 1400-1800.
Fee: £4.00/free/£2.50.
Facilities: P T(2 hrs) ① 🐴 (on leads)

Little Easton (nr. Great Dunmow)
The Gardens of Easton Lodge Map ref. D/E4
Warwick House, Easton Lodge
Tel: (01371) 876979 Web: www.eastonlodge.co.uk
23 acres of beautiful historic gardens, famous for their
peaceful atmosphere. Featuring the splendid formal
gardens created by leading Edwardian designer Harold
Peto. Former home of the Countess of Warwick.
Times: Open 25 Mar-30 Oct, Fri-Sun, 1200-1800.
Fee: £3.80/£1.50/£3.50.
Facilities: ⊗ P T(2 hrs) ① ⅂ 🐴 (on leads) 🖫

Little Easton (nr. Great Dunmow)
Little Easton Manor and Barn Theatre Map ref. D/E4
Park Road
Tel: (01371) 872857
Little Easton Manor has gardens, lakes and fountains. Also
The Barn Theatre, angling, a caravan and rally site and
refreshments.
Times: Open Jun-Sept, daily, 1400-1700 by
appointment only.
Fee: £2.50/free/£2.00.
Facilities: P T(2 hrs) ① ⅂ 🐴 🖫

Messing (nr. Tiptree)
Red House Visitor Centre Map ref. I5
School Road
Tel: (01621) 815219
Sensory and artists gardens, pond, children's play area and
junior farm. Coffee shop, plant and craft sales.
Times: Gardens open all year, daily, 0930-1600. Farm and
shop open Mon-Fri, 0930-1600.
Fee: Free.
Facilities: P T(2 hrs) ① ⅂ 🐴 (on leads)

RHS Garden, Hyde Hall, Rettendon

Norpar Flowers Map ref. D9
Navestock Hall
Tel: (01277) 374968 Web: www.norpar.co.uk
Dried flowers grown and dried on the premises.
Demonstrations, country walk, 10th C. church and antique
farm implement museum.
Times: Open all year, Mon-Sat 1000-1700, Sun 1100-
1700, closed some Mons, please telephone to check.
Fee: Free.
Facilities: 🅿 T(2 hrs) 🛆 🛉

Blake Hall Gardens and Museum Map ref. D7
Bobbingworth
Tel: (01277) 362502 Web: www.blakehall.co.uk
Twenty five acres of beautiful gardens, with many species of
trees, peat and herbaceous borders, old ice house, rose
garden and tropical house. Also World War II museum.
Times: Open 25 Mar-28 Sept, Good Fri and Sat-Wed,
1100-1700.
Fee: £3.00/£1.50/£3.00/£8.00.
Facilities: 🅿 🖼 T(1½ hrs) 🛆 🛉

RHS Garden Hyde Hall Map ref. G9
Buckhatch Lane
Tel: (01245) 400256 Web: www.rhs.org.uk
28 acre garden with all year round interest, including dry
garden, roses, flowering shrubs, perennial borders and
alpines. National Collection of Viburnum. New garden for
wildlife.
Times: Open Jan-Sept, daily, 1000-1800. Oct-Dec, daily,
1000-dusk. Last entry 1 hr before closing. Closed 25 Dec.
Fee: £4.50/£1.00
Facilities: 🛆 🅿 T(3 hrs) 🛆 🛆

For even more
information visit
our website at
www.visiteastofengland.com

Westlands Garden Map ref. G9
Chalk Street
Tel: (01245) 400902 Web: www.westlandnursery.co.uk
A 0.75 acre enthusiast's garden, with many features of
interest, in attractive rural setting. Adjacent hardy plant
nursery and tearoom.
Times: Open 1 May-30 Sept, Wed-Sun, 1000-1700.
Fee: £2.00.
Facilities: 🅿 T(1 hrs) 🛆

Bridge End Gardens Map ref. C/D2
Tel: (01799) 510445
Victorian garden featuring fine trees, garden ornaments,
a rose garden, Dutch garden, pavilions and a hedge maze.
Times: Open all year, daily, 0800-dusk. Contact Tourist
Information Centre for opening times of maze.
Fee: Free.
Facilities: 🛆 T(1½ hrs)

The Thaxted Garden for Butterflies Map ref. E3
Aldboro Lodge, Park Street
Tel: (01371) 830780
A 1-acre retirement garden especially planted and
developed to be attractive to butterflies and moths.
Exhibition of photographs of the butterflies that have
visited the garden.
Times: Open 1 May-1 Oct, daily, 0900-1700.
Fee: Free.
Facilities: 🅿 🖼 T(30 mins)

See Also:
Audley End House and Park, Saffron Walden, page 40
Cressing Temple Barns, Cressing, nr Braintree,page 53
Firstsite@ The Minories Art Gallery, Colchester, page 72, 73
Hylands House, Widford, nr Chelmsford, page 40
Ingatestone Hall, Ingatestone, page 39
Layer Marney Tower, nr Colchester, page 40
Leez Priory, Hartford End, nr Braintree, page 39
Museum of Harlow, page 75
Paycockes, Coggeshall, page 39
Sir Alfred Munnings Art Museum, Dedham, page 74

HERTFORDSHIRE

Benington (nr. Stevenage)
Benington Lordship Gardens Map ref. H10
Tel: (01438) 869228 Web: www.beningtonlordship.co.uk
Edwardian garden and historic site. Ornamental, vegetable,
rose/water garden. Herbaceous borders, lakes and
contemporary sculptures.
Times: Open 5-20 Feb, daily, 1200-1600; 25 Jun-3 Jul,
daily, 1400-1700; also Bank Hol Suns 1400-1700 and Bank
Hol Mons 1200-1700. By appointment at other times.
Fee: £3.50/free.
Facilities: 🅿 🚌 T(1 hr) 🏃 🎋

Enfield
Capel Manor Gardens Map ref. I14
Bullsmoor Lane
Tel: (0208) 366 4442 Web: www.capel.ac.uk
Thirty acres of richly planted themed gardens including
Italianate maze, historical gardens and Japanese garden.
Gardening Which? Magazine demonstration/theme
gardens. National Gardening Centre with specially designed
gardens.
Times: Open all year, Jan-4 Mar, Mon-Fri, 1000-1800; 5
Mar-31 Oct, daily, 1000-1800; 1 Nov-Dec, Mon-Fri, 1000-
1800. Last admission at 1630.
Fee: £5.00/£2.00/£4.00/£12.00.
Facilities: 🅿 T(2-3 hrs) 🍴 🎋 🛍 🖼

Enfield
Myddelton House Gardens Map ref. I14
Bulls Cross
Tel: (01992) 702200 Web: www.leevalleypark.com
A garden for all seasons, created by famous plantsman,
expert botanist and author E.A. Bowles. Unusual varieties
and rarities of plants. Home to the National Collection
of award-winning Bearded Iris.
Times: Open Apr-Sept, Mon-Fri, 1000-1630. Oct-Mar,
Mon-Fri, 1000-1500. Suns and Bank Hol Mons from
27 Mar-Oct, 1200-1600.
Fee: £2.30/£1.70/£1.70.
Facilities: 🅰 🅿 🚌 ♨ T(1½ hrs) 🏃 🎋

Hitchin
St. Pauls Walden Bury Garden Map ref. F10
St. Pauls Walden Bury
Tel: (01438) 871218
Formal woodland garden laid out in about 1730, and
covering 60 acres with temples, statues, lake, ponds and
flower gardens. The childhood home of the late Queen
Mother.
Times: Open 17 Apr and 8 May, Sun, 1400-1900. Also
5 Jun 1200-1530 (followed by concert at 1600).
Fee: Open days £3.50/50p/£3.50.
Facilities: 🅿 T(1-2 hrs) 🍴 🎋 🎋 🖼

St. Albans
The Gardens of the Rose Map ref. E13
Chiswell Green
Tel: (01727) 850461 Web: www.rnrs.org
The Royal National Rose Society's Garden, including the
international trials of new roses. New garden being
constructed during 2005.
Times: Part of garden may open from June, please contact
for details.
Fee: Please contact for details of admission prices.
Facilities: 🅰 🅿 T(1-3 hrs) 🎋 🎋

See Also:

NORFOLK

Attleborough

Peter Beales Roses Map ref. I9
London Road
Tel: (01953) 454707 Web: www.classicroses.co.uk
2¹/2 acres of beautiful rose gardens set in rural
surroundings. Sweet Briar Bistro and shop.
Times: Nursery: Mon-Sat, 0900-1700, Sun and Bank Hol,
1000-1600. Bistro: Mon-Sat, 0930-1630, Sun and Bank
Hol, 1030-1530, Fri and Sat 1900-2100 (pre-book). Shop:
Mon-Sat, 0900-1700, Sun and Bank Hol, 1000-1600.
Fee: Free.
Facilities: ⊛ 🅿 T(1-2 hrs) 🏃 ⊛ ⩋ 🐾 (on leads) 🈴

Bayfield (nr. Holt)

Natural Surroundings Map ref. I3
Bayfield Estate
Tel: (01263) 711091 Web:
www.naturalsurroundings.org.uk
8 acres of demonstration gardens, orchid meadow and
woodland walk. Shop, sales area and light refreshments.
Red squirrels and family events all summer.
Times: Open 12 Feb-13 Mar, Thurs-Sun, 1000-1600, 15
Mar-2 Oct, Tues-Sun, 1000-1700, 3-31 Oct,Thurs-Sun,
1000-1600, 1-30 Nov, Fri-Sat, 1000-1600, 1-17 Dec, Sun,
1000-1600. Closed 18 Dec-Feb (half-term).
Fee: £2.50/£2.00/£2.00/£8.50(family).
Facilities: 🅿 T(1¹/2 hrs) ⊛ ⩋ 🐾(on leads).

Beeston Regis (nr. Sheringham)

Priory Maze and Gardens Map ref. K2
Cromer Road
Tel: (01263) 822986 Web: www.priorymazegardens.com
Norfolk's only traditional hedge maze set in 10 acres of
tranquil and natural woodland, meadow and stream
gardens - only 600m from the sea. Plant centre.
Times: Open 25 Mar-31 Oct, daily 1000-1700 (1730 in
summer). Also May-Aug late night on Thurs closes 2000.
Closed 26 Dec.
Fee: £4.00/£2.00/£3.50.
Facilities: ⊛ Q 🅿 ⛺ ⩇ ⩫ T(2 hrs) ⊛ 🈴

East Ruston (nr. Stalham)

East Ruston Old Vicarage Garden Map ref. M4
Tel: (01692) 650432
Web: www.e-ruston-oldvicaragegardens.co.uk
A 20-acre exotic garden separated into sections including
the Tropical Borders, Mediterranean Garden, Sunken
Garden, Autumn Borders, Kitchen Garden and Wildflower
Meadows.
Times: Open 25 Mar-29 Oct, Wed, Fri-Sun and Bank Hols,
1400-1730.
Fee: £4.00/£1.00.
Facilities: ⊛ 🅿 T(2 hrs) ⊛ ⩋

Erpingham (nr. Aylsham)

Alby Crafts Gardens Map ref. K4
Cromer Road
Tel: (01263) 761226 Web: www.albycrafts.co.uk
4¹/2 acres of island beds and borders, separated by wide
expanses of grass. Specimen trees and wide variety of
unusual plants and shrubs. Four ponds and bridge.
Times: Open Mar-Oct, Tues-Sun and Bank Hol Mon,
1000-1700.
Fee: £2.50/free.
Facilities: ⊛ Q 🅿 T(1¹/2 hrs) ⊛

Gooderstone (nr. Swaffham)

Gooderstone Water Gardens Map ref. E8
The Street
Tel: (01603) 712913
Created in 1970 from a wet meadow, the gardens cover
6¹/2 acres, with trout stream, four ponds, waterways,
mature trees, colourful plants, nature trail and thirteen
bridges
Times: Open all year, daily. Please contact for further
details.
Fee: £4.00/£1.00/£3.00.
Facilities: 🅿 T(1¹/2 hrs) ⊛ ⩋ 🐾 (on leads)

Oxburgh Hall Gardens

Grimston (nr. King's Lynn)

Congham Hall Herb Garden Map ref. D5

Lynn Road

Tel: (01485) 600250 Web: www.conghamhallhotel.co.uk

Garden with over 650 varieties of herbs in formal beds, with wild flowers and a potager garden. Over 250 varieties of herbs for sale in pots.

Times: Open 27 Mar-end Sept, Sun-Fri, 1400-1600.

Fee: Free.

Facilities: 🅿 🚌 T(30 mins) ✗ ⬤

Heacham (nr. Hunstanton)

Norfolk Lavender Limited Map ref. D3

Caley Mill

Tel: (01485) 570384 Web: www.norfolk-lavender.co.uk

Home of the National Collection of Lavenders. See many varieties of lavender and a large miscellany of herbs. Hear about the harvest, and the ancient process of lavender distillation.

Times: Open 2 Jan-31 Mar, daily, 1000-1600. 1 Apr-31 Oct, daily, 1000-1700. 1 Nov-31 Dec, daily, 1000-1600. Closed 25, 26 Dec and 1 Jan.

Fee: Free.

Facilities: ⬤ Q 🅿 T(4 hrs) ✗ ⬤ ➤ (on leads) ▣

Mannington (nr. Saxthorpe Corpusty)

Mannington Gardens and Countryside Map ref. J4

Mannington Hall

Tel: (01263) 584175 Web: www.manningtongardens.co.uk

Gardens with a lake, moat, woodland and an outstanding rose collection. There is also a Saxon church with Victorian follies and countryside walks and trails with guide booklets.

Times: Walks open all year, daily, 0900-dusk. Gardens open 1 May-25 Sept, Sun, 1200-1700. 1 Jun-31 Aug, Wed-Fri, 1100-1700.

Fee: £4.00/free/£3.00 Car park £2.00.

Facilities: ⬤ 🅿 T(2 hrs) ✗ ⬤ ⚲ ▣

Norwich

The Plantation Garden Map ref. K/L7

4 Earlham Road

Tel: (01603) 621868 Web: www.plantationgarden.co.uk

A rare surviving example of a private Victorian town garden, created between 1856-1897 in a former medieval chalk quarry and undergoing restoration by volunteers.

Times: Open all year, daily, 0900-1800 (or dusk in summer).

Fee: £2.00/free.

Facilities: 🚌 ⚖ T(2 hrs) ⚲ ▣

Raveningham (nr. Loddon)

Raveningham Gardens Map ref. N9

The Stables

Tel: (01508) 548152 Web: www.raveningham.com

Extensive gardens surrounding an elegant Georgian house, provide the setting for many rare, variegated and unusual plants and shrubs with sculptures, parkland and a church.

Times: Open 27, 28 Mar; 1, 2, 29, 30 May; 28, 29 Aug, 1400-1700. Also 2 days in Jun, please contact for details.

Fee: £2.50/free/£2.00.

Facilities: 🅿 T(1½ hrs) ⬤ ➤ (on leads)

South Walsham

Fairhaven Woodland and Water Garden Map ref. M6/7
School Road
Tel: (01603) 270449
Web: www.norfolkbroads.com/fairhaven
Delightful natural woodland and water garden, with private
broad and a 950 year old oak tree. Spring flowers,
candelabra primulas, azaleas and rhododendrons.
Times: Open all year, daily, 1000-1700. May-Aug, Wed and
Thurs, 1000-2100. Closed 25 Dec.
Fee: £4.00/£1.50/£3.50.
Facilities: ◉ 🄿 🚌 T(3 hrs) 🏃 ⑪ 🚻 🐾 (on leads) ♿

West Acre (nr. Swaffham)

West Acre Gardens Map ref. E6
Tel: (01760) 755562
D-shaped walled garden. Extensive display beds with year-
round interest and beauty. Huge range of unusual plants
for sale
Times: Open 1 Feb-30 Nov, daily, 1000-1700.
Fee: Free.
Facilities: 🄿 T(2 hrs) 🐾 ♿

Wroxham

Hoveton Hall Gardens Map ref. M6
Tel: (01603) 782798
Approximately 15 acres of gardens in a woodland setting,
with a large walled herbaceous garden and a Victorian
kitchen garden. Woodland and lakeside walks.
Times: Open 25 Mar-4 Sept, Wed, Fri and Sun, also Thurs
in May and June, 1030-1700.
Fee: £4.00/£1.50/£4.00.
Facilities: ◉ 🄿 T(2 hrs) ⑪ 🚻

See Also:
Blickling Hall, Gardens and Park, nr Aylsham, page 43
Bressingham Steam Experience and Gardens,
nr Diss, page 105
Felbrigg Hall, nr Cromer, page 43
Hales Hall Barn and Gardens, Loddon, page 59
Houghton Hall, page 43
Oxburgh Hall, Oxborough, page 43
Pensthorpe Nature Reserve and Gardens, nr Fakenham,
page 191
Sandringham, nr Kings Lynn, page 44
Sheringham Park, page 192
Shirehall Museum and Abbey Gardens, Little Walsingham,
page 89

SUFFOLK

Benhall (nr. Saxmundham)

The Walled Garden Map ref. M7
Park Road
Tel: (01728) 602510 Web: www.thewalledgarden.co.uk
A nursery where almost 1,500 varieties of plants are sold
and raised. A large garden divided by Yew hedges provides
an opportunity to see many of the plants grown to
maturity.
Times: Open 1 Jan-15 Feb, Tues-Sat, 0930-dusk;
16 Feb-3 Dec, Tues-Sun and Bank Hol 0930-1700; 4-21
Dec, Tues-Sat 0930-dusk.
Fee: Free.
Facilities: 🄿 T(1 hr) ♿

Autumn Crocuses at Felbrigg Hall

Coddenham (nr. Ipswich)

Shrubland Gardens Map ref. I9

Shrubland Park

Tel: (01473) 830221 Web: www.shrublandpark.co.uk

Extensive Italianate Victorian garden laid out by Sir Charles Barry in historic parkland. Formal beds, fountains, loggia, wild garden, fine trees and a series of follies.

Times: Open 27 Mar-4 Sept, Sun and Bank Hol Mon, 1400-1700.

Fee: £3.00/£2.00/£2.00.

Facilities: ▣ T(1¹/₂ hrs) ⼌

East Bergholt

East Bergholt Place Garden Map ref. H11

Tel: (01206) 299224

The garden was laid out at the turn of the century, and covers 15 acres, with fine trees, shrubs, rhododendrons, camellias and magnolias. Specialist plant centre in walled garden.

Times: Open 1 Mar-30 Sept, daily, 1000-1700. Closed 27 Mar.

Fee: £2.50/free.

Facilities: ⊛ ▣ T(2 hr) ⼌

Halesworth

Woottens Plants Map ref. N5

Blackheath, Wenhaston

Tel: (01502) 478258 Web: www.woottensplants.co.uk

Plantmans nursery specialising in auriculas, bearded iris, hemerocallis, pelargoniums, hardy perennials and ornamental grasses. Frequently featured in the press and on television. Display garden.

Times: Open all year, daily, 0930-1700. Closed 25 Dec-2 Jan.

Fee: Free.

Facilities: ▣ T(1¹/₂ hrs) ▨

Abbey Gardens, Bury St. Edmunds

Helmingham Hall

Helmingham

Helmingham Hall Gardens Map ref. J8

Tel: (01473) 890363 Web: www.helmingham.com

A moated and walled garden, with many rare roses, and possibly the best kitchen garden in Britain. New rose garden and herb and knot garden created in the early 1980's.

Times: Open 1 May-18 Sept, Sun, 1400-1800.

Fee: £4.50/£2.50/£4.00.

Facilities: ⊛ ▣ T(2 hrs) ⼌ ⼌ ♞ (on leads) ▨

Kelsale (nr. Saxmundham)

Laurel Farm Herbs Map ref. M6

Main Road (A12)

Tel: (01728) 668223 Web: www.theherbfarm.co.uk

Well established herb garden to view. Specialist herb grower with a large range of culinary and medicinal pot grown plants. Established since 1985.

Times: 1 Jan-28 Feb, Wed, Thurs and Fri 1000-1500; 1 Mar-30 Jun, Wed-Mon, 1000-1700; 1 Jul-31 Oct, Mon-Fri 1000-1700; 1 Nov-31 Dec, Wed, Thurs and Fri 1000-1500. Also open by appointment.

Fee: Free.

Facilities: ⊛ ▣ T(1 hr) ▨

For even more information visit our website at www.visiteastofengland.com

Stanton (nr. Bury St. Edmunds)

Wyken Hall Gardens and Wyken Vineyards Map ref. F5/6
Tel: (01359) 250287 Web: www. wykenvineyards.co.uk
Seven acres of vineyard and 4 acres of garden, surrounding
an Elizabethan manor house. Woodland walks and 16th C.
barn containing a restaurant, cafe and shop.
Times: Garden open 1 Apr-30 Sept, Mon-Fri and Sun,
1400-1800. Retaurant cafe and shop open daily 1000-
1800, also Fri and Sat evenings for dinner from 1900.
Fee: £3.00/free.
Facilities: 🅿 T(2 hrs) ⓘ 🐾 (on leads) ♿

Thornham Magna (nr. Eye)

The Thornham Walled Garden Map ref. H/I5
Tel: (01379) 788700
Web: www.thornhamwalledgarden.com
Restored Victorian glasshouses in the idyllic setting of a
2 acre walled garden, with fruit trees, wide perennial
borders and a collection of East Anglian geraniums, and
fern house.
Plant sales
Times: Open 2 Jan-31 Mar, daily, 1000-1600. 1 Apr-30
Sept, daily, 0900-1700. 1 Oct-24 Dec, daily, 1000-1600.
Fee: Free.
Facilities: 🅿 🚌 T(1 hr) 🪑 🐾 (on leads) ♿

See Also:
Brandon Country Park, Brandon, page 193
Guildhall, Hadleigh, page 44
Haughley Park, nr Stowmarket, page 44
Hengrave Hall, nr Bury St Edmunds, page 45
Ickworth House, Park and Gardens, Horringer, nr Bury St
Edmunds, page 45
Kentwell Hall and Gardens, Long Melford, page 46, 47
Lavenham Guildhall of Corpus Christi, page 46
Little Hall, Lavenham, page 46
Melford Hall, Long Melford, page 47
Somerleyton Hall and Gardens, nr Lowestoft, page 45, 47

For even more
information visit
our website at
www.visiteastofengland.com

Ickworth House

Nurseries & Garden Centres

CAMBRIDGESHIRE

Cambridge

Notcutts (Ansells) Garden Centres Map ref. H11
High Street, Horningsea, Cambridge CB5 9JG
Tel: (01223) 860320   Web: www.notcutts.co.uk
Discover a world of ideas and inspiration around every corner for you, your home and your garden. From fabulous plants to gifts and treats galore, there's so much to see. Gift ideas from around the world, houseplants, books, silk flowers, 3,000 varieties of hardy plants (with a 2 year replacement guarantee), pet centre, restaurant, expert friendly advice about seasonal and bedding plants, garden furniture and barbecues. Keep an eye open for regular offers on key garden products. Notcutts open 7 days a week, free car-parking. ⊛ P ⑪ ♿

Peterborough

Notcutts Garden Centres Map ref. D5
Oundle Road, Orton Waterville, nr. Peterborough PE2 5UU
Tel: (01733) 234600   Web: www.notcutts.co.uk
Discover a world of ideas and inspiration around every corner for you, your home and your garden. From fabulous plants to gifts and treats galore, there's so much to see. Gift ideas from around the world, houseplants, books, fresh cut and silk flowers, 3,000 varieties of hardy plants (with a 2 year replacement guarantee), pet centre, restaurant, expert friendly advice about seasonal and bedding plants, garden furniture and barbecues. Keep an eye open for regular offers on key garden products. Notcutts open 7 days a week, free car-parking plus children's play area. ⊛ P ⑪ ♿

ESSEX

Ardleigh (nr. Colchester)

Notcutts Garden Centres Map ref. L4
Station Road, Ardleigh CO7 7RT
Tel: (01206) 230271   Web: www.notcutts.co.uk
Discover a world of ideas and inspiration around every corner for you, your home and your garden. From fabulous plants to gifts and treats galore, there's so much to see. Gift ideas from around the world, houseplants, books, 3,000 varieties of hardy plants (with a 2 year replacement guarantee), expert friendly advice about seasonal and bedding plants, garden furniture and barbecues. Keep an eye open for regular offers on key garden products. Notcutts open 7 days a week, free car-parking plus children's play area. ⊛ P ♿

East Bergholt

The Place For Plants Map ref. H11
East Bergholt Place Garden, East Bergholt CO7 6UP
Tel: (01206) 299224
Plant Centre and Garden for specialist and popular plants, voted 7th most recommended nursery in the Country (Gardeners' Favourite Nurseries, by Leslie Geddes-Brown). A plant centre has been set up in the Victorian Walled Garden at East Bergholt Place stocked with an excellent range of plants, shrubs, trees, climbers, herbaceous plants, ferns, grasses, bamboo's, herbs etc. and a selection of terracotta pots and garden sundries. Situated 2 miles east of the A12 on B1070, on the edge of East Bergholt. Plant Centre opens daily, 1000-1700 (closed Easter Sun).
⊛ 𝙿 ⚥ ⬛

HERTFORDSHIRE

Bragbury End (nr. Stevenage)

The Van Hage Garden Company Map ref. H10
Bragbury Lane, Bragbury End, nr. Stevenage SG2 8TJ
Tel: (01438) 811777 Fax: (01438) 815485
Café: (01438) 813172 Web: www.vanhage.co.uk
Junction 7, off A1(M) at Stevenage South, follow signs A602 to Ware. A series of listed farm buildings linked together, each retaining many original features and individuality. The emphasis is on top-quality plants and inspirational displays in the award winning Plant Nursery and Houseplant Department. The courtyard Café serves a fine selection of homemade food. Other attractions include a children's play area and Christmas Grotto. Information, Free Parking, Coaches (limited at weekends), WC, Disabled Facilities, Wheelchairs, Baby Changing.
⊛ 𝙿 T(3 hrs) ⍟ ⋔ ⬛

Chenies (nr. Rickmansworth)

The Van Hage Garden Company Map ref. C14
Chenies, nr. Rickmansworth WD3 6EN
Tel: (01494) 764545 Fax: (01494) 762216
Web: www.vanhage.co.uk
Junction 18, M25 on A404 towards Amersham. Established over 23 years ago this delightful garden centre, nestling in the Hertfordshire/Buckinghamshire countryside, offers customers a fantastic selection of both indoor and outdoor plants. Staff are always on hand to offer comprehensive information, and the centre is full of inspirational ideas for the garden. Coffee Shop, Aquatics, BBQ's, Garden Buildings, Garden Furniture, Hard Landscape, Statues, Christmas Grotto.
⊛ 𝙿 T(3 hrs) ⍟ ⋔ ⬛

Great Amwell (nr. Ware)

The Van Hage Garden Company Map ref. I12
Great Amwell, nr. Ware SG12 9RP
Tel: (01920) 870811 Fax: (01920) 871861
Web: www.vanhage.co.uk
On A1170 (Junction 25 off M25). One of Europe's top gardening retailers offering an outstanding selection of products and inspirational displays to meet all gardening requirements. Van Hage is a leisure destination for the whole family, with landscaped animal gardens, seasonal events and attractions, and a 400 seater air-conditioned restaurant with a courtyard setting - you can spend the whole day here. Don't miss our Christmas Wonderland which includes a free Santa's Grotto, the ultimate festive shopping experience. Entrance to Garden Centre FREE. Disabled, Information, Parking (Ample - FREE), Coaches, WC, Shops, Catering - Hot Meals, Snacks, Beverages, Self-service, Groups welcome. ⊛ 𝙿 T(3 hrs) ⍟ ⋔ ⬛

St. Albans

Aylett Nurseries Limited Map ref. F13
North Orbital Road, St. Albans AL2 1DH
Tel: (01727) 822255 Web: www.aylettnurseries.co.uk
Undoubtedly one of the best Garden Centres in the
southeast. Famous for our Dahlias having been awarded
Gold medals by the Royal Horticultural Society for 36
consecutive years. In spring our greenhouses are well worth
a visit to see our geraniums, fuchsias, hanging baskets and
other summer bedding plants. Our plant area is a
gardener's paradise, with all year round displays.
Houseplants are another speciality. Light lunches and
snacks are available at our Coffee House. Visit our Gift
Shop before you leave. Christmas Wonderland opens mid-
Oct. Open daily including Sun except Easter Sun,
Christmas and Boxing Day. ▣ ◗T(1-2 hrs) ⑭ ⬛

St. Albans

Notcutts Garden Centres Map ref. F13
Hatfield Road, Smallford, nr. St. Albans AL4 0HN
Tel: (01727) 853224 Web: www.notcutts.co.uk
Discover a world of ideas and inspiration around every
corner for you, your home and your garden. From fabulous
plants to gifts and treats galore, there's so much to see.
Gift ideas from around the world, houseplants, books,
fresh cut and silk flowers, 3,000 varieties of hardy plants
(with a 2 year replacement guarantee), pet centre,
restaurant, expert friendly advice about seasonal and
bedding plants, garden furniture and barbecues. Keep an
eye open for regular offers on key garden products.
Notcutts open 7 days a week, free car-parking. ⑳

NORFOLK

Attleborough

Peter Beales Roses Map ref. I9
London Road, Attleborough NR17 1AY
Tel: (01953) 454707 Fax: (01953) 456845
Email: Sales@classicroses.co.uk
Web: www.classicroses.co.uk
A large and world famous collection of roses, featuring over
1100 rare, unusual and beautiful varieties of which 250 are
unique. The National Collection of Rosa Species is held
here. Browse through 2¹/2 acres of gardens. Container roses
available in the summer months, or order for winter
delivery. Experts are always on hand for advice or help in
the selection of new varieties. Open Mon-Fri, 0900-1700;
Sat, 0900-1700; Sun and Bank Hols, 1000-1600.
Catalogue free on request. New Sweet Briar Shop and
Bistro open. ⑳ ▣ T(1-2 hrs) ⫍ ⑭ ⤶ ✦ (on leads) ⬛

Hatfield House Garden

Fakenham

Bressingham (nr. Diss)

Blooms of Bressingham Map ref. J11
Bressingham, nr. Diss IP22 2AB
Tel: (01379) 688585
Three miles west of Diss on A1066. Designed to excite and inspire 21st century gardeners, this unique two acre Plant Centre, adjacent to world famous Bressingham Steam Experience and Gardens (featuring the "Dad's Army Exhibition"), gives bigger, better choice for creative gardeners. The famous Blooms range of quality plants, and an increased product range incorporates a new "life-style" approach to gardening. Add the innovative "Into-Food" Café, all set in a striking structure, and it's a must for a great day out. Open: Daily, 0900-1800, Mar-Oct; 0900-1700, Nov-Feb (except Christmas Day/Boxing Day). Plant Centre Sun Trading Hours are:- 1100-1700. See also entry for Bressingham Steam Experience and Gardens under Machinery & Transport on page (105) and Into-Food Café under Afternoon Teas on page (159). 🅿 🚗 🎪 🎋 🕎 🛍

Fakenham Garden Centre Map ref. G4
Mill Road, Hempton, Fakenham NR21 7LH
Tel: (01328) 863380
Web: www.fakenhamgardencentre.co.uk
Fakenham Garden Centre has so much to offer all under one roof. Our wide selection of indoor and outdoor plants from all over the world will be sure to inspire you. For that special occasion we have a selection of gifts, books and clothing. To entertain the children we have a pet and aquatic centre. Our Coffee Shop offers a tantalising selection of hot and cold food. Our trained staff are always at hand for expert advice. Free car parking, disabled facilities and toilets with baby changing facilities. We are open 7 days a week, Mon-Sat 0900-1730; Sun 1000-1600.
🅫 🅿 🍴 🎋 🛍

Blickling Hall, Garden and Park

Gressenhall (Nr. Dereham)

Norfolk Herbs Map ref. H6
Blackberry Farm, Dillington, nr. Gressenhall,
Dereham NR19 2QD
Tel: (01362) 860812
Web: www.norfolkherbs.co.uk.
(Approx. 1 mile north of Dereham on the B1110, now signed as the B1146, take the first left to Dillington and we are approx. 1¹/2 miles on right). Norfolk's specialist Herb Farm, in a beautiful wooded valley renowned for its wildlife. Visitors may browse through a vast array of aromatic, culinary and medicinal herb plants, and learn all about growing and using herbs. Open Apr-Jul, daily; Aug, Tue-Sun, 0900-1800. For group visits or visiting Sept to March, please telephone first.
🅫 🅿 T(30 mins) 🎋 🎋 🛍

King's Lynn
African Violet Centre Map ref. B6
Terrington St. Clement, nr. King's Lynn PE34 4PL
Tel: (01553) 828374 Web: www.africanvioletcentre.ltd.uk
The African Violet and Garden Centre offers a wide variety of plants for any enthusiast. Known for our African Violets we boast the best in Britain. A winner of many Chelsea Gold Medals, we place ourselves as the perfect venue, whatever the weather. Our centre enables visitors to share in the secrets and discover the wonderful world of African Violets. Spacious Garden and Gift Shop, Café serving light lunches, children's play area. Ample parking, coach parties welcome. Talks/demonstrations by appointment. Situated by the A17, five miles from King's Lynn. FREE ADMISSION! Open daily: 0900-1700; Sun 1000-1700. Closed Christmas/New Years Day only. ☺ Q P ⚲ ⬛

Heacham (nr. Hunstanton)
Norfolk Lavender Ltd Map ref. D3
Caley Mill, Heacham (on A149) PE31 7JE
Tel: (01485) 570384 Fax: (01485) 571176
Web: www.norfolk-lavender.co.uk
The Fragrant Plant Meadow and Conservatory offer a wide selection of scented plants to add to our lavenders, herb plants and garden collection. Also tours (May-Sept) - learn about the harvest and ancient distillation process. The Gift Shop stocks the full range of Norfolk Lavender's famous fragrant products with a wide choice of other gifts to suit all pockets. Miller's Tearoom - specialising in locally baked cakes, scones, cream teas and lunches. The National Collection of Lavenders. FREE ADMISSION. Open Apr-Oct 1000-1700; Nov-Mar, 1000-1600.
☺ Q P T(4 hrs) ⚲ ⬛ ⌁ (on leads) ⬛

Norwich
Notcutts Garden Centres Map ref. K8
Daniels Road (Ring Road), Norwich NR4 6QP
Tel: (01603) 453155 Web: www.notcutts.co.uk
Discover a world of ideas and inspiration around every corner for you, your home and your garden. From fabulous plants to gifts and treats galore, there's so much to see. Gift ideas from around the world, houseplants, books, fresh cut and silk flowers, 3,000 varieties of hardy plants (with a 2 year replacement guarantee), pet centre, coffee shop, plus expert friendly advice about seasonal and bedding plants, garden furniture and barbecues. Keep an eye open for regular offers on key garden products. Notcutts open 7 days a week, free car-parking. ☺ P ⚲ ⬛

page 127

Reymerston (nr. Norwich)

Thorncroft Clematis Nursery Map ref. 18
The Lings, Reymerston, nr. Norwich NR9 4QG
Tel: (01953) 850407 Web: www.thorncroft.co.uk
Come and visit our nursery and garden in the 'heart' of the Norfolk countryside. Our family run nursery stocks many beautiful and unusual clematis cultivars.
Open Tues-Sat, 1000-1600, Closed Sun & Mon. Open Bank Hol Mon. Directions - PLEASE NOTE we are NOT in the village of Reymerston. The nursery is on the B1135, exactly halfway between Wymondham and Dereham.
⊛ P 🔥

SUFFOLK

Weston (nr. Beccles)

Winter Flora
Plant and Home Décor Centre Map ref. N3
Hall Farm, Weston, nr. Beccles NR34 8TT
Tel: (01502) 716810
This family business which began in 1969 is no longer known only for dried flowers. Winter Flora has one of the best selections of silk flowers in East Anglia, a plant centre containing a tempting array of unusual and traditional flowers and shrubs all strengthened by helpful design and plant advice. Numerous treasures reside in the very special plant centre run by Steve Malster, a dedicated plants man who nevertheless maintains the keenest prices, while the large show garden offers many a pleasant spot to sit and gain respite. Coffee Shop with homemade fare. 1¹/2 miles south of Beccles on the A145. Open daily 1000-1700. Closed Easter Day, 24 Dec-2 Jan inclusive.

Woodbridge

Notcutts Garden Centres Map ref. K9
Ipswich Road, Woodbridge IP12 4AF
Tel: (01394) 445400 Web: www.notcutts.co.uk
Discover a world of ideas and inspiration around every corner for you, your home and your garden. From fabulous plants to gifts and treats galore, there's so much to see. Gift ideas from around the world, houseplants, books, silk flowers, 3,000 varieties of hardy plants (with a 2 year replacement guarantee), restaurant, expert friendly advice about seasonal and bedding plants, garden furniture and barbecues. Keep an eye open for regular offers on key garden products. Notcutts open 7 days a week, free car-parking plus children's play area. ⊛ P 🍴 🔥

Norfolk Lavender

Animal & Bird Collections

BEDFORDSHIRE

Aspley Guise
HULA Animal Rescue: South Midlands Animal Sanctuary
Map ref. B7
Glebe Farm, Salford Road
Tel: (01908) 584000 Web: www.hularescue.org
A 17-acre registered agricultural holding, headquarters of
the registered charity founded in 1972. Visitors can see
round the animal houses, and feed the resident ponies,
pigs, goats and cows.
Times: Open all year, Sat, Sun and Bank Hols, 1300-1500.
Also 16 Jan, 20 Feb, 27 Mar, 1 May, 5 Jun, 10 Jul, 14 Aug,
18 Sept, 23 Oct, 27 Nov, 1300-1600. Closed 24 Dec-2 Jan.
Fee: £1.00/50p.
Facilities: ⊛ 🅿 ⇌ T(2 hrs) 🐾

Biggleswade
**The English School of Falconry - Bird of Prey and
Conservation Centre** Map ref. F6
Old Warden Park, Old Warden
Tel: (01767) 627527 Web: www.shuttleworth.org
One of the country's largest collections of birds of prey
(over 300), including rare species. Walk-through barn owl
aviary and daily displays featuring different birds of prey.
Times: Open 1 Feb-31 Oct, daily, 1000-1600 (1700 in
summer months).
Fee: £7.50/free/£6.50.
Facilities: 🅿 T(5 hrs) 🍴 🎋 🔲

Dunstable
Whipsnade Wild Animal Park Map ref. C11
Tel: (01582) 872171 Web: www.whipsnade.co.uk
Whipsnade Wild Animal Park has over 2,500 animals set in
600 acres of beautiful parkland. Fun-filled and informative
daily events run throughout the day.
Times: Open all year daily, 1 Jan-26 Mar, 1000-1600; 27
Mar-17 Sept, Mon-Sat, 1000-1800, Sun and Bank Hol
1000-1900; 18 Sept-1 Oct 1000-1800; 2-29 Oct,
1000-1700; 30 Oct-31 Dec, 1000-1600. Closed 25 Dec.
Fee: £14.50/£11.00/£12.50/£46.00.
Facilities: 🅿 🚐 T(5 hrs) 🍴 🎋 🔲

Leighton Buzzard
Mead Open Farm Map ref. B10
Stanbridge Road, Billington
Tel: (01525) 852954 Web: www.meadopenfarm.co.uk
Wide range of farm animals, including pets corner. Indoor
and outdoor play areas, daily hands on activities and
tractor/trailer rides.
Times: Open all year, Jan, daily, 1000-1600; Feb-Oct, daily,
1000-1700; Nov-Dec, daily, 1000-1600. Closed 23-31 Dec.
Fee: £4.75/£3.75/£4.25/£17.00 (2004 prices).
Facilities: Q 🅿 T(4 hrs) 🍴 🎋 🔲

Slip End (nr. Luton)
Woodside Animal Farm Map ref. D11
Woodside Road
Tel: (01582) 841044 Web: www.woodsidefarm.co.uk
100's of farm and exotic animals to see and feed. Indoor
and outdoor play areas, tractor rides, animal encounters,
trampolines and crazy golf. Farm shop, pet store and coffee
shop.
Times: Open all year, daily, summer 0900-1800, winter
0900-1700. Closed 25, 26 Dec and 1 Jan.
Fee: £5.95/£4.95/£4.95.
Facilities: 🅿 🚐 T(3 hrs) 🍴 🎋 🔲

Thurleigh (nr. Bedford)
Thurleigh Farm and Adventure Playground Map ref. D4
Cross End
Tel: (01234) 771597 Web: www.thurleighfarmcentre.co.uk
Working farm with indoor and outdoor play facilities.
Trampoline centre. Meet and feed the animals both large
and small. Nature trail. Tearoom and special
seasonal attractions.
Times: Open all year, daily, 1000-1800. Closed 10, 11, 17,
18, 24, 25, 25 and 31 Jan, 1, 7, 8 and 28 Feb, 1, 7 and 8
Mar. Closed 25 Dec-2 Jan.
Fee: £3.50/£5.00(child £4.00 during term time)
Facilities: 🅿 🚐 T(4 hrs) 🍴 🎋

Wilden (nr. Bedford)
Bedford Butterfly Park Map ref. E5
Renhold Road
Tel: (01234) 772770 Web: www.bedford-butterflies.co.uk
Set in landscaped hay meadows, the park features a
tropical glasshouse where visitors walk through lush foliage
with butterflies flying. Tearoom, gift shop, trails and
playground.
Times: Open 8 Jan-11 Feb, Thurs-Sun, 1000-1600; 12 Feb-
30 Oct, daily, 1000-1700; 31 Oct-18 Dec, Thurs-Sun,
1000-1600.
Fee: £4.50/£2.75/£3.50/£13.00(family).
Facilities: ⊛ Q G 🅿 T(2½ hrs) 🍴 🎋 🔲

Woburn
Woburn Safari Park Map ref. C8
Woburn Park
Tel: (01525) 290407 Web: www.woburnsafari.co.uk
Drive through the safari park with 30 species of animals in natural groups just a windscreen's width away, plus the action-packed Wild World Leisure Area with shows for all.
Times: Open all year. 1 Jan-6 Mar, Sat and Sun, also 12-20 Feb, daily, 1100-1500 (last entry); 12 Mar-30 Oct, daily, 1000-1700 (last entry); 5 Nov-31 Dec, Sat and Sun, 1100-1500 (last entry).
Fee: Please contact for details of admission prices.
Facilities: ⊛ Q ℙ T(6 hrs) ⑨ 🛆

CAMBRIDGESHIRE

Godmanchester
Wood Green Animal Shelters Map ref. E10
King's Bush Farm, London Road
Tel: (08701) 904090 Web: www.woodgreen.org.uk
Europe's busiest animal rescue and rehoming site with lots to see, including farm animals, cats, dogs and small animals. Some permanent residents, others awaiting caring new homes.
Times: Open all year, daily, 1000-1600. Closed 25, 26 Dec.
Fee: Free.
Facilities: ⊛ ℙ T(1½ hrs) 𝕂 ⑨ 🛆 🐾

Linton
Linton Zoo Map ref. I13
Hadstock Road
Tel: (01223) 891308 Web: www.lintonzoo.com
The zoo has big cats, lynx, wallabies, lemurs, toucans, parrots and reptiles, a wonderful combination of beautiful gardens and wildlife.
Times: Open all year, daily, please contact for times. Closed 25 and 26 Dec.
Fee: £6.50/£4.50 (up to 13 yrs)/£6.00.
Facilities: ℙ 🚌 T(6 hrs) 𝕂 ⑨ 🛆 🛆

Sawtry
Hamerton Zoo Park Map ref. C8
Tel: (01832) 293362 Web: www.hamertonzoopark.com
A wildlife park with tigers, lemurs, marmosets, meerkats,
wallabies, and a unique bird collection with rare and exotic
species from around the world.
Times: Open all year, daily, from 1030. Closed 25 Dec.
Fee: £6.50/£4.50/£5.50.
Facilities: 🅿 T(3 hrs) ⓘ 🎋 ⬛

Shepreth (nr. Royston)
Shepreth Wildlife Park (Willersmill) Map ref. G13
Station Road
Tel: (01763) 262226 Web:
www.sheprethwildlifepark.co.uk
A great day out for the whole family. See tigers, puma, lynx,
wolves, reptiles and many more, at one of East Anglia's
major attractions.
Times: Open all year, daily, summer, 1000-1800; winter,
1000-dusk. Closed 25 Dec.
Fee: £6.00/£4.50/£5.00.
Facilities: Q 🅿 T(4 hrs) ⓘ 🎋

Woodhurst (nr. Huntingdon)
The Raptor Foundation Map ref. E9
The Heath, St. Ives Road
Tel: (01487) 741140 Web: www.raptorfoundation.org.uk
A collection of injured birds of prey and wild birds. Hand-
reared owls used for fund raising for the hospital. Tearoom,
gift shop, craft village and falconry flying area.
Times: Open all year, daily, 1000-1700. Closed 25 Dec and
1 Jan.
Fee: £3.50/£2.00/£2.50.
Facilities: ⊛ Q 🅿 T(3 hrs) 🕏 ⓘ 🎋 ⬛

See Also:
Sacrewell Farm and Country Centre, Thornhaugh, page 69
Wimpole Hall and Home Farm, nr Royston, page 38

ESSEX

Billericay
Barleylands Farm Centre Map ref. F10
Barleylands Road, Billericay, Essex, CM11 2UD
Tel: (01268) 290229 Web: www.barleylands.co.uk
Great fun for everyone at our fun farm centre. Children can
explore the adventure playground, have bundles of bounces
on our giant trampolines and bouncy castle, race around
the farm on the mini tractors or get creative in the gigantic
sandpit! We have lots of friendly farm animals to meet and
feed with cute and cuddlies in the pets corner. You can also
take an educational trip through our Bygone Farming
Experience. Enjoy a delicious snack in our Tea Room or
bring your own picnic. Miniature Steam Train also on
site(Sun only). Also see Barleylands Craft Village.
Times: Open 1 Mar-31 Oct, daily, 1000-1700.
Fee: £3.00/£3.00/£3.00.
Facilities: ⊛ Q 🅿 🚻 T(2 hrs) ⓘ 🎋 ⬛

Bocking
Dorewards Hall Farm Map ref. G5
Church Street
Tel: (01376) 324646 Web: www.dorewardshall.com
Historical working farm and shop in the pretty village of
Bocking. Events and seasonal activities.
Times: Open all year, daily, 0900-1730.
Fee: £1.00.
Facilities: 🅿 T(1 hr) ⓘ 🎋 🐾 (on leads)

Colchester
Colchester Zoo Map ref. J5
Maldon Road, Stanway
Tel: (01206) 331292 Web: www.colchester-zoo.co.uk
One of Europe's finest zoos, with over 200 species in 60 acres of gardens. New Playa Patagonia Sealion experience with 24 metre tunnel under the water. Don't miss the African Zone with the chance to feed the elephants and giraffes.
Times: Open all year, daily, from 0930. Closed 25 Dec.
Fee: £11.99/£6.99/£8.99. Please confirm prices before you visit.
Facilities: Q P T(6 hrs)

Mistley
Mistley Place Park Animal Rescue Centre Map ref. M3
New Road
Tel: (01206) 396483
Twenty five acres of woodlands and lakeside walks with goats, horses, sheep, rabbits, ducks, gift shop and a nature trail.
Times: Open all year, Tues-Sun and Bank Hol Mon, 1000-1800 (or dusk if earlier). Open daily in school hols.
Fee: £3.00/£2.00/£2.50.
Facilities: P T(2 hrs)

Nazeing (nr. Harlow)
Ada Cole Rescue Stables Map ref. B7
Broadlands, Broadley Common
Tel: (01992) 892133 Web: www.adacole.co.uk
A horse rescue charity with 47 acres of paddocks and stables. Gift shop, information room, and pet's corner.
Times: Open all year, daily, 1400-1630. Closed 25 Dec and 1 Jan.
Fee: £1.50/free.
Facilities: P T(1½ hrs) (on leads)

For even more information visit our website at
www.visiteastofengland.com

South Weald (nr. Brentwood)
Old MacDonalds Educational Farm Park Map ref. D9
Weald Road
Tel: (01277) 375177 Web: www.oldmacdonaldsfarm.org.uk
We tell the whole story of British livestock farming, keeping rare breeds, cattle, pigs, sheep, shire horses and poultry, red squirrels, owls, otters and lots more.
Times: Open all year, daily, 1000-1700 (in summer closes 1800). Closed 25, 26 Dec.
Fee: £3.25/£2.00/£2.75.
Facilities: P T(2 hrs)

South Woodham Ferrers
Marsh Farm Country Park Map ref. H9
Marsh Farm Road
Tel: (01245) 321552
Web: www.marshfarmcountrypark.co.uk
A farm centre with sheep, a pig unit, free-range chickens, milking demonstrations, an indoor and outdoor adventure play area, nature reserve, walks, picnic area and pet's barn.
Times: Open mid Feb-end Oct, daily, from 1000. Nov-mid Dec. Sat, Sun 1000-1600.
Fee: £5.60/£3.00/£4.00/£16.50 (2004 prices).
Facilities: Q P T(3 hrs)

South Woodham Ferrers
Tropical Wings Butterfly and Bird Gardens Map ref. H9
Wickford Road
Tel: (01245) 425394 Web: www.tropicalwings.co.uk
Over 6,000 sq ft of tropical house, home to free-flying exotic butterflies, birds and tropical plants. Outdoor bird gardens. Children's play area.
Times: Open 2 Jan-11 Feb, please telephone for details; 12 Feb-30 Apr, Mon-Sun, 1030 1630; 1 May-30 Sept, Mon-Sun, 0930-1730; 1 Oct-20 Nov, Mon-Sun, 1030-1630; 21 Nov-31 Dec, please telephone for details.
Fee: £5.25/£3.50/£4.25/£15.00(family).
Facilities: P T(3 hrs)

Southend-on-Sea
Southend Sea Life Adventure Map ref. I11
Eastern Esplanade
Tel: (01702) 601834 Web: www.sealifeadventure.co.uk
The very latest in marine technology brings the secrets of the
mysterious underwater world closer than ever before. An
amazing underwater tunnel allows an all-round view. Daily
talks and presentations.
Times: Open all year, daily, from 1000 (last admission 1700).
Closed 25 Dec.
Fee: £5.75/£4.25/£4.50.
Facilities: Q ▤ ▭ ⇌ T(1½ hrs) ⓘ

Waltham Abbey
Lee Valley Park Farms Map ref. A8
Stubbins Hall Lane, Crooked Mile
Tel: (01992) 892781 Web: www.leevalleypark.com
Two farms in one. Hayes Hill, a traditional-style farm with
visitor facilities, including tearooms and play area. Holyfield
Hall, a modern arable farm. Also information centre on the
whole of the Lee Valley Regional Park.
Times: Open 2 Jan-31 Mar, Mon-Fri, 1000-1630, Sat, Sun,
Bank Hols, 1000-dusk; 1 Apr-31 Oct, Mon-Fri, 1000-1630,
Sat, Sun, Bank Hols, 1000-1730; 1 Nov-31 Dec, Mon-Fri,
1000-1630, Sat, Sun, Bank Hols, 1000-dusk. Closed 25, 26
Dec, 1 Jan.
Fee: £4.50/£3.50/£4.00.
Facilities: ⊛ ▤ T(3½ hrs) ⓘ ⼌

Wethersfield (nr. Braintree)
Boydells Dairy Farm Map ref. F3
Tel: (01371) 850481 Web: www.boydellsdairy.co.uk
A small dairy farm where you can watch the milking of cows,
sheep and goats. Also pigs, poultry and bees. Goat and
donkey cart rides. Farm shop.
Times: Open 26 Mar- 30 Sept, Fri-Sun and Bank Hols, also
daily during Essex school Hols 1400-1700.
Fee: £3.50/£2.50.
Facilities: ▤ ▭ T(2 hrs) ⼓ ⼌ ⬚

Widdington (nr. Saffron Walden)
Mole Hall Wildlife Park Map ref. D3
Tel: (01799) 540400 Web: www.molehall.co.uk
Park with otters, chimps, guanaco, lemurs, wallabies, deer, a
butterfly pavilion, attractive gardens, picnic/play areas and
pet's corner.
Times: Open all year, daily 1030-1800. Closed 25 Dec.
Fee: £5.50/£3.80/£4.00.
Facilities: ⊛ ▤ T(2½ hrs) ⓘ ⼌ ⬚

See Also:
Clacton Pier (seaquarium), page 139
Hainault Forest Country Park, Chigwell, page 184
Layer Marney Tower, nr Colchester, page 40
Red House Visitor Centre, Messing, page 115

HERTFORDSHIRE

Broxbourne
Paradise Wildlife Park Map ref. I13
White Stubbs Lane
Tel: (01992) 470490 Web: www.pwpark.com
A marvellous day out for the family with many daily
activities, children's rides, catering outlets, picnic areas,
paddling pool and an excellent range of animals.
Times: Open 1 Jan-28 Feb, daily, 1000-1700 (or dusk if
earlier). 1 Mar-31 Oct, daily, 0930-1800. 1 Nov-31 Dec,
daily, 1000-1700 (or dusk if earlier). Closed 25 Dec.
Fee: £10.00/£7.00/£7.00/£32.00.
Facilities: ⊛ G ▤ ▭ T(5 hrs) ⓘ ⼌ ⬚

Letchworth Garden City
Standalone Farm Map ref. G8
Wilbury Road
Tel: (01462) 686775
An open farm with cattle, sheep, pigs, poultry, shire horses
a wildfowl area, natural history museum, farm walk and
daily milking demonstration.
Times: Open 1 Mar-30 Sept, daily, 1100-1700.
Fee: £3.95/£2.95/£2.95/£15.95.
Facilities: ⊛ ▤ T(3 hrs) ⼌ ⓘ

Whitwell
Waterhall Farm and Craft Centre Map ref. F10
Tel: (01438) 871256
An open farm featuring rare breeds, and offering a 'hands-on' experience for visitors. Craft centre and tea-room.
Times: Open all year, Sat, Sun and school holidays. Nov-Mar 1000-1600, Mar-Nov 1000-1700.
Fee: £2.75/£1.75/£1.75.
Facilities: 🅿 🚃 T(3 hrs) 🗘 🗮 🏌

See Also:
Activity World and Farmyard Funworld, Bushey, page 146
Aldenham Country Park, Elstree, page 188

London Colney
Willows Farm Village Map ref. F13
Coursers Road
Tel: (01727) 822444
Web: www.willowsfarmvillage.com
At the unique Willows Farm Village families discover their true animal instincts, roaming free in the countryside and running wild with the adventure activities. Daft Duck Trials, Bird-o-batic falconry displays and country fun fair.
Times: Open 12 Mar-30 Oct, daily, 1000-1730.
Fee: £8.50/£7.50(2004 prices).
Facilities: ⊛ Q 🅿 T(4 hrs) 🗘 🗮

NORFOLK

Banham
Banham Zoo Map ref. I10
The Grove
Tel: (01953) 887771 Web: www.banhamzoo.co.uk
Wildlife spectacular, which will take you on a journey to experience some of the world's most exotic, rare and endangered animals, including tigers, leopards and zebra.
Times: Open all year, daily, from 1000. Closing times have seasonal variations. Closed 25 and 26 Dec.
Fee: Please contact for details of admission prices.
Facilities: ⊛ Q 🅿 T(4-6 hrs) 🗘 🗮 🔲

Filby (nr. Great Yarmouth)
Thrigby Hall Wildlife Gardens Map ref. O7
Tel: (01493) 369477 Web: www.thrigbyhall.co.uk
A wide selection of Asian mammals, birds, reptiles, tigers, crocodiles and storks. A 250-year-old landscaped garden with play area and willow pattern gardens.
Times: Open 1 Jan-31 Mar, daily, 1000-1600; 1 Apr-31 Oct daily, 1000-1700; 1 Nov-31 Dec, daily, 1000-1600.
Fee: £7.50/£5.00/£6.50.
Facilities: ⊛ Q ▣ T(3 hrs) ⟋ ⊛ ㄷ ▧

Frettenham (nr. Norwich)
Hillside Animal Sanctuary Map ref. L6
Hill Top Farm, Hall Lane
Tel: (01603) 736200 Web: www.hillside.org.uk
Visit our rescued farm animals - cows, sheep, goats, horses, ponies and donkeys. Information centre and gift shop.
Times: Open 25-28 Mar, 1300-1700; 3 Apr-29 May, Sun, 1300-1700; 5 Jun-29 Aug, Sun, Mon, 1300-1700; 4 Sept-30 Oct, Sun, 1300-1700; open every Bank Hol Mon, 1300-1700.
Fee: £4.00/£2.00/£2.00.
Facilities: Q ▣ ▭ T(2 hrs) ⊛ ㄷ ♞ (on leads) ▧

Fritton (nr. Great Yarmouth)
Redwings Visitor Centre Map ref. O8
Caldecott Hall
Tel: 0870 040 0033 Web: www.redwings.co.uk
A sanctuary for horses, ponies and donkeys. Stroll along the paddock walks, visit the gift shop and information centre or adopt a rescued horse.
Times: Open 19 Mar-31 Oct, daily during school hols; Sun-Wed, at all other times, 1000-1600.
Fee: £3.60/£1.60/£2.50/£10.00(family).
Facilities: ▣ T(3 hrs) ⊛ ㄷ ♞ (on leads) ▧

Great Witchingham
Norfolk Wildlife Centre and Country Park Map ref. J6
Fakenham Road
Tel: (01603) 872274 Web: www.norfolkwildlife.co.uk
A large collection of British and European wildlife in 40 acres of parkland with a pet's corner, play areas, model farm and clear-water trout pool. Reptile house. This is not a zoo.
Times: Open Feb half term, then weekends until Easter. Easter-end Oct, daily, 1000-1700 (last admission 1600).
Fee: £6.95/£5.50/£5.95/£23.00(family).
Facilities: ▣ ▭ T(3-4 hrs) ⊛ ㄷ

Great Yarmouth
Amazonia Map ref. P7
Central Seafront
Tel: (01493) 842202
Web: www.amazonia-worldofreptiles.net
One of the largest collections of reptiles in the country, set in a beautiful tropical garden for the ultimate jungle experience.
Times: Open 5 Feb-30 Oct, daily, 1000-1700.
Fee: £4.50/£3.75/£4.00.
Facilities: ▭ T(30 mins) ⟋ ⊛ ㄷ ▧

Great Yarmouth
Great Yarmouth Sealife Centre Map ref. P7
Marine Parade
Tel: (01493) 330631 Web: www.sealife.co.uk
The centre takes visitors on a fascinating seabed stroll from local waters to tropical depths, including starfish, sharks, stingrays and shrimps. 'Lost City of Atlantis' with underwater tunnel.
Times: Open all year, daily, from 1000. Closed 25 Dec.
Fee: £6.95/£4.95/£5.95(2004 prices).
Facilities: ▭ ⇌ T(2 hrs) ⊛ ㄷ ▧

Hunstanton
Hunstanton Sea Life Sanctuary Map ref. D3
Southern Promenade
Tel: (01485) 533576 Web: www.sealsanctuary.co.uk
A breath-taking display of British marine life. Over 2,000 fish from 200 different species. Ocean tunnel, rock pools, seal rehabilitation centre, otters and penguins.
Times: Open all year, daily, 1000-1600; Closed 25 Dec.
Fee: £7.95/£4.95/£5.50/£24.80(family).
Facilities: ▭ T(2 hrs) ⊛ ㄷ ▧

Long Sutton
Butterfly and Wildlife Park Map ref. A5
Tel: (01406) 363833
Web: www.butterflyandwildlifepark.co.uk
One of Britain's largest walk-through butterfly houses. Insectarium, pet's corner, reptiles and falconry displays (eagles, owls and falcons) and Playfort
Times: Open 19 March-30 Jun, daily, from 1000-1700; 1 Jul-11 Sept, daily, 1000-1730; 12 Sept-6 Nov, daily, 1000-1600. Last admission 1 hr before closing.
Fee: £5.50/£3.80/£4.80/£17.00.
Facilities: ⊛ ▣ T(5 hrs) ⊛ ㄷ ▧

For even more information visit our website at www.visiteastofengland.com

Reedham
Pettitt's Animal Adventure Park Map ref. N8
Camphill
Tel: (01493) 700094 Web: www.pettittsonline.co.uk
A family park, which includes animals galore including
birds of prey, chickens, ducks, miniature Falabella horses,
goats, monkeys, parrots, peacocks, rheas and wallabies.
Play area.
Times: Open 19 Mar-30 Oct, daily, 1000-1700/1730.
Fee: £7.95/£7.95/£5.85/£31.00.
Facilities: ⊛ 🅿 🚼 ⪰ T(6 hrs) ⑪ 𝘈

Scoulton (nr. Watton)
Melsop Farm Park Map ref. H8
Melsop Farm, Ellingham Road
Tel: (01953) 851943
Farm park (rare breeds centre). 17th C. thatched Listed
house, set in 11 acres of rural Breckland countryside.
Indoor and outdoor play areas.
Times: Open 1 Jan-21 Mar, Sat, Sun and school hols; 22
Mar-30 Oct, Tues-Sun and Bank Hol Mon; 31 Oct-31 Dec,
Sat, Sun and school hols, 1000-1700. Closed 25, 26 Dec.
Fee: £4.50/£3.50/£3.50.
Facilities: ⊛ 🅿 T(3 hrs) ⑪ 𝘈 🅱

Snetterton (nr. Attleborough)
ILPH Hall Farm Map ref. H10
Tel: (01953) 498898 Web: www.ilph.org
Visit the centre for horses and ponies in beautiful
countryside. See the work of the International League for
the Protection of Horses. Visit the coffee and gift shops.
Times: Open 5 Jan-21 Dec, Wed, Sat, Sun 1100-1600.
Fee: Free.
Facilities: ⊛ 🅿 T(2 hrs) 🧍 ⑪ 𝘈 🏇 🅱

Snettisham (nr. Hunstanton)
Park Farm Snettisham Map ref. D4
Tel: (01485) 542425
Web: www.parkfarms-snettisham.co.uk
Unique red deer safari tours, a visitor centre, adventure
play area, crafts centre, art gallery, tearoom and souvenir
shop. Indoor and outdoor activities include farm animals
and pets.
Times: Open 1 Feb-31 Oct, daily, 1000-1700. 1 Nov-31
Dec, please ring for information. Closed 25 and 26 Dec.
Fee: £4.95/£3.95/£4.25. Farm and Deer Safari in season,
£8.50/£6.50/£7.50.
Facilities: ⊛ 🍴 🅿 T(5 hrs) 🧍 ⑪ 𝘈 🏇 🅱

West Runton (nr. Sheringham)
Norfolk Shire Horse Centre Map ref. K3
West Runton Stables
Tel: (01263) 837339
Web: www.norfolk-shirehorse-centre.co.uk
Shire horses are demonstrated, working twice daily. Native
ponies and a bygone collection of horse-drawn machinery.
There is also a children's farm.
Times: Open 24 Mar-28 Oct, daily except Sat (unless Bank
Hol), 1000-1700. Closed Fri in Sept and Oct.
Fee: £5.50/£3.50/£4.50.
Facilities: ⊛ 🅿 T(3 hrs) ⑪ 𝘈 🏇

Wroxham
Junior Farm at Wroxham Barns Map ref. M5
Tunstead Road, Hoveton NR12 8QU
Tel: (01603) 783762 Web: www.wroxham-barns.co.uk
10 acres of converted barns and farmland with something
for everyone. Meet, feed and learn about the friendly
farmyard animals at Junior Farm. Wroxham Barns new
Children's Fair with train, Indian canoes, trampolines, mini
wheel and chicken slide (and much more besides) its great
fun. Resident craftsmen, gift and clothes shops, food and
fudge shops and tearoom.
Times: Open all year, daily, 1000-1700. Closed 25, 26 Dec
and 1 Jan. Fair (seasonal).
Fee: Free admission and parking. Junior Farm £2.75 per
person (under 3s free). Fair rides individually priced. See
also our entry under Stop & Shop on page 167
Facilities: ⊛ 🍴 🅿 T(3 hrs) ⑪ 𝘈 🅱

See Also:
Fritton Lake Country World, nr Great Yarmouth, page 190
Playbarn, nr Norwich, page 147
Roots of Norfolk, Gressenhall, page 88.

SUFFOLK

Baylham (nr. Ipswich)
Baylham House Rare Breeds Farm Map ref. I9
Mill Lane, Baylham, Suffolk IP6 8LG.
Tel: (01473) 830264
E-mail: gdo@baylham-house-farm.co.uk
Web: www.baylham-house-farm.co.uk
Rare Breeds Farm with cattle, sheep, pygmy goats, poultry
and pigs, including Maori pigs called Kune Kunes. The
main area of the farm is wheelchair and pushchair friendly.
River walk. Picnic area. Disabled toilet. Visitor's Centre with
information, gifts, souvenirs and refreshments. Every child
gets a free bag of animal food.
Times: Open 12 Feb-30 Oct, daily, from 1100.
Fee: £4.00/£2.00/£3.00, under 4's free.
Facilities: ☺ 🅿 T(1 hr) 🕺 ⑨ 🍴 🅱

Fritton Lake Country World

Kessingland (nr. Lowestoft)
Suffolk Wildlife Park Map ref. O3
Tel: (01502) 740291 Web: www.suffolkwildlifepark.co.uk
Discover the ultimate African adventure, set in 100 acres of
coastal parkland. Experience close encounters with rhino,
lions, giraffes, buffalo and many more.
Times: Open all year, daily, from 1000. Please phone for
closing times. Closed 25 and 26 Dec and 1 Jan.
Fee: Please contact for details of admission prices.
Facilities: ☺ Q 🅿 T(4-6 hrs) ⑨ 🍴 🅱

Earsham (nr. Bungay)
Otter Trust Map ref. L3
Tel: (01986) 893470 Web: www.ottertrust.org.uk
A breeding and conservation headquarters, with the largest
collection of otters in the world. There are also lakes with a
collection of waterfowl and deer.
Times: Open 25 Mar-30 Sept, daily, 1030-1800, last
admission 1700.
Fee: £6.00/£3.00.
Facilities: 🅿 T(2 hrs) ⑨ 🍴

Newmarket
National Stud Map ref. A7
Tel: (01638) 663464 Web:
www.nationalstud.co.uk
A conducted tour which includes top thoroughbred
stallions, mares and foals, and gives an insight into the day
to day running of a modern stud farm.
Times: Open 1 Mar-30 Sept, Mon-Sat, tours at 1115 and
1430; Sun, tour at 1430. Plus autumn racedays tour at
1115.
Fee: £5.00/£3.50/£4.00/£15.00.
Facilities: ⊛ Q 🅿 🚽 T(1½ hrs) 🖈 ⑪ 🎋 ⑤

Wickham Market
Easton Farm Park Map ref. K8
Easton
Tel: (01728) 746475 Web: www.eastonfarmpark.co.uk
Free daily pony rides, pat-a-pet and egg collecting. Lots of
farm animals to meet and feed. Play areas, chicks hatching,
Suffolk Punch horse talks and woodland/river walks.
Times: 12-20 Feb, 1030-1600; 19 Mar-25 Sept, 1030-
1800; 22 Oct-30 Oct, 1030-1600.
Fee: £5.50/£4.00/£5.00(2004 prices).
Facilities: ⊛ Q 🅿 T(4 hrs) ⑪ 🎋 🐕(on leads)

Stonham Aspal (nr. Stowmarket)
Redwings Rescue Centre Map ref. I7
Stonham Barns, Pettaugh Road
Tel: 0870 040 0033 Web: www.redwings.co.uk
Home to thirty rescued horses, ponies and donkeys
including Harry Potter, a Shetland pony with a club foot.
Displays, gifts, refreshments and 'adopt a pony'.
Times: Open 25 May-30 Sept, daily, 1000-1600.
Fee: £3.50/£1.50/£2.50.
Facilities: 🅿 T(3 hrs) 🎋 🐕(on leads) ⑤

Wickham Market
Valley Farm Camargue Horses Map ref. L8
Valley Farm Riding and Driving Centre
Tel: (01728) 746916 Web: www.valleyfarmonline.co.uk
Britain's only herd of breeding Camargue horses, as
featured on television. Animal collection including camel
and Suffolk Punches. Horse riding charged separately
Times: Open all year, daily, 1000-1630. Closed 25 and 26
Dec.
Fee: £2.00/£1.00.
Facilities: 🅿 T(2 hrs) 🖈 ⑪ 🎋 🐕(on leads) ⑤

See Also:
Kentwell Hall and Gardens, Long Melford, page 46, 47
Museum of East Anglian Life, Stowmarket, page 100

Stonham Aspal (nr. Stowmarket)
Suffolk Owl Sanctuary Map ref. I7
Stonham Barns, Pettaugh Road
Tel: (01449) 711425
Web: www.suffolk-owl-sanctuary.org.uk
Outdoor flying arena, featuring frequent demonstrations of
birds of prey in flight. Woodland walk, red squirrel
enclosure, and aviaries with most species of British owls
and raptors. Information centre.
Times: Open all year, daily, summer, 1000-1700; winter,
1000-1630. Closed 23 Dec-2 Jan.
Fee: Free. Donations appreciated.
Facilities: 🅿 T(2 hrs) ⑪ 🎋 ⑤

Amusement/ Theme Centres & Parks

CAMBRIDGESHIRE

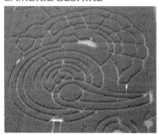

Milton (nr. Cambridge)
The Milton Maize Maze Map ref. H11
Rectory Farm Shop, A10 Milton Bypass
Tel: (01223) 860374
Web: www.rectoryfarmshop.co.uk
A giant walk through puzzle to challenge any age! A field full of family fun. Farm shop. New for 2004 - pets' paddock and small coffee shop.
Times: Maze open 16 Jul-4 Sept, daily, 1000-1700 (last entry at 1615).
Fee: £3.50/£2.50/£12.00 (family).
Facilities: 🅿 T(2 hrs) ⓘ 🚹

ESSEX

Braintree
The Original Great Maze Map ref. F5
Blake House Craft Centre
Tel: (01376) 553146 Web: www.maze.info
This challenging maize maze is known as one of the biggest mind benders in the world. It has more than five miles of pathways laid out in over 10 acres of the idyllic north Essex countryside.
Times: Open 10 Jul-11 Sept, daily, 1000-1700.
Fee: £4.50/£2.50/£3.50.
Facilities: 🅿 🚌 T(2-5 hrs) ⓘ 🚹 🚹

Clacton-on-Sea
Clacton Pier Map ref. N6
Tel: (01255) 421115 Web: www.clactonpier.co.uk
Fun pier with fairground rides, arcades, shops, cafes, restaurants, side shows, children's play area and seaquarium.
Times: Open all year, daily, from 1000. Rides open 1 Mar-end Oct. Closed 25 Dec.
Fee: Free. Individual charges for rides/attractions.
Facilities: 🚌 🚌 T(3 hrs) ⓘ 🚹

Colchester
PC Arena Map ref. K4
14 Queen Street
Tel: (01206) 542905
Web: www.pcarenas.com/colchester2.htm . . . .
East Anglia's only themed multiplayer PC gaming arena. Play all the latest games against your friends, or others. Lighting and an excellent sound system add to the atmosphere.
Times: All Year, Mon-Fri, 0900-1800; Sat, 0900-1900; Sun 1000-1600.
Fee: £3.50 per hour
Facilities: 🚌 🚌 T(1 hr)

Colchester
Quasar at Rollerworld Map ref. K4
Eastgates
Tel: (01206) 868868 Web: www.rollerworld.co.uk
East Anglia's largest quasar (laser game) arena. Futuristic briefing room, space age vesting room and industrial wasteland arena, complimented by fully interactive lights, UV effects, smoke generators and sub bass sound system.
Times: Open all year, please contact for further details.
Fee: Please contact for details of admission prices.
Facilities: ⓘ 🅿 🚌 🚌 T(2 hrs) ⓘ

Adventure Island, Southend-on-Sea

Colchester
Rollerworld Map ref. K4
Eastgates
Tel: (01206) 868868 Web: www.rollerworld.co.uk
Great Britain's largest roller-skating rink, 25m x 50m maple floor. RollerHire, RollerCafe and RollerBar - stunning sound and light show.
Times: Open all year, please contact for further details.
Fee: Please contact for details of admission prices.
Facilities: ⊛ 🅿 🚻 ⇌ T(2-3 hrs) 🚻 📷

Great Dunmow
Coco Nuts Play Ltd Map ref. E5
Ford Farm, Braintree Road
Tel: (01371) 874111 Web: www.coconutsplay.co.uk
Children's indoor adventure play and party centre. Three level adventure frame(includes ball pools/slides), summer garden and coco's café.
Times: Open all year, daily. Closed 25-28 Dec.
Fee: Under 5's £2.95, over 5's £3.95
Facilities: 🅿 T(2 hrs) 🚻 📷

Rayleigh
Megazone Laser Arena Map ref. H10
The Warehouse Centre, 7 Brook Road
Tel: (01268) 779100 Web: www.rayleighmegazone.co.uk
A game of stealth, strategy and skill, played in the laser arena in Essex with the most advanced laser system.
Times: Open all year, Mon-Fri, 1500-2200; Sat and Sun, 1000-2200; school hols, 1000-2300. Closed 25 Mar, 25, 26 Dec and 1 Jan.
Fee: Non-member £3.95, member £3.50.
Facilities: ⊛ 🅿 T(1½ hrs) 🏃 📷

Southend-on-Sea
Adventure Island Map ref. I11
Sunken Gardens West, Western Esplanade
Tel: (01702) 443400 Web: www.adventureisland.co.uk
One of the best value 'theme parks' in the South East, with over 40 great rides and attractions, for all ages. No admission charge, you only 'pay if you play'!
Times: Open Jan-Mar, Sat and Sun; Easter-early Sept, daily; Sept-31 Dec, Sat and Sun, from 1100. Also open school half terms.
Fee: Free. Individual charges for rides/attractions.
Facilities: Q 🚻 ⇌ T(3-4 hrs) 🚻 🍴 🐕

Southend-on-Sea
Kursaal Map ref. I11
Eastern Esplanade
Tel: (01702) 322322 Web: www.kursaal.co.uk
The Kursaal has something for everyone. Among the features are ten pin bowling, a sports bar with big screen entertainment, amusement machines, rides, McDonalds, and the Rendezvous Casino.
Times: Open all year, daily, 1000-late. Closed 25 Dec.
Fee: Free. There are charges for bowling etc - prices vary, so please contact for details.
Facilities: 🅿 🚻 ⇌ T(2½ hrs) 🚻 📷

Clacton Pier

Southend-on-Sea
Mr B's Space Chase Quasar Map ref. I11
5/8 Marine Parade
Tel: (01702) 467720
A quasar arena situated within a family entertainment centre with prize bingo and video games.
Times: Open all year, daily and summer school half terms, 1000-2400. Closed 25 Dec.
Fee: Free. Quasar £2.50 per 15 mins.
Facilities: ⛴ ⇌ T(20 mins) 🐕

Southend-on-Sea
Southend-on-Sea Pier Map ref. I11
Western Esplanade
Tel: (01702) 215620 Web: www.southendpier.co.uk
The world's longest pleasure pier. Train ride along the pier. Pier Museum at North Station, amusements, novelty shop, restaurant and licensed public house. Guided tours at Lifeboat House.
Times: Open all year, daily from 0800. Please telephone hotline for closing times.
Fee: Free. Train £3.00/£1.50/£1.50/£7.20 (family). Walk and ride £2.20/£1.20/£1.20/£4.80 (family).
Facilities: ⊛ ⛴ ⇌ T(2 hrs) 🕯 ⼞ 🚾

Walton-on-the-Naze
Walton Pier Map ref. O5
Pier Approach
Tel: (01255) 672288 Web: www.waltonpier.co.uk
Adult and junior rides (one price to pay - ride all day wristbands). Family amusement area, tenpin bowling, Pirate Pete's soft play area, Seaspray Diner, Mermaid Bar and fishing.
Times: Open all year. Weekends only in low/winter season. Daily during school holidays and Jun. Telephone hotline for exact opening times 01255 682400.
Fee: Free. Individual charges for rides/attractions.
Facilities: ⊛ T(2 hrs) 🕯 🐕 (on leads) 🚾

See Also:
Gnome Magic, Dedham, page 114
House on the Hill Toy Museums Adventure, page 78

NORFOLK

Dereham
Big Apple Map ref. H6
Station Road
Tel: (01362) 696910 Web: www.thebigapple.co.uk
Family entertainment centre with ten pin bowling, laserquest, kids play, pool and video games.
Times: Open all year, daily, 1000-2200 or later. Closed 25 Dec.
Fee: Ten pin bowling £3.75/£2.75/£2.75.
Facilities: ▯ T(1hr 30 mins) 🕯 🚾

Great Yarmouth
Britannia Pier Map ref. P7
Marine Parade
Tel: (01493) 842914 Web: www.britannia-pier.co.uk
Traditional seaside pier with amusement arcades, children's rides, fun fair, restaurants and bars. Theatre with summer season shows.
Times: Open 25 Mar-end Oct, daily, from 0900.
Fee: Free.
Facilities: ⛴ ⇌ T(2-3 hrs) 🕯 🐕

Great Yarmouth
Joyland Map ref. P7
Marine Parade
Tel: (01493) 844094
Delightful family fun park for young children. Rides include the world famous snails and Tyrolean tub twist. Huge Toytown Mountain with Spook Express kiddie coaster.
Times: Open 12-20 Feb, daily; 26 Feb-18 Mar, Sat, Sun; 19 Mar-Nov, daily 1200-1800. Extended opening hours during holiday periods.
Fee: Free. Individual charges (tokens) for rides/attractions.
Facilities: Q ⛴ ⇌ T(1 hr) 🕯 ⼞ 🐕

Great Yarmouth
Louis Tussauds House of Wax Map ref. P7
18 Regent Road
A waxworks exhibition with torture chambers, a chamber of horrors, hall of funny mirrors and family amusement arcade.
Times: Open all year, daily, from 1100.
Fee: £3.00/£2.00/£9.00 (family)(2004 prices).
Facilities: 🚻 ♿ T(1 hr)

Great Yarmouth
Merrivale Model Village Map ref. P7
Marine Parade
Tel: (01493) 842097
A miniature world of town and countryside - now under new ownership. Landscaped gardens with many models, including working fairground, garden railway and museum of the old Penny Slot Machine.
Times: Open 25 Mar-30 Oct, daily 1000-1700.
Illuminations 4 July-3 Sept, 1000-2100.
Fee: £4.00/£3.50/£3.50.
Facilities: Q 🚻 ♿ T(1 hr) 🍴 🐾 (on leads) ♿

Great Yarmouth
The Mint Map ref. P7
31 Marine Parade
Tel: (01493) 842968 Web: www.thurston.uk.com
Family entertainment centre, including 'Quasar' the live action laser game.
Times: Open all year, daily, 0900-2300.
Fee: Quasar Centre £2.99/£2.99 for 15 mins.
Facilities: 🚻 ♿ T(30 mins)

Great Yarmouth
Pleasure Beach Map ref. P7
South Beach Parade
Tel: (01493) 844585 Web: www.pleasure-beach.co.uk
9 acre leisure park, with Rollercoaster, Skydrop, Log flume, Twister, Monorail, Galloping Horses, Caterpillar, Disko and Fun House. Height restrictions are in force on some rides.
Times: Open Mar-Oct. Please contact for opening days and times.
Fee: Free. Individual charges for rides/attractions.
Facilities: ⊙ 🚻 ♿ T(2-3 hrs) 🍴 🖾 🐾

Lenwade (nr. Norwich)
The Dinosaur Adventure Park Map ref. J6
Weston Park
Tel: (01603) 876310 Web: www.dinosaurpark.co.uk
A unique family day out. Attractions include the dinosaur trail, woodland maze, secret animal garden, Climb-a-Saurus, adventure play areas, education centre and lots more.
Times: Open 19 Mar-11 Sept, daily, 1000-1700. 12 Sept-23 Oct, Fri-Sun, 1000-1700. 24-30 Oct, daily, 1000-1700.
Fee: Please contact for details of admission prices.
Facilities: ⊙ Q 🖾 T(4 hrs) 🍴 🖾 ♿

South Creake (nr. Fakenham)
South Creake Maize Maze Map ref. F4
Compton Hall
Tel: (01328) 823224 Web: www.amazingmaizemaze.co.uk
Seven acres of maze to get lost in! Set in 18 acres of unspoilt Norfolk countryside. Crazy golf and panning for gold.
Times: Open 9 Jul-4 Sept, daily, 1000-1800.
Fee: Maze £3.50/£2.50/£2.50/£10.00. Panning for gold and crazy golf £1.50/£1.50/£1.50.
Facilities: Q 🖾 T(4 hrs) 🍴 🖾 ♿

Wroxham
Wroxham Barns Children's Fair Map ref. M5
Tunstead Road
Tel: (01603) 784118 Web: www.wroxham-barns.co.uk
Children's rides including ferris wheel, train, adventure riverboat ride, trampolines, giant slide, jumping jack and kiddies rollercoaster - plus lots more.
Times: Open 19 Mar-10 Apr, daily; 16 Apr-1 May, Sat and Sun; 2 May-4 Sept, daily, 1100-1700.
Fee: Free. Individual charges for rides, £5 for 9 tokens.
Facilities: 🖾 T(2 hrs) 🍴 🖾

See Also:
Langham Glass Maize Maze, nr Holt, page 89

SUFFOLK

Farnham (nr. Saxmundham)
Friday Street Farm Shop - Maize Maze Map ref. M7
Tel: (01728) 602783
Maize maze with quiz. Enjoy hours of fun trying to locate the answers hidden in a few miles of paths. The maze takes a new shape every year and is suitable for all ages.
Times: Open mid Jul-Sept, daily, 0900-1630.
Fee: £3.00/£2.50/£8.00 (family).
Facilities: 🖾 T(3 hrs) 🍴 🖾 🐾 ♿

Felixstowe
Golf FX Map ref. L11
Manning's Amusement Park, Sea Road
Tel: (01394) 282370
Indoor adventure golf with 13 holes of skill, fun and surprises. Suitable for all the family.
Times: Open all year, daily, 1000-2100. Closed 25 Dec.
Fee: £2.00.
Facilities: 🛏 T(30 mins) 🎫 🐕

Felixstowe
Manning's Amusement Park Map ref. L11
Sea Road
Tel: (01394) 282370
Traditional children's amusement park with rides and attractions. Nightclub, sportsbar, amusement arcade and Sunday market.
Times: Open all year, please contact for opening days and times. Children's rides open Easter-30 Sept, Sat, Sun and school hols, 1100-1800. Closed 25 Dec.
Fee: Child £3.00
Facilities: 🛏 T(2 hrs) 🎫 🐕 🔲

Ipswich
Ipswich Town Football Club Stadium Tours Map ref. I/J10
Portman Road
Tel: (01473) 400555 Web: www.itfc.co.uk
See behind the scenes at a top football club. From the dressing room to the directors' box - the tour gives you a unique access 'behind the blues'.
Times: By appointment only - contact (01473) 400555 for full details.
Fee: £7.50/£5.00/£5.00/£22.00.
Facilities: 🅿 🛏 ♿ T(1½ hrs) 🚶

Lowestoft
The East Point Pavilion Visitor Centre Map ref. P2
Royal Plain
Tel: (01502) 533600 Web: www.visit-lowestoft.co.uk
A glass, all-weather Edwardian-style structure with a large indoor play area called Mayhem (for children aged 2-12). Small souvenir shop, restaurant, tearooms and Tourist Information Centre.
Times: Open 25 Mar-10 Apr, daily; 16, 17, 23, 24, 30 Apr; 1, 7, 8, 14, 15, 21, 22 May; 28 May-5 Jun, daily; 8, 11, 12, 15 Jun; 18 Jun-4 Sept, daily, 7, 10, 11, 14, 17, 18, 24 and 25 Sept.
Fee: £13.75/£11.50.
Facilities: 🅦 🅀 🅿 🛏 ♿ T(1 hr) 🎫 🏛

Lowestoft
New Pleasurewood Hills Leisure Park Map ref. P2
Leisure Way, Corton
Tel: (01502) 586000 Web: www.pleasurewoodhills.com
Fifty acres of rides, attractions and shows. Tidal wave watercoaster, log flume, chairlift and two railways, pirate ship, parrot/sealion shows, go-karts, rattlesnake coaster and Mega-Drop Tower.
Times: Open 25 Mar-10 Apr; daily; 16, 17, 23, 24, 30 Apr; 1, 7, 8, 14, 15, 21, 22 May; 28 May-5 Jun, daily; 8, 11, 12, 15 Jun; 18 Jun-4 Sept, daily; 7, 10, 11, 14, 17, 18, 24 and 25 Sept.
Fee: £13.75/£11.50.
Facilities: 🅦 🅿 🛏 T(6 hrs) 🎫 🏛 🔲

Southwold
Southwold Pier Map ref. O5
North Parade
Tel: (01502) 722105
Web: www.southwoldpier.co.uk
New pier, completed in 2002 - the first built in the UK for over 45 years. Amusements, exhibition - history of piers and seaside holidays, bar/restaurant, gift shop and tea room.
Times: Open 1 Jan-30 Apr, daily, 1000-1600. 1 May-30 Sept, daily, 1000-2200. 1 Oct-31 Dec, daily, 1000-1600. Closed 25 Dec.
Fee: Free.
Facilities: 🅦 🅿 🛏 T(3 hrs) 🎫 🏛 🐕 🔲

Children's Indoor Play Centres

BEDFORDSHIRE

Dunstable
Toddler World Map ref. C/D10
Dunstable Leisure Centre, Court Drive
Tel: (01582) 604307 Web: www.activityworld.co.uk
Indoor adventure play area for children under the height
limit of 1.2m.
Times: Open all year, daily, 0930-1700. Closed 25, 26 Dec
and 1 Jan.
Fee: Child £2.95.
Facilities: 🅿 T(1 hr) 🛈

CAMBRIDGESHIRE

Peterborough
Activity World Map ref. D5
Padholme Road East
Tel: (01733) 314446 Web: www.activityworld.co.uk
An indoor and outdoor adventure playground, plus the
Laser Maze arena.
Times: Open all year, daily, 0930-1830. Closed 25, 26 Dec
and 1 Jan.
Fee: School term weekdays £1.00/£2.95. Weekends/Hols
£1.00/£3.95. Children under 1 metre £2.95.
Facilities: 🅿 🍴 T(1½ hrs) 🛈 🚻

Peterborough
Big Sky Adventure Play Map ref. C6
24 Wainman Road, Shrewsbury Avenue, Woodston
Tel: (01733) 390810
An indoor children's soft play activities centre, with electric
mini go-karts and a monorail rocket ship ride. Trampoline
arena, plus six metre climbing wall.
Times: Open all year, daily, 1030-1800. Closed 25, 26 Dec
and 1 Jan.
Fee: Main play area £4.75. Pre-school play area £3.75. Extra
charge for go-karts, monorail and climbing wall.
Facilities: 🅿 T(2 hrs) 🛈 🚻 ♿

ESSEX

Clacton-on-Sea
Play Rascals Map ref. N6
Rascals House, Telford Rd, Gorse Lane Ind Estate
Tel: (01255) 475755
Giant children's indoor play centre, with seperate toddler
section. Restaurant.
Times: Open all year, daily 1000-1800. Closed 24-26 Dec
and 1 Jan.
Fee: 1-4yrs £3.50/5-12yrs £4.50.
Facilities: 🅿 🍴 ♿ T(2 hrs) 🛈

Wimpole Hall and Home Farm. Arrington

Colchester
Childsplay Adventureland Map ref. K4
Clarendon Way
Tel: (01206) 366566
Web: www.childsplayadventureland.com
Indoor play facility for under 9's. ROSPA safety inspected.
Ball pools, slides and special area for babies/toddlers.
Times: Open all year, daily, 0930-1830. Closed 25 Dec.
Fee: Child (under 5) £3.45. Child (over 5) £3.95.
Facilities: Q ☐ � 〒 T(2 hrs) 🛈 ⬚

Colchester
Go Bananas Map ref. K4
9-10 Mason Road, Cowdray Centre
Tel: (01206) 761762 Web: www.go-bananas.co.uk
Children's indoor adventure playground. 3-storey adventure
frame for 5-12 year-olds, an under 5's play village, climbing
wall, spaceball ride and cafeteria.
Times: Open all year, daily, 0930-1830. Closed 25, 26 Dec
and 1 Jan.
Fee: Child (under 5) £3.50. Child (5-12yrs) £4.20.
Facilities: Q ☐ 🚍 〒 T(2 hrs) 🛈

Halstead
Tumblewood Map ref. H3
Whitehouse Business Park, Whiteash Green
Tel: (01787) 474760 Web: www.tumblewood.co.uk
Children's indoor adventure playground with facilities for
parties. Separate play areas and baby/toddler area.
Times: Open all year, daily, 1000-1800. Closed 25, 26 Dec
and 1 Jan.
Fee: Child (under 5) £2.95. Child (over 5) £3.45.
Facilities: ⊛ ☐ 🚍 T(2 hrs) 🛈

Southend-on-Sea
Kids Kingdom Map ref. I11
Garon Park, Eastern Avenue
Tel: (01702) 462747
Web:www.kidskingdomsouthend.com
Exciting range of indoor adventure play activities for
children up to 12 years of age. Slides, inflatables, ball
ponds, swing bridges, and special under 5 section.
Times: Open all year, Mon-Fri, 0930-1800. Sat 0930-1900,
Sun 1000-1800. Closed 25, 26 Dec and 1 Jan.
Fee: Child (under 5) £3.50. Child (over 5) £4.50.
Facilities: ☐ 🚍 T(1½ hrs) 🛈

HERTFORDSHIRE

Bishop's Stortford
Little Legs Playhouse Map ref. K10
Unit 3, Birchanger Industrial Estate, Stansted Road
Tel: (01279) 656646 Web: www.littlelegsplayhouse.co.uk
Children's indoor soft play centre with cafeteria and private
party rooms. Under 4's area with non-walker section.
Larger over 4's apparatus with many features.
Times: Open all year, Mon, 1200-1730; Tues-Sun, 1000-
1730. Closed 24-26, 31 Dec and 1 Jan.
Fee: Various, please contact for further details.
Facilities: ☐ T(2-3 hrs) 🛈 ⬚

Hatfield Forest

Bushey

Activity World and Farmyard Funworld Map ref. E/F15

The Lincolnsfield Children's Centre, Bushey Hall Drive

Tel: (01923) 219902 Web: www.lincolnsfields.co.uk

The best of both worlds for children. Activity World is a giant indoor adventure playground. Farmyard Funworld has lots of animals to see and feed in our outdoor farmyard and play area.

Times: Open all year, daily, 1000-1800. Last admission one hour before closing time. Closed 25, 26 Dec and 1 Jan.

Fee: Child (under 2) £1.50/Child (under 5) £4.00/Child (over 5) £5.00/Adult £1.00. Special discounts on term time weekdays.

Facilities: T(4 hrs)

Hatfield

Activity World Map ref. G12

Longmead, Birchwood

Tel: (01707) 270789 Web: www.activityworld.co.uk

A large children's indoor adventure play centre with 6,000 sq ft of giant slides, ball pools and mazes. Birthday parties are catered for and special schemes for playgroups.

Times: Open all year, daily, 0930-1830. Closed 25, 26 Dec and 1 Jan.

Fee: Child £2.95. Weekends and school holidays £3.95, Toddlers under 1 mtr all times £2.95.

Facilities: T(1½ hrs)

Hatfield

Toddler World Map ref. G12

The Galleria, Comet Way

Tel: (01707) 257480 Web: www.activityworld.co.uk

Indoor adventure play area for children under the height limit of 1.2m.

Times: Open all year, Mon-Sat, 1000-1800; Sun, 1100-1700. Closed 25, 26 Dec and 1 Jan.

Fee: Child £2.95.

Facilities: T(1 hr)

Sawbridgeworth

Adventure Island Playbarn Map ref. K11

Parsonage Lane

Tel: (01279) 600907

A £200,000 high-quality barn conversion into an indoor children's play centre incorporating a toddler area for the under 3's, soft play, slides and much more.

Times: Open all year, Tues-Sun 100-1800, Bank Hols, 1000-1600. Closed 24-27 Dec and 1 Jan.

Fee: Child from £1.30-£3.80.

Facilities: T(1½ hrs)

NORFOLK

Cromer

Funstop Map ref. K3

Exchange House, Louden Road

Tel: (01263) 514976

A children's indoor adventure centre with a giant slide, ball pond, tubes, scrambling nets and a special under-3's area.

Times: Open Jan-May, Fri-Sun and daily during school hols, May-Jun, Thurs-Sun and daily during school hols, Jul-Sept, daily, Oct-Dec, Fri-Sun and daily during school hols, 1000-1800. Closed 25-26 Dec.

Fee: Child (under 3) £2.20. Child (over 3) £3.50.

Facilities: T(2 hrs)

Knapton (nr. Mundesley)

Elephant Playbarn Map ref. M4

Mundesley Road

Tel: (01263) 721080 Web: www.elephantplaybarn.co.uk

A converted Norfolk barn filled with exciting toys for the under 8's. Also a fully enclosed courtyard with pedal toys and an adventure play area.

Times: Open all year, Wed-Sun, 1000-1600. Closed 20 Dec-4 Jan.

Fee: Child £4.00.

Facilities: T(2 hrs)

Fishing by the River Thet, Thetford

Poringland (nr. Norwich)
The Playbarn Map ref. L8
West Green Farm, Shotesham Road
Tel: (01508) 495526 Web: www.theplaybarn.co.uk
Children's indoor and outdoor play centre. Designed for
age 7 and under. Large barn and courtyard, beach barn,
children's farm, riding school and after school club.
Times: Open all year, Mon-Fri, 0930-1530; Sun, 1000-
1700. Closed 25, 26 Dec and 1 Jan.
Fee: £1.00/£4.00.
Facilities: ⊛ Q 🄿 🚻 T(2 hrs) 🕉 ⑪ 🎋 🖳

SUFFOLK

Bury St. Edmunds
Activity World Playcentre Map ref. D/E6/7
Station Hill
Tel: (01284) 763799 Web: www.activityworld.co.uk
Indoor children's playground, including giant drop slide,
tumble tower, dizzy doughnut and giant ball pit.
Times: Open all year, Mon-Sat, 0930-1830. Please contact
for Christmas opening dates.
Fee: Child under 5's Mon-Fri, term time£3.50. Under 5's
weekend £4.25. Over 5's standard £4.25.
Facilities: 🄿 🚻 ⇌ T(1¹/₂ hrs) ⑪

Martlesham Heath
Kidz Kingdom Map ref. K10
Gloster Road
Tel: (01473) 611333 Web: www.kingpinbowling.co.uk
Four level structure with slides, ball pools, rope bridge,
aerial runways, tots soft play and large bouncy attractions.
Also Laser King, a 20 gun laser maze.
Times: Open all year, daily - times vary, please contact for
details. Closed 25 and 26 Dec.
Fee: Please contact for details of admission prices.
Facilities: 🄿 🚻 T(2 hrs) ⑪

Stowmarket
Playworld/Ocean Adventure Map ref. H7/8
Mid-Suffolk Leisure Centre, Gainsborough Road
Tel: (01449) 674980
A children's indoor play area for the under 10's, with a
wide range of inflatables, laser game, grand prix cars, bikes
and more.
Times: Playworld - open 30 Apr-4 Sept, Mon-Fri, 0930-
1900; Sat and Sun, 0900-1800. Ocean Adventure - open all
year, Mon-Fri, 0930-1900; Sat and Sun, 0900-1800. Closed
24 Dec-1 Jan.
Fee: Child (under 2) £1.80. Child (over 2) £3.15(2004
prices).
Facilities: ⊛ 🄿 🚻 ⇌ T(1¹/₂ hrs) ⑪ 🎋

Leisure Pools

BEDFORDSHIRE

Bedford
Bedford Oasis Beach Pool Map ref. D5/6
Cardington Road
Tel: (01234) 272100 Web: www.bedford.gov.uk
Fun pool with two giant waterslides, spa baths, bubble
burst area, lazy river ride, outside water lagoon, water
cannon, wave machine and water mushroom.
Times: Open all year. Weekdays in term times, 1200-1930;
weekdays in holidays, 1100-1930; weekends, 0945-1830.
Other sessions available.
Fee: £2.90-£4.90/£2.40-£3.90.
Facilities: ⊛ 🄿 🚻 ⇌ T(2-3 hrs) ⑪ 🖳

CAMBRIDGESHIRE

Cambridge
Parkside Pools Map ref. H11
Gonville Place
Tel: (01223) 446100
Web: www.cambridge.gov.uk/leisure/parkside.htm
Eight lane 25 metre pool, diving pool, two giant flume
rides, children's water area and health suite.
Times: Open all year daily.
Fee: Prices vary depending upon activity.
Facilities: ⊛ 🚻 ⇌ T(2-3 hrs) ⑪ 🖳

ESSEX

Chelmsford
Riverside Ice and Leisure Centre Map ref. F7
Victoria Road
Tel: (01245) 615050 Web: www.riversideiceandleisure.com
National sized ice arena, and three swimming pools
including flume ride and triple-diving platform. Fitness
centre, sports hall, squash and children's indoor adventure
playground.
Times: Open all year. Please contact for further details.
Fee: Prices vary depending upon activity.
Facilities: ⊛ 🄿 🚻 ⇌ T(2-3 hrs) ⑪ 🖳

**For even more
information visit
our website at
www.visiteastofengland.com**

Colchester
Colchester Leisure World Map ref. K4
Cowdray Avenue
Tel: (01206) 282000
Web: www.colchesterleisureworld.co.uk
Leisure pool with flumes, wave machine and rapids ride.
Separate fitness pool, sports hall, squash courts and 'Aqua
Springs' sauna/spa experience.
Times: Open all year. Please contact for further details.
Fee: Prices vary depending upon activity.
Facilities: ☼ Ⓟ 🛏 ⚌ T(2-3 hrs) ⑪ 🛍

Maldon
Blackwater Leisure Centre Map ref. I7
Park Drive
Tel: (01621) 851898 Web: www.blackwaterleisure.co.uk
Leisure pool with jungle river, flume ride and jacuzzi bubble
ledge. Toddler pool. Gym, sauna and sports hall.
Times: Open all year. Please contact for further details.
Fee: Prices vary depending upon activity.
Facilities: ☼ Ⓟ 🛏 T(2-3 hrs) ⑪ 🛍

HERTFORDSHIRE

Broxbourne
Lee Valley Leisure Pool Map ref. I13
New Nazeing Road
Tel: (01992) 467899 Web: www.leevalleypark.com
Large indoor pool with beach area, fountain and wave
machine. Toddlers' soft play area and fitness suite.
Times: Open all year, Mon-Fri, 0600-2200; Sat, 0800-
1800; Sun, 0800-1900.
Fee: Prices vary depending upon activity.
Facilities: ☼ Ⓟ T(2-3 hrs) ⑪ 🛍

Hemel Hempstead
Aquasplash Map ref. D12/13
Leisureworld, Jarman Park
Tel: (01442) 292203
Indoor tropical water park with space bowl, super flume,
tyre ride, drag race, multi slide, falling rapids and lazy river.
Times: Open all year, daily during school hols, closed Mon
and Tues in term time.
Fee: £4.90/£4.10/£3.50/£15.80.
Facilities: Ⓟ 🛏 ⚌ T(2-3 hrs) ⑪ 🛍

Letchworth Garden City
North Herts Leisure Centre Map ref. G8
Baldock Road
Tel: (01462) 679311 Web: www.leisure-centre.com
Tropical leisure pool with wave machine, giant flume, swan
slide and inflatable. Health and fitness studio, sports hall
and squash courts.
Times: Open all year, Mon 0800-2200;Tues-Fri 0700-2200;
Sat, 1100-1915; Sun, 0700-1730; Bank Hols, 1000-1800.
Fee: Prices vary depending upon activity.
Facilities: ☼ Ⓟ 🛏 ⚌ T(2-3 hrs) ⑪ 🛍

NORFOLK

Great Yarmouth
Marina Leisure Centre Map ref. P7
Marine Parade
Tel: (01493) 851521
Web: http://marina.leisureconnection.co.uk
Leisure pool with aqua slide and wave machine. Children's
indoor soft play area. Piazza with summer entertainment.
Times: Open all year, Mon-Fri, 0630-2200; Sat and Sun,
0900-2200.
Fee: Prices vary depending upon activity. Swimming -
£3.10/£2.70/£2.70.
Facilities: ☼ 🛏 ⚌ T(2-3 hrs) ⑪ 🛍

Hunstanton
Oasis Leisure Centre Map ref. D3
Central Promenade
Tel: (01485) 534227 Web: www.west-norfolk.gov.uk
Indoor pool with flume ride. Main sports hall with bowls
and multi-sport activities. Squash court, fast tanning
sunbeds and fitness suite.
Times: Open all year. Times vary according to season,
contact for details.
Fee: Prices vary depending upon activity.
Facilities: ☼ Ⓟ 🛏 T(2-3 hrs) ⑪ 🛍

Norwich
Aqua Park and Jumping Jacks Map ref. K/7
Norwich Sport Village and Hotel, Hellesdon
Tel: (01603) 788898 Web: www.norwichsportvillage.com
Aqua Park is fun for all the family, with two giant flumes,
ride the rapids and laze in the bubble bay. Competition
and toddlers pool. Jumping Jacks indoor children's
adventure playground.
Times: Mon-Sat,0630-2200, Sun 0630-1800. Jumping
Jacks Mon-Fri 1100-1730, Sat and Sun 1100-1730. Closed
25 and 26 Dec.
Fee: Aqua Park (off peak) £4.35/£3.00/£3.10/£11.40
(family). Aqua Park (peak) £5.35/£3.50/£13.40 (family).
Jumping Jacks £1.50.
Facilities: 🅿 T(2 hrs) ⑪ 🖥

Sheringham
The Splash Leisure Pool Map ref. J/K2
Weybourne Road
Tel: (01263) 825675 Web: www.northnorfolk.org
Tropical leisure pool with giant 150ft waterslide and wave
machine. Children's paddling area. Sun terrace, saunas,
activity hall and health/fitness studios.
Times: Open all year. Times vary according to season,
contact for details.
Fee: Prices vary depending upon activity.
Facilities: ⊛ 🅿 🚭 ⇌ T(2-3 hrs) ⑪ 🖥

Thetford
Waterworld Map ref. F/G11
Breckland Leisure Centre, Croxton Road
Tel: (01842) 753110 Web: www.breckland.gov.uk
Fun leisure pool with wave machine, rapids, water cannon,
flume and spa pool. Competition pool and fitness centre.
Times: Open all year, please telephone for details.
Fee: Prices vary depending upon activity.
Facilities: ⊛ 🅿 🚭 ⇌ T(2-3 hrs) ⑪

SUFFOLK

Bury St. Edmunds
Bury St. Edmunds Leisure Centre Map ref. D/E6/7
Beetons Way
Tel: (01284) 753496 Web: www.stedmundsbury.gov.uk
Leisure pool with two water flumes, water cannon, pirate
galleon and beach area. Also competition pool, sauna-
world, sports hall and fitness studio.
Times: Open all year, Mon-Fri, 0630-2230; Sat, 0830-
1930; Sun, 0830-2100; Bank Hols, 0900-2100. Contact for
specific opening times for each activity.
Fee: Prices vary depending upon activity.
Facilities: ⊛ 🅿 🚭 T(2-3 hrs) ⑪

Felixstowe
Felixstowe Leisure Centre Map ref. L11
Undercliff Road West
Tel: (01394) 670411
Web: www.suffolkcoastal.gov.uk/leisure
Leisure pool with slides. Sauna, steam room, fitness/health
suite and indoor bowls rink. Children's indoor soft play.
Times: Open all year, Mon-Fri 0700-2200, Sat and Sun
0800-2200.
Fee: Prices vary depending upon activity.
Facilities: ⊛ 🚭 T(2-3 hrs) ⑪ 🖥

Ipswich
Crown Pools Map ref. I/J10
Crown Street
Tel: (01473) 433655 Web: www.ibcsport.co.uk
Leisure pool with wave machine and fountains, set in a sub
tropical atmosphere. Also 25 metre competition pool and
health suite.
Times: Open all year. Please telephone for times.
Fee: Prices vary depending upon activity.
Facilities: ⊛ 🚭 T(2-3 hrs) ⑪

Sudbury
Kingfisher Leisure Centre Map ref. E10
Station Road
Tel: (01787) 375656
Web: http://kingfisher.leisureconnection.co.uk
Leisure complex featuring swimming pool with water flume
and beach area. Spa pool, fitness studio, health suite and
sauna.
Times: Open all year, Mon-Fri, 0630-2200; Sat, 0700-
1900; Sun, 0830-1730.
Fee: Prices vary depending upon activity.
Facilities: ⊛ 🅿 🚭 ⇌ T(2-3 hrs) ⑪

Felixstowe

A Taste of the East

FOOD FROM THE SEA

With its long coastline, it is little surprise that some of the region's great food specialities are its seafood. Along the Norfolk coast, try mussels from Stiffkey, lobsters from Sheringham, and Cromer's famous crabs, regarded as some of the best in the country. At Great Yarmouth, once a major fishing port, sample smoked kippers and bloaters. And at Aldeburgh in Suffolk, be sure to sample the fish and chips – arguably the best in the whole world!

Essex is a great place for sea food. In Colchester oysters have been farmed since Roman Times, and every October the town holds a private oyster festival attended by the Mayor. Mersea Island is now the centre of the "English Natives" oyster industry. South from here, samphire, "the asparagus of the sea" grows along the coast, whilst Maldon is the only place in the country where sea water is used to make crystalline salt (recommended by Delia Smith). Further south is the fishing village of Leigh-on-Sea where you can try cockles and jellied eels.

Visit Lowestoft for the annual Fish Fayre, when the town celebrates its fishing heritage. Learn more about the herring industry, which was once a mainstay of the town, look round an old fishing boat or a smart new coastal research vessel, and most importantly, taste and buy food fresh from the sea.

From the inland waterways of the Fens, a local delicacy is eel, a common fish in this area, alongside bream, roach, rudd, pike and zander.

PORK, POULTRY AND GAME

Pork and all its related products is the prime meat of the region. You'll find it hard to find a better sausage than the Old Epping, the Royale Cambridge, the much prized, royal warranted Newmarket, or the sagey Lincolnshire. There are pork pies and haslet (sausage meat loaf wrapped in lacy caul fat), Huntingdonshire fidget pies (made with gammon forehock, sliced potatoes, onions, cooking apples, cider and covered with pastry made with flour and lard), and famous Essex and Suffolk hams and bacons.

Traditionally Suffolk hams were sweet-cured with black treacle, brown sugar and hot beer. Hams were cooked in the kitchen copper with a bunch of hay in the bottom to stop them sticking, and this imparted a special flavour.

Bacon was prepared from the sides and smoked in the farmhouse or cottage, or it could be taken to the local "smoky house"" often owned by the local craftsman who could use up his sawdust and oak chippings. The sawdust was damped down to make it smoke and the bacon or ham might take three weeks to be cured and smoked.

During the early 18th century, droves of turkeys and geese were made to walk from Norwich to the London markets, with their feet coated with tar for protection. Today the county of Norfolk is home to poultry producer Bernard Matthews.

Game is plentiful in the rich corn-growing areas of the East of England, and it figures prominently on local menus in the winter. The flat fens and salt marshes provide very tasty wild duck, whole rabbit and hare is used in many local dishes. Pheasants were originally introduced into England by the Romans as an ornamental bird, and plenty abound in the East of England. At certain times of the year you can purchase delicious venison from Woburn Abbey's naturally reared deer.

MILLS AND BAKERIES

Most of the region's farmland grows cereal crops such as wheat, barley, corn, rye and maize. The region produces about 25% of the whole cereal production of Britain. Wheat is used to produce flour for making cakes, biscuits and bread, and because of this, the turning sails and waterwheels of historic mills have been part of life in the East of England for over 800 years.

The family firm of Jordan's, has been milling since 1855, and is renowned today for its crunchy breakfast cereals and bars. You can visit Jordan's mill shop at Holme Mills near Biggleswade. In Hertfordshire, the Mill Green Museum and Mill in Hatfield sells freshly milled flour, whilst at Kingsbury Watermill in St Albans, delicious waffles are the speciality. Head to Norfolk windmills of Great Bircham and Denver to try delicious bread and cakes made using the freshly milled flour.

In Bedfordshire, try a clanger – a local delicacy of baked suet crust with savoury meat at one end, and something sweet at the other – a complete meal in one handy parcel, originally made for the men-folk labouring in the fields. Pick one up from Gunns Bakery in Sandy. And whilst in the county of Bedfordshire, you may like to know that the tradition of afternoon tea was started at Woburn Abbey, by Anna Maria, the 7th Duchess of Bedford.

FRUIT AND VEGETABLES

The East of England is famous for its fruit and vegetables. The Fens, known as "the food basket of Britain", is noted for its rich dark peaty soil, which grows wonderful fruit as well as cereals, flowers and vegetables.

Surrounding Wisbech, you will find apple orchards and soft fruits, whilst carrots and celery thrive around Ely. Indeed, they thrive so well that 70% of all British celery comes from within 10 miles of Ely! In Hertfordshire, you might spot watercress growing on farms in the Whitwell area. The region is also well known for the growing of asparagus, and in the summer, you can enjoy the "asparagus of the sea" – the samphire which grows so well along the East Anglian coast.

Pick up some of this delicious fruit and vegetable produce from the many markets and farm shops throughout the region, or pick-your-own fruit from strawberries, raspberries and gooseberries to apples, pears and plums.

The jam and preserve manufacturers, Elsenham, Wilkin and Sons, Cartwright and Butler, and Chivers are all local to the East of England. Visit the museum and tearoom at Wilkin and Sons in Tiptree where the first jams were made in 1885.

If you have the chance, try a couple of traditional local specialities. Apple dumplings (apples wrapped in shortcrust pastry and baked with sultanas), or biffins (dried apples cooked in the oven overnight) and once sold in Norwich. Sometimes these were flattened and coated with sugar.

NAUGHTY BUT NICE!

Look out for delicious ice-cream made from only the purest ingredients, hand-made chocolates and fudge, or visit Great Yarmouth for the biggest seaside rock shop in the world. For "something really steamy", try a hot mustard from the famous selection of Colmans. The mustard makers have been associated with Norwich since 1814, and you can visit the Mustard Shop in the city.

BEER, CIDER AND WINE

There are many famous brewers to be found in the region, including Greene King, Adnams, Elgoods, Charles Wells, Ridley's and Batemans, to name just a few. Some of these offer a brewery tour where you can see the whole process for yourself, and then refresh your taste buds with a pint of real ale, matured naturally in the cask.

As well as being the source of one of the purest of natural spring waters, Hadham

Water, Hertfordshire was once known as the "cradle of the malting industry", its rich barley harvest providing the essential ingredient of beer. Malting took place throughout the area, and by 1855 there were 44 breweries in Hertfordshire. Today this tradition continues with McMullen and Sons, who have been brewing beer in Hertford for over 170 years.

Cider has been associated with Suffolk for over 600 years, and was a common drink until the introduction of beer in the 18th century, which resulted in its decline. In Norfolk, visit Whin Hill Cider , where the drink is brewed in an 18th century flint barn at Wells-next-the-Sea.

Nearly 2000 years ago the Romans planted vines on various sites around Great Britain, but the combination of low rainfall and limestone/chalk soils made them particularly successful in the east. By 1086, more than 40% of Britain's recorded vineyards were in the East of England. Today there are more than forty vineyards, ranging from small back garden undertakings, to large commercial concerns. Many of the vineyards are open for guided tours and tastings, including Chilford Hall Vineyard in Cambridgeshire where you can learn how English wine is made, and appreciate the subtle differences between Chilford's quality wines.

Turn to page 160 for more breweries and vineyards in the region which welcome visitors.

Restaurants

CAMBRIDGESHIRE

Cambridge

Arundel House Hotel Map ref. G11
Chesterton Road, Cambridge CB4 3AN
Tel: (01223) 367701 Fax: (01223) 367721
Email: info@arundelhousehotels.co.uk
Web: www.arundelhousehotels.co.uk
Elegant, privately owned, 103 bedroom, 19th C. Victorian terrace hotel beautifully located overlooking the River Cam and open parkland, only a few minutes walk from the historic city centre and famous University colleges. The hotel is well known for its friendly relaxed atmosphere and has a reputation for providing some of the best food in the area, at very modest prices, in its award winning restaurant. The hotel's magnificent Victorian style conservatory, which overlooks an attractive walled garden adjacent to the bar, offers an alternative menu throughout the day, including cream teas, with additional seating outside. The hotel facilities also include a large car park.

Duxford (nr. Cambridge)

Duxford Lodge Hotel Map ref. H13
Ickleton Road, Duxford CB2 4RT
Tel: (01223) 836444 Fax: (01223) 832271
Email: admin@duxfordlodgehotel.co.uk
Web: www.duxfordlodgehotel.co.uk
Beautiful gardens, village setting just south of Cambridge, and close to Duxford Air Museum, the pretty villages of Essex and Suffolk and Newmarket Races. The attractive hotel has much going for it. Beautifully maintained public rooms and delightful bedrooms provide a relaxed informal atmosphere. Modern French cooking is the theme for 'Le Paradis' Restaurant, one of only a few 2 Rosette Restaurants in the Cambridgeshire area. Tourist Board Gold award for Quality. Cheerful enthusiastic service and an excellent wine list. Lunch from £10.99, Dinner from £27.50, Sun lunch £17.95, children under 10 half price. Private dining our speciality.

A PLACE TO EAT -
A PLACE TO MEET

Looking for more than just good food when you go out for a meal? Look no further than the award-winning Barn Brasserie where freshly prepared food using the East of England's finest produce is just one of the many things to look forward to. Set in the heart of stunning countryside and yet just a few minutes from the A12 near Colchester, this fabulous oak-beame[d] converted barn offers a dinin[g] experience and ambiance unrivalled [in] the region. With a choice of men[u] starting from just £5·99*, there's n[o] need to wait for a special occasio[n] because it's the experience you'[re] looking for at the price you want [to] pay. Our professional and frien[dly] team are waiting to welcome you.

BARN BRASSERIE GREAT TEY
BOOK YOUR TABLE NOW ON
01206 212345

* Terms and conditions apply.

ESSEX

Ely

The Old Fire Engine House Map ref. 18
25 Saint Mary's Street, Ely CB7 4ER
Tel: (01353) 662582 Fax: (01353) 668364
Web: www.theoldfireenginehouse.co.uk
The Old Fire Engine House is a restaurant and gallery, which has been owned and run by the same family since 1968. An 18th C. brick building close to Ely Cathedral, it has a large walled garden, friendly staff and an informal atmosphere. The cooking is based on local ingredients and classic English dishes form the mainstay of the menus. There is an extensive wine list and afternoon teas are also served. Art Gallery features monthly exhibitions of work by regional and national artists. Open for coffee, lunch, tea and dinner - telephone for details. ⊛ P 🍴 ≈ 🍷 🅱

Felsted (nr. Great Dunmow)
Reeves Restaurant Map ref. F5
Rumbles Cottage, Braintree Road, Felsted,
nr. Great Dunmow CM6 3DJ
Tel: (01371) 820996 Web: www.dreeves@btclick.com
In the centre of the picturesque and historic village of Felsted, an enchanting Grade II Listed building provides an idyllic setting for Reeves Restaurant. Relax and enjoy superb food freshly prepared by our two highly experienced chefs. Menus to entice with a contemporary twist on traditional fine dining. Open Wed - Sat for simple and stylish lunches. Evenings a la carte menu and Sunday is traditional lunch. ⊛ 🍴

Huntingdon
The Old Bridge Hotel Map ref. D9
1 High Street, Huntingdon PE29 3TQ
Tel: (01480) 424300 Web: www.huntsbridge.co.uk
The ultimate 'country hotel in a town'. The lounges extend into a really splendid conservatory with attractive and comfortable cane chairs and tables. Here one can enjoy exceptional brasserie style food. There is also a top-class, panelled restaurant with a wine list regularly named as one of the finest in the UK, including a selection of 20 wines served by the glass. Enjoy tea, coffee and drinks (including a fine selection of real ales) any time of day in the comfortable lounge and bar or outside on the patio. Open: daily. Average prices: 3 course restaurant meal £24.00. Brasserie meals from £4.50. ⊛ P 🍴 ≈ 🍷

Great Tey (nr. Colchester)
The Barn Brasserie Map ref. I4
Great Tey, nr. Colchester CO6 1JE
Tel: (01206) 212345 Fax: (01206) 211522
Web: www.barnbrasserie.co.uk
The Barn Brasserie, Great Tey, can be found just a five minute journey along the A120 from the main A12 near Colchester. Set in the heart of beautiful countryside, this award-winning conversion of a Grade Two Listed 16th C. barn is one of the most popular and successful restaurants in the region. Offering fantastic dining with a range of set menus as well as a superb a la Carte menu, and a choice of 100 fine wines, the Barn Brasserie has a reputation for excellent service, excellent food and excellent value for money. Open all day every day with plenty of car parking. ⊛ P 🍷 🅱

Messing (nr. Colchester)
Crispin's Map ref. I5
The Street, Messing, nr. Colchester CO5 9TR
Tel: (01621) 815868
Crispin's, built around 1475, is an oak-beamed, candlelit restaurant with en-suite rooms, with four-poster beds. B&B for two is £57.50. It's international cuisine is outstanding, and the restaurant is open from 1930 Wed-Sat and for lunch on Sun. We are just a few miles from the A12 south of Colchester.

Nayland
The White Hart Inn Map ref. F11
11 High Street, Nayland CO6 4JF
Tel: (01206) 263382 (reservations)
Fax: (01206) 263638 Email: Nayhart@aol.com
Web: www.whitehart-nayland.co.uk
An Inn located in an old coaching house in the heart of Constable Country. Countryside-style cooking with French flair, and the use of seasonal local produce. Wedding Licence. Private function room and terrace available. Light fare lunch menu with á la carte in the evenings. Restaurant and guestrooms open 7 days a week. Six bedrooms with en-suite facilities available seven days a week. 🅿 〽 ⬛

Pleshey

HERTFORDSHIRE

St. Albans
Waffle House Map ref. F13
Kingsbury Watermill Museum Limited,
St. Michael's Street, St. Albans AL3 4SJ
Tel: (01727) 853502 Fax: (01727) 730459
Freshly baked, Belgian-style waffles are the star attraction in this delightfully informal venue on the outskirts of town. The menu ranges from best-seller ham and mushroom to pecan with butterscotch sauce. The kitchen cares about quality, making use of organically farmed beef, stoneground flour and free-range eggs. Situated next to a historic watermill, museum and gift shop. Eat in the rustic dining room (once the Miller's Parlour), or outside in the shade of huge parasols. Open: Mon-Sat, 1000–1800. Sun and Bank Hols, 1100–1800 (1700 winter). Waffles from £2.10 to £7.00. £12.00 per head for three courses, without drinks (unlicensed). ⬛ 🅿 🛏 ⬛ 〽 ⬛

NORFOLK

Attleborough
Sweet Briar Bistro Map ref. I9
Peter Beales Roses, London Road, Attleborough NR17 1AY
(Leave the A11 at the roundabout South of the town)
For table reservations and evening dining -
Tel: (01953) 450134
Our licensed Sweet Briar Bistro is set amidst the secluded gardens of Peter Beales Classic Roses. Experience fine dining, freshly prepared food and a friendly service. Contemporary a la Carte menu on Saturday evenings and other evenings on request. Extensive daytime menu from light bites to delicious mouth-watering meals. Group bookings and parties welcome. Booking Essential. Open 7 days a week, including Bank Hols, Mon-Sat 0930-1630; Sun and Bank Hols 1030-1530; Fri and Sat evening and other evenings on request 1900-2100. ⬛

Aylsham
The Walpole Arms Map ref. K5
The Common, Itteringham, Nr Aylsham NR11 7AR
Tel: (01263) 587258
Fax: (01263) 587074
Email: goodfood@thewalpolearms.co.uk
Just a couple of miles from both Blickling and Mannington
Halls. The Walpole Arms is an oak beamed 18th century
country pub and restaurant serving exceptional food for
which it has received numerous awards including a
Michelin "Bib Gourmand'. Run by former Masterchef
producer, Richard Bryan, The Walpole offers a range of
real ales including the celebrated 'Walpole Ale' and a dozen
wines by the glass. As well as a vine covered terrace, there
are two peaceful gardens in which to enjoy summer eating,
and at lunch time a snack menu is offered in addition to
the a la carte. Booking is strongly recommended.
Open 1200-1500 and 1800-2300 (Food 1200-1400 and
1900- 2100) 🅿 🕙 🐕 📶

Burgh Castle (nr. Great Yarmouth)
Church Farm Hotel & Restaurant Map ref. O8
Church Road, Burgh Castle, nr. Great Yarmouth
NR31 9QG
Tel: (01493) 780251
Fax: (01493) 780480
Email: enquiries@church-farm.uk.Net
Church Farm nestles beside Breydon Water where the rivers
Waveney and Yare meet opposite the Berney Arms
Windmill, giving the most beautiful spectacular views of Norfolk.
The towns of Gorleston and Great Yarmouth are 10
minutes drive away with their entertainments, beaches
and shops. 🕙

Thetford
The Mulberry Map ref. F/G11
11 Raymond Street, Thetford IP24 2EA
Tel: (01842) 820099
A Victorian themed restaurant in the heart of the old town,
specialising in homemade, traditional and vegetarian food.
Child friendly and non smoking with a delightful courtyard
garden for teas and coffee. Full a la carte service, lunch and
evenings. Open 1000-1400 and 1800-2100, Mon-Sat;
Average price for 3 courses £20.00.

SUFFOLK

Bury St. Edmunds
The Priory Hotel and Garden Restaurant
Map ref. D/E6/7
Tollgate, Bury St. Edmunds IP32 6EH
Tel: (01284) 766181 Fax: (01284) 767604
Email: reservations@prioryhotel.co.uk
Web: www.prioryhotel.co.uk
The Priory Hotel and Garden Restaurant is set within
extensive gardens, surrounded by historic Priory flint walls.
The Grade II listed hotel offers a warm welcome and high
levels of individual service, whilst you enjoy the Priory's
hospitality, comfort, charm and tranquility. All rooms are
en-suite. Free parking for over 70 cars.
🅿 🛏 ⇌ 🕙 🐕 📶

Ipswich
The Galley Restaurant Map ref. I/J10
25 St. Nicholas Street, Ipswich IP1 1TW
Tel: (01473) 281131 Web: www.galley.uk.com
This attractive restaurant has an outstanding reputation for
the finest food, wines and friendly efficient service. Short
walk from town centre and nearby marina development.
International cuisine, seafood specialities; daily specials
and vegetarian dishes. Alfresco dining. Open for lunch
1200-1400; dinner 1800 until late; Tues-Sat. ⊛

Woodbridge
The Galley Restaurant Map ref. K9
21 Market Hill, Woodbridge IP12 4LX.
Tel: (01394) 380055 Web: www.galley.uk.com
Set in a period building with views over the thriving market
square. The ground floor is a casual walk-in affair and the
upstairs boasts a beautifully appointed 70 cover restaurant.
A leisurely stroll from the quayside, daily specials are always
available. Quality international cuisine and a wide choice of
fine wines. Open Tues-Sat 1200-1400; 1830 until late; Sun
lunch 1200-1400. ⊛

Hadleigh
The Marquis of Cornwallis Map ref. G10
Upper Street, Upper Layham, nr. Hadleigh, Ipswich IP7 5JZ
Tel: (01473) 822051
Web: www.themarquisofcornwallis.com
Nestled in Constable countryside, The Marquis of
Cornwallis offers a truly traditional welcome. The candle-lit
ambience provides the perfect atmosphere for sampling
and enjoying its real ales, country wines and traditional
English country menu. Perched on the rim of the valley, the
Marquis' garden rolls down to the River Brett and provides
the perfect location to watch the sun set over the vale.
Open daily, we have no petty restrictions, with patrons able
to eat in one of the bars, the dining room or the garden.
⊛ P 🍴 🐕

Afternoon Teas

CAMBRIDGESHIRE

Ely
Steeplegate Map ref. I8
16-18 High Street, Ely CB7 4JU
Tel: (01353) 664731
Proprietor: Mr J S Ambrose. Seats: 40. Home-made cakes,
scones and fresh cream teas, served in an historic building
backing onto the cathedral. Craft goods also sold. Small
groups welcome. Open: Daily except Sun. ⊛ 🍴 ⇌ 🍴

ESSEX

Aldham (nr. Colchester)
Mill Race Garden Centre Coffee Shop Map ref. J4
New Road, Aldham, nr. Colchester CO6 3QT
Just off the A1124, formerly A604 at Ford Street.
Tel: (01206) 242521 Web:
www.millracegardencentre.co.uk
Enjoy home-made and speciality cakes, cream teas or light
lunches in our conservatory style coffee lounge or courtyard
garden. Riverside garden and boat hire, large plant centre,
silk and dried flower shop and giftware. Aquatic Centre
opening 2005. Open daily including Sun 0930-1700. ⊛ P
🍴 🐕 🐕 🏵

Ingatestone
Café du Jardin Map ref. E9
Ingatestone Garden Centre, Roman Road,
Ingatestone CM4 9AU
Tel: (01277) 353268
Web: www.ingatestone-gardencentre.co.uk
Café du Jardin has established a good reputation for home
cooked lunch and home baked cakes. It is in attractive
gardens where you can sit in warm weather to enjoy the
food and gardens. Come once and you'll come again!
Open 7 days a week. P T(2 hrs) 🍴 🏵

NORFOLK

Bressingham (nr. Diss)
Into-Food Café Map ref. J11
Blooms of Bressingham, Bressingham, nr. Diss IP22 2AB
Tel: (01379) 688585
Three miles west of Diss on A1066. This impressive building
was completed in Spring 2000, and the Tea Rooms
renamed. Distinctive daily menus all at a reasonable cost,
provide delicious snacks, lunches or tea-time treats in this
unique setting, with an outside decking area an added
attraction. Open: Daily, 0900-1730, Sun 1030 - 430, Mar-
Oct; 0900-1630, Nov-Feb (except Christmas Day/Boxing
Day). See also entry for Blooms of Bressingham under
Nurseries & Garden Centres on page 105.

Heacham (nr. Hunstanton)
Norfolk Lavender Ltd Map ref. D3
Caley Mill, Heacham (on A149) PE31 7JE
Tel: (01485) 571965/570384
Web: www.norfolk-lavender.co.uk
Locally baked cakes and scones and cream teas a speciality.
Lunches available all year and log fire Oct-Apr. Miller's
Tearoom in the middle of lavender/herb gardens and fragrant
meadow. Seats: 120 all year, 88 in summer. Free admission.
Open Apr-Oct, 1000-1700; Nov-Mar, 1000-1600. Average
price: £2.70. ◎ Q P T(4 hrs) ƒ ⑪ ⋔ (on leads) ▣

Thursford (nr. Fakenham)
Thursford Collection Map ref. H4
Thursford, nr. Fakenham NR21 0AS
Tel: (01328) 878477
Our "Treasures in Store" museum houses majestic old road
engines, mechanical organs and old-fashioned fairground
rides. Live Wurlitzer shows and music from mechincal pipe
organs. Old farm buildings transformed into a small village
with a touch of Charles Dickens' England house the gift shops
and famous Christmas shop. Afternoon cream teas on the
lawn. Teas, light refreshmants and hot meals also served in our
Barn.
Admission: £5.50/£3.00/£5.20. ◎ Q P T(2½ hrs) ⑪ 冈 ▣

Beccles
The Parish Lantern Map ref. N2/3
Exchange Square, Beccles NR34 9HH
Tel: (01502) 711700
A rich mix of crafts, gifts, clothes, pictures and jewellery
housed in this part 17th C. listed building. Set in the
historic market town of Beccles, which features a wealth of
period buildings leading down to the River Waveney,
'Gateway to the Broads'. Open Mon-Sat, 0900-1700. ◎

SUFFOLK

Walberswick
The Parish Lantern Map ref. O5
On the Village Green, Walberswick IP18 6TT
Tel: (01502) 723173
Visit our celebrated tea room and courtyard garden. Enjoy
morning coffee, light lunches, cream teas and home-baked
cakes. Original crafts, gifts, clothes and pictures. Set in the
unspoilt beauty of the fishing village of Walberswick. Open:
1 Mar-Christmas Eve, daily from 1000. Jan and Feb, Fri, Sat
and Sun only, from 1000. ◎

Wingfield (nr. Diss)
Wingfield Arts Tea Room Map ref. J/K4/5
Church Road, Wingfield IP21 5RA
Tel: (01379) 384505 Fax: (01379) 384034
Email: info@wingfield-arts.co.uk
Web: www.wingfield-arts.co.uk
Enjoy traditional homemade cakes in the unique
atmosphere of our medieval barn or on our sunny terrace
with views across the sculpture garden and rolling Suffolk
landscape. Our friendly staff can offer an extended
selection of specialist teas and cordials and during the
Autumn our menu is revised to include winter warmer
snacks. We are the only tea room in the area and free entry
to Wingfield Arts site means that you can visit as often as
you like! We welcome group bookings - set teas and light
lunches for groups should be arranged in advance. Open:
Easter-Dec, Wed-Sun 2-5pm. ◎ P ⑪ ▣

Breweries & Vineyards

CAMBRIDGESHIRE

Linton
Chilford Hall Vineyard Map ref. I13
Chilford Hundred Limited, Balsham Road, Linton,
nr. Cambridge CB1 6LE
Tel: (01223) 895625 Web: www.chilfordhall.co.uk
Taste and buy award winning wines from the largest
vineyard in Cambridgeshire. See the grapes growing in the
eighteen acre vineyard, learn how English wine is made and
appreciate the subtle difference between each of the
Chilford quality wines. Also on sale, a range of local
specialities - browse and buy! Take the A11/A1307 then
just follow - 'Chilford Hall Vineyard' signs.
Times: Open 1 Mar-31 Oct, Fri, Sat and Sun, 1100-1730.
Group visits by arrangement throughout the year.
Fee: Vineyard tours £5.50.
Facilities: ❀ 🄿 T(2 hrs) 🏃 ⑨ ☴ 🐕 🛆

Wisbech
Elgood's Brewery and Garden Map ref. H4
North Brink Brewery
Tel: (01945) 583160 Web: www.elgoods-brewery.co.uk
Independent family brewery established in 1795. Visitors
can watch traditional methods of brewing and sample a
range of real ales. 4-acre garden contains many features
and maze.
Times: Open 26 Apr-29 Sept, Tues-Thurs, 1130-1630.
Fee: Brewery, garden and tasting £6.00. Garden only
£2.50.
Facilities: ❀ 🄿 T(2 hrs) 🏃 ⑨ 🛆 (garden and visitor centre)

ESSEX

Boxted (nr. Colchester)
Carter's Vineyards Map ref. K3
Green Lane
Tel: (01206) 271136 Web: www.cartersvineyards.co.uk
Vineyards and a winery with an alternative energy project
and a conservation area. Fishing facilities (day licence) are
available.
Times: Open 28 Mar-31Oct, daily, 1100-1700.
Fee: £3.50.
Facilities: Q 🄿 T(2 hrs) 🏃 ☴ 🐕 🛆

East Mersea
Mersea Vineyard Map ref. L6
Rewsalls Lane
Tel: (01206) 385900 Web: www.merseawine.com
10 acre site (established 1985) overlooking the Blackwater
and Colne estuaries. Tasting and vineyard walk. Conducted
tours of winery and vineyard by appointment only.
Times: Vineyard tours by appointment only.
Fee: Free. Vineyard tours £3.50.
Facilities: ❀ 🄿 T(1 hr)

Felsted (nr. Great Dunmow)
Felsted Vineyard Map ref. F5
The Vineyards, Crix Green
Tel: (01245) 361504
Set on a 12 acre site. Working vineyard and brewery - see
how wine is made and how to brew. Children welcome to
view animals.
Times: Open all year, Sat and Sun, 1000-dusk. Closed 24
Dec-1 Jan. Other times by appointment.
Fee: Free.
Facilities: 🄿 🍽 T(1½ hrs) ☴

Great Bardfield
Bardfield Vineyard Map ref. F3
Great Lodge
Tel: (01371) 810776
Web: www.thegreatlodgeexperience.com
The vineyard was planted in 1990, on a south facing slope
behind a Grade I listed brick and tile barn built by Anne of
Cleves. The aromatic grape varieties are hand-picked.
Times: Open 21 Mar-30 Sept, daily, 1000-2200 by prior
arrangement, please contact for details.
Fee: £4.75.
Facilities: 🄿 T(1½ hrs) 🏃 ☴

For even more
information visit
our website at
www.visiteastofengland.com

Purleigh (nr. Maldon)
New Hall Vineyards Map ref. H8
Chelmsford Road
Tel: (01621) 828343 Web: www.newhallwines.co.uk
Guided tours of the vineyards, with a trail through the vines and the cellars where wine can be tasted. Also visit the press house with slide shows. See fermentation/bottling.
Times: Open all year, Mon-Fri, 1000-1700; Sat and Sun, 1000-1530.
Fee: Free.
Facilities: T(2-3 hrs)

NORFOLK

Ickburgh (nr. Thetford)
Iceni Brewery Map ref. F9
3 Foulden Road
Tel: (01842) 878922
Tours of the brewery, featuring traditional and new methods of brewing and the history of brewing. Free tasting. Hop Garden and new shop open.
Times: Open all year, Mon-Fri, 0830-1630.
Fee: Free.
Facilities: T(20 mins)

Wells-next-the-Sea
Whin Hill Cider Map ref. G2
Stearmans Yard
Tel: (01328) 711033 Web: www.whinhillcider.co.uk
Cider works in an 18th C. flint barn. Exhibits of cider making equipment, mugs and glasses. Visitors can see bottling, labeling and blending. Opportunity to taste/purchase ciders and apple juice.
Times: Open 2 Apr-26 Jun, Sat and Sun, 1100-1730. 1 Jul-31 Aug, Tues-Sun, 1100-1730. 4 Sept-30 Oct, Sat and Sun, 1100-1730.
Fee: Free.
Facilities: T(30 mins)

Woodbastwick (nr. Wroxham/Hoveton)
Woodforde's Brewery Shop and Visitor Centre
Map ref. M6
Broadland Brewery
Tel (01603) 722218 Web: www.woodfordes.co.uk
Woodforde's cask ale brewery shop and visitor centre. Various displays and video of the brewing process. The Fur and Feather Inn is located next door, which is the brewery tap and restaurant.
Times: Open all year, Mon-Fri, 1030-1630. Sat, Sun and Bank Hol Mon, 1130-1630. Closed 25 and 26 Dec.
Fee: Free.
Facilities: T(1½ hrs)

SUFFOLK

Bungay
St. Peter's Brewery and Visitor Centre Map ref. L3
St. Peter's Hall, St. Peter South Elmham
Tel: (01986) 782322 Web: www.stpetersbrewery.co.uk
Opened in 1996, this unique working brewery is housed in 19th C. farm buildings. Restaurant/bar in medieval moated hall dating from 13th C. Brewery shop and visitor centre.
Times: Open all year. Brewery tours - Fri-Sun and Bank Hols, every hour between 1200-1600. Visitor centre and shop - Mon-Fri, 0900-1700; Sat, Sun and Bank Hol Mon, 1100-1700.
Fee: Brewery tours/tastings £4.00.
Facilities: Q T(1 hr)

Bury St. Edmunds

Greene King Brewery Visitor Centre Map ref. D/E6/7
Westgate Street
Tel: (01284) 714297 Web: www.greeneking.co.uk
Museum providing an insight into the history and art of brewing. Informative and fun tour of the working brewhouse, including a tutored tasting of the beers. Shop and off license.
Times: Open all year, Museum and shop, Mon-Sat, 1000-1700; Sun, 1200-1600. Tours, Mon-Sat at 1100 and 1400. Closed Good Friday, 25 and 26 Dec. Evening tours Wed, Thurs, Fri by arrangement.
Fee: Museum £2.00/£1.00/£1.50/£5.00. Tours £6.00 (over 12s only).
Facilities: T(2½ hrs)

Framlingham

Shawsgate Vineyard Map ref. L7
Badingham Road
Tel: (01728) 724060 Web: www.shawsgate.co.uk
An attractive 15-acre vineyard with a modern, well-equipped winery, vineyard walk, guided tours, wine tastings, picnic area, children's play area and shop.
Times: Open all year, daily, 1030-1700. (Oct-early March 1100-1600). Last tours half hour before closing.
Fee: £5.00/free/£4.00.
Facilities: T(45 mins)

Ilketshall St. Lawrence (nr. Halesworth)

Suffolk Apple Juice and Cider Place Map ref. M4
Cherry Tree Farm
Tel: (01986) 781353
Traditional apple pressing equipment can be seen ready for use. Explanations given on its use, and quality single apple juices and ciders can be sampled and bought.
Times: Open 31 Mar-2 Nov, Mon, Tues and Thurs-Sat, 0900-1300 and 1400-1800. Closed 25 and 26 Dec.
Fee: Free.
Facilities: T(30 mins)

Kirtling (nr. Newmarket)

Sascombe Vineyards Map ref. B8
The Thrift
Tel: (01440) 783100
Organic site with alternative energy, traditional architecture, consultations, talks, mineral water, honey and fine organic dessert-style wines wholesale and retail.
Times: Open at any time by appointment only.
Fee: £3.50.
Facilities: T(1 hr)

Shotley (nr. Ipswich)

Witenagemot Wines Ltd Map ref. K11
Witenagemot, Below Church
Tel: (01473) 787016 Web: www.witenagemot.co.uk
19 acre vineyard with views over the River Orwell and out to sea. Believed to be ancient vineyard site (5/6th C.) Carp lake, winery and river walks.
Times: Please contact for details.
Fee: Please contact for details.
Facilities: T(2½ hrs)

See Also:

Ickworth House, Park and Gardens, Horringer, nr Bury St Edmunds, page 45
Wyken Hall Gardens and Wyken Vineyards, Stanton, nr Bury St Edmunds, page 122

Carter's Vineyards, Boxted

Stop & Shop

CAMBRIDGESHIRE

steeplegate

Ely
Steeplegate Map ref. I8
16-18 High Street, Ely CB7 4JU
Tel: (01353) 664731
Unusual gifts of good taste in Craft Gallery beside the
cathedral. Tearoom. We sell woodwork, books, ceramics,
jewellery, lace and toys. Open all year, daily except Sunday,
0900-1730. ⊛ ▭ ⇌ ⑪

ESSEX

Billericay
Barleylands Craft Village Map ref. F9
Barleylands Farm, Barleylands Road, Billericay CM11 2UD
Tel: (01268) 290219 Email: info@barleylands.co.uk
Web: www.barleylands.co.uk
Come and visit our Craft Village where you can experience
over 30 specialist workshops where local people
demonstrate and sell their crafts. You can enjoy a delicious
snack in our Tea Room or bring your own picnic to enjoy in
our landscaped courtyards. Easy access for all, with a flat
level surface and lifts to upper levels. FREE Entry and
parking. Open all year, closed Mondays. Groups welcomed-
notice appreciated. Also on site Fun Farm Centre - see
Barleylands Farm Centre. ⊛ Q ℙ ▭ T(2 hrs) ⑪ 卅
🐕 ⌷

Braintree
Blake House Craft Centre Map ref. F5
Blake End, nr. Braintree CM77 6SH
Tel: (01376) 552553
Web: www.blakehousecraftcentre.co.uk
The courtyard of listed farm buildings, which have been
converted into craft shops, specialized businessess and
restuarant/tearoom. Open all year. Some units open 7
days a week ,including tea room, and bank holidays 1000-
1700 closed 25 Dec-3 Jan.
ℙ ▭ T(2 hrs) ⑪ ⌷

Brentwood
Hazle Ceramics Workshop Map ref. D10
Stallion's Yard, Codham Hall, Great Warley,
nr. Brentwood CM13 3JT
Tel: (01277) 220892 Web: www.hazle.com
See where the award-winning collectable ceramic wall
plaques, "A Nation of Shopkeepers" are made. Hobby
ceramic painting sessions on Fri/Sat and school hols -
phone for details/book. Open all year, Fri-Sat and Bank
Hols, 1100-1700. Shop open Tues-Sat. Closed 24 Dec-
4 Jan. ⊛ ℙ T(1 hr) ⑪ ⌷

Chelmsford
Moulsham Mill Map ref. F7
Parkway, Chelmsford CM2 7PX
Tel: (01245) 608200 Web: www.moulshammill.co.uk
A mill on the site of an ancient watermill, dating back to
Domesday. The watermill is not working, and has been
restored to a retail craft and business centre. Refreshments
available. Open all year, Mon-Sat, 0900-1700. Closed on
all Bank Hols. ℙ ▭ ⇌ T(1½ hrs) ⑪ ⌷

Colchester
GfB : the Colchester Bookshop Map ref. K4
92 East Hill, Colchester CO1 2QN
Tel: (01206) 563138
Web: www.gfb.uk.net
Browse through five rooms of fascinating books on
literature, art, philosophy, history, science and local
interest, less than 5 minutes walk from Colchester Castle,
just beyond Hollytrees Museum and the Minories Art
Gallery, at the top of East Hill. Good books also bought.
Open Mon-Sat, 1000-1730. ▣ ▄▄ T(1 hr)

Colchester

Dedham
Dedham Art and Craft Centre Map ref. L3
High Street
Tel: (01206) 322666
One of East Anglia's leading Art and Craft Centres in a
beautiful converted red brick 18thC church in an area of
outstanding natural beauty. Spread over 3 extensive floors
with many interesting and original displays by artists and
craft workers.
Times: Open all year every day 1000-1700 except
Christmas day and Boxing day.
Fee: Free.
Facilities: ⊛ ▄▄ T(1 hr) ⓘ

Saffron Walden
Debden Antiques Map ref. D3
Elder Street, Debden, nr. Saffron Walden CB11 3JY
Tel: (01799) 543007 Web: www.debden-antiques.co.uk
A large collection of fine antiques for the home and
garden, displayed in a magnificent 17th C. Essex barn.
Outside is a lovely courtyard and a large private car park.
Open all year, Tues-Sat 1000-1730; Sun and Bank Hols,
1100-1600. ▣ T(1 hr)

NORFOLK

VISIT

THE BLACK SHEEP SHOP

THE BLACK SHEEP SHOP AND
NEW COUNTRYWEAR COLLECTION
Aylsham
Black Sheep Shop - Black Sheep Jerseys Map ref. K5
9 Penfold Street, Aylsham NR11 6ET
Tel: (01263) 733142/732006
Email: Email@blacksheep.ltd.uk
Web: www.blacksheep.ltd.uk
The Black Sheep shop is now a 'must see' when visiting
Norfolk. The world famous British made jerseys and
accessories are still a reason in themselves to visit. Now our
country and casual wear ranges are stronger than ever: Mat
de Misaine, Sebago, Chatham and Weird Fish are just a few
of the ranges that have been introduced, giving excellent
choice for both men and women. Clothes have never
looked this good! Free colour catalogue on request. Open
Mon-Fri, 0900-1750; Sat, 1000-1700; closed Sun. Free
customer parking. ⊛

NORFOLK CHILDREN'S BOOK CENTRE

Between Aylsham and Cromer
Norfolk Children's Book Centre Map ref. K4
Wayside, Alby NR11 7HB
Tel: (01263) 761402 Web: www.ncbc.co.uk
Surrounded by fields, the Centre displays one of the best collections of children's and teachers' books in East Anglia. Here you will find a warm welcome and expert advice. You can browse through the latest and the classics in both fiction and non-fiction. We also sell story cassettes, videos and cards. Find out more about the Centre on www.ncbc.co.uk or telephone (01263) 761402. Open daily, Mon-Sat, 1000-1700, closed Bank Hols. Teachers welcome anytime, please phone. Find us between Aylsham and Cromer just off the A140. Look out for the signposted turn 500 metres north of Alby Craft Centre.

Cley-next-the-Sea
Made in Cley Map ref. I2
High Street, Cley-next-the-Sea, Holt NR25 7RF
Tel: (01263) 740134
Web: www.madeincley.co.uk
Hand-thrown domestic and sculptural Pottery in stoneware, porcelain and raku, contemporary jewellery in silver and gold, and prints. Everything is made on the premises and exhibited in a Regency shop which is itself of historical interest. Open daily, all year round. Free parking in village.

Cromer
Bond Street Antiques (inc BRIGGS) Map ref. K3
6 Bond Street, Cromer NR27 9DA
Tel: (01263) 513134
Goldsmiths, Silversmiths and Jewellers, incorporating Gem Test Centre. Gems, jewellery, Amber, gifts and objects d'art. Top prices paid for gold, silver and antiques. Valuations for Insurance and Probate. Member of The National Association of Goldsmiths and Fellow of The Gemmological Association of Great Britain.

Erpingham (nr. Aylsham)
Alby Crafts Map ref. K4
Cromer Road, Erpingham, nr. Norwich NR11 7QE
Tel: (01263) 761590 Web: www.albycrafts.co.uk
Alby Crafts is set amongst superb gardens in beautifully converted farm buildings. Browse in the working studios of some of Norfolk's finest crafts people, including a sculptor, artist, wood turner, silversmith and needleworker. Purchase from them directly or commission your own piece of work. Visit the tearooms, gift and book shop, and the Gallery selling quality British crafts. Or take a relaxing stroll in the beautiful 4^1/$_2$ acre gardens. Open 1000-1700, Tues-Sun (and Bank Hols), from 2nd weekend in Jan-24 Dec.

Shopping in St. Albans

Norwich Market

Sutton (nr. Stalham)
Sutton Pottery Map ref. N5
Church Road, Sutton, Norwich NR12 9SG
Tel: (01692) 580595 Web: www.suttonpottery.com
Follow brown tourist signs from A149 south of Stalham, then fingerposts through Sutton. Malcolm Flatman has been making stoneware pottery in this small workshop since 1977. He designs and creates additions to a large range of practical, repeatable, microwave-proof and dishwasher-safe tableware in a spectrum of glazes.He also makes many decorative pieces and lamps, and revels in bespoke designs and "one-off" items. Visit the workshop to view work in progress, to discuss your special pottery requirements, or to purchase from existing regular stock. Price list and pottery by post. Website catalogue and order form. Cards welcome. Usually open Mon-Fri 0900-1800, throughout the year, but please telephone before a special journey. Free admission. ⊛ 🅿 T(15 mins) 🔲

Great Yarmouth
Candlemaker and Model Centre Map ref. N7
Mill Road, Stokesby, nr. Great Yarmouth NR29 3EY
Tel: (01493) 750242 www.candlemaker-norfolk.co.uk
Situated 9 miles from Great Yarmouth on the banks of the River Bure. Boasts England's largest variety of handcrafted candles, with many that are unique. The candle showroom and workshop is open 1 Apr-31 Oct, 0900-1700, Tues-Sat; closed Sun and Mon. Free admission. Free parking and river moorings. Candle making courses are now available.
⊛ 🅿 T(1 hr) 🔨 🏇 🐕 🔲

Norfolk Lavender Ltd Map ref. D3
Caley Mill, Heacham (on A149) PE31 7JE
Tel: (01485) 570384
Set in the ground floor of Caley Mill, the Gift Shop contains a very wide range of gifts for all the family. There are items to suit every pocket, masses of choice and frequent new ideas. The Old Barn houses the Lavender Shop where you can buy Norfolk Lavender's fragrant products: The English Lavender, Rose, Lily of the Valley and Norfolk Lavender for Men. Open Apr-Oct, 1000-1700; Nov-Mar, 1000-1600. Average price: £2.70. ⊛ Q 🅿 T(4 hrs) 🔨 👹 🐕 (on leads) 🔲

Wroxham
Wroxham Barns Map ref. M5
Tunstead Road, Hoveton NR12 8QU
Tel: (01603) 783762 Web: www.wroxham-barns.co.uk
At the finest rural crafts centre in Norfolk, resident craftsmen bring traditional and contemporary skills to life and produce unique items. From paintings to pine furniture, from apple juice to stained glass, there is something for everyone. A stunning choice of gifts, cards, toys and clothing is available in our shops, together with a selection of tempting foods and homemade fudges. Our tearoom serves delicious cakes and lunches, and children will love Junior Farm and Wroxham Barns Children's Fair. Open daily from 1000-1700 (except Dec 25/26 and Jan 1). Admission is free. Junior Farm £2.75 per person, under 3's free. Fair seasonal - rides priced individually. Guide dogswelcome. ◉ Q ⊡ T(3 hrs) ⑪ ☴ ⬛

SUFFOLK

Aldringham (nr. Leiston)
Aldringham Craft Market Map ref. N7
Aldringham, nr. Leiston IP16 4PY
Tel: (01728) 830397

Family business, established 1958. Three relaxed and friendly galleries offering wide and extensive ranges of British craft products, original paintings, etchings and prints; studio, domestic and garden pottery, wood, leather, glass, jewellery, toys, kites, games, books, maps and many other good things including dolls houses and furniture, ladies' clothes, toiletries and hardy perennial plants. We only stock sensibly-priced, high quality products. Easy car parking; children's play area; coffee shop. Open all year, Mon-Sat, 1000-1730; Sun, 1000-1700.

NURSEY & SON LTD

Bungay
Nursey & Son Ltd Map ref. L3
12 Upper Olland St, Bungay NR35 1BQ
Tel: (01986) 892821
Email: tnursey@aol.com
Web: www.nurseyleather.co.uk
Established 1790. Jerkins, gilets, jackets, leather and suede jackets, leather trousers, sheepskin coats, slippers, gloves, hats, rugs etc. The factory shop has a good selection especially for gifts, handbags, wallets, purses, also a wide variety of sub-standard products and oddments. Open Mon-Fri, 1000-1300 and 1400-1700. Nov, Dec and Jan, open 6 days a week. Access, Visa. ◉ 🅿 🛏

Debenham
Carters Teapot Pottery Map ref. J7
Low Road, Debenham IP14 6QU
Tel: (01728) 860475 Fax: (01728) 861110
Email: info@cartersteapots.com
Web: www.cartersteapots.com
It doesn't have to be tea time to visit this Pottery making highly collectable teapots, in the beautiful village of Debenham. Visitors can see from the viewing area how these world renowned teapots are made and painted by hand. Pottery shop selling teapots, mugs and quality seconds. Situated just off the High Street, follow the teapot signs. Parking available. Tea, coffee and light refreshments in the conservatory. Open Mon-Fri, 0900-1730; Sat and Bank Hols, 1030-1630; Sun, 1400-1700. ◉ ⑪

Monks Eleigh (nr. Lavenham)
Corn Craft and SummerHouse Map ref. G9
Bridge Farm, Monks Eleigh IP7 7AY
Tel: (01449) 740456 Email: rwgage@lineone.net
Web: www.corncraft.co.uk
Situated in converted farm buildings in the heart of Suffolk Countryside between Hadleigh and Lavenham, specialising in the traditional craft of Corn Dolly making, practised on the farm for many years. Also selling a large range of unusual gifts, flowers and crafts.
NEW **The SummerHouse** selling beautiful and unusual furniture and gifts for the garden and home, offering original design ideas and accessories, with interior design service. The Tea Room, recently extended to provide seating for 80 people, serving home made refreshments, including light lunches. **Country Creations** hobby and craft material shop. Easy parking. Open everyday throughout the year, Mon-Sat, 1000-1700; Sun, 1100-1700. ◉ 🅿 T(3 hrs) ⑪ 🏷

Walberswick

The Parish Lantern Map ref. O5

On the Village Green, Walberswick IP18 6TT

Tel: (01502) 723173

Set in a Grade II listed Georgian building with courtyard garden, The Parish Lantern offers good quality crafts, gifts, clothes and pictures, as well as delicious cream teas and light lunches. The unspoilt sea-side village of Walberswick, with it's picturesque harbour and sandy beach, has long attracted writers and artists, and was once the home of architect and designer Charles Rennie Mackintosh. Close to Minsmere R.S.P.B. Reserve and Dunwich Heath, and just a short ferry ride (in summer) or a pleasant walk from Southwold. Open: 1 Mar-Christmas Eve, daily from 1000. Jan and Feb, Fri, Sat and Sun only, from 1000. ⊛

Woolpit (nr. Bury St. Edmunds)

Elm Tree Gallery Map ref. F7

The Old Bakery, Woolpit, nr. Bury St. Edmunds IP30 9QG

Tel: (01359) 240255

An Aladdin's cave of attractive, good quality crafts and gifts, housed in The Old Bakery, a timber-framed building dating from c.1550. The extensive range includes jewellery, textiles, wood, ceramics - including locally crafted Clarecraft figures, Moorcroft pottery and Harmony Kingdom, and one of the best selections of greetings cards in the region. Children's gifts. Light refreshments available all day, but limited seating available. Open: All year, Tues-Sat 1000-1800 (closed Bank Hols). Also open every day in Dec until Christmas, 1000-1800. ⊛ ⌷

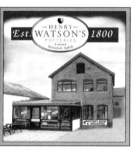

Wattisfield

Watson's Potteries Map ref. G5

Wattisfield IP22 1NH

Tel: (01359) 251239 Web: www.henrywatson.com

Henry Watson's Ltd has been manufacturing pottery for over 200 years. Our country gift shop offers a wide choice of excellent quality seconds, including the famous 'Original Suffolk Collection' of terracotta kitchenware and the Charlotte Watson fine cream earthenware range all at factory shop prices plus many other exciting and interesting gift ideas. After browsing, enjoy light refreshments in the relaxed surroundings of our coffee shop. Open Mon-Sat, 0930-1700; Sun, 1100-1700. Find us: On the A143 between Bury St. Edmunds and Diss. ⊛

Travel the Norfolk Coast with
an award winning service

COAST*H*OPPER

New year round timetable booklet available now

Plan days out along the beautiful Norfolk Coast without the car...
hop on and off the **COAST*H*OPPER** bus service from Hunstanton to Cromer
Information on services linking to this award winning service and our 2004
photographic competition is available in the CoastHopper booklet and on the
Passenger Transport Unit website: www.passengertransport.norfolk.gov.uk

Br*o*ads Hopper
Your passport to the heart of the Norfolk Broads

BroadsHopper is for everyone as it operates just like any other bus service. It's
perfect for visiting, shopping or just enjoying the Norfolk Broads. You don't have
to have a bike to use this service, although the cycle trailer is available for those
who wish to take their bike with them for free!

Linking Blickling Hall to Acle via Wroxham, serving key locations on route, it's the
perfect way for visitors and locals to explore and enjoy this beautiful area.

The BroadsHopper also links with other local bus and train services which
is ideal for those who wish to extend their journey into Norwich
or Great Yarmouth.

**For your copy of the CoastHopper or BroadsHopper bus
timetable visit your local Tourist Information Centre, library
or order your copy from the Norfolk County Council,
Customer Service Centre on:**

0844 800 8003

(lines open Monday to Friday)

Norfolk County Council
at your service

Countryside

You're never far from the sea in the East of England - the coastline curves from west-facing Hunstanton right around to Southend and the mouth of the River Thames. Long stretches of coastline are remote and peaceful, and are a habitat for birds and favourite haunt of birdwatchers and lovers of wildlife. There are unspoilt beaches, nature reserves, fishing villages, and some of the finest sand dunes and salt marshes in Britain. The backwaters, creeks and mudflats of the Essex coast are a quiet and lonely paradise for yachting enthusiasts as well as sea birds.

What better way to explore the countryside than drifting and dreaming on the waterways? The Broads National Park is home to some of the rarest wildlife in Britain. The Cambridgeshire waterways are renowned for the wide Fenland sky-scapes, and the Lee Valley Park forms a green "corridor" through Hertfordshire and Essex, right to London.

It's not all water - discover ancient woodlands, wide expanses of sandy heathland where the stone curlew nests, and dense grasslands, rich in flowers. Visit the great forests of Thetford and Rendlesham where you can cycle and walk along forest tracks, and climb on giant play sculptures.

To the west of the region are the gentle hills of the chalky Dunstable Downs and the Greensand Ridge, named for the amazing green colour of the stone. The Ashridge Estate runs along the main ridge of the Chiltern Hills, with beech woodlands and chalk downland supporting a rich variety of wildlife.

AROUND THE COASTLINE

Our tour around the coastline of East Anglia starts in Norfolk, at the Wash, England's largest tidal estuary, and an important winter feeding area for wildfowl. Nearby Old Hunstanton is noted for the only red and white striped cliffs in the country, made up of carrstone and red/white chalk. At Holkham, take a walk on the huge private beach backed by pine trees. Continue past the little port of Wells-next-the-Sea, where the beach huts are in a crazy huddle, to the delight of artists and photographers. At Stiffkey and Morston the saltmarshes are some of the oldest on the coast, and in summer are turned purple by the sea lavender. From here you can take a boat trip to see the seals on the three mile long sand and shingle spit of Blakeney Point. Alternatively enjoy the views over Britain's first designated nature reserve from Cley's windmill - you might spot bitterns, oystercatchers and avocets.

At Weybourne, cliffs rich in fossils rise from the marshlands, and you can jump aboard the North Norfolk Railway for a ride along the coast to Sheringham. It is surrounded by attractive heath and woodland, such as Sheringham Park, one of Humphry Repton's most outstanding achievements. Continuing past Cromer, the crumbling cliffs and high-piled sand dunes between Overstrand and Winterton-on-Sea are in a constant battle with the sea, as seen at Happisburgh (noted for its red/white striped lighthouse) where buildings are toppling over the edge.

On now to Suffolk, to England's most easterly point, Lowestoft Ness. From here head south past Covehithe's severely eroded cliffs to Southwold. Take the little ferry over the River Blyth to Walberswick (famous for its crabbing contest), for a walk along the beach to Dunwich, where the 12th C. capital of East Anglia was washed away by the sea. Nearby is Dunwich Heath, a unique remnant of the once extensive 'Sandlings' - great in late summer, when the heather is in bloom. The adjacent RSPB Minsmere Nature Reserve is famous for its rich habitat of reedbeds, artificial lagoons and woodland. Continue south to Aldeburgh to visit the marshes/wetland of North Warren, or take a walk to Snape for a boat trip on the River Alde. Further south is Europe's largest vegetated shingle spit, Orford Ness - home to many bird species and seaside flora and cared for by the National Trust. Close by is Havergate Island, an important nature reserve. Stop off next at Shingle Street, where you can search for amber. At Bawdsey, take the ferry across the River Deben, which winds downstream past low-wooded hills and sailing hamlets to Woodbridge. Passing Felixstowe, you reach the windswept sand/shingle peninsula of Landguard Point, on the northern banks of the estuary of the Rivers Orwell and Stour.

The southern banks of the River Stour are in Essex. They are steep and wooded, and are one of the most important areas in Britain for breeding birds. Heading south are the Walton Backwaters, a solitary wilderness of tidal saltings, mud/sand flats and reed-fringed islands and a paradise for birdwatchers and sailors. The Naze is a headland of grass

and gorse jutting out into the sea - its 70 feet high cliffs (rich in fossils) are being severely eroded away by the sea. Between Brightlingsea and Burnham-on-Crouch is a series of pretty river estuaries and creeks, once the haunt of smugglers. Pay a visit to Britain's most easterly island at Mersea, reached by a causeway. The Blackwater estuary with its open water and mudflats is important for wintering birds. Two islands sit in the estuary, the private Osea, and Northey - the site of the Battle of Maldon in 991. Look out for the Thames sailing barges in this area. Between the Rivers Blackwater and Crouch is the Dengie Peninsula, where much of the countryside, once waterlogged, was reclaimed in the 17th C. by Dutch engineers to create rich farming land. Further south is the remote Foulness Island, the fourth largest off the coast of England, and the inter-tidal flats/marshes of Maplin Sands, a haven for wildfowl.

INLAND WATERS

Broads National Park

Broadland is a unique and fascinating place, so timeless and natural that it's hard to believe that this landscape is man-made. In the Middle Ages, much of the natural woodland in this area was felled, and people were looking for another source of fuel. They found it in the peaty marshes around the rivers. Huge pits were excavated - not very deep, but many were very large considering all the digging was done by hand. The sea level began to rise and the peat diggings started to flood. Today, these flooded pits are the shallow lakes we know as the Broads, and the best way to discover this landscape is by boat.

The Norfolk Broads are home to some of Britain's rarest wildlife. In spring, listen out for the odd "booming" sound of the bittern, sounding like a muffled for horn. The whole of Hickling Broad is a nature reserve, bounded by reed and sedge beds, oak woodland and waterscapes. This attracts ospreys, spoonbills, and avocets, and is a good place to see the rare swallowtail butterfly and the Norfolk Hawker dragonfly. Ranworth Broad is one of the few broads totally free from boat traffic. Visit the Broads Wildlife Centre, a thatched building which floats on the broad and is a

excellent viewpoint for watching birds and wildlife. By contrast, Oulton Broad on the River Waveney near Lowestoft, is great for sailing cruising, powerboats and windsurfing. Visit www.broads-authority.gov.uk

Dedham Vale

The Dedham Vale is famous worldwide, through the paintings of John Constable, and many of the scenes which brought him inspiration can still be seen today. This fine lowland landscape on the border of Suffolk and Essex is dissected by the winding course of the attractive River Stour. Grazing meadows, ancient woodlands and hedgerows provide habitats for many species of flora and fauna. Leave your car at home and discover this beautiful area on foot or by bicycle.
Visit www.dedhamvalestourvalley.org

The Fens

Cambridgeshire's Fenland is known for its dramatic skies and spectacular sunsets, as well as for its wildlife. Habitats include the extensive system of drainage ditches which carry water from the peatlands, the surviving areas of fenlands washes, and red field and alder and willow carr. It is home to birds such as the Whooper and Bewick's Swan, Blacktailed Godwit and Ruff, as well as an enormous variety of wetland plants and insects.

The Ouse Washes, cutting diagonally across the Cambridgeshire fens, is one of the world's finest wetlands where hundreds of thousands of ducks and swans gather to overwinter. Boating on the River Nene, Cam and Great Ouse is atmospheric and tranquil with rivers and drains meandering through Fenland countryside and attractive villages. Visit www.fenswaterways.com

Grand Union Canal

The Grand Union Canal, the most famous and prosperous of all the British canals, was opened in 1806 and linked London with the rapidly expanding industrial Midlands. The canal gives great opportunities for boating, walking, fishing and cycling, passing through Leighton Buzzard in Bedfordshire and through Tring, Berkhamsted, Watford and Rickmansworth (visit the Batchworth Lock Canal Centre) in Hertfordshire. Visit www.waterscape.com

Lee Valley Park

A mosaic of farmland, nature reserves, green open spaces and waterways, inlaid with centres for leisure, sport, heritage and entertainment. It stretches along the banks of the River Lea from the more rural areas of Hertfordshire and Essex down into the heart of London's East End. 200 species of birds can be seen on the wetlands, including internationally important populations for Gladwell and Shoveler ducks attracted by the great area of open water. The bittern is one of the Park's rare winter visitors. Visit www.leevalleypark.org.uk

OPEN COUNTRYSIDE

Ashridge Estate - This area of around 4,000 acres of ancient woodland, commons and chalk downland, supports a rich variety of wildlife. It runs along the main ridge of the Chiltern Hills, on the borders of Hertfordshire and Buckinghamshire. There is an extensive network of footpaths. Next to the visitor centre is the 105ft high monument (erected 1832) to the third Duke of Bridgewater, Francis Thomas Egerton, "the father of British inland waterways". Visit www.nationaltrust.org.uk and www.chilternsaonb.org

The Brecks - A unique mix of forest, heath and farmland which once covered a huge area. This landscape was created by prehistoric farmers as they cut back the trees to make clearings for crops, and by the constant grazing of sheep and rabbits. 'Breck' is land once cultivated, then a few years later, allowed to return to the wild. Later large areas were planted over with forestry. The pockets of remaining heath-land are fiercely protected today - a rich haven for many rare species of flora and fauna. The area is also dotted with historical sites - burial mounds, deserted villages and Neolithic flint mines. Visit www.brecks.org

The Chilterns -This is a landscape of rolling chalk hills, farmland, quiet valleys, charming brick and flint villages, and magnificent beechwoods (planted in the 18th C. to provide valuable timber to the local furniture-making industry). Rich in flora and fauna - the woodlands are carpeted with bluebells in spring, whilst in the autumn, the trees are turned to magnificent golden colours. Look out also for the kite, a bird of prey re-introduced here in the early 1990s. The area is excellent for cycling, horse-riding and walking. Visit www.chilternsaonb.org

The Dunstable Downs - This is the highest point in the East of England at 244m (801 feet), providing superb views over Bedfordshire and the Vale of Aylesbury. Part of the Chiltern Hills, they were formed by chalk deposited on the seabed when the area was still underwater about 70 million years ago. This is a great place for a picnic, and for flying kites - you can buy them from the countryside centre, which also has a downs exhibition. There are miles of footpaths, ancient remains (burial mounds), and an abundance of plants and wildlife - or you could take a flight in a glider. Visit www.nationaltrust.org.uk and www.chilternsaonb.org

Dunstable Downs, Bedfordshire

Epping Forest - Covering some 6,000 acres, this is the largest public open space in the vicinity of London, although it is only a tenth of its original size. Dating from ancient times, it once formed part of the great royal hunting forest of Essex, whose function was to supply deer for the monarch. In 1878, the 'Epping Forest Act' was passed, and the management of the forest was given to the Corporation of London. Today the forest stretches for about 12 miles, and is noted for its fine woodlands (hornbeams, beech and oak), heath, reed fringed ponds and grassland. Visit www.cityoflondon.gov.uk/living_environment/open_spaces

The Greensand Ridge - A narrow ridge of sandstone running for about 40 miles from Leighton Buzzard to Gamlingay. Iron deposits give the stone a distinctive rust-brown colour, and in some areas 'glauconite' (an iron-bearing mineral) colours the stone an amazing green - the origin of the name 'Greensand'. Today you can see it used in local villages, churches, walls and bridges. The ridge is well-wooded because the sandy soils derived from the greensand are low in nutrients, and so make poor agricultural land. Another key feature of the area is the number of historic estates, such as Woburn. Visit www.greensand-trust.org.uk

The Sandlings - An area of lowland heaths which once stretched right along the Suffolk coastline. Created by prehistoric farmers as they cut back the trees to make clearings for crops - then later the grazing of sheep and rabbits prevented the trees from growing back, allowing heather and gorse to spread. In the 1920s, large areas of forestry were planted. Today the remaining heath-land is fiercely protected and managed - a rich haven for many species of flora and fauna. Visit www.suffolkcoastandheaths.org

Thetford Forest Park - Britain's largest lowland pine forest, covering over 50,000 acres. Created in the 1920s, the forest is a patchwork of both Corsican and Scots pines, heath-land and broadleaves, intersected with broad sandy rides and tracks. Rich in animal, bird and plant life - look out for deer, bats and the park's emblem, the red squirrel. Visitors can discover the peace and tranquillity of the forest, or enjoy a great family day out, with numerous way-marked walks, cycle trails, picnic sites and special events. The forest is also rich in archaeological sites, such as Grimes Graves. Regular programme of events. Visit www.forestry.gov.uk

Countryside Organisations

The Broads Authority
18 Colegate, Norwich, Norfolk NR3 1BQ
Tel: (01603) 610734   www.broads-authority.gov.uk

English Nature
Bedfordshire & Cambridgeshire, Ham Lane House, Ham Lane, Nene Park, Orton Waterville, nr. Peterborough, Cambs PE2 5UR Tel: (01733) 405850
Essex & Hertfordshire, Harbour House, Hythe Quay, Colchester, Essex CO2 8JF Tel: (01206) 796666
Norfolk, 60 Bracondale, Norwich, Norfolk NR1 2BE
Tel: (01603) 620558
Suffolk, Regent House, 110 Northgate Street, Bury St. Edmunds, Suffolk IP33 1HP
Tel: (01284) 762218   www.english-nature.gov.uk

Essex Wildlife Trust (EWT)
Abbotts Hall Farm, Great Wigborough, nr. Colchester, Essex CO5 7RZ
Tel: (01621) 862960   www.essexwt.org.uk

Forest Enterprise - East Anglia Forest District
Santon Downham, nr. Brandon, Suffolk IP27 0TJ
Tel: (01842) 810271   www.forestry.gov.uk

The National Trust - Regional Office for East Anglia
Angel Corner, 8 Angel Hill, Bury St. Edmunds, Suffolk IP33 1UZ
Tel: 0870 609 5388   www.nationaltrust.org.uk

Norfolk Wildlife Trust (NWT)
Bewick House, 22 Thorpe Road, Norwich, Norfolk NR1 1RY
Tel: (01603) 625540   www.wildlifetrust.org.uk/norfolk

The Royal Society for the Protection of Birds (RSPB)
Regional Office for East Anglia
Stalham House, 65 Thorpe Road, Norwich, Norfolk NR1 1UD
Tel: (01603) 661662   www.rspb.org.uk

Suffolk Wildlife Trust (SWT)
Brooke House, The Green, Ashbocking, Suffolk IP6 9JY
Tel: (01473) 890089   www.wildlifetrust.org.uk/suffolk

The Wildlife Trust (Bedfordshire & Cambridgeshire)
The Manor House, Broad Street, Great Cambourne, Cambridge, CB3 6DH.
Tel: (01954) 713500   www.wildlifetrust.org.uk/bcnp

The Wildlife Trust (Hertfordshire)
Grebe House, St. Michaels Street, St. Albans, Hertfordshire AL3 4SN
Tel: (01727) 858901   www.wildlifetrust.org.uk/herts

Cycling

The East of England is perfect cycling country, with quiet roads, byways and tracks meandering through the landscape. The peaceful countryside and pretty villages will delight you, as will the many enticing tea shops and inns. Historic windmills, watermills, moated halls, grand houses, flint-built churches, and charming cottages are all here to be discovered along your way. There are some great off-road tracks in forests, country parks, and around reservoirs, where cycling is safe for all the family, and you can hire bikes at some of these places. Best of all, the hills are so gentle that you don't have to be superman or woman to enjoy days out touring by bike. Here are some ideas to get you started.

OFF-ROAD BIKING

Bedfordshire: Marston Vale Millennium Country Park, 4- and 6-mile routes around lake, cycle hire available. Tel: 01234 767037.

Cambridgeshire: 10-mile circuit around Grafham Water near Huntingdon. Tel: 01480 812154.

Essex: Cycling opportunities in many of the country parks in Essex such as the Flitch Way, which runs for 15 miles along the old Bishop's Stortford to Braintree railway. Contact Essex County Council. Tel: 01245 437118.

Norfolk: 9-mile Bure Valley Path between Aylsham and Wroxham or numerous trails at the Kelling Heath Holiday Park at Weybourne, near Holt, cycle hire available. Details at www.cyclenorfolk.co.uk.

Suffolk: Rendlesham Forest Centre, near Woodbridge, forest rides of 6 and 12-miles. Alton Water, south of Ipswich, 8 mile mainly off-road route around the reservoir (cycle hire available). Thetford Forest, rides starting at High Lodge Forest Centre, Brandon (cycle hire available).

DAY RIDES

Route maps and information about places of interest and places to stay are available for each of the following day rides, many of which are circular. Contact East of England Tourist Board on 0870 225 4852 to purchase the Cycling Discovery Maps.

Bedfordshire:
The Great Ouse: 25 miles, starting in Bedford and exploring the Ouse Valley with its ancient limestone villages and medieval bridges.
The Thatchers Way: 24 miles, starting in Bedford, taking in picturesque thatched cottages, a collection of flying machines, and the unique Swiss Garden.

Cambridgeshire:
Katherine's Wheels: 15 miles, including 10 miles off-road around Grafham Water (near Huntingdon).
Peterborough Green Wheel (North): 29 miles, including cream-coloured villages and prehistoric remains.
Apples & Ale: 13 miles, from Wisbech through fruit orchards to a Georgian brewery.

Essex:
Two Rivers' Way: 25 miles, from Burnham-on-Crouch via weather-boarded villages, sailing hamlets and England's oldest Saxon chapel.
Witchfinder's Way: 27 miles, from Harwich, visiting the haunts of Matthew Hopkins, the Witchfinder General.

Hertfordshire:
Roisia's Path: 28 miles starting from Therfield (near Royston) with panoramic views and timber-framed villages.
Romans and Royalty: 16 miles, taking in St Albans and Hatfield.
Literary Landscapes: 25 miles, from Welwyn with visit to George Bernard Shaw's country retreat

Norfolk:
The Brecks: 20 miles, from Swaffham through heath and pine forests.
Lost Villages of Breckland: 23 miles, from village of Gressenhall, near Dereham.
The Bishop's Chapel: 23 miles, from Dereham via a ruined Norman chapel
Nelson's Norfolk: 29 miles, from Fakenham including Lord Nelson's birthplace and the pilgrimage centre of Little Walsingham
Lords of the Manor: 29 miles, by country estates, starting from Aylsham

Suffolk:
The Miller's Trail: 23 miles, starting at the village of Ixworth near Bury St Edmunds.
The Jockey's Trail: 28 miles, starting in Newmarket and taking in stud farms.
Churches, Copses and Country Lanes: 24 miles including crumbling cliffs and historic churches.

LONG DISTANCE ROUTES

Essex Cycle Route: 250 miles of cycling between Epping and Harwich through beautiful countryside and charming villages and towns. Dip into small setions or try some of the loops and links around it. The route links with the National Cycle Network Route 1 (Hull to Harwich). A guide to the route (priced £2.50) is available from Essex County Council on 01245 437118

Fens Cycle Way: discover the unique panorama of the Fens, criss-crossed by waterways. This cycle pack contains two separate loops, starting at Wisbech (40 miles) and Ely (34 miles). Pack includes two maps, and an information guide with places to stay and cycle hire. Contact East of England Tourist Board on 0870 225 4852.

Harwich to Hull: The 369 mile long distance route from Harwich to Hull is part of the National Cycle Network being developed by the cycling charity Sustrans. It includes a choice of routes through some of the most attractive countryside in the region. Contact Sustrans on 0845 113 0065.

The Heart of Suffolk Cycle Route: a fully signed circular route of 78 miles through the rural heartland of Suffolk, using a mixture of mainly quiet roads and well-surfaced tracks. This route connects to the National Cycle Network Route 1 (Hull to Harwich). A saleable map/guide to the cycle route (including places to stay) is available from the Mid Suffolk Tourist Information Centre at Stowmarket on (01449) 676800, or visit www.heartofsuffolk.com for further information.

Norfolk Coast Cycleway: 103 miles from King's Lynn to Great Yarmouth using quiet roads and lanes just inland from the coast. Dip into small sections or loops, or ride the entire route. Connects to National Cycle Network Route 1 (Hull to Harwich) Maps for a small charge from Cromer Tourist Information Centre, 01263 512497, or for a more detailed guide visit www.cycle-norfolk.co.uk

The Painters' Trail: 69 miles starting from Manningtree (Essex) or Sudbury (Suffolk) through the Stour Valley, source of artistic inspiration for John Constable, and birthplace of Thomas Gainsborough. Contact East of England Tourist Board on 0870 225 4852.

The Suffolk Coastal Cycle Route: explore an area of outstanding natural beauty, with peaceful countryside and unspoilt coastline. This cycle pack details a fully signed circular route of 88 miles (shorter options available), on two fold-out maps, together with information on places to stay and off-road forest rides. This route connects to the National Cycle Network Route 1 (Hull to Harwich). The saleable pack is available from the East of England Tourist Board on 0870 225 4852.

ORGANISED CYCLING HOLIDAYS

Needham Market
Suffolk Cycle Breaks
Bradfield Hall Barn, Alder Carr Farm, PO Box 82, Needham Market IP6 8BW
Tel: (01449) 721555 Fax: (01449) 721707
Email: enquiry@cyclebreaks.com
Web: www.cyclebreaks.com www.walkingbreaks.com
Gentle cycling and walking holidays in Suffolk and Norfolk. Luggage transfer and accommodation pre-arranged. ⊛

MORE CYCLING INFORMATION

Bedford Tourist Information Centre, 01234 215226 (twelve easy rides around the town).
Braintree TIC 01376 550066 (routes in Colne Valley).
The Brecks, 01842 765400 or visit www.brecks.org (cycling pack of five routes).
Chilterns Conservation Board, 01844 271300 (cycling leaflet).
Countryside Access Team, 01603 223284, or visit www.countrysideaccess.norfolk.gov.uk
Countryside Services Team, Cambridgeshire County Council, 01223 717445, or visit www.cambridgeshire.gov.uk/sub/cntryside (range of leaflets).
East of England Tourist Board, 0870 225 4852, or visit www.eastofenglandtouristboard.com
Essex County Council on 01245 437118 or visit www.essexcc.gov.uk
Hertfordshire County Council, www.hertsdirect.org (routes in Hertfordshire).
Mid Bedfordshire Tourist Information Centre, 01767 682728 (three day rides in the county).
Suffolk County Council on www.visit-suffolk.org.uk
Sustrans, 0845 113 0065, or visit www.sustrans.org.uk (national cycling information including East of England).

For even more information visit our website at **www.visiteastofengland.com**

Walking

Walk by the sea, along river valleys, through woodland or heathland. You are spoilt for choice in the East of England and there's no better way to get to know the place than on foot. What's more, the countryside is scattered with many good pubs and afternoon tea stops ready to welcome thirsty travellers. Looking for a challenge? Walk one of our long distance routes which will take you through some of the best countryside in the region. Or choose your area, and contact the tourist information centre (see page 209) or the following people for a wealth of local walking information:

Cambridgeshire County Council, Countryside Services Team, 01223 717445
www.cambridgeshire.gov.uk/sub/cntryside
Essex County Council, Public Rights of Way Team, 01245 437274 www.essexcc.gov.uk
Hertfordshire County Council, Countryside Management Service www.hertsdirect.org/cms
Norfolk County Council, Countryside Access Team, 01603 223284 www.countrysideaccess.norfolk.gov.uk
Suffolk County Council, 01473 264775, www.visit-suffolk.org.uk

LONG DISTANCE COASTAL WALKS

The Peddar's Way and Norfolk Coast Path (93 miles) - runs from Knettishall Heath Country Park (Suffolk) to Cromer (Norfolk). Official trail guide by Bruce Robinson, and published by Aurum Press (ISBN: 1-85410-852-2). Basic route and accommodation guide from Sheila Smith, Caldcleugh, Old Buckenham, nr. Attleborough, Norfolk NR17 1RU. Tel: (01953) 861094. www.nationaltrail.co.uk/peddarsway
The Stour and Orwell Walk (42 miles) - runs from Felixstowe (Suffolk) to Manningtree (Essex). Saleable guide available from The Suffolk Coast and Heaths Unit, Dock Lane, Melton, nr. Woodbridge, Suffolk IP12 1PE. Tel: (01394) 384948.
The Suffolk Coast and Heaths Path (50 miles) - linear walk along the Suffolk coastline from Felixstowe to Lowestoft. Saleable guide available from The Suffolk Coast and Heaths Unit, Dock Lane, Melton, nr. Woodbridge, Suffolk IP12 1PE. Tel: (01394) 384948.
The Weavers' Way (61 miles) - follows the Norfolk coastline from Cromer to Great Yarmouth. Maps and information at www.countrysideaccess.norfolk.gov.uk. Accommodation guide from Sheila Smith, Caldcleugh, Old Buckenham, nr. Attleborough, Norfolk NR17 1RU. Tel: (01953) 861094.

LONG DISTANCE INLAND WALKS

The Angles Way (78 miles) - linear walk running from Great Yarmouth (Norfolk) to Knettishall Heath Country Park (Suffolk). Saleable guide to route available from Sheila Smith, Caldcleugh, Old Buckenham, nr. Attleborough, Norfolk NR17 1RU. Tel: (01953) 861094.
Black Fen Trail (65 miles) - way-marked circular Cambridgeshire route linking Ely, March and Downham Market. Information on walk (including other Fenland trails) from Fens Tourism, Springfields, Camelgate, Spalding, Lincolnshire PE12 6EU. Tel: (01775) 764888.
The Essex Way (81 miles) - linear walk stretching right across the county from Epping to Harwich. Saleable guide from Essex County Council, County Hall, Chelmsford, Essex CM1 1QH. Tel: (01245) 437291.
The Fen Rivers Way (50 miles) - runs from Cambridge to The Wash in Norfolk. Saleable guide to route available from Bernard Hawes, 52 Maid's Causeway, Cambridge, Cambridgeshire CB5 8DD. Tel: (01223) 560033.
The Greensand Ridge Walk (40 miles) - runs through Bedfordshire from Leighton Buzzard to Gamlingay. Leaflet (send self-addressed envelope) from The Greensand Trust, The Forest Office, Haynes West End, Bedfordshire MK45 3QT. Tel: (01234) 743666.
The Hereward Way (110 miles) - runs from Oakham (nr. Stamford), through Cambridgeshire via Peterborough, March, Ely and Brandon to East Harling in Norfolk. A leaflet covering the Cambridgeshire section is available from the Countryside Services Team (Cambridgeshire County Council) on (01223) 717445.
The Hertfordshire Way (166 miles) - circular route around the county. Saleable guide available from The Friends of the Hertfordshire Way, 53 Green Drift, Royston, Hertfordshire SG8 5BX. Tel: (01763) 244509.
The Iceni Way (98 miles) - from Knettishall Heath Country Park (Suffolk) to Sandringham and Hunstanton (Norfolk). Saleable guide from Sheila Smith, Caldcleugh, Old Buckenham, nr Attleborough, NR17 1RU. Tel: (01953) 861094.
The Icknield Way Path (105 miles) - runs from Ivinghoe Beacon (Buckinghamshire) to Knettishall Heath Country Park (Suffolk), passing through parts of Bedfordshire and Hertfordshire. Saleable guide available from the Icknield Way Association, 19 Boundary Road, Bishop's Stortford, Hertfordshire CM23 5LE. Tel: (01279) 504602.
The Lea Valley Walk (50 miles) - runs from Luton, (Bedfordshire) via Hertfordshire to London's East End. Saleable guide available from the Lee Valley Park Information Centre, Stubbins Hall Lane, Crooked Mile, Waltham Abbey, Essex EN9 2EG. Tel: (01992) 702200.

The Ouse Valley Way (26 miles) - runs from Bluntisham to Eaton Socon, following Cambridgeshire's River Great Ouse. It can be shortened into six circular routes. Saleable guide from Huntingdon TIC. Tel: (01480) 388588.

The Roach Valley Way (23 miles) - circular walk around south-east Essex. Saleable guide to route available from PROW Team, Essex County Council, County Hall, Chelmsford, Essex CM1 1QH. Tel: (01245) 437291.

The St. Peter's Way (45 miles) - Essex linear walk from Chipping Ongar to Bradwell-on-Sea. Saleable guide to route available from PROW Team, Essex County Council, County Hall, Chelmsford, Essex CM1 1QH. Tel: (01245) 437291.

The Sandlings Path (60 miles) - inland route through Suffolk's lowland heaths (Sandlings) between Ipswich and Southwold. Saleable guide available from The Suffolk Coast and Heaths Unit, Dock Lane, Melton, nr. Woodbridge, Suffolk IP12 1PE. Tel: (01394) 384948.

The Stour Valley Path (60 miles) - linear walk from Newmarket (Suffolk) to Manningtree (Essex). Saleable guide from The Dedham Vale and Stour Valley Countryside Project, c/o Suffolk County Council, Environment and Transport Department, St. Edmund House, Rope Walk, Ipswich, IP4 1LZ. Tel: (01473) 583176.

The Three Forests Way (60 miles) - circular walk linking the ancient forests of Epping, Hainault and Hatfield in Essex. Saleable guide to route available from PROW Team, Essex County Council, County Hall, Chelmsford, Essex CM1 1QH. Tel: (01245) 437291.

Golf

Many golf clubs in the region welcome visitors. Contact the nearest Tourist Information Centre (see page 209) for more golfing centres, and see page 206 for golfing holidays.

Searles Golf Resort and Country Club Map ref. D3
South Beach, Hunstanton PE36 5BB
Tel: (01485) 536010 Fax: (01485) 533815
Web: www.searles.co.uk
9 hole, par-34 resort golf course designed in a links style, with good large greens and enhanced by natural features. Open to the public on a 'pay and play' basis, the course provides a challenge for both experienced and novice golfers alike, with a large 10-bay driving range offering a chance to practice before hitting the course proper. Club hire available. New Country Club overlooking the course is now open and serving refreshments, daytime snacks and evening meals. Changing and shower facilities also provided. Area also incorporates two fishing lakes, bowling green and astro-putting course. Societies welcome.
◉ P 🚂 ⑪ 🖼️

Peterborough
Orton Meadows Golf Course Map ref. C6
Ham Lane, Orton Waterville PE2 5UU
Tel: (01733) 237478
Email: Enquiries@ortonmeadowsgolfcourse.co.uk
Web: www.ortonmeadowsgolfcourse.co.uk
18 holes, 5613 yards Par 67. Top Pay As You Play Course with lakes and streams in picturesque setting surrounded by trees. Booking necessary. Club/Trolley hire available. Web: www.experiencedgolfclubs.co.uk
Orton Meadows hosts Eastern England's only Golf Factory Clearance Shop providing excellent value and top quality refurbished second hand clubs. ◉ P ⑪

Peterborough
Orton Meadows Pitch & Putt Course Map ref. C6
Ham Lane, Orton Waterville PE2 5UU
Tel: (01733) 237478
This 12 hole Pitch & Putt Course is very popular with players of all ages and all levels, and provides fun for all the family. An introduction to the game for those who would like to take up golf, or opportunity for players to improve their short game. Clubs and Balls provided. ◉

Peterborough
Thorpe Wood Golf Course Map ref. C5
Thorpe Wood PE3 6SE
Tel: (01733) 267701
Email: Enquiries@thorpewoodgolfcourse.co.uk
Web: www.thorpewoodgolfcourse.co.uk
18 holes, 7086 yards, Par 73. Top UK Pay As you Play Course designed by Peter Alliss and Dave Thomas (designers of The Belfry), set in undulating parkland maintained in superb condition and always open whatever the weather. Popular with golfers of all ages/abilities. Booking necessary. Club/Trolley hire available. ◉ P ⑪

Country Parks & Nature Reserves

BEDFORDSHIRE

Bedford
Priory Country Park Map ref. D6
Tel: (01234) 211182
Over 300 acres of open space with two lakes and riverside.
Fishing facilities, water sports, bird-watching hides, guided
walks and talks.
Times: Open at any reasonable time. Please contact for
Visitor Centre opening times.
Fee: Free.
Facilities: ⊛ ℙ T(1½ hrs) ⨍ ⟑ ⟟

Dunstable
Dunstable Downs Countryside Centre Map ref. C11
Whipsnade Road
Tel: (01582) 608489 Web: www.nationaltrust.org.uk
Scenic views over the vale of Aylesbury. Countryside Centre
where kites, souvenirs and publications can be purchased.
Site of Specific Scientific Interest.
Times: Countryside Centre open 1 Jan-24 Mar, Sat, Sun
and Bank Hols, 1000-1600. 25 Mar-31 Oct, Mon-Sat,
1000-1700; Sun and Bank Hols, 1000-1800. 1 Nov-31
Dec, Sat, Sun and Bank Hols, 1000-1600. Closed 25 Dec.
Fee: Free.
Facilities: ⊛ ℙ T(2 hrs) ⨌ ⟑ ⟟ NT

Harrold
Harrold-Odell Country Park Map ref. B4
Carlton Road
Tel: (01234) 720016 Web: www.ivelandouse.co.uk
A 150-acre country park with three lakes and riverside.
Posted walks in meadow, lakeside and by river. Visitors
centre with tearoom and facilities.
Times: Open all year, daily, at any reasonable time.
Fee: Free.
Facilities: ⊛ ℙ ⟚ T(2½ hrs) ⨌ ⟑ ⟟

Luton
John Dony Field Centre Map ref. E10
Hancock Drive, Bushmead
Tel: (01582) 486983
Web: www.luton.gov.uk/enjoying/museums
Natural history site with displays featuring local/natural
history, conservation and archaeology.
Times: Open 31 Mar-24 Dec, 0930-1645
Fee: Free.
Facilities: ⊛ ℙ T(1 hr) ▣

RSPB Lodge Nature Reserve, Sandy, Bedfordshire

Luton
Sundon Hills Country Park Map ref. D9
Sundon
Tel: (01582) 608489 Web: www.nationaltrust.org.uk
Chalk downland within the Chilterns Area of Outstanding
Natural Beauty, a Site of Specific Scientific Interest, and
adjoining the Icknield Way long distance footpath.
Outstanding landscape views.
Times: Open at any reasonable time.
Fee: Free.
Facilities: ⊛ ℙ T(2 hrs) ⟑ ⟟ NT

Marston Moretaine
The Marston Vale Millennium Country Park Map ref. C7
Tel: (01234) 767037 Web: www.marstonvale.org
Country park with visitor centre. Bike hire, exhibition, café and
bar, bistro, art gallery and shop. Rare wetland habitat.
Times: Open all year, daily, 1000-1600 (closes 1800 during
school hols in July and Aug). Closed 25, 26 Dec and
1 Jan.
Fee: Free. Charge for wetlands reserve: £2.50/£1.75/£1.75
Facilities: ℙ ⟚ ⥱ T(2 hrs) ⨍ ⨌ ⟟

Sandy
RSPB Lodge Nature Reserve Map ref. F6
Tel: (01767) 680541 Web: www.rspb.org.uk
A reserve with mixed woodland and heathland supporting a
wide variety of birds and wildlife. Also formal gardens
which are run by organic methods open to the public.
Times: Open all year, Mon-Fri, 0900-1700; Sat and Sun,
1000-1700. Closed 25 and 26 Dec.
Fee: £3.00/£1.00/£1.50/£6.00.
Facilities: ⊛ ℙ ⥱ T(3 hrs) ⟑

See Also:
Moggerhanger Park, nr Bedford, page 37

CAMBRIDGESHIRE

Babraham (nr. Cambridge)
Wandlebury Country Park Map ref. H12
Wandlebury Ring, Gog Magog Hills
Tel: (01223) 243830 Web: www.cpswandlebury.org
Countryside park and nature reserve, the site of an Iron Age
ring ditch. Woodlands, circular walks, wildlife and public
footpaths leading to a Roman road.
Times: Open all year, daily, dawn-dusk.
Fee: £2.00 car park charge.
Facilities: ▣ 🚻 T(2 hrs) 🚶 🎋 🐕

Brampton (nr. Huntingdon)
Brampton Wood Map ref. C10
Tel: (01954) 713500 Web: www.wildlifetrust.org.uk/bcnp
Consists primarily of ash and field maple with hazel
coppice. Supports wide variety of plants and animals, and
is particularly well known for butterflies.
Times: Open all year, daily, any reasonable time.
Fee: Free.
Facilities: ▣ T(4 hrs) 🐕

Fowlmere (nr. Royston)
RSPB Fowlmere Nature Reserve Map ref. G13
Tel: (01763) 208978 Web: www.rspb.org.uk
An 100-acre nature reserve incorporating a nature trail and
three bird-watching hides. Attractions include unspoilt
wetland scenery and birdlife including the kingfisher.
Times: Open at any reasonable time.
Fee: Free, donations appreciated.
Facilities: ⊛ ▣ T(2hrs) 🚶 🎋

Gamlingay (nr. Sandy)
Gamlingay Wood Map ref. D12
Tel: (01954) 713500 Web: www.wildlifetrust.org.uk/bcnp
Ancient ash and maple wood, which grows on a mixture of
soils and contains an unusual variety of woodland types.
Special habitat for mosses, fungi and insects. New
woodland creation project.
Times: Open all year, daily, any reasonable time.
Fee: Free.
Facilities: ▣ T(2 hrs) 🐕

Grafham (nr. Huntingdon)
Grafham Water Map ref. C10
Tel: (01480) 812154 Web: www.anglianwater.co.uk
Water park with extensive views, sailing, trout fishing,
nature reserve, trails and walks, picnic areas, play areas,
refreshments and gift shop.
Times: Open 3 Jan-20 Mar, Mon-Fri, 1100-1500, Sat, Sun
1100-1600. 21 Mar-28 Oct, Mon-Fri, 1100-1600; Sat, Sun,
1100-1700. 29 Oct-18 Dec, Mon-Fri, 1100-1500. Sat, Sun
1100-1600.
Fee: Car park charge £2.00 all day
£1.00 for 1 hr.
Facilities: ⊛ ▣ T(3 hrs) ⑪ 🎋 🐕 (on leads) ♿

Grafham Water

Huntingdon

Hinchingbrooke Country Park Map ref. D9

Brampton Road

Tel: (01480) 451568

Web: www.huntsleisure.org/countryside/hinchingbrooke

Open grasslands, meadows, woodlands and lakes covering 180 acres with a wealth of wildlife. Ideal for family outings and picnics. Visitor centre.

Times: Open at any reasonable time.

Fee: Free.

Facilities: ⊛ 🅿 T(2 hrs) ⓘ 🛒 ✝ 🔲

Longstowe (nr. St. Neots)

Hayley Wood Map ref. E12

Tel: (01954) 713500 Web: www.wildlifetrust.org.uk/bcnp

Mostly ancient woodland of oak, ash and maple - resplendent with bluebells and oxlips in spring. Whilst in summer the rides and glades are filled with wildflowers and butterflies.

Times: Open at any reasonable time.

Fee: Free.

Facilities: T(2 hrs) ✝

March

RSPB Ouse Washes Map ref. H7

Welches Dam

Tel: (01354) 680212 Web: www.rspb.org.uk

Nature reserve in the heart of the Fens, with ten bird-watching hides, visitor centre and a programme of events.

Times: Open at any reasonable time.

Fee: Free

Facilities: ⊛ 🅿 T(2 hrs) ✝

Wildfowl and Wetlands Trust, Welney

Milton (nr. Cambridge)

Milton Country Park Map ref. H11

Cambridge Road

Tel: (01223) 420060 Web: www.scambs.gov.uk

Milton Country Park comprises 95 acres of woodland, grass and water areas with many sites for picnics, and a play area for children.

Times: Open all year, daily, from 0800. Closing times vary throughout the year.

Fee: Free.

Facilities: ⊛ 🅿 🛒 T(2 hrs) 🛒 ✝

St. Neots

Paxton Pits Nature Reserve Map ref. D11

High Street, Little Paxton

Tel: (01480) 406795 Web: www.paxton-pits.org.uk

Restored gravel pits, made up of lakes, meadows, grassland, scrub and woodland. Famous for its nightingales in summer and wildfowl in winter. Visitor centre, trails and bird-watching hides.

Times: Open all year, daily, dawn-dusk.

Fee: Free.

Facilities: 🅿 T(3 hrs) 🛠 🛒 ✝

Waresley

Waresley and Gransden Woods Map ref. E12

Tel: (01954) 713500 Web: www.wildlifetrust.org.uk/bcnp

Both woods are fine examples of the ancient woodland which once covered much of the boulder clay uplands in this area. Both woods are ash and oak. New Woodland creation project.

Times: Open at any reasonable time.

Fee: Free.

Facilities: 🅿 T(2 hrs) ✝

Welney

Wildfowl and Wetlands Trust Map ref. I6

Hundred Foot Bank

Tel: (01353) 860711 Web: www.wwt.org.uk

A wetland nature reserve of 1,000 acres attracting large numbers of ducks and swans in winter, waders in spring and summer, plus a range of wild plants and butterflies.

Times: Open all year, daily, 1000-1700. Also open until 2000 for swan evenings on the following days: 1 Jan-28 Feb, 10 Nov-23 Dec, 28-30 Dec, Wed-Sun. Closed 25 Dec only.

Fee: £3.90/£2.50/£3.20/£10.00(family).

Facilities: ⊛ Q 🅿 T(2 hrs) ⓘ 🛒

For even more information visit our website at www.visiteastofengland.com

Wicken (nr. Soham)
Wicken Fen National Nature Reserve Map ref. I10
Tel: (01353) 720274 Web: www.wicken.org.uk
The last remaining undrained portion of the great Fen levels of East Anglia, rich in plant and invertebrate life, and good for birds. Also a working windpump and restored Fen cottage. Café.
Times: Open all year, daily, dawn-dusk. Visitor Centre Tues-Sun and Bank Hol Mon, 1000-1700. Closed 25 Dec.
Fee: £4.10/£1.30/£4.10.
Facilities: ❀ 🅿 T(2½ hrs) ⚲⑪ ⋔ 🛉 NT

Wicken Fen National Nature Reserve

See Also:
Wimpole Hall and Home Farm, nr Royston, page 38

ESSEX

Basildon
Langdon Visitor Centre and Nature Reserve Map ref. F10
Third Avenue, Lower Dunton Road
Tel: (01268) 419103 Web: www.essexwt.org.uk
460 acres of meadow, woodland and plotland gardens. Eighteen miles of footpaths and bridleways. A former plotland home, The Haven, has been restored to 1930s style, and is open as a museum.
Times: Open all year, Tues-Sun, 0900-1700; Bank Hol Mon, 0900-1700. Closed 25 and 26 Dec.
Fee: Free.
Facilities: 🅿 T(2 hrs) ⚲⑪ ⋔ 🛉

Billericay
Hanningfield Reservoir Visitor Centre Map ref. G9
Hawkswood Road
Tel: (01268) 711001 Web: www.essexwt.org.uk
The visitor centre has refreshments, toilets, gift shop and full disabled access. It will help you discover the 100-acre nature reserve on the shores of Hanningfield Reservoir. Bird hides and walks.
Times: Open all year, Tues-Sun, 0900-1700. Open Mon during summer months, please contact for details. Closed 25 and 26 Dec.
Fee: Free. Donations appreciated.
Facilities: 🅿 T(2 hrs) ⋔

Braintree
Great Notley Country Park and Discovery Centre
Map ref. F/G5
Tel: (01376) 347134
Ecologically built discovery centre with permanent exhibition of ecological principals. Wind turbine. Set within a 100 acre country park, providing beautiful walks around lakes, meadows and woods.
Times: Open all year. Tues-Fri, 1000-1600; Sun, 1000-1600. Closed 25-28 Mar, 21 Dec-3 Jan.
Fee: Free.
Facilities: 🅿 T(1-2 hrs) ⚲ ⑪ ⋔ 🛝

Brentwood
Thorndon Country Park Map ref. E10
The Avenue
Tel: (01277) 211250 Web: www.essexcc.gov.uk
Public open space of 540 acres. Woodlands, meadows, picnic and barbeque areas. Fishing lake and two visitor centres. Horse, cycle and walking routes.
Times: Open all year, daily, 0800-dusk.
Fee: Free.
Facilities: 🅿 🚌 ⇌ T(2 hrs) ⑪ ⋔ 🛉

Chigwell
Hainault Forest Country Park Map ref. C10
Romford Road
Tel: (0208) 500 7353 Web: www.hainaultforest.co.uk
600 acres of ancient woodland, a lake and rare breeds farm. Visitor and interpretation centre.
Times: Open all year, daily, 0700-dusk.
Fee: Free.
Facilities: 🅿 🚌 T(2 hrs) ⑪ ⋔ 🛉 🛝

Clacton-on-Sea
Holland Haven Country Park Map ref. O5
Tel: (01255) 253235
Unspoilt coastal grazing marshes with footpaths through meadows. Cliff-top walks to Frinton-on-Sea. Birdwatchinghides. Access to beaches.
Times: Open at any reasonable time.
Fee: Free.
Facilities: ❀ 🅿 🚌 T(2 hrs) ⋔ 🛉

Colchester
High Woods Country Park Map ref. K4
Visitors Centre, Turner Road
Tel: (01206) 853588
A 330 acre country park situated to the north of central
Colchester, with a variety of landscape and wildlife. Visitor
centre, toilets, bookshop and small shop.
Times: Visitor Centre open, 1 Jan-31 Mar, Sat and Sun,
1000-1600. 1 Apr-30 Sept, Mon-Sat, 1000-1630; Sun,
Bank Hols 1100-1730. 1 Oct-31 Dec, Sat and Sun, 1000-
1600. Closed 24, 25 Dec.
Fee: Free.
Facilities: ⊛ Q 🅿 T(2 hrs) ✗ 🎋 🏌 📷

Corringham (nr. Stanford-le-Hope)
Langdon Hills Country Park Map ref. F11
One Tree Hill
Tel: (01268) 542066 Web: www.essexcc.gov.uk
Country park consisting of Westley Heights and One Tree
Hill. Picnic areas, wildflower meadows and ancient
woodlands overlooking the Thames estuary.
Times: Open all year, daily, 0800-dusk.
Fee: Free.
Facilities: ⊛ 🅿 🚍 ♿ T(5 hrs) 🎋 🏌

Danbury (nr. Chelmsford)
Danbury and Lingwood Commons Map ref. H7/8
Tel: 0870 609 5388 Web: www.nationaltrust.org.uk
Danbury Common is composed of a mixture of woodland,
scrub, grassland and heath. Napoleonic defences are
evidence of Danbury's military past.
Times: Open at any reasonable time.
Fee: Free. Donations for parking.
Facilities: ⊛ 🅿 T(2 hrs) 🏌 NT

Danbury (nr. Chelmsford)
Danbury Country Park Map ref. H8
Woodhill Road
Tel: (01245) 222350 Web: www.essexcc.gov.uk
Country park set in the gardens and old deer park of
Danbury Palace. Walled garden, lakes and woodland.
The site offers a place for quiet recreation.
Times: Open all year, daily, 0800-dusk. Closing times are
displayed at the entrance to the site car parks.
Fee: Free. Car parking charges (upto 1 hr) £1.00, all day
£2.00.
Facilities: 🅿 T(1½ hrs) 🎋 🏌

East Mersea
Cudmore Grove Country Park Map ref. L6
Bromans Lane
Tel: (01206) 383868 Web: www.essexcc.gov.uk
Situated next to the entrance of the Colne estuary, the park
consists of grassland and a sandy beach, ideally suited to
walking, picnics, informal games and wildlife watching.
Times: Open all year, daily, 0800-dusk.
Fee: Car park charge - £1.00 per hour, £2.00 all day.
Facilities: Q 🅿 T(1½ hrs) 🎋 🏌 📷

Fingringhoe (nr. Colchester)
Fingringhoe Wick Nature Reserve Map ref. L5
South Green Road
Tel: (01206) 729678 Web: www.essexwt.org.uk
125 acres of woodland, lakes and saltmarsh on the Colne
estuary, with nature trails and eight hides. Observation
room, tower and gift shop.
Times: Open 1 Jan-24 Dec, Tues-Sun and Bank Hol Mon,
0900-1700. Open 27-31 Dec. Closed 25 and 26 Dec.
Fee: £1.00/50p.
Facilities: ⊛ Q 🅿 T(4 hrs) ✗ 🎋 🏌(on lead and restricted
walkway)

Hylands Park, Chelmsford

Ayot Green, Hertfordshire

Gosfield (nr. Halstead)
Gosfield Lake Resort Map ref. G4
Church Road
Tel: (01787) 475043 Web: www.gosfieldlake.co.uk
A leisure park with something for everyone. Lake with
fishing, water-skiing and children's playground.
Times: Open 1 Apr-2 Nov, daily, 0900-dusk.
Fee: £1.00/50p/50p. Extra charges for activities.
Facilities: P T(2 hrs) 🖰 ⩜ ♈

Hadleigh
Hadleigh Castle Country Park Map ref. H11
Chapel Lane
Tel: (01702) 551072 Web: www.essexcc.gov.uk
Large area of unspoilt countryside (fields and woodland),
with superb views over the Thames estuary. Remains of
castle close by, picnic areas, horse rides, bird hides and
way-marked trails.
Times: Open all year, daily, 0800-dusk.
Fee: Free (car park charge).
Facilities: P 🚽 ⇌ T(2 hrs) ⩜ ♈

Harwich
RSPB Stour Estuary Nature Reserve Map ref. O3
Tel: (01773) 328006 Web: www.rspb.org.uk
The Stour Estuary is one of the most important estuaries in
Britain for breeding birds, with internationally important
numbers of grey plovers, knots, redshanks and dunlin.
Times: Open any reasonable time. Closed for 1 day over
Christmas, please contact for details.
Fee: Free. Donations appreciated.
Facilities: ⊛ P ⇌ T(3 hrs) 🖍 ⩜ ♈

Layer de la Haye (nr. Colchester)
Abberton Reservoir Visitor Centre Map ref. K5
Church Road
Tel: (01206) 738172 Web: www.essexwt.org.uk
Nature reserve providing superb bird-watching over the
1,200 acre expanse of Abberton Reservoir. Shop with
toilets and displays. Adult and children's activities.
Times: Open all year, Tues-Sun, 0900-1700. Closed 25 and
26 Dec.
Fee: Free. Donations appreciated.
Facilities: Q P T(3 hrs) ⩜

Leigh-on-Sea
Belfairs Nature Reserve Map ref. I11
Eastwood Road North
Tel: (01702) 520202 Web: www.southend.gov.uk
Woodland gardens and walks. Golf course, pitch and putt
and 92-acre nature reserve.
Times: Open all year, daily.
Fee: Free.
Facilities: ⊛ P 🚽 T(2½ hrs) 🖰 ⩜ ♈

Little Wigborough (nr. Colchester)
Copt Hall Marshes Map ref. K5
Tel: 0870 609 5388 Web: www.nationaltrust.org.uk
Site of Specific Scientific Interest. The salt marshes are rich
in overwintering wildfowl and wading birds. Grass
headland paths give access to the sea wall.
Times: Open at any reasonable time.
Fee: Free.
Facilities: ⊛ P T(2 hrs) ♈ NT

Pitsea (nr. Basildon)
Wat Tyler Country Park Map ref. G11
Pitsea Hall Lane
Tel: (01268) 550088 Web: www.basildon.gov.uk
125 acres of thorn woodland, meadows, coastal grassland,
saltings and ponds. Motorboat museum, adventure play
area, craft units, boat pond and miniature railway.
Times: Open all year, daily, 0900-dusk.
Fee: Free.
Facilities: P ⇌ T(3 hrs) 🖍 🖰 ⩜ ♈ 🖾

Rayleigh
Hockley Woods Map ref. H10
Main Road, Hockley
Tel: (01702) 203078
Ancient semi natural woodland, 300 acres - freedom to
roam. Picnic area, play area and two self guided trails.
Horse routes. Rare animals, birds and insects. Local nature
reserve.
Times: Open at any reasonable time.
Fee: Free.
Facilities: P T(3½ hrs) ⩜ ♈

Rayne (nr. Braintree)
Flitch Way Country Park Map ref. C/D/E/F/G5
Rayne Station Centre, Station Road
Tel: (01376) 340262 Web: www.essexcc.gov.uk
15 miles of linear country park along the old Bishop's
Stortford to Braintree railway. Rayne Station Centre has
been renovated, and now has an exhibition of local
heritage.
Times: Open all year, daily, dawn-dusk. Rayne Station
Centre open all year, daily, 0800-1700. Exhibition Room
open all year, Sun, 1300-1600.
Fee: Free.
Facilities: ◉ ▣ 🚻 ⚡ T(2 hrs) 📷 🐾

Romford
Bedfords Park Visitor Centre Map ref. C9/10
Broxhill Road
Tel: (01708) 748646 Web: www.essexwt.org.uk
Set in the grounds of Bedfords Park, an historic parkland
site, the Visitor Centre is built on the site of the former
mansion. Exotic trees and superb views over area. EWT.
Times: Open all year, Tues-Sun, 0900-1700. Closed 25 and
26 Dec.
Fee: Free.
Facilities: ▣ T(2 hrs)

South Ockendon
Belhus Woods Country Park Map ref. D11
Romford Road, Aveley
Tel: (01708) 865628 Web: www.essexcc.gov.uk
A mixed landscape of ancient woodlands, grasslands and
lakes created from gravel extraction. Offering quiet
recreation, including fishing, walking and bird watching.
Visitor Centre.
Times: Open all year, daily, 0800-dusk.
Fee: Free (car park £1 per hr, £2 all day).
Facilities: ◉ ▣ 🚻 T(3 hrs) 💷 📷 🐾

South Weald (nr. Brentwood)
Weald Country Park Map ref. D9
Weald Road
Tel: (01277) 261343 Web: www.essexcc.gov.uk
Visitor Centre with interactive exhibition. Gift shop, light
refreshments, deer paddock, country walks, fishing, lakes
and own horse-riding.
Times: Open all year, daily, 0800-dusk Visitor Centre open
Tues-Sun and Bank Hols 1000-1600(closed later in
summer).
Fee: Free. Car park charge - 1 hour £1.00, over 1 hour
£2.00.
Facilities: ◉ ▣ T(5 hrs) 📷 💷 📷 🐾 ♿

Takeley (nr. Bishop's Stortford)
Hatfield Forest Map ref. D5
Tel: (01279) 870678 Web: www.nationaltrust.org.uk
Over 400 hectares of ancient coppice woodland, grassland,
magnificent pollarded trees, two ornamental lakes, 18th C.
Shell house and stream.
Times: Open all year, at any reasonable time. Vehicle
access to forest, 1 Apr-31 Oct, daily, 1000-1700.
Fee: Free, car park charge.
Facilities: ◉ ▣ T(2hrs) 📷 💷 📷 🐾 NT

Lee Valley Park

Waltham Abbey
River Lee Country Park Map ref. A8
Situated on either side of the River Lea, between Waltham
Abbey and Broxbourne
Tel: (01992) 702200 Web: www.leevalleypark.com
Unique patchwork of lakes, waterways, green open spaces
and countryside areas, covering 1,000 acres. A haven for
wildlife - great for cycling, walking, angling and bird-
watching. Dragon-fly sanctuary.
Times: Open all year, daily, dawn-dusk.
Fee: Free.
Facilities: ◉ ▣ 🚻 ⚡ T(2 hrs) 💷 📷 🐾

See Also:
Chelmer and Blackwater Navigation, Chelmsford, page 202
Hedingham Castle, Castle Hedingham, page 52
Hylands House, nr Chelmsfrod, page 40
Marks Hall Garden and Arboretum, Coggeshall, page 114
Marsh Farm Country Park, South Woodham Ferrers,
page 132
Royal Gunpowder Mills, Waltham Abbey, page 79

HERTFORDSHIRE

Berkhamsted
Ashridge Estate Map ref. C12
Ringshall
Tel: (01442) 851227 Web: www.nationaltrust.org.uk
Six square miles of woodlands, commons, chalk downland
and farmland, with the focal point of the Bridgewater
Monument. Visitor centre.
Times: Estate open all year. Visitor Centre open 19 Mar-11
Dec, Mon-Fri, 1300-1700; Sat and Sun, 1200-1700.
Fee: Monument £1.20/60p.
Facilities: ⊛ 🅿 T(2 hrs) ⊙ ⋔ 🔊 NT

Elstree
Aldenham Country Park Map ref. F15
Aldenham Road
Tel: (0208) 953 9602 Web: www.hertsdirect.org/aldenham
Meadow and woodland consisting of 175 acres with Rare
Breeds Farm, playgrounds, angling, nature trail and toilets.
Refreshments. Site of 'Winnie the Pooh's' 100 Aker Wood.
Times: Open Jan-Feb, daily, 0900-1600. Mar-Apr, daily,
0900-1700. May-Aug, daily, 0900-1800.
Sept-Oct, daily, 0900-1700. Nov-Dec, daily, 0900-1600.
Closed 25 Dec.
Fee: Car park £4.00.
Facilities: ⊛ 🅿 T(4 hrs) ⊙ 🎄 ⋔

Hertford
Hertford Heath and Balls Wood Map ref. H/I12
Tel: (01727) 858901 Web: www.wildlifetrust.org.uk/herts
Rare Hertfordshire open heathland and 'heathy' pools
attract dragonflies, butterflies and heathland birds. The
site varies from mature coppiced woodland, mixed
deciduous trees and conifer plantations through to areas of
open heathland.
Times: Open at any reasonable time.
Fee: Free
Facilities: T(3 hrs) ⋔

Rickmansworth
Rickmansworth Aquadrome Map ref. D15
Frogmoor Lane, off Harefield Road
Tel: (01923) 776611
100 acres of water, woodland and semi-landscaped
parkland with walks (including scenic Alder trail), picnic
and BBQ areas, children's playground, day fishing tickets
and water sports.
Times: Open all year, daily, dawn-dusk.
Fee: Free.
Facilities: 🅿 T(1 hr) ⊙ 🎄 ⋔ 🔊

Rickmansworth
Stocker's Lake Nature Reserve Map ref. D15
Tel: (01727) 858901
Offering a 3km circular walk, with hides, the reserve is
home to a huge range of waterfowl, finches and thrushes
and the largest heronry in Hertfordshire.
Times: Open at any reasonable time.
Fee: Free.
Facilities: 🅿 T(2½ hrs) ⋔

St Margarets
Amwell Quarry Nature Reserve Map ref. J12
Ware
Tel: (01727) 858901 Web: www.wildlifetrust.org.uk/herts
Primarily a flooded former gravel extraction, Amwell Quarry
also offers reedbed, marsh and willow woodland. It is an
excellent breeding site for wetland birds and is being
enhanced as a habitat for the elusive Bittern(occasionally
seen on site).
Times: Open at any reasonable time.
Fee: Free.
Facilities: T(30 mins) ⋔

Stanstead Abbots
RSPB Rye Meads Nature Reserve Map ref. J12
Rye Meads Visitor Centre, Rye Road
Tel: (01992) 708383 Web: www.rspb.org.uk
Rye Meads has a wide range of wetland habitats and is
particularly suited to family visits. The reed bed, open water
and meadows attract many different birds.
Times: Open all year, daily, 1000-1700 (or dusk if earlier).
Closed 25 and 26 Dec.
Fee: Free.
Facilities: ⊛ 🅿 🚻 ⇌ T(3 hrs) 🎄 🔊

Ashridge Estate, Hertfordshire

For even more
information visit
our website at
www.visiteastofengland.com

Stevenage
Fairlands Valley Park Map ref. G10
Tel: (01438) 353241
Web: www.stevenage-leisure.co.uk/fairlands
120 acres of parkland, including watersports, dinghy,
windsurfing and powerboat courses. Private tuition and
angling. Play area, cafe and disabled toilets on site.
Times: Open all year at any reasonable time.
Fee: Free.
Facilities: ⊕ 🅿 🚌 T(2 hrs) 🚻 🎋 🐕 ♿

Tring
College Lake Wildlife Centre Map ref. B12
Bulbourne (off B488)
Tel: (01865) 775476 Web: www.bbowt.org.uk
Created from a worked-out chalk quarry, College Lake has
been transformed into an outstanding centre for wildlife.
Visitor centre, farming/wildlife museum, bird hides and two
mile walk.
Times: Visitor permit required from Warden's office on
request. Open all year, daily (except Mon), 1000-1700.
Fee: Free.
Facilities: 🅿 ⚡ T(3-4 hrs) 🎋 ♿

Tring
Wilstone Reservoir Nature Reserve Map ref. B12
Tel: (01727) 858901 Web: www.wildlifetrust.org.uk/herts
The reservoir supplies water to the Grand Union Canal and
was built in 1802, later extended. It is an important refuge
for summer ducks. A hide and viewing areas provide good
views of waterfowl and waders in the autumn/winter.
Times: Open at any reasonable times.
Fee: Free.
Facilities: 🅿 T(1½ hrs) 🐕

Ware, Hertfordshire

Fairlands Valley Park, Stevenage, Hertfordshire

Waltham Cross
Cedars Park Map ref. I13/14
Theobalds Lane
Tel: (01992) 785537 Web: www.broxbourne.gov.uk
Steeped in history - this magnificent park hosts the remains
of Theobalds Palace, first visited by Elizabeth I in 1564.
Ornamental gardens, lake, pets' corner, rose walk and
arboretum.
Times: Open all year, daily, 1000-dusk.
Fee: Free.
Facilities: ⊕ 🅿 🚌 ⚡ T(1 hr) 🚻 🎋 🐕 ♿

Welwyn Garden City
Stanborough Park Map ref. G12
Stanborough Road
Tel: (01707) 327655 Web: www.welhat.gov.uk
Stanborough Park is a high quality public open space
providing a focus of activity for many varied user groups.
Watersports centre, nature trail, picnic areas and fishing.
Times: Open all year, daily, at any reasonable time.
Fee: Free
Facilities: 🅿 T(2 hrs) 🚻 🎋 🐕 ♿

See Also:
Hatfield House, Park and Gardens, Hatfield, page 41, 42
Knebworth House, Park and Gardens, page 41, 42
River Lee Country Park, Waltham Abbey, page 187

NORFOLK

Blakeney

Blakeney Point National Nature Reserve Map ref. H/12
Tel: 0870 609 5388 Web: www.nationaltrust.org.uk
One of Britain's foremost bird sanctuaries, the point is a
3¹/2 mile long sand and shingle spit noted in particular for
its colonies of breeding terns. Seals can also be seen.
Times: Open all year, daily, any reasonable time.
Fee: Car park £2.50.
Facilities: ⊛ 🅿 🛏 T(3 hrs) ➤ NT

Cley-next-the-Sea

NWT Cley Marshes Nature Reserve Map ref. I2
Coast Road
Tel: (01263) 740008
Web: www.wildlifetrust.org.uk/norfolk
Coastal nature reserve, with an international reputation.
Popular with bird-watchers who come to see migrant and
wading birds. Visitor centre overlooks the reserve.
Times: Reserve open all year, daily, dawn-dusk. Closed 25,
26 Dec. Visitor centre open late Mar-early Dec, daily,
1000-1700(reduced times Nov and Dec).
Fee: £3.75/free (members).
Facilities: 🅿 🛏 T(1-6 hrs) 🎞 🖥

Foxley (nr. Dereham)

NWT Foxley Wood Map ref. I5
Tel: (01603) 625540
Web: www.wildlifetrust.org.uk/norfolk
The largest ancient woodland in the county (320 acres),
with three nature trails existing around the site. The wood
is well used by naturalists, the general public and schools.
Times: Open all year, daily (except Thurs), 1000-1700.
Fee: Free.
Facilities: 🅿 T(2 hrs) 🏃 (by appointment) 🎞

Fritton (nr. Great Yarmouth)

Fritton Lake Country World Map ref. O8
Church Lane
Tel: (01493) 488208 Web: www.frittonlake.co.uk
A 250-acre centre with a children's assault course, putting,
adventure playground, golf, fishing, boating, wildfowl,
heavy horses, cart rides and falconry flying displays.
Times: Open 19 Mar-30 Oct, daily, 1000-1730 (closes
1700 in Oct). Also 5 Nov-17 Dec, Sat, but please telephone
to confirm.
Fee: £6.50/£4.50/£5.50.
Facilities: ⊛ 🍵 🅿 🛏 T(4 hrs) 🏃 🖤 🎞 🖥

Cley-next-the-Sea

Great Yarmouth

RSPB Berney Marshes Nature Reserve (and Breydon Water) Map ref. O7/8

Tel: (01493) 700645 Web: www.rspb.org.uk

Huge expanse of open space, grazing marshes and mudflats. Breydon Water is Britain's most easterly estuary. Home to tens of thousands of wintering and breeding wildfowl and waders.

Times: Open all year, daily, any reasonable time.

Fee: Free.

Facilities: ⊕ ≋ T(2 hrs) ⋒ ⋔ (on leads)

Hickling

NWT Hickling Broad National Nature Reserve

Map ref. N5/6

Stubb Road

Tel: (01692) 598276

Web: www.wildlifetrust.org.uk/norfolk

Nature reserve beside the largest area of open water in the Broads. Dykes, marshes, fens and woodland, with a visitors centre and water trail. Wintering and resident birds.

Times: Open all year, daily. Visitor's centre open, mid Apr-mid Sept, 1000-1700.

Fee: £3.00/free(members). Booking essential for water trail boat trip (extra charge).

Facilities: ▣ T(1-5 hrs) ⋒ ⋒

Holme-next-the-Sea (nr. Hunstanton)

Holme Bird Observatory Reserve (Norfolk Ornithologist's Association) Map ref. D2

Broadwater Road

Tel: (01485) 525406 Web: www.noa.org.uk

Nature reserve with over 320 species of birds recorded since 1962. One of 18 bird observatories in the UK. Various species of dragonfly. Over 50 species of flora.

Times: Open all year, Tues-Sun and Bank Hol Mons, 0900-1700 (or dusk, if earlier). Closed 25, 26 Dec.

Fee: £3.00.

Facilities: ▣ T(2-3 hrs) ⋔

Holt

Holt Country Park Map ref. J3

Norwich Road

Tel: (01263) 516001 Web: www.northnorfolk.org

100 acre, mainly coniferous woodland, with children's play area, waymarked trails and a small visitor centre. An observation tower offers attractive views.

Times: Open all year, at any reasonable time.

Fee: Free. Car park charge £1.00.

Facilities: ⊕ ▣ T(2 hrs) ⋒ ⋔

King's Lynn

The Green Quay Environmental Discovery Centre

Map ref. C5/6

Marriott's Warehouse, South Quay

Tel: (01553) 818500 Web: www.thegreenquay.co.uk

Set beside the River Great Ouse, the centre promotes the conservation of The Wash estuary and local wildlife. Film shows, bird viewing gallery and hydroponics.

Times: Open 3 Jan-24 Dec, Mon-Wed, Sat, Sun, 1000-1700, Thurs, Fri 1000-2100.

Fee: £1.00/50p/£1.00.

Facilities: T(1 hr) ⋒ ⋒

Mundford

Lynford Arboretum Map ref. F9

Tel: (01842) 810271 Web: www.forestry.gov.uk

A nationally important collection of over 200 species of broad-leaved and coniferous trees. Spring and Autumn are particularly stunning.

Times: Open at any reasonable time.

Fee: Free.

Facilities: ⊕ ▣ T(3 hrs) ⋒ ⋒

Pensthorpe (nr. Fakenham)

Pensthorpe Nature Reserve and Gardens Map ref. H4

Tel: (01328) 851465 Web: www.pensthorpe.com

Collection of rare and native water birds and migratory visitors. Lakeside, woodland, wildflower meadows, river walks and bird hides. The Millennium Garden. Cafe, shop and play area.

Times: Open 1 Jan-31 Mar, daily, 1000-1600. 1 Apr-31 Dec, daily, 1000-1700. Closed 25, 26 Dec and 1 Jan.

Fee: £6.00/£3.00/£5.00/£15.00(family).

Facilities: ⊕ Q ▣ T(3-5 hrs) ⋒ ⋒ ⋒

Little Ouse River

Cley Mill

Ranworth
NWT Broads Wildlife Centre Map ref. M6
Tel: (01603) 270479
Web: www.wildlifetrust.org.uk/norfolk
A nature trail and conservation centre with displays showing history and wildlife. Gallery with telescopes and binoculars over-looking the Ranworth Broad Nature Reserve.
Times: Wildlife centre open 1 Apr-31 Oct, daily, 1000-1700. Boardwalk open all year.
Fee: Free.
Facilities: 🅿 🚌 T(1 hr) 🎋

Sheringham
Sheringham Park Map ref. J3
Upper Sheringham
Tel: (01263) 821429 Web: www.nationaltrust.org.uk
One of Humphry Repton's most outstanding achievements, this landscape park contains fine mature woodlands, and a large woodland garden with rhododendrons and azaleas. Stunning views of coast.
Times: Open all year, daily, dawn-dusk.
Fee: Car park £3.00.
Facilities: ⚘ 🅿 T(3 hrs) 🎋 🐕 (on leads) **NT**

Snettisham (nr. Hunstanton)
RSPB Snettisham Nature Reserve Map ref. D4
Tel: (01485) 542689 Web: www.rspb.org.uk
At Snettisham you can enjoy one of the country's greatest wildlife spectacles. As the rising tide covers The Wash, waders, ducks and geese move up the beach onto the pools.
Times: Open at any reasonable time.
Fee: Free.
Facilities: ⚘ 🅿 T(3 hrs) 🎋

Strumpshaw (nr. Norwich)
RSPB Strumpshaw Fen Nature Reserve Map ref. M7
Low Road
Tel: (01603) 715191 Web: www.rspb.org.uk
Extensive trails take visitors through unspoilt broadland scenery and habitats - woodland, meadows, fens and reed beds. A great variety of wildlife can be seen. Three bird-watching hides.
Times: Open all year, dawn-dusk. Information Centre, open 1 Jan-31 Mar, daily, 0900-1600; 1 Apr-31 Oct, daily, 0900-1700; 1 Nov-31 Dec, daily, 0900-1600. Closed 25 Dec.
Fee: £2.50/50p/£1.50/£5.00.
Facilities: ⚘ 🅿 T(3 hrs) 🎋

Titchwell (nr. Hunstanton)
RSPB Titchwell Marsh Nature Reserve Map ref. E2
Main Road
Tel: (01485) 210779 Web: www.rspb.org.uk
Nature reserve with three bird-watching hides and two trails. Visitor centre with large shop, food servery, car park and toilets
Times: Open 1 Jan-14 Feb, daily, 0930-1600; 15 Feb-13 Nov, daily, 0930-1700; 14 Nov-31 Dec, daily 0930-1600. Closed 25 and 26 Dec.
Fee: Car park £3.00.
Facilities: ⚘ Q 🅿 🚌 T(2½ hrs) 🎋 🐕 🛏 ♿

NWT Broads Wildlife Centre, Ranworth

Weeting (nr. Brandon)
NWT Weeting Heath National Nature Reserve
Map ref. E10
Tel: (01842) 827615
Web: www.wildlifetrust.org.uk/norfolk
A nature reserve with grassy heath, pine plantation, meres and associated wildlife. There is also a self-guided nature trail and access to the hides.
Times: Open 1 Apr-31 Aug, daily, dawn-dusk.
Fee: £2.00/free.
Facilities: P T(1 hr) (by appointment)

See Also:
Blickling Hall, nr Aylsham, page 43
Felbrigg Hall, nr Cromer, page 43
Holkham Hall, Wells next the Sea, page 42, 44
Mannington Gardens and Countryside, page 119
Oxburgh Hall, Oxborough, page 43
Sandringham, nr Kings Lynn, page 44
Wolterton Park, nr Aylsham, page 43

SUFFOLK

Aldeburgh
RSPB North Warren Nature Reserve Map ref. N7/8
Thorpe Road
Tel: (01728) 688481 Web: www.rspb.org.uk
Delightful reserve consists of grazing marshes, reedbeds, heath and woodland. Good for wildfowl in winter, and butterflies and dragonflies in summer. Marsh harriers, nightingales and bitterns.
Times: Open all year, daily, any reasonable time.
Fee: Free.
Facilities: P T(2 hrs) (on leads)

Bradfield St. George (nr. Bury St. Edmunds)
Bradfield Woods Map ref. E7
Tel: (01473) 890089
Web: www.wildlifetrust.org.uk/suffolk
One of Britain's finest ancient woodlands - a haven for wildlife. A working wood, it has been under continuous management since 1252, supplying local needs for firewood and hazel products. SWT.
Times: Open at any reasonable time.
Fee: Free.
Facilities: P T(2 hrs) (on leads)

Brandon
Brandon Country Park Map ref. C3
Bury Road
Tel: (01842) 810185
Web: www.suffolkcc.gov.uk/e-ant-t/countryside
30 acres of landscaped parkland, with a lake, walled garden, tree trail and forest walks. Visitor centre open daily. Play area, plant stall and off-road cycle loops.
Times: Park open all year, daily, dawn-dusk. Visitor centre open 1 Jan-28 Feb, daily, 1000-1600. 1 Mar-31 Oct, Mon-Fri, 1000-1700; Sat and Sun, 1000-1730. 1 Nov-31 Dec, daily, 1000-1600.
Fee: Free.
Facilities: P T(1½ hrs)

Reedham Ferry

Brandon
Go Ape! Hire Wire Forest Adventure. Map ref. D3
High Lodge Forest Centre, Thetford Forest
Between Brandon and Thetford (off B1107)
Tel: 0870 444 5562 Web: www.goape.co.uk
Go Ape! is a spectacular aerial course of zip slides,
scramble nets and rope bridges at heights of up to 35 feet
off the forest floor. Go Ape! is an exhilarating test of agility,
courage and determination. Minimum age 10 years.
Minimum height 4ft 7ins. Under 18s must be accompanied
by a participating adult. Booking strongly recommended.
See our advertisement on page 208
Times: 12-20 Feb, daily; 19 Mar-30 Sept, daily; 1 Oct-30
Nov, Sat and Sun. Times vary, please telephone to confirm.
Fee: Please telephone for details.
Facilities: 🄿 T(2½ hrs) ⑪ 🎋

Brandon
High Lodge Forest Centre Map ref. D3
Between Brandon and Thetford (off B1107)
Tel: (01842) 810271 Web: www.forestry.gov.uk
High Lodge nestles in the heart of the Thetford Forest Park.
Centre offers walking, cycling (cycle hire), high ropes
course, adventure playground, shop and restaurant.
Times: Open all year, daily, 0900-dusk. Closed 25 Dec.
Fee: £4.00 per car.
Facilities: ⊛ Q 🄿 T(4 hrs) ⑪ 🎋 🐾(on leads)

Bury St. Edmunds
Nowton Park Map ref. E7
Nowton Road
Tel: (01284) 763666 Web: www.stedmundsbury.gov.uk
Previously a country estate, with 170 acres of woodland
and pasture. Some formal recreation. All-weather pitch and
two football pitches. Children's play area. Visitor centre.
Times: Open all year, daily, 0830-dusk. Visitor centre open
Sat and Sun, 1100-1700 (closes 1600 in winter). Closed
24, 25 Dec.
Fee: Free.
Facilities: ⊛ 🄿 🛏 ⇌ T(2 hrs) 🎋 🐾 (on leads)

Carlton Colville (nr. Lowestoft)
Carlton Marshes Map ref. O2
Burnt Hill Lane
Tel: (01502) 564250
Web: www.wildlifetrust.org.uk/suffolk
Over 100 acres of grazing marsh, fens and peat pools, set
in the Waveney Valley. It is the Broads in miniature. Flower-
studded marshes and wintering birds. Visitor Centre. SWT.
Times: The reserve is open all the time but the centre is
only open some weekends and occasionally during the
week.
Fee: Free.
Facilities: 🄿 T(2 hrs) 🎋 🐾 (on leads)

Clare
Clare Castle Country Park Map ref. C10
Malting Lane
Tel: (01787) 277491
Web: www.suffolkcc.gov.uk/e-ant-t/countryside
A small country park, incorporating the remains of a castle
and a Victorian railway station, in a 30-acre site fronting
onto the River Stour.
Times: Open all year, daily, dawn-dusk.
Fee: Free.
Facilities: ⊛ 🄿 🛏 T(2 hrs) 🎋 🐾

Dunwich
Dunwich Heath Coastal Centre and Beach Map ref. O6
Tel: (01728) 648505 Web: www.nationaltrust.org.uk
Remnant of the once extensive Sandling Heaths, and one of
Suffolk's most important nature conservation areas. Many
excellent walks and access to beach. Coastguard cottages
with observation room, tearoom and shop.
Times: Heath open all year, daily, dawn to dusk. Tearoom
and shop open 2 Jan-28 Feb, Sat and Sun, 1000-1600; 1 -
31 Mar, Wed-Sun,1000-1600; 1 Apr-31 Oct, Wed-Sun,
1000-1700, 1 Nov-31 Dec, Wed-Sun 1000-1600. Also
daily during school hols.
Fee: Free. Car park charge £2.10.
Facilities: ⊛ 🄿 T(2-3 hrs) ⑪ 🎋 🐾 🖾 NT

Felixstowe
Trimley Marshes Map ref. K11
Tel: (01473) 890089
Web: www.wildlifetrust.org.uk/suffolk
Exciting wetland reserve created entirely from arable land
alongside the River Orwell, unbeatable for its sheer number
and species of birds. Wonderful estuary views. Visitor
Centre. SWT.
Times: Open at any reasonable time.
Fee: Free.
Facilities: T(4 hrs) 🐾 (on leads)

Dunwich Heath Coastal Centre and Beach

Hadleigh
RSPB Wolves Wood Map ref. H10
Tel: (01255) 886043 Web: www.rspb.org.uk
Wolves Wood is one of the few remaining areas of the ancient woodland that used to cover East Anglia. Wide variety of birds, plants and animals.
Times: Open at any reasonable time.
Fee: Free.
Facilities: T(1 hr)

Knettishall (nr. Thetford)
Knettishall Heath Country Park Map ref. F4
Tel: (01953) 688265
Web: www.suffolkcc.gov.uk/e-ant-t/countryside
Park with 375 acres of Breckland heath and mixed woodlands, with access to the River Ouse along walks. Picnic areas, toilets, and the starting point for The Peddar's Way, Angles Way and Icknield Way long distance footpaths.
Times: Open all year, daily, 0900-dusk.
Fee: Free.
Facilities: T(2 hrs)

Lackford (nr. Bury St. Edmunds)
Lackford Lakes Map ref. D6
Tel: (01284) 728706
Web: www.wildlifetrust.org.uk/suffolk
Lackford Lakes lies beside the River Lark, and have been created from former gravel pits. A superb site for wildfowl in both winter and summer. Visitor Centre. SWT.
Times: Open 1 Jan-31 Mar, Wed-Sun, 1000-1600; 1 Apr-31 Oct, Wed-Sun, 1000-1700; 1 Nov-31 Dec, Wed-Sun, 1000-1600. Closed for Christmas, please phone for details.
Fee: Free.
Facilities: T(2 hrs)

Snape Maltings

Needham Market
Needham Lake and Local Nature Reserve Map ref. H8
Tel: (01449) 727150 Web: www.midsuffolkleisure.co.uk
A large man-made lake and nature reserve, with picnic and educational facilities, on the outskirts of Needham Market. Tarmac pathway around the lake.
Times: Open at any reasonable time.
Fee: Free.
Facilities: T(1 hr)

Orford
Orford Ness National Nature Reserve Map ref. N9
Tel: (01394) 450900 Web: www.nationaltrust.org.uk
A 10 mile long vegetated shingle spit on the Suffolk coast. It is a national nature reserve and a former top secret military test site. Waymarked trails and displays.
Times: Open 26 Mar-25 Jun, Sat. 28 Jun-1 Oct, Tues-Sat. 8-29 Oct, Sat. Ferries leave Orford Quay from 1000-1400. Last ferry leaves the Ness at 1700.
Fee: National Trust members, £3.90/£1.95. Non-members, £5.90/£2.95.
Facilities: T(2½ hrs) NT

Orford
RSPB Havergate Island Map ref. M/N9
Tel: (01394) 450732 Web: www.rspb.org.uk
Small island set in the River Ore. Mainly a coastal lagoon reserve, important for avocets, terns and other waders. Wildfowl in winter, and a variety of flora in summer.
Times: Visits must be pre-booked, please telephone RSPB Minsmere on (01728) 648281. Open 1 Jan-31 Mar, 1st Sat of each month. 1 Apr-31 Aug, 1st and 3rd weekends, and every Thurs. 1 Sept-31 Dec, 1st Sat of every month.
Fee: £5.00/£2.50.
Facilities: T(5 hrs)

Reydon (nr. Southwold)
Hen Reedbed Map ref. N4
Tel: (01473) 890089
Web: www.wildlifetrust.org.uk/suffolk
A blend of reedbeds, fens, dykes and pools created in 1999 to provide new breeding habitat for bittern and other wildlife. A rich mosaic of wetland habitats. SWT.
Times: Open at any reasonable time.
Fee: Free.
Facilities: T(2 hrs) (on leads)

For even more information visit our website at **www.visiteastofengland.com**

Stutton (nr. Ipswich)
Alton Water Map ref. I11
Holbrook Road
Tel: (01473) 328268 Web: www.anglianwater.co.uk
Largest area of inland water in Suffolk. Visitor centre with
cafeteria, panoramic views and cycle hire. Nature reserves,
eight mile walk/ten mile cycle track, watersports centre and
fishing.
Times: Open all year. Gates open - summer, 0700-2030;
winter, 0700-1800. Visitor Centre - daily in summer, 1000-
1700; weekends, Bank Hols and school hols only in winter,
1000-dusk.
Fee: Free. Car Park, peak times £2.00, off peak £1.00.
Facilities: ⊛ 🅿 🚻 T(3 hrs) 🍴 🎋 🐕

Thornham Magna (nr. Eye)
Thornham Walks Map ref. H/I5
Tel: (01379) 788345 Web: www.midsuffolkleisure.co.uk
12 miles of walks through parkland, woods, meadow and
farmland of the Thornham Estate. The walks include a
surfaced path suitable for push chairs and wheelchairs.
Times: Open all year, daily, 0900-1800.
Fee: Free. Car park charge, Mon-Sat £2.00; Sun and Bank
Hols £2.50.
Facilities: ⊛ 🅿 T(2 hrs) 🍴 🎋 🐕 (on leads)

West Stow (nr. Bury St. Edmunds)
West Stow Country Park Map ref. D5
Icklingham Road
Tel: (01284) 728718
Web: www.stedmundsbury.gov.uk/weststow.htm
Country park with woodland, river, lake, nature trails,
walks and bird hides. Large car park with picnic area.
Visitor centre with displays, cafeteria and shop.
Times: Open all year, daily, summer 0800-2000; winter
0800-1700.
Fee: Free.
Facilities: ⊛ 🅿 T(2 hrs) 🍴 🎋 🐕 (on leads)

Westleton (nr. Saxmundham)
RSPB Minsmere Nature Reserve Map ref. N/O6
Tel: (01728) 648281 Web: www.rspb.org.uk
RSPB's flagship reserve on the Suffolk coast, with bird-
watching hides and nature trails, year-round events and
guided walks. Visitor centre with large shop and tearoom.
Times: Reserve open all year, daily (except Tues), nature
trails 0900-2100 (or dusk if earlier). Closed 29 Mar, 25-27
Dec, 3 Jan. Visitor centre open daily (except Tues) - Jan-Dec
0900-1600.
Fee: £5.00/£1.50/£3.00/£10.00.
Facilities: ⊛ 🅿 T(3 hrs) 🍴 🎋

Woodbridge
Sandlings Forests Map ref. L/M9, M8, N5/6
Tel: (01394) 450164 Web: www.forestry.gov.uk
The Sandlings covers woods in Rendlesham, Tangham and
Dunwich. Diverse mix of conifer plantations, interspersed
with broadleaved areas, lowland heath and wetland areas.
Forest Centre at Rendlesham with circular walks, cycle trails
and adventure playground.
Times: Open all year, daily, any reasonable time.
Fee: Free. Car park charge £1.00.
Facilities: ⊛ 🅿 T(2½ hrs) 🍴 🎋 🐕

See Also:
Ickworth House, Park and Gardens, nr Bury St Edmunds,
page 45
Walberswick Visitor Centre, page 100.

Saffron Walden, Essex

Mills

BEDFORDSHIRE

Bromham (nr. Bedford)
Bromham Mill Map ref. C5
Bridge End
Tel: (01234) 824330 Web: www.bedfordshire.gov.uk
Restored watermill in working condition. Wholemeal
stoneground flour for sale. Refreshments overlooking River
Great Ouse. Art gallery, craft sales and picnic site.
Times: Open 27 Mar-30 Oct, Sun and Bank Hol Mon,
1300-1700.
Fee: Donations requested.
Facilities: ◉ P ⛽ T(1½ hrs) ⓘ ⋒

Stevington (nr. Bedford)
Stevington Windmill Map ref. C5
Tel: (01234) 228330 Web: www.bedfordshire.gov.uk
A fully-restored 18th C. postmill. Entry is via keys which are
available from the pubs in the village for a small returnable
deposit.
Times: Open all year, daily, 1000-1900 (or dusk if earlier).
Collect keys from the pubs in the village.
Fee: Free.
Facilities: ◉ P T(1 hr)

CAMBRIDGESHIRE

Houghton (nr. Huntingdon)
Houghton Mill Map ref. E9
Tel: (01480) 301494 Web: www.nationaltrust.org.uk
A large, timber-built watermill on an island in the River Ouse,
with much of the 19th C. mill machinery intact and some
restored to working order.
Times: Open 2 Apr-29 May, Sat and Sun, 1300-1700. 30
May-28 Sept, Sat-Wed, 1300-1700. 1-30 Oct, Sat and Sun,
1300-1700.
Fee: £3.20/£1.50/£7.00 (family).
Facilities: ◉ P ⛽ T(1 hr) ⓘ ⋒ NT

Swaffham Prior
The Windmill Map ref. I10/11
Tel: (01638) 741009 Web: www.fostersmill.co.uk
Four sailed working windmill, built in 1857, and worked
commercially until 1946. Restored by the present owner,
and producing stoneground flours. Visitors can climb the
mill. Photographic display.
Times: Open 9 Jan; 13 Feb; 13 Mar; 10 Apr; 8 May;
12 Jun; 10 Jul; 14 Aug; 11 Sept; 9 Oct; 13 Nov; 11 Dec,
1300-1700.
Fee: Free. Donations appreciated.
Facilities: P T(30 mins) 𝕏

Wicken (nr. Soham)
Wicken Corn Windmill Map ref. I9
23 High Street
Tel: (01664) 822751 Web: www.geocities.com/wickenmill
One of the country's finest windmills, built in the 19th C.
Probably the world's only working 12-sided smock
windmill. The mill grinds wholemeal flour on open days.
Times: Open 1 Jan, 5 Feb; Mar-Nov first Sat and Sun in
month; 3 Dec; also 28 Mar and Summer Bank Hols, 1000-
1730.
Fee: Free. Donations appreciated.
Facilities: P T(1 hr) 𝕏

See Also:
Anglesey Abbey, Gardens and Lode Mill, nr Cambridge,
page 39
Sacrewell Farm and Country Centre, nr Peterborough,
page 69
Wicken Fen National Nature Reserve, nr Soham, page 184

Thorpeness Windmill

ESSEX

Aythorpe Roding
Aythorpe Roding Postmill Map ref. D6
Tel: (01245) 437663 or (07887) 662177
An 18th C. postmill (the largest remaining in Essex) restored to working order. It is winded by a fantail arrangement, which runs along a stone track around the mill.
Times: Open 24 Apr; 8, 29 May; 26 Jun; 31 Jul; 28 Aug; 11, 25 Sept, 1400-1700.
Fee: Free.
Facilities: ⊕ T(2 hrs)

Bocking (nr. Braintree)
Bocking Windmill Map ref. G4
Church Street
Tel: (01376) 341339
Postmill built in 1721. Small collection of historic agricultural items.
Times: Open 2, 8 May, 1000-1700. 30 May, 26 Jun, 31 Jul, 29 Aug, 1400-1700.
Fee: Free. Donations appreciated.
Facilities: P 🚻 T(1 hr) ⁊ 🛏

Colchester
Bourne Mill Map ref. K4
Bourne Road
Tel: (01206) 572422 Web: www.nationaltrust.org.uk
The mill was originally built as a fishing lodge in 1591, and features stepped Dutch Gables. There is a mill pond, and some of the machinery, including the waterwheel is working.
Times: Open 1 Jun-31 Aug, Tues and Sun, 1400-1700. Please to confirm times.
Fee: £2.00/£1.00 (2004 prices).
Facilities: ⊕ P T(2 hrs) 🛏 NT

Finchingfield
Finchingfield (Duck End) Postmill Map ref. F3
Tel: (01245) 437663 or (07887) 662177
A small, simple, mid-18th C. feudal or estate-type postmill with a wooden wind shaft and one pair of stones.
Times: Open 17 Apr; 8, 15 May; 19 Jun; 17 Jul; 21 Aug; 11, 18 Sept, 1400-1700.
Fee: Free.
Facilities: ⊕ T(2 hrs)

Mountnessing (nr. Ingatestone)
Mountnessing Windmill Map ref. E9
Roman Road
Tel: (01245) 437663 or (07887) 662177
An early 19th C. postmill restored to working order. Visitors may climb the windmill and see the wooden machinery.
Times: Open 8, 15 May; 19 Jun; 17 Jul; 21 Aug; 11, 18 Sept; 1400-1700.
Fee: Free.
Facilities: ⊕ P T(1³/4 hrs) 🛏

Rayleigh
Rayleigh Windmill and Museum Map ref. H10
Mill Hall Car Park, Bellingham Lane
Tel: (01268) 771072
A windmill with sails but no mechanism. On the ground floor, the museum has bygones and local artefacts.
Times: Open 2 Apr-24 Sept, Sat, 1030-1300.
Fee: 20p/10p.
Facilities: P 🚻 ⚖ T(30 mins) 🛏

Stansted Mountfitchet
Stansted Mountfitchet Windmill Map ref. C4
Millside
Tel: (01279) 647213
Brick tower windmill built in 1787. Not working, but contains most of original machinery. Scheduled ancient monument.
Times: Open 27-28 Mar, 3 Apr; 1, 2, 8, 29, 30 May; 5 Jun; 3 Jul; 7, 28, 29 Aug; 4 Sept; 2 Oct, 1400-1800.
Fee: 50p/25p.
Facilities: 🚻 ⚖ T(45 mins) ⁊ 🛏

Stock (nr. Ingatestone)
Stock Towermill Map ref. F9
Mill Lane
Tel: (01245) 437663 or (07887) 662177
A 19th C. towermill, recently restored to working order and typical of the latest in millwrights techniques just before windmills became obsolete.
Times: Open 10 Apr; 8 May; 12 Jun; 10 Jul; 14 Aug; 11 Sept; 9 Oct, 1400-1700.
Fee: Free.
Facilities: ⊕ P T(2 hrs)

Thorrington (nr. Wivenhoe)
Thorrington Tidemill Map ref. L5
Brightlingsea Road
Tel: (01245) 437663 or (07887) 662177
An early 19th C. tidal watermill, restored by Essex County Council. Visitors may climb to the top of the mill.
Times: Open 27 Mar; 24 Apr; 8, 29 May; 26 Jun; 31 Jul; 28 Aug; 11, 25 Sept, 1400-1700.
Fee: Free.
Facilities: ⊕ P T(1³/4 hrs)

HERTFORDSHIRE

Cromer (nr. Buntingford)
Cromer Windmill Map ref. H9
Tel: (01279) 843301 Web: www.hertsmuseums.org.uk
Hertfordshire's sole-surviving postmill. Video and audio display. Exhibitions on Hertfordshire's windmills, the history of Cromer Mill and the restoration of the mill.
Times: Open 8 May-11 Sept, Sun, 2nd and 4th Sat in month, 1430-1700.
Fee: £1.50/25p.
Facilities: P T(1 hr) 🛖🎭 ⛩

Ivinghoe (nr. Tring)
Ford End Watermill Map ref. B11
Station Road (B488)
Tel: (01582) 600391 Web: www.fordendwatermill.co.uk
Grade II listed watermill first recorded 1616 on site of an earlier mill. Now restored to working order as it was in late 1800s. Stoneground wholemeal flour for sale when milling.
Times: Open 25* Mar; 2*, 8*, 22, 30* May; 12, 26 Jun; 10, 24 Jul; 14, 28, 29* Aug; 11, 25* Sept. 1430-1730.
* - indicates milling demonstrations on these dates between 1500-1700.
Fee: £1.20/40p.
Facilities: P 🚻 T(1 hr) ⛩

St. Albans
Kingsbury Watermill Map ref. F13
St. Michael's Street
Tel: (01727) 853502
A 16th C. watermill with working machinery, a collection of farm implements, an art gallery and gift shop. There is also the Waffle House tearoom and restaurant.
Times: Open all year. Summer - Mon-Sat, 1000-1800; Sun, 1100-1800. Winter - Mon-Sat, 1000-1700; Sun, 1000-1700. Closed 25 and 26 Dec.
Fee: £1.50/75p.
Facilities: 🅰 P T(30 mins) 🎭

St. Albans
Redbournbury Watermill Map ref. E12
Redbournbury Lane
Tel: (01582) 792874 Web: www.redbournmill.co.uk
An 18th C. working watermill with riverside walks. Organic flours and bread for sale.
Times: Open 27 Mar-2 Oct, Sun, 1400-1730, Bank Hols and special weekends 1030-1730.
Fee: £1.50/80p.
Facilities: P 🚻 T(1½ hrs) 🎭

See Also:
Mill Green Museum and Mill, Hatfield, page 81.

NORFOLK

Acle
Stracey Arms Drainage Mill Map ref. N/O7
Tel: (01603) 222705 Web: www.norfolkwindmills.co.uk
An exhibition of photographs, and the history of drainage mills in Broadland. A restored drainage mill with access by two ladders to the cap showing the brakewheel and gears.
Times: Open Easter-end Sept, daily, 0900-2000.
Fee: 70p/30p.
Facilities: 🅰 P T(30 mins) 🐕 🐾

Cley-next-the-Sea
Cley Mill Map ref. I2
Tel: (01263) 740209 Web: www.cleymill.co.uk
A towermill used as a flourmill until 1918, and then converted to a guesthouse in 1983. Built in the early 1700s, it is an outstanding example of a preserved mill with sails.
Times: Open 31 Mar-30 Sept, daily, 1400-1700.
Fee: £2.00/£1.00/£1.00.
Facilities: P 🚻 T(30 mins)

Denver (nr. Downham Market)
Denver Windmill Map ref. C8
Sluice Road
Tel: (01366) 384009 Web: www.denvermill.co.uk
A fully restored windmill, with all its internal machinery. Unique guided tours to the top of the tower. Visitor's centre, tearoom and bakery.
Times: Open all year, Mon-Sat 1000-1700, Sun 1200-1700 (1 Jan-31 Mar and 1 Nov-30 Dec closes 1600). Closed 25-28 and 31 Dec and 1 Jan.
Fee: £3.50/£2.00/£3.00/£9.00(family).
Facilities: P T(2 hrs) 🛖🎭 ⛩ 🐾

Hunsett Mill

Great Bircham (nr. Kings Lynn)
Bircham Mill Map ref. E4
Tel: (01485) 578393 Web: www.birchamwindmill.co.uk
Beautifully restored windmill and on-site working bakery.
Tea rooms serve homebaked scones, cakes and light
lunches. Gift shop, garden, animals, play-area and
cycle hire.
Times: Open 20 Mar-30 Sept, daily, 1000-1700.
Fee: £3.00/£1.75/£2.75.
Facilities: ⊛ Q 🄿 🚂 T(2 hrs) ⑪ 🐈

Great Yarmouth
Berney Arms Windmill Map ref. O8
Tel: (01493) 857900 Web: www.english-heritage.org.uk
A most splendid, and the highest remaining Norfolk
marshmill with seven floors. Built in the late 19th C. by
millwrights Stolworthy, and situated on Halvergate Marsh.
Access by boat or train only.
Times: 24 Mar-30 Sept open by appointment for groups
only.
Fee: £2.00/£1.00/£1.50.
Facilities: ⊛ ⇌ T(30 mins) ㅟ EH

Horsey (nr. Great Yarmouth)
Horsey Windpump Map ref. O5
Tel: (01493) 393904 Web: www.nationaltrust.org.uk
Situated on the edge of Horsey Mere, this windmill is four
storeys high - the gallery affording splendid views across the
marshes.
Times: Open 5-31 Mar, Sat and Sun, 1000-1630. 1 Apr-30
Jun, Wed-Sun, 1000-1630. 1 Jul-31 Aug, daily, 1000-1630.
1 Sept-30 Oct, Wed-Sun, 1000-1630.
Fee: £2.00/£1.00.
Facilities: ⊛ 🄿 T(1½ hrs) ⑪ 🎇 NT

Letheringsett (nr. Holt)
Letheringsett Watermill Map ref. I3
Riverside Road
Tel: (01263) 713153
Web: www.letheringsettwatermill.co.uk
An historic working watermill with an iron water wheel and
main gearing restored with an additional vintage Ruston
Hornsby oil engine. Flour, animal and pet feed are for sale.
Times: Open all year, May-Sept, Mon-Fri, 1000-1700; Sat,
0900-1300. Oct-Apr, Mon-Fri, 0900-1600; Sat, 0900-1300
Banl Hol Sun only, 1400-1700. Closed 25 Mar, Bank Hol
Mons and some days at Christmas and New Year.
Fee: Working demonstrations £3.50/£2.00/£3.00. Non-
demonstration days £2.50/£1.50 (2004 prices).
Facilities: 🄿 T(1½ hrs)

Old Buckenham (nr. Attleborough)
Old Buckenham Mill Map ref. I10
Green Lane
Tel: (01603) 222705 Web: www.norfolkwindmills.co.uk
The largest diameter cornmill in the country built in 1818.
The mill is static but contains much machinery. It had five
sets of stones when operating.
Times: Open 10 Apr, 8 May, 12 Jun, 10 Jul, 14 Aug, 11
Sept, 1400-1700.
Fee: 70p/30p.
Facilities: ⊛ 🄿 🚂 T(45 mins)

Starston (nr. Harleston)
Starston Windpump Map ref. L11
Tel: (01379) 852393
Restored windpump (1832). A hollow postmill built to
supply water to Home Farm, Starston. Access by footpath,
150yds from off-road parking.
Times: Open at any reasonable time.
Fee: Free.
Facilities: 🄿 🚂 T(30 mins)

SUFFOLK

Herringfleet (nr. Lowestoft)
Herringfleet Marshmill Map ref. N1
Tel: (01473) 264755
The last surviving smock drainage mill (19th C.) in the
Broads area, and the last full-size working windmill in the
country with four common sails and a tailpole. Access on
foot only.
Times: Open 8 May, Sun, 1300-1700. Open other
occasional Suns throughout the year, please contact for
details.
Fee: Free.
Facilities: ⊛ 🄿 T(1 hr)

Holton St. Peter (nr. Halesworth)
Holton Saint Peter Postmill Map ref. M4/5
Mill House
Tel: (01986) 872367
A restored 18th C. post windmill with four sails and a working fantail.
Times: Open 30 May and 29 Aug, 1000-1800. Exterior open at all reasonable times.
Fee: Free.
Facilities: ⊛ ⊨ ≽ T(30 mins)

Pakenham (nr. Bury St. Edmunds)
Pakenham Water-Mill Map ref. F6
Mill Road
Tel: (01359) 270570
An 18th C. working water-mill on a Domesday site, with a 1904 Blackstone oil engine, mill pool, short river walk, picnic and barbecue area. Stone-ground flour for sale.
Times: Open 25 Mar-30 Sept, Sat, Sun and Bank Hols, 1400-1730. Milling demonstrations 7 Apr, 5 May, 2 Jun, 7 Jul, 4 Aug, 1 Sept, 0900-1130. By appointment at other times.
Fee: £2.50/£1.50/£2.00.
Facilities: ⃞ T(1½ hrs) Ж ⼘ ⼙

Saxtead Green (nr. Framlingham)
Saxtead Green Postmill Map ref. K6/7
Tel: (01728) 685789 Web: www.english-heritage.org.uk
An elegant white windmill, dating from 1796. A fine example of a traditional Suffolk postmill. Climb the stairs to the 'buck' to see the machinery, all in working order.
Times: 24 Mar-30 Sept, Fri, Sat, 1200-1700.
Fee: £2.60/£1.30/£2.00.
Facilities: ⊛ T(1 hr) Ж (audio tours) EH

Thelnetham (nr. Diss)
Thelnetham Windmill Map ref. G4
Mill Road
Tel: (01473) 727853
A tower windmill, built in 1819, with four very large patent sails driving two pairs of millstones. In full working order.
Times: Open 28 Mar, 29 May, 3 Jul, 7, 28 Aug, 4 Sept, 1100-1700.
Fee: £1.50/25p.
Facilities: ⃞ T(1 hr) Ж

Thorpeness
Thorpeness Windmill Map ref. N/O7
Tel: (01394) 384948
Web: www.suffolkcoastandheaths.org
A working windmill housing displays on the Suffolk Coast and Heaths, Thorpeness village and information on the workings of the mill.
Times: Open 25-28 Mar, 1100-1300 and 1400-1700; 1 Apr-30 Jun, Sat, Sun and Bank Hol Mon, 1100-1300 and 1400-1700. 1 Jul-31 Aug, Mon-Fri, 1400-1700; Sat and Sun, 1100-1300 and 1400-1700. 3, 4, 10 and 11 Sept, 1100-1300 and 1400-1700.
Fee: Free.
Facilities: T(45 mins) ⼙

Woodbridge
Buttrums Mill Map ref. K9
Burkitt Road
Tel: (01394) 382045 Web: www.tidemill.org.uk
A fine six storey towermill which is now fully restored with sails and machinery. There is also a display on history and machinery.
Times: Open 27 Mar-2 May , Sun and Bank Hols, 1400-1730. 7 May-27 Aug, Sat, Sun and Bank Hols, 1400-1730. 28 Aug-25 Sept, Sun, Bank Hols, 1400-1730.
Fee: £1.50/25p.
Facilities: ⊛ ⃞ ⊨ ≽ T(45 mins) Ж

Woodbridge
Woodbridge Tidemill Map ref. K9
Tidemill Quay
Tel: (01728) 746959 Web: www.tidemill.org.uk
A completely restored 18th C. tidalmill. Built in 1793, and used until 1957. The machinery works at varying times, subject to tides.
Times: Open 25-28 Mar, 2-30 Apr, Sat and Sun; 1 May-30 Sept, daily; 1-30 Oct, Sat and Sun, 1100-1700.
Fee: £2.00/£1.00/£1.00.
Facilities: ⊨ ≽ T(40 mins)

See Also:
Museum of East Anglian Life, Stowmarket, page 100.

Boat Trips

CAMBRIDGESHIRE

Cambridge
Riverboat Georgina Map ref. H11
Jubilee Gardens, Jesus Lock, Chesterton Road
Tel: (01223) 307694 Web: www.georgina.co.uk
River cruises with a 1st class service in the magnificent
surroundings of the River Cam. Private charter available.
Times: Please contact for details of opening times.
Fee: Various rates, please contact for details.
Facilities: 🅿 ⛟ T(2 hrs) 🔋

Peterborough
Key Ferry Cruises Map ref. C5
The Embankment
Tel: (01933) 680743
30 min river trips from Ferry Meadows Country Park, with
full commentary. Private charter trips from Peterborough.
Times: Please contact for details of opening times.
Fee: £2.20/£1.20/£2.20 (2004 prices).
Facilities: T(1 hr) 🍴

ESSEX

Chelmsford
Chelmer and Blackwater Navigation Map ref. G/H/17
Paper Mill Lock, North Hill, Little Baddow
Tel: (01245) 225520 Web: www.cbn.co.uk
Historic canal with 14 miles of towpath - excellent for
walkers, boaters and anglers. Canal centre at Paper Mill
Lock offers a teashop, boat hire and river trips aboard the
barge 'Victoria'.
Times: Canal centre open all year. River trips between
Apr-Oct.
Fee: Canal centre free. Charge for boat hire and river trips.
Facilities: 🅿 ⛟ T(2 hrs) 🍴 🔋

HERTFORDSHIRE

Broxbourne
The Lady of Lee Valley Map ref. I13
Lee Valley Boat Centre Limited, Old Nazeing Road
Tel: (01992) 462085
Web: www.riverleecruises.co.uk www.leevalleyboats.co.uk
Regular river cruises - public trips and private hire (some
with meals/refreshments), aboard 'The Lady of Lee Valley'.
Also day boats and hourly electric/rowing boats available.
Times: Open 1 Jan-31 Oct, 1-31 Dec, daily, 1000-1800.
Please contact for times of cruises.
Fee: Various - please contact for details.
Facilities: ⊛ 🅿 ⇌ T(1-5 hrs) 🛏 🍴 🔋

NORFOLK

Barton Turf
RA Boat Trip Map ref. M5/6
Gay's Staithe, Barton Broad
Tel: (01692) 670779 Web: www.broads-authority.gov.uk
Trips on Barton Broad aboard the solar-powered RA. Enjoy
a high tech boating experience and hear about Clear Water
2000 - Europe's leading lake restoration project.
Times: Open Apr, May and Oct weekends, Bank Hols and
local half term, departing at 1000, 1130, 1400 and 1530.
Jun-Sept, daily, departing at 1000, 1130, 1400 and 1530.
Fee: £4.50/£3.50/£3.50/£10.00 (family).
Facilities: ⊛ 🅿 T(1½ hrs) 🍴 🛏 🔋

Blakeney
Bishops Boats Seal Trips Map ref. H/12
Tel: (01263) 740753 Web: www.bishopsboats.co.uk
A boat trip to see the seals and birds on Blakeney Point.
See many species of birds, and both grey and common
seals in the colony of approximately 500.
Times: All year please contact for details, as times vary due
to tides.
Fee: £6.00/£4.00.
Facilities: 🅿 ⛟ T(2 hrs) 🍴 🛏 🍴

Punting at Cambridge

Horning
Mississippi River Boat Map ref. M6
Lower Street
Tel: (01692) 630262 Web: www.southern-comfort.co.uk
Double-decker paddle steamer, which can carry 100 passengers for sightseeing trips and private parties. Three public trips are arranged daily with excellent commentary. Full bar facilities are available plus hot drinks and snacks.
Times: Open Apr-Oct, Mon-Fri, sailings at 1030, 1300 and 1500. Sun 1300 and 1500, also some Sats.
Fee: £5.20/£4.60. Booking essential.
Facilities: 🅿 T(2 hrs) 🐕

Horning
Norfolk Broads Yachting Co Ltd Map ref. M6
Southgates Yacht Station, Lower Street NR12 8PF
Tel: (01692) 631330 Fax: (01692) 631133
Email: info@nbyco.com Web: www.nbyco.com
The Norfolk Broads Yachting Company runs the largest fleet of sailing yachts on the Norfolk Broads. The fleet consists of Gaff or Bermudan rigged 2-8 berth yachts. Plus the Wherry yacht "White Moth" 10 berth (skippered). Weekly, short break or daily hire available. Also sailing and rowing dinghies and day boats for hire by the hour, day or week. ⊛ 🅸 🐕

Hunstanton
Searles Sea Tours Map ref. D3
South Beach PE36 5BB
Tel: (07831) 321799 or (01485) 534444
Web: www.seatours.co.uk
A choice of 5 guided sea tours providing educational fun for all ages and leaving from Hunstanton's central promenade. Take a trip along the coastline to capture panoramic views of Hunstanton's cliffs and coastline, aboard the 'Wash Monster' (LARC) or DUKW amphibious landing craft. Or take the 'Sandbank Special' and discover the strange creatures of the Wash just at the bottom of the ramp! Take the MV Sealion on the 2-hour, 14-mile sea tour to view the beautiful seals of the Wash, with full commentary given. Please contact for times and fees. Coach parties welcome, but please book to avoid disappointment. ⊛ T(3 hrs) 🏊 🐕

Ludham
Wildlife Water Trail Map ref. N6
How Hill
Tel: (01692) 678763 Web: www.broads-authority.gov.uk
A water trail by electric launch, through the marshes and fens of How Hill Nature Reserve with a guide. Includes short walk to bird hide.
Times: Open 25 Mar-31 May, Sat, Sun, Bank Hols, Easter week and local half term, hourly from 1100-1500. 1 Jun-30 Sept, hourly from 1000-1700. 2-31 Oct, Sat and Sun and local half term, hourly from 1100-1500.
Fee: £4.00/£3.00/£3.00/£8.00 (family).
Facilities: ⊛ 🅿 T(50 mins) 🏊 🍴

Morston (nr. Blakeney)
Beans Seal Trips Map ref. H2
Tel: (01263) 740505 Web: www.beansboattrips.co.uk
A family run business for over 50 years, offering daily boat trips to see the seals and birds in their natural habitat on and around Blakeney Point nature reserve.
Times: Open 1 Jan-31 Mar, Sat-Mon and Wed. 1 Apr-31 Oct, daily, 1 Nov-31 Dec, Sat-Mon and Wed (times depend on tides). Closed 25 Dec.
Fee: £6.00/£4.00.
Facilities: 🅿 🚌 T(2 hrs) 🏊 ⊛ 🍴 🐕 🅸

Morston (nr. Blakeney)
Temple Seal Trips Map ref. H2
Tel: (01263) 740791 Web: www.sealtrips.co.uk
Boat trips to see the common and grey seals basking on Blakeney Point, an internationally famous bird sanctuary. Red and white boats depart from Morston Quay.
Times: Open all year, daily, times vary according to tide. Please phone for details.
Fee: £6.00/£4.00.
Facilities: 🅿 🚌 T(2 hrs) 🍴 🐕 🅸

Ranworth

Helen of Ranworth Boat Trip Map ref. M6
The Staithe
Tel: (01603) 270453 Web: www.broads-authority.gov.uk
Two hour trips from Ranworth on Helen (an electric ferry) show what travel was like on a Broads reed lighter - a vessel that traditionally used to carry bundles of reed.
Times: Open 25 Mar-30 Oct, Mon-Sat at 1015. Also ferry service from Ranworth Staithe to Broads Wildlife Centre, afternoons, every half hour.
Fee: £5.50/£4.50/£4.50/£12.00. Ferry 80p/40p/80p.
Facilities: T(2 hrs)

Wroxham and Potter Heigham

Broads Tours Ltd Map ref. L/M6 and N6
The Bridge (Wroxham) and The Bridge (Potter Heigham)
Tel: Wroxham (01603) 782207, Potter Heigham (01692) 670711 Web: www.broads.co.uk
Leading passenger boat company on the Norfolk Broads. Enjoy a relaxing and informative trip from either Wroxham (double decker and traditional style passenger boat) or Potter Heigham (traditional style passenger boat).
Times: Open Mar-Oct, please contact for further details.
Fee: Varies depending on tour taken, contact for details.
Facilities: T(2½ hrs) (Wroxham only) (Wroxham only)

SUFFOLK

Beccles

Liana Boat Trip Map ref. N2/3
The Quay, Fen Lane
Tel: (01502) 713196 Web: www.broads-authority.gov.uk
A trip on the Liana offers Edwardian style, travelling along the River Waveney, looking at its scenery and wildlife. Trips go towards Geldeston or Aldeby depending on tides.
Times: Open Easter week; Apr-May, Sat, Sun and Bank Hols and local half term week; Jun-Sept, daily, Oct, Sat, Sun and local half term week at 1100, 1415 and 1545.
Fee: £4.50/£3.50/£3.50/£10.00 (family).
Facilities: T(1½ hrs)

Flatford (nr. East Bergholt)

River Stour Trips Map ref. H12
Opposite Bridge Cottage, Flatford Mill
Tel: (01787) 313199 Web: www.riverstourtrust.org
Boat trips on Stour Trusty II, an elegant electric launch designed in Edwardian style. 30 minute round trips to Fen Bridge, or longer charters to Dedham, Stratford or Brantham.
Times: Trips from 25 Mar-2 Oct, Sun, Bank Hols and Wed. Charters on other days by arrangement. Please contact for further details.
Fee: Please contact for prices.
Facilities: T(1-3 hrs)

Ipswich

Orwell River Cruises Limited Map ref. I/J10
Orwell Quay, Ipswich Wet Dock
Tel: (01473) 836680 Web: www.orwellrivercruises.com
Cruises down the historic and beautiful River Orwell, to Pin Mill, Harwich Harbour and the UK's largest container port at Felixstowe. Themed musical evenings. Private charters.
Times: Regular public cruises - please contact 01473 258070 for days and times.
Fee: Harwich Harbour Cruise: £10.50/£5.25/£8.50/£26.00 Pin Mill Cruise £8.00/£4.25/£6.50/£21.00 (family).
Facilities: T(3½ hrs)

Orford

Lady Florence River Cruises Map ref. N9
Orford Quay
Tel: (07831) 698298 Email: lady-flo@keme.co.uk
Web: www.lady-florence.co.uk
Based at Orford Quay. River cruises with brunch, lunch, dinner and champagne sunsets, within the Rivers Alde and Ore. Cruise passes Aldeburgh, The National Trust's Orford Ness and Havergate Island.
Times: Open all year, daily, brunch 0930-1200; lunch 1200-1600; dinner Apr-Aug 1600-2000. Champagne sunset Sept-Oct 1600-1830. Please phone for a leaflet, details or prices.
Fee: Prices from £16.95 per person, minimum. Prices depend on the time of year, and food/drinks chosen.
Facilities: T(upto 4 hrs)

Oulton Broad

Waveney River Tours Ltd Map ref. O2

Mutford Lock

Tel: (01502) 574903/(07769) 731389

Web: www.waveneyrivertours.com

Daily sailings and private parties. River cruises on the 'Waveney Princess' or 'Enchantress'. Visits to Burgh Castle on Wed, and a day trip to Beccles on Fri.

Times: Open 25 Mar-28 Oct, daily, 0830-1730.

Fee: Please contact for prices.

Facilities: ⛴ ⇌ T(1 hr to whole day)

Southwold

Coastal Voyager Map ref. O5

Southwold Harbour

Tel: (07887) 525082

Web: www.coastalvoyager.co.uk

Coastal Voyager has it all - offering a variety of sea trips and river cruises departing from Southwold harbour. Including high speed blast trip (^{1}/2hr) and trips along the River Blyth, such as a 3^1/2hr cruise to Blythburgh.

Times: Open all year, please contact for further details.

Fee: High speed blast trip £16.00/£8.00. 3^1/2hr river cruise £20.00/£10.00.

Facilities: 🅿 T(3½ hrs) 🍴 ⊓ 🗓

Sudbury

River Stour Trips Map ref. E10

The Granary, Quay Lane

Tel: (01787) 313199 Web: www.riverstourtrust.org

Boat trips on Rosette, an elegant electric launch designed in Edwardian style. Trips through the picturesque water meadows to Ballingdon, Cornard and Henny. Occasional steam launch trips. Tearoom with home-made cakes.

Times: Trips from 27 Mar-2 Oct, Sun, Bank Hols and Wed. Charters on other days by arrangement. Please contact for further details.

Fee: Please contact for prices.

Facilities: 🅿 ⇌ T(1-4 hrs) 🍴 🗓 ⊓ 🕴

Waldringfield (nr. Woodbridge)

Deben Cruises Map ref. K10

Waldringfield Boatyard, The Quay

Tel: (01473) 736260

Cruises along the picturesque River Deben, aboard the M.V. Jahan. Trips to Woodbridge or Felixstowe Ferry. Commentary on history of river. Snacks and drinks onboard.

Times: Open 1 May-31 Sept - please contact for days and times.

Fee: £6.00.

Facilities: 🍴 🅿 T(2 hrs)

Oulton Broad

Fun Activities, Holidays & Tours

BEDFORDSHIRE

Thurleigh (nr. Bedford)
Monster Events Centre Map ref. D4
Milton Road
Tel: (01234) 771904 Web: www.monster-events.co.uk
Off-road activity centre for all ages. Activities include quad
bikes, 4x4, monster truck and radio control trucks. All
activities must be pre-booked in advance.
Times: By appointment only.
Fee: Prices vary depending upon activity.
Facilities: ▣ T(1-3 hrs) ⑪ ⬓

NORFOLK

Awayadays
Stone Cottage, Front Road, Wood Dalling,
Norwich NR11 6RN
Tel: (01263) 587005 Web: www.awayadays.com
Regular one to seven day tours of the East of England,
Norfolk and Norwich for individuals, groups and people
with special interests. Open top City sightseeing bus tours
of Norwich and Great Yarmouth. Packages can include
attractions, accommodation and luxury travel. No car
needed. Disabled catered for. ⊛

Hilltop Outdoor Centre Map ref. K3
'Old Wood', Sheringham NR26 8TS
Tel/Fax: (01263) 824514
Web: www.hilltopoutdoorcentre.co.uk
Set in 25 acres of wood/fields. Adventure Days, and three to
five day Summer Camps offer:- abseiling, giant zip wire,
treetop trail, air rifles, trail bikes, archery, assault course,
climbing wall, heated outdoor pool, crate stacking, bridges,
high ropes and orienteering. Families and parties welcome,
B&B available. ⊛

Searles Golf Resort and Country Club Map ref. D3
South Beach, Hunstanton PE36 5BB
Tel: (01485) 536010 Fax: (01485) 533815
Web: www.searles.co.uk
9 hole, par-34 resort golf course designed in a links style,
with good large greens and enhanced by natural features.
Open to the public on a 'pay and play' basis, the course
provides a challenge for both experienced and novice
golfers alike, with a large 10-bay driving range offering a
chance to practice before hitting the course proper. Club
hire available. New Country Club overlooking the course is
now open and serving refreshments, daytime snacks and
evening meals. Changing and shower facilities also
provided. Area also incorporates two fishing lakes, bowling
green and astro-putting course. Societies welcome.
⊛ ▣ 🚌 ⑪ ⬓

SUFFOLK

Kennett (nr. Newmarket)
'Wildtracks' Off-road Activity Park Map ref. B6
Chippenham Road
Tel: (01638) 751918 Web: www.wildtracksltd.co.uk
Off-road activity park with military vehicles, 4x4 Range
Rovers, quads, karts, clay shooting and motocross bikes.
Times: Open 1st Sun in every month, 1000-1600. Other
times by arrangement.
Fee: Various. Entry to park £6.00 per car.
Facilities: ◉ 🅿 ⇌ T(2-3 hrs) 🛇 🍴 🐕 (on leads)

Needham Market
Suffolk Cycle Breaks
Bradfield Hall Barn, Alder Carr Farm, PO Box 82,
Needham Market IP6 8BW
Tel: (01449) 721555 Fax: (01449) 721707
Email: enquiry@cyclebreaks.com
Web: www.cyclebreaks.com www.walkingbreaks.com
Gentle cycling and walking holidays in Suffolk and Norfolk.
Luggage transfer and accommodation pre-arranged. ◉

Newmarket
National Horseracing Museum
Minibus Tours Map ref. A7
99 High Street, Newmarket CB8 8JH
Tel: (01638) 667333 Web: www.nhrm.co.uk
Behind the scenes tours of Newmarket's racing industry.
Our daily tour departs at 0920 (except Sundays) and gives
you a fascinating insight into the world of horse racing. The
tour includes a visit to a trainer's yard, and equine
swimming pool and an opportunity to see the horses on
the gallops. Also available is a programme of Special Tours
including the ever popular all day Introduction to Racing,
where you will be accompanied to the races by an expert
guide. As well as explaining the complexities of racing they
will be able to take you down to the start and on a visit to
the jockey's weighing room.
◉ 🚌 ⇌ T(2½ hrs) 🍴 🛇 🍴

Thetford

Go Ape! High Wire Forest Adventure   Map ref. D3
Thetford Forest High Lodge Visitor Centre
Thetford Suffolk IP27 0TJ
Tel: 0870 444 5562 Web: www.goape.co uk
E.Mail: info@goape.co.uk
Go Ape! is a spectacular aerial course of zip slides,
scramble nets and rope bridges at heights of up to 35ft off
the forest floor. Go Ape! is an exhilarating test of agility,
courage and determination. Whether friends and family,
schools, youth groups or corporate parties, Go Ape!
provides fun laughter and adventure. Minimum age 10
years. Minimum height 4ft 7ins. Under 18s must be
accompanied by a participating adult. See website for
opening and admission charges. Pre-bookings strongly
recommended. To book, call the booking hotline on 0870
4445562 or book online at www.goape.co.uk (credit card
required).
⊛ ₽ T(2½-3 hrs) ⑪ ⼌ ⼍

Thorpeness

Thorpeness Village   Map ref. N/O7
Tel: 01728 452176 Web: www.thorpeness.co.uk
This pretty seaside village was created by Glencairn Stuart
Ogilvie, whose aim was to provide healthy, fun packed
holidays for families. Boat hire is available on Thorpeness
Meare, whilst The Country Club has 7 tennis courts. The
Club's original wings have been converted into apartments,
some with sea views. Thorpeness Hotel and Golf Club
offers comfortable accommodation, good food and a
superb 18-hole golf course, laid out by James Braid in
1922. Guests can enjoy a variety of holiday packages all
year round ⊛ ₽ ⑪ ⼍

Tourist Information

With so much to see and do in this area, it's impossible for us to mention all of the places you can visit. Tourist Information Centres (TICs) have plenty of information on all the things that you can do and places you can visit. TICs can book accommodation for you, in their own area, or further afield using the 'Book A Bed Ahead' Scheme. They can also be the ideal place to purchase locally made crafts or gifts, as well as books covering a wide range of local interests.

* Not open all year.

BEDFORDSHIRE

Bedford, St. Paul's Square.
Tel: (01234) 215226
Email: touristinfo@bedford.gov.uk
Web: www.bedford.gov.uk
Dunstable, The Library, Vernon Place.
Tel: (01582) 471012
Email: dunstable-tic@bedfordshire.gov.uk
Web: www.visitbeds-luton.com
Luton, Central Library, St. George's Square.
Tel: (01582) 401579
Email: tourist.information@luton.gov.uk
Web: www.lutononline.gov.uk
Mid Bedfordshire, 5 Shannon Court, High Street, Sandy.
Tel: (01767) 682728
Email: tourist.information@midbeds.gov.uk
Web: www.midbeds.gov.uk

Limited information is also available from the following Bedfordshire information points:
Ampthill, Mid Beds District Council, The Limes, Dunstable Street. Tel: (01525) 402051
Woburn Heritage Centre *, Old St. Mary's Church, Bedford Street. Tel: (01525) 290631

CAMBRIDGESHIRE

Cambridge, The Old Library, Wheeler Street.
Tel: 0906 586 2526 (charged at 60p per min)
Email: tourism@cambridge.gov.uk
Web: www.visitcambridge.org
Ely, Oliver Cromwell's House, 29 St. Mary's Street.
Tel: (01353) 662062
Email: tic@eastcambs.gov.uk Web: www.eastcambs.gov.uk
Huntingdon, The Library, Princes Street.
Tel: (01480) 388588
Email: hunts.tic@huntsdc.gov.uk
Web: www.huntsleisure.org
Peterborough, 3-5 Minster Precincts.
Tel: (01733) 452336
Email: tic@peterborough.gov.uk
Web: www.peterborough.gov.uk

St. Neots, The Old Court, 8 New Street.
Tel: (01480) 388788
Email: stneots.tic@huntsdc.gov.uk
Web: www.huntsleisure.org
Wisbech and the Fens, 2-3 Bridge Street.
Tel: (01945) 583263
Email: wisbech@eetb.info Web: www.fenland.gov.uk

ESSEX

Braintree, Town Hall Centre, Market Square.
Tel: (01376) 550066
Email: braintree@eetb.info Web: www.enjoybraintree.co.uk
Brentwood, Pepperell House, 44 High Street.
Tel: (01277) 200300
Email: brentwood@eetb.info
Web: www.brentwood-council.gov.uk
Clacton-on-Sea, Town Hall, Station Road.
Tel: (01255) 423400 Email: emorgan@tendringdc.gov.uk
Web: www.essex-sunshine-coast.org.uk
Colchester, 1 Queen Street.
Tel: (01206) 282920
Email: vic@colchester.gov.uk
Web: www.colchesterwhatson.co.uk
Harwich, Iconfield Park, Parkeston
Tel: (01255) 506139
E-mail: tic@harwichconnexions.co.uk
Web: www.harwichconnexions.co.uk
Maldon, Coach Lane.
Tel: (01621) 856503
Email: tic@maldon.gov.uk Web: www.maldon.gov.uk
Saffron Walden, 1 Market Place, Market Square.
Tel: (01799) 510444
Email: tourism@uttlesford.gov.uk
Web: www.uttlesford.gov.uk
Southend-on-Sea, Pier Entrance, Western Esplanade
Tel: (01702) 215120 Email: vic@southend.gov.uk
Web: www.southend.gov.uk
Thurrock, Moto Services, M25, Grays.
Tel: (01708) 863733
Email: tourist.information@thurrock.gov.uk
Web: www.thurrock.gov.uk
Waltham Abbey, 2-4 Highbridge Street.
Tel: (01992) 652295 Email: walthamabbey@eetb.info
Web: www.walthamabbey.org.uk

Limited information is also available from the following Essex information points:

Burnham-on-Crouch, The Old Customs House, The Quay.
Tel: (01621) 784962 Email: communityinfo@tiscali.co.uk
Braintree, Freeport, Charter Way, Chapel Hill.
Tel: (01376) 348168
Chelmsford, Rail Station, Duke Street.
Tel:(01245) 283400
South Woodham Ferrers, 34 Baron Road.
Tel: (01245) 327200 Email: swfcic@chelmsfordbc.gov.uk
Walton-on-the-Naze *, Princes Esplanade.
Tel: (01255) 675542
Witham, Town Hall, 61 Newland Street.
Tel: (01376) 502674 Email: witham_tourism@yahoo.co.uk

HERTFORDSHIRE

Birchanger Green, Welcome Break Services,
Junction 8, M11 Motorway.
Tel: (01279) 508656
Bishop's Stortford, The Old Monastery, Windhill.
Tel: (01279) 655831
Email: tic@bishopsstortford.org
Web: www.bishopsstortford.org
Hemel Hempstead, Marlowes.
Tel: (01442) 234222
Email: stephanie.canadas@dacorum.gov.uk
Web: www.dacorum.gov.uk
Hertford, 10 Market Place.
Tel: (01992) 584322
Email: hertford@eetb.info Web: www.hertford.net
Letchworth Garden City, 33-35 Station Road.
Tel: (01462) 487868
Email: tic@letchworth.com Web: www.letchworth.com
St. Albans, Town Hall, Market Place.
Tel: (01727) 864511
Email: tic@stalbans.gov.uk Web: www.stalbans.gov.uk

Limited information is also available from the following Hertfordshire information points:
Baldock, Baldock Library, Simpson Drive.
Tel: (01438) 737333
Berkhamsted, Berkhamsted Library, Kings Road.
Tel: (01438) 737333
Borehamwood, Central Reception, Civic Offices,
Elstree Way.
Tel: (0208) 207 2277
Email: customer.services@hertsmere.gov.uk
Buntingford, The Manor House, High Street.
Tel: (01763) 272222
Email: btc.manorhouse@btclick.com
Cheshunt, One Stop Shop (personal callers only),
Windmill Lane.
Harpenden, Town Hall, Leyton Road.
Tel: (01582) 768278

Email: harpenden.town.council@hertscc.gov.uk
Hitchin, 27 Churchyard.
Tel: (01462) 453335 Email: htci@hitchin.net
Hoddesdon, One Stop Shop (personal callers only),
42 Tower Centre.
Rickmansworth, Three Rivers House, Northway.
Tel: (01923) 776611
Email: enquiries@threerivers.co.uk
Stevenage, Central Library, Southgate.
Tel: (01438) 737333
Tring, 99 Akeman Street.
Tel: (01442) 823347 Email: info@tring.gov.uk
Waltham Cross, One Stop Shop (personal callers only),
123 High Street.

NORFOLK

Aylsham, Bure Valley Railway Station, Norwich Road.
Tel: (01263) 733903
Email: aylsham.tic@broadland.gov.uk
Web: www.broadland.gov.uk
Burnham Deepdale, Deepdale Farm.
Tel: (01485) 210256 Email: info@deepdalefarm.co.uk
Web: www.deepdalefarm.co.uk
Cromer, Prince of Wales Road.
Tel: (01263) 512497
Email: cromertic@north-norfolk.gov.uk
Web: www.northnorfolk.org
Diss, Mere's Mouth, Mere Street.
Tel: (01379) 650523
Email: dtic@s-norfolk.gov.uk
Web: www.south-norfolk.gov.uk
Downham Market *, The Priory Centre, 78 Priory Road.
Tel: (01366) 383287
Email: downham-market.tic@west-norfolk.gov.uk
Web: www.west-norfolk.gov.uk
Great Yarmouth *, Marine Parade.
Tel: (01493) 842195
Email: tourism@great-yarmouth.gov.uk
Web: www.great-yarmouth.co.uk
Holt *, 3 Pound House, Market Place.
Tel: (01263) 713100
Email: holttic@north-norfolk.gov.uk
Web: www.northnorfolk.org
Hoveton *, Station Road.
Tel: (01603) 782281
Email: hovetoninfo@broads-authority.gov.uk
Web: www.broads-authority.gov.uk
Hunstanton, Town Hall, The Green.
Tel: (01485) 532610
Email: hunstanton.tic@west-norfolk.gov.uk
Web: www.west-norfolk.gov.uk
King's Lynn, The Custom House, Purfleet Quay.
Tel: (01553) 763044
Email: kings-lynn.tic@west-norfolk.gov.uk

Web: www.west-norfolk.gov.uk
Norwich, The Forum, Millennium Plain.
Tel: (01603) 727927
Email: tourism@norwich.gov.uk Web: www.norwich.gov.uk
Sheringham *, Station Approach.
Tel: (01263) 824329
Email: sheringhamtic@north-norfolk.gov.uk
Web: www.northnorfolk.org
Swaffham *, Market Place.
Tel: (01760) 722255
Email: swaffham@eetb.info Web: www.breckland.gov.uk
Thetford, 4 White Hart Street.
Tel:(01842) 820689 Email:info@thetfordtourism.co.uk
Wells-next-the-Sea *, Staithe Street.
Tel: (01328) 710885 Email: wellstic@north-norfolk.gov.uk
Web: www.northnorfolk.org
Wymondham *, Market Cross, Market Place.
Tel: (01953) 604721
Email: wymondhamtic@btconnect.com
Web: www.wymondham-norfolk.co.uk

Limited information is also available from the following
Norfolk information points:
Dereham *, Church House, Church Street.
Tel: (01362) 698992 Email: derehamtourism@tesco.net
Great Yarmouth, Town Hall, Hall Plain.
Tel: (01493) 846345
Email: tourism@great-yarmouth.gov.uk
Harleston, The Xchange, 5 Exchange Street.
Tel:(01379) 855066
Email: info@visitwaveneyvalley.com
Little Walsingham *, Shirehall Museum, Common Place.
Tel: (01328) 820510
Email: walsingham.museum@farmline.com
Loddon *, The Old Town Hall, 1 Bridge Street.
Tel: (01508) 521028
Ludham *, Toad Hole Cottage Museum, How Hill.
Tel: (01692) 678763
Email: toadholeinfo@broads-authority.gov.uk
Potter Heigham *, The Staithe. Tel: (01692) 670779
Email: potterinfo@broads-authority.gov.uk
Ranworth *, The Staithe. Tel: (01603) 270453
Email: ranworthinfo@broads-authority.gov.uk
Stalham *, The Museum of the Broads, The Staithe.
Tel: (01692) 581681
Watton *, The Clock Tower, High Street.
Tel: 07818 670694

SUFFOLK

Aldeburgh, 152 High Street.
Tel: (01728) 453637 Email: atic@suffolkcoastal.gov.uk
Web: www.suffolkcoastal.gov.uk

Beccles *, The Quay, Fen Lane.
Tel: (01502) 713196
Email: becclesinfo@broads-authority.gov.uk
Web: www.broads-authority.gov.uk
Bury St. Edmunds, 6 Angel Hill.
Tel: (01284) 764667 Email: tic@stedsbc.gov.uk
Web: www.stedmundsbury.gov.uk
Felixstowe, 91 Undercliff Road West.
Tel: (01394) 276770
Email: ftic@suffolkcoastal.gov.uk
Web: www.suffolkcoastal.gov.uk
Flatford *, Flatford Lane.
Tel: (01206) 299460 Email: flatfordvic@babergh.gov.uk
Web: www.visit-suffolk.org.uk
Ipswich, St. Stephens Church, St. Stephens Lane.
Tel: (01473) 258070
Email: tourist@ipswich.gov.uk Web: www.ipswich.gov.uk
Lavenham *, Lady Street.
Tel: (01787) 248207 Email: lavenhamtic@babergh.gov.uk
Web: www.visit-suffolk.org.uk
Lowestoft, East Point Pavilion, Royal Plain.
Tel: (01502) 533600 Email: touristinfo@waveney.gov.uk
Web: www.visit-lowestoft.co.uk
Mid Suffolk, Wilkes Way, Stowmarket.
Tel: (01449) 676800 Email: tic@midsuffolk.gov.uk
Web: www.visit-suffolk.org.uk
Newmarket, Palace House, Palace Street.
Tel: (01638) 667200 Email: newmarket@eetb.info
Web: www.visit-suffolk.org.uk
Southwold, 69 High Street.
Tel: (01502) 724729
Email: southwold.tic@waveney.gov.uk
Web: www.visit-southwold.co.uk
Sudbury, Town Hall, Market Hill.
Tel: (01787) 881320 Email: sudburytic@babergh.gov.uk
Web: www.visit-suffolk.org.uk
Woodbridge, Station Buildings.
Tel: (01394) 382240 Email: wtic@suffolkcoastal.gov.uk
Web: www.suffolkcoastal.gov.uk

Limited information is also available from the following
Suffolk information points:
Brandon, 31 High Street. Tel: (01842) 814955
Hadleigh, The Library, 29 High Street.
Tel: (01473) 823778
Email: hadleigh.library@libher.suffolkcc.gov.uk
Haverhill, The Library, Camps Road.
Tel: (01440) 703971
Email: infocentre.haverhill@libher.suffolkcc.gov.uk
Mildenhall *, Mildenhall Museum, 6 King Street.
Tel: (01638) 715484

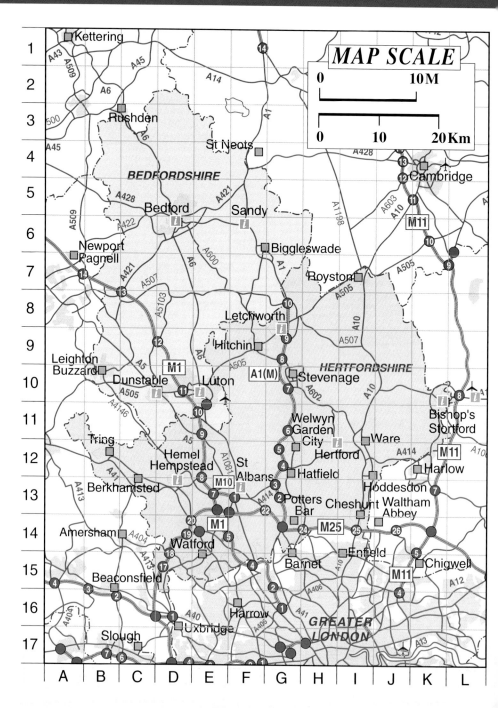

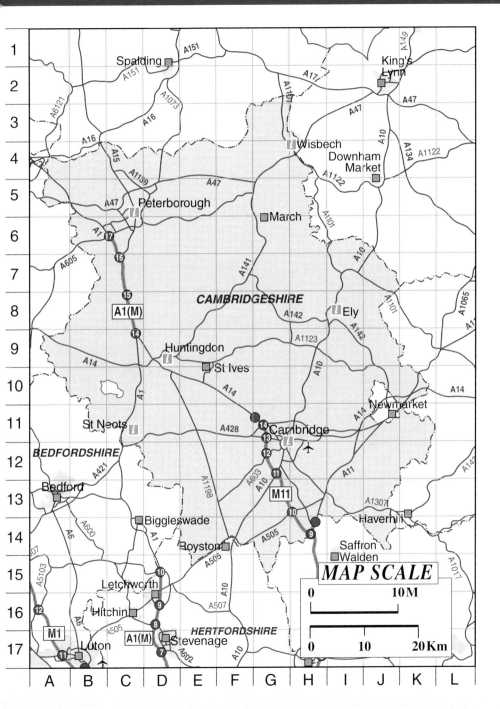

MAP SCALE

0	10M

0	10	20 Km

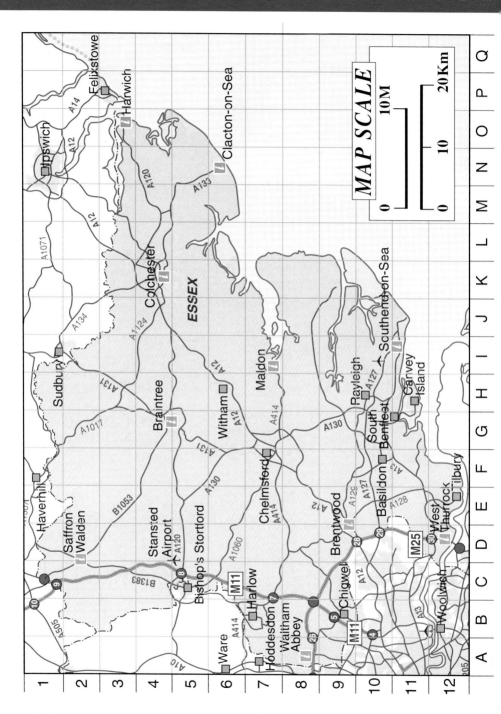

MAP SCALE

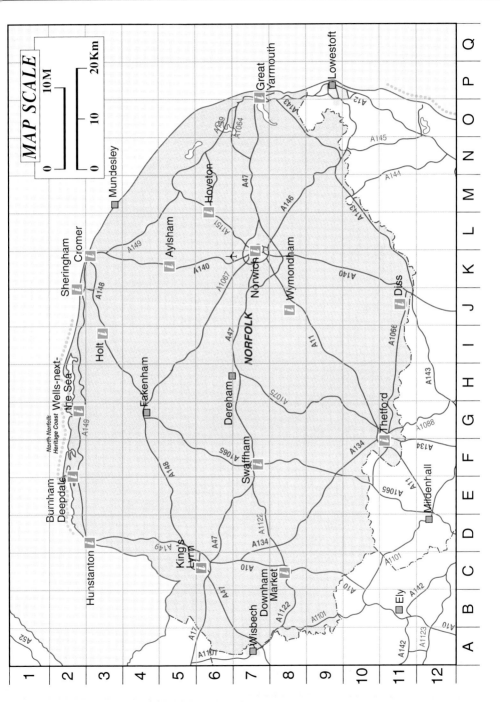

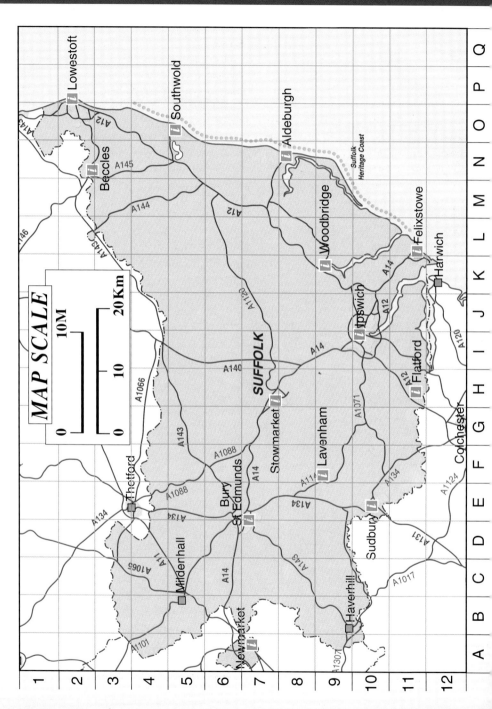

Index